MOD!
A VERY BRITISH STYLE

Also by Richard Weight

Patriots:
National Identity in Britain, 1940–2000

Modern British History:
The A–Z Guide
(with Mark Garnett)

MOD!

A VERY BRITISH STYLE

RICHARD WEIGHT

THE BODLEY HEAD
LONDON

Published by The Bodley Head 2013

4 6 8 10 9 7 5 3

Copyright © Richard Weight 2013

Richard Weight has asserted his right under the Copyright, Designs
and Patents Act 1988 to be identified as the author of this work

First published in Great Britain in 2013 by
The Bodley Head
Random House, 20 Vauxhall Bridge Road,
London SW1V 2SA

www.bodleyhead.co.uk
www.vintage-books.co.uk

Addresses for companies within The Random House Group Limited can be found at:
www.randomhouse.co.uk/offices.htm

The Random House Group Limited Reg. No. 954009

A CIP catalogue record for this book
is available from the British Library

ISBN 9780224073912

The Random House Group Limited supports The Forest Stewardship
Council® (FSC®), the leading international forest-certification organisation.
Our books carrying the FSC label are printed on FSC®-certified paper.
FSC is the only forest-certification scheme supported by the leading
environmental organisations, including Greenpeace. Our
paper procurement policy can be found at
www.randomhouse.co.uk/environment

Typeset by Palimpsest Book Production Ltd, Falkirk, Stirlingshire

Printed and bound in Great Britain by
Clays Ltd, St Ives PLC

For my mother
Angela Weight
who taught me the value of modernism

Objects that are really modern stay so for a long time. If one hears of an item of clothing that is out of date the very next season then one can be sure it was never truly modern, but only falsely professed to being such.

Adolf Loos, 'Why a Man Should Be Well Dressed',
Vienna, 1898

Contents

Part Two

Acknowledgements

My first thanks go to my agent Bill Hamilton and to Will Sulkin of Random House for getting this book commissioned and for keeping faith during the years it took to get *Mod!* to market. My editor at the Bodley Head, Jörg Hensgen, put time and energy into knocking my thoughts and writing into shape that went beyond the call of duty; and he usually did so with humour as well as honesty. Sulkin and Hensgen are, quite simply, British publishing at its best. Professors Peter Hennessy and Martin Daunton gave occasional but equally valuable support from the wings, reminding me why these two great scholars have been mentors to me in the twenty years since I decided to become a professional historian.

I owe a huge debt to my Senior Research Assistant, Chris Gomersall. His intuitive handling of sources and the intellectual stimulus he provided at project meetings were invaluable. My research assistant in the United States, Kelsie Baher, mined useful material from afar. Kelsie, together with the best of my American students from Boston to Berkeley, Chicago to Florida, helped me to see how different British youth culture has been to its American counterpart, for all the superficial similarities that are so often assumed in the mass media.

Many friends and colleagues have sustained me since my last book was published; rest assured that I know who you all are. A close circle continually showed, in the words of Jim Frank, that they had my 'best interests at heart'. They include Jim himself, Nick Black and Ed Davie. Ed's 'clean living under difficult circumstances' was an inspiration and he provided valuable practical support during the completion of this book. Bronwen Rice's expert transcribing of interviews saved me time under pressure. Thanks also to Anna for her Olympian performances at crucial times during the race.

There are also people who will never know how much they helped: the Reverend Nicholas George and various members of the Anglican congregation of St Giles' Church, Camberwell; the staff at Caravaggio's restaurant in Camberwell (*grazie*, Fernando); the players and staff at Tottenham Hotspur FC, especially during our best season since the 1960s (cheers, 'arry); Dr Roger Durston and Mr Colin Hopper, the likes of whom make the NHS such a great institution; and finally, the Blue Note jazz musicians long dead whose music was my muse for many of the days and nights that I struggled to make sense of British youth culture.

The journalist Jonh Ingham lent me his considerable expertise when interviewing some of the fascinating figures who spoke to me about their experience and views of popular Modernism in its various forms. I would like to thank, in no particular order, Mary Quant, Sir Terence Conran, Nick Hornby, William Hunt, Steve White, Norman Jay, Simon Napier-Bell, Prince Buster, Stephen Jones, Sheryl Garratt, Robert Elms, Billy Bragg, Mike Pickering, Margaret Calvert, Peter York, Owen Hatherley, Angela McRobbie, Humphrey Ocean, Gilles Peterson, Richard Williams, Eddie Piller, Paul Tunkin, Don Letts, Greil Marcus and Sir Paul Smith.

And finally, a posthumous and eternal thank you goes to my late father, Phil Strong, whose love, support, intellectual rigour, musical tastes and all-round style have continued to shape my life in the years since his premature death at the age of forty-nine.

All errors of judgement and accuracy that readers may discern in the finished product are entirely my own, and I welcome any constructive comments through my website: mail@richardweight.com

Richard Weight
Camberwell and Whitstable
December 2012

Author's Note

While I argue that Britain's first youth culture was a popular form of twentieth-century modernism I do not believe the two are synonymous. Therefore, when I refer to the movement in its conventionally artistic form – be it the poetry of T. S. Eliot or the architecture of Le Corbusier – 'modernism' appears in lower case. When I refer to any variant of the youth culture – either the term 'Modernism' used by its founders or 'Mod' as it became known in its more commercial form – the word is capitalized.[1]

INTRODUCTION
The Simple Things You See Are All Complicated

Hope I die before I get old.
  The Who, 'My Generation', 1965

Pop music *is* the classical music of now.
  Paul McCartney, 1968[1]

AMPHETAMINES, JEAN-PAUL SARTRE AND JOHN LEE HOOKER

This is a book for anyone who has experienced the thrill and frustration of being young since Winston Churchill stepped on to a balcony on 8 May 1945 to tell a jubilant crowd: 'This is *your* victory'. Many who stood beneath that balcony in Whitehall celebrated their victory by getting drunk, dancing and having sex, often with virtual strangers, in London's alleyways and public gardens. Yet as war veterans all over Britain settled down to enjoy the longest period of peace and prosperity in the nation's history, they watched with a mixture of amusement, contempt and horror as a gap opened up between those who had fought for freedom and the young men and women who were reaping the benefits without appearing to value the sacrifices made by their elders. 'I fought the war for your sort', says a bowler-hatted City gent to the Beatles in the film *A Hard Day's Night*, angry that four sharp-suited youths have invaded his first-class train carriage and are playing pop music on a transistor radio. 'I bet you're sorry you won,' is Ringo's memorable response.

Over the next decades the gulf would widen between young people and those who had never experienced youth culture. The latter were the veterans of an age when art and entertainment were regarded as separate pursuits stemming from different cultures with different values; when monarchs and politicians did not court rock stars and fashion designers; when parading your sexual preferences or drug habits could end your career, not bolster your popularity; and when youth culture had not been curated in museums, recorded in documentaries or studied by academics. Today popular music and fashion are an accepted part of national life, valued as art forms, commodities and as a collective experience. Youth cultures that were once derided as ephemeral or amoral, and which had set out to mock the past and the values of their parents, have become common ground for subsequent generations. Pete Townshend's famous line, 'Hope I die before I get old', now seems absurd not so much because Townshend overvalued youth but because the youth culture he helped to create proved to be so robust and regenerative that it survived the ravages of time.

Mod! is a book about the first distinctively British youth cult and the artistic and social influence it has had. What became known as Mod was an amalgam of American and European music, fashion and design that left its mark not only on a variety of subsequent youth cults but also on British culture as a whole. At its peak in the mid-1960s, Mod became shorthand for what it meant to be a modern Briton; it helped to shape popular ideas about social relationships, taste, lifestyle and national identity at a time when the British Empire was being dismantled and American consumerism was changing British society.

Although its precise origins are, as David Fowler observes, 'shrouded in darkness: literal and metaphorical',[2] its early history can be pieced together from oral testimony. A few hundred style-conscious men and women who named themselves 'Modernists' after their love of modern jazz started the movement in Soho in 1959, where they went from all parts of London to have fun and strike a pose. It seems to have gestated in the capital for three years, developing its style codes and precepts. There are no accurate statistics for the size of the movement at any given time, but we do know that between 1962 and 1967 Mod became a national and international movement. Celebrated and demonised in equal measure by the mass media, commercially exploited by young entrepreneurs as well as established business, it seems to have involved millions of people, from the few trend-setting 'faces' at its core, to the many more on its periphery, known as 'tickets', who bought a ride on it at one time or another. When it became associated in the mid-1960s with the emergence of British rock music, the movement acquired artistic figureheads like the Who. But because Mod was more than a particular style of music, it survived changing musical tastes as well as disillusionment with Swinging London. Over the following decades Mod found its way into glam rock and punk, Britpop and rave, which together formed a canon of British youth culture that continues to be referenced – and enjoyed – by the less tribal, digitally connected young Britons of the early twenty-first century.

When the British Music Experience opened its doors at the O2 in 2009, aiming to tell the story of popular music in Britain since the 1950s, the owner and impresario Harvey Goldsmith chose as its logo the red, white and blue Mod 'target'. Early Mods had adopted the insignia of the Royal Air Force in wry reference to the military elite whom Churchill had lauded as 'the Few' during the Battle of Britain in 1940. Seventy years later at the O2, the target, which once signified membership of a different, subcultural elite, had become instead a unifying symbol for British youth culture as a whole.

Mod emerged at a time when consumer society was promising not only huge improvements to working-class life but an escape from class altogether, into a new state of being, called 'youth'. As Jon Savage explained:

The Allies won the war at exactly the moment that America's latest product was coming off the production line . . . The post-war spread of American values would be spearheaded by the Teenager. This new type was the ultimate psychic match for the times: living in the now, pleasure-seeking, product-hungry, embodying the new global society where social inclusion was to be granted through purchasing power.[3]

The prospect of greater inclusion in British society, both as consumers and as producers of taste, is what drove the original Mods to fetishise clothes, music, gadgets and grooming.

Mods affronted society because hitherto the British working classes had not been regarded as arbiters of taste, or even as shoppers of note beyond their need for essential goods and services. As Andy Bennett has written, 'rather than accentuating issues of class divisions, post-war consumerism offered young people the opportunity to break away from their traditional class-based identities and adopt new, self-constructed forms of identity'.[4] Shopping with taste and parading the results, as much as casual sex and drug-taking, is what disturbed so many older Britons about the movement.

Mod is the closest the British have come to constructing their own version of the American Dream – a mobilising, energising legend of opportunity which rebuked the snobbery and deference that conspired to give Britain one of the lowest levels of social mobility in the capit-alist world. The Who's first manager, Pete Meaden, memorably defined the Mod ethos as 'clean living under difficult circumstances'.[5] It was the aspiration to live well, whatever your social background or mate-rial circumstances; to be smart mentally and sartorially in order to make the most of your opportunities; to belong to a nationwide tribe and enjoy the status and comfort it gave you.

The English poet Thom Gunn said of Elvis Presley that 'he turns revolt into a style, prolongs / The impulse to a habit of the time'.[6] If so, then Mods turned revolt into a lifestyle. Appropriately perhaps, the term 'lifestyle' was coined in 1929 by an Austrian Freudian psychi-atrist, Alfred Adler, to describe a set of goals and ideals through which individuals, driven by a sense of inferiority, try to attain an ersatz perfection, often through material consumption. Without any coherent ideology or manifesto, Mod became a focal point for the aspirations of upwardly mobile British youth as the consumer society disrupted old certainties about class. 'Mods', wrote Mary Quant in her best-selling memoir of 1966, 'represent the whole new classless spirit that has grown out of the Second World War . . . Once, only the rich, the Establishment set the fashion . . . There was a time when clothes were a sure sign of a woman's social position and income group. Not now. Snobbery has gone out of fashion, and in our shops you will find duchesses jostling with typists to buy the same dresses.'[7]

Of course, neither snobbery nor misogyny ended because typists and duchesses were buying the same dresses in Quant's King's Road boutique, or because men began to wear pink shirts and use moisturiser. But sociologists in the 1970s argued that 'subcultures' operated under the surface of mainstream society, challenging prejudice through rituals of dress and behaviour. Although criticised since for ascribing too much political intent to style, their analysis of Mod as a cheeky parody of middle-class smartness has yet to be bettered. As Dick Hebdige wrote: 'The Mods invented a style which enabled them to negotiate between school, work and leisure, and which concealed as much as it stated . . . the Mods undermined the conventional meaning of "collar, suit and tie", pushing neatness to the point of absurdity . . . they were a little *too* smart, somewhat *too* alert, thanks to amphetamines.'[8]

Formed against the backdrop of American global supremacy and European decline, Mod was a uniquely British amalgam of American and European culture. Originally, one Mod explains, 'hardly anything we did came from the UK.' Another agrees: 'Back then it was all existentialism and rhythm and blues . . . Amphetamines, Jean-Paul Sartre and John Lee Hooker: that was being a Mod.'[9] The original Modernists loved modern jazz and admired the sharp-suited style of figureheads like Miles Davis, who had taken it from French and Italian fashion. Later, Mods embraced American rhythm and blues and soul, and through this music they identified with black America, a world they had no experience of but with which they empathised as a stratum of society not accorded its due because of social prejudice.

At the same time young Britons reclaimed their popular culture from the slavish transatlantic mimicry which had characterised it since the 1930s. Mods created a distinctly British hybrid by mixing American music with West European forms, from the classical tradition to the English music hall. In fashion, they combined casual American styles, such as sportswear, with a smarter, more colourful and flamboyant tradition, which sprang from Western Europe's more liberal attitudes to sex and sexuality.

Mod therefore spearheaded a cultural renaissance that tempered the Americanisation of Britain and helped to define what it meant to be British at a crucial period when the nation was coming to terms with the decline in its global power. For some, it has even compensated for that decline. As the *New Musical Express* put it in 1965, 'We may be regarded as a second-class power in politics, but at any rate we now lead the world in pop music!'[10] Although British pop music briefly stimulated interest in Mod among young Americans, Mod's popularity did not long survive the end of Beatlemania. In Britain, on the other hand, Mod inspired and helped to establish a series of interrelated youth cultures over the next half-century. What made the movement so successful was that it challenged the American domination of British popular culture while also celebrating the best of what America offered to the world.

Mods consciously drew on the European tradition of the dandy, which fashion historian Christopher Breward (echoing Pete Meaden) defined as 'a mannered denial of sordid realities . . . through the deliberate manipulation of appearance'.[11] In everything from their sharp Italian suits and scooters to their admiration for Continental film stars and sportsmen, Mods were eager to engage with European popular culture and to challenge prejudices about Europe that were deeply embedded in the British psyche after centuries of conflict with Continental powers. Spared the horrors of war, young Mods found Western Europe not a threat but a source of pleasure and inspiration, 'a land of plenty' in much the same way as America.

Sipping a cappuccino in a sun-kissed piazza in Rome during the 1960s was as remote an experience as riding Route 66 in a Cadillac – unless you were lucky enough to be a pop or film star – so for many British teenagers such dreams remained pleasures of the imagination until they were affluent enough to travel abroad in the 1970s and 80s. In the meantime, such pleasures had to be enjoyed second-hand. A cappuccino made with an imported Gaggia machine in Newcastle was still a cappuccino – even if the froth was blown into your face by a stiff breeze from the North Sea. Mods' adoption of Continental style at a time when older Britons continued to view Europe with suspicion only widened the generation gap – yet it contributed to making Britain a more cosmopolitan place in the late twentieth century.

A WHOLE CLIMATE OF OPINION

This book contends that Mod was not just the first distinctively British youth culture, and the first to have an impact beyond its teenage constituency, but that it was in essence a popular form of modernism – that stream of creativity in Europe and America that began in the early twentieth century as an avant-garde reaction to mainstream aesthetics, morality and politics.

Mostly through its crucible, the Bauhaus school of architecture and design, by the early 1930s the modern movement had gained traction in Britain largely through commercial design. Millions of first-time homeowners, particularly those moving to the new suburbs, may have lived in mock 'Tudorbethan' houses, but modern design – from clean Bauhaus through to the glitzier art deco – shaped these little castles and their surroundings. It changed much of their furniture and decor; it left its mark on the streamlined cars, coaches and trains that took commuters to work in the city at ever greater speeds; it shaped the design of offices and the new mass-production factories, like the Hoover plant in Perivale; and it influenced the look of labour-saving gadgets like the vacuum cleaner, which gave those who could not afford domestic servants more time for leisure. Modernist design was evident in the promenades, hotels and ballrooms of England's seaside resorts, the telephones and radio sets, and the architecture of the Odeon cinemas and the BBC's original Broadcasting House, all of which housed the new mass media that connected people from across different regions into a common culture. Modernism even shaped the electricity pylons that powered most of this new world and bestrode the ancient countryside like invading robots from H. G. Wells's *War of the Worlds*.

After the Second World War, liberal ideas of modernity and progress gained more currency in Britain. Of course, it was not the first time that Britons had thought they were 'modern' and associated that with urban life in an industrial society. However, the vision of a more centrally planned economy and society, in the vanguard of aesthetic improvement, technological innovation and social mobility, was a ventricle in the heart of the fragile liberal consensus that emerged in the era of reconstruction between 1945 and 1970. The historians Martin Daunton and Bernhard Rieger have concluded that: 'In the trans-formed postwar world, the established stories of British modernity emphasizing historical continuity lost their earlier persuasiveness. Viewed from this perspective, the Second World War, rather than the Great War, proved the more prominent watershed in bringing about a recasting of the meanings of British modernity.'[12]

The liberal narrative of modernity, from Bauhaus to Beveridge, may have been politically disrupted by the changing fortunes of the Labour Party but consumers' demand for visibly contemporary products did not abate, nor did they cease to use that material culture to express their personal sense of modernity. After the Second World War, mass-market modernism reached a new audience hungry for relief from austerity, and it was in the 1950s that Swedish design became popular, initially among the affluent and educated middle classes who were more receptive to the Continental lifestyle. Promoted by intellectuals like Herbert Read and Nikolaus Pevsner, and presented to the public at the 1951 Festival of Britain (and annually at the Ideal Home Exhibition), Swedish design combined the rational and geometric principles of Bauhaus with the use of natural materials like wood, which appealed to consumers in Britain, where the Arts and Crafts Movement still had an influence on popular taste. Modernism was thus absorbed through being adapted to native traditions. In his study of the subject, Ian Christie wrote: 'No longer avant-garde, Modernism had become, to borrow Auden's phrase, "a whole climate of opinion" – and in doing so, in a final extended irony, it had achieved something that many of its avant-garde progenitors had desired: the reintegration of art and life.'[13] According to the art critic Charles Harrison,

Modernism may fruitfully be thought of as a form of tradition, but one maintained in a kind of critical tension with the wider surrounding culture. The tradition in question is one in which what is carried forward is not a given stylistic canon, but rather a kind of disposition or tendency . . . To think of modernism in these terms is to suggest a strong alternative to the identification of modernist art simply with the avant-garde enterprises of the early twentieth century.[14]

It is this broader definition of modernism that can also be applied to Mod. As I will show in this book, from the 1960s onwards this 'disposition or tendency' towards the modern created a unique form of popular music, fashion and design, which came to stand not only as an expression of youth but a component of British culture as a whole, in the process broadening the cultural sources of patriotism and defining what it meant to be British.

While it was not the first time that members of a European youth movement had embraced urban modernity, it was the first time in

Britain that such a movement came primarily from the working classes; it then made creative and commercial alliances with middle-class youth to whom modernist style and ideas also offered moments of liberation. Mod thereby gave modernism a fresh impetus by taking the movement's aesthetic style and some of its democratic precepts to a new mass market, bigger than any it had been able to reach during the 1930s or 1950s. That market was driven by the ideas of youth and social progress and fuelled by affluence and consumerism. By 1966, *Design* magazine was hoping that 'one day Carnaby Street could rank with Bauhaus as a descriptive phrase for a design style, when cutlery and furniture design could swing like The Supremes'.[15]

The trend in which modernist design was linked directly to commercial youth culture owed much to British followers of American Pop Art like Richard Hamilton, Lawrence Alloway and Peter Blake, who launched their ideas in 1956 at an ICA exhibition called 'This Is Tomorrow'. Pop Art's democratic ethos successfully challenged the nation's aesthetic elite, such as Herbert Read, who had promoted a temperate British version of Continental modernism while rejecting what they saw as the vulgarity of American mass culture. In *Pop Design: From Modernism to Mod*, the critic Nigel Whiteley observed that

Although Pop did not bring about the widespread and permanent changes its devotees would have wished, it did transform the habits and outlook of the great majority in terms of design. It realised Richard Hamilton's description of the characteristics of popular culture as 'expendable, low-cost, mass-produced, young, witty, sexy, glamorous, and Big Business' . . . The intellectual structure of design theory had crumbled . . . All the applied arts – and in many cases the fine arts – aspired to the condition of fashion.[16]

The popularisation of Mod, epitomised by Carnaby Street's becoming a tourist attraction, dismayed some of the movement's founders, less because they objected to retailers cashing in on their style than because it encroached on their status, which was validated by a precise definition of style and attendant consumer choices. Like some of the intellectual founders of modernism in the 1920s, the original Mods of the 1960s displayed all the elitism of the Establishment they were attacking and which, ultimately, they wanted to join. Yet the watering down of its original ethos did not mark the death of Mod. On the contrary, it triumphantly emerged from the shadows of subculture into the glare of the mainstream – the first youth movement to fully achieve that feat. What Mod lost in its ability to rebel and shock it gained in influence by appealing to a wider audience.

As well as helping to take modernism to market, Britain's first youth culture repositioned modernism back in the city where it had begun as an avant-garde movement. Mods celebrated the city in opposition to the suburbs and satellite towns where most of them had been raised. They attacked the social conservatism of suburbia – its focus on work, family and routine – setting it against the exciting cosmopolitanism, vibrancy and eroticism of the city. Michael Bracewell has written eloquently about suburbia's huge impact on British pop 'as the prime incubator of English outsiders and artists':

Culturally – to say nothing of spiritually – suburbia has been a place to come home to that doubles as a place to escape from . . . a state of statelessness in which environment presents itself as a proposition of conformism, the weight of which inspires rebellion as much as obedience . . . In suburbia, the teenage outsiders must make do with taking over the bus-shelter from dusk till midnight as a meeting-place and venue for illicit activities – reversing the creed of suburbia's shrine to respectable commuting by having nowhere to go, and leaving their own bored art of graffiti as defiant evidence of their act of desecration.[17]

In its reaction against the tedium of suburbia Mod embraced the modernist design that was evident in the clothes of Mary Quant, the haircuts of Vidal Sassoon, the album covers of Peter Blake and, most of all, the design and retail empire of Terence Conran. Conran cut his teeth providing designs for the Festival of Britain, collaborated with Quant on her King's Road boutique, championed Bauhaus design, founded Habitat and invented flat-pack furniture. As he later wrote:

Modernism seemed to offer a chance to reshape the world in an exciting way. It also fitted in perfectly with the democratic spirit of the times; people didn't want to go back to the old elitism. We felt that we were in the perfect position to put the Bauhaus ideals into practice . . . Habitat did for the home what designers like Mary Quant, Barbara Hulanicki and Ossie Clark were doing for clothes. We were part of a minor revolution in taste instigated by young people.'[18]

This idea that youth culture was ushering in a democratisation of taste was prevalent among designers, artists and critics. As the interior designer David Hicks concluded in 1968 in his book, *On Living – with Taste*: 'In the past taste filtered down from the aristocracy to the landed gentry and, in turn, to the butchers and grocers. Now . . . an office girl in Oxford Street is invariably better dressed than a president's wife and a telephone operator will have better taste than a baronet.'[19] One of the original members of the cult, Richard Barnes, reflected in 1979:

Once discovered by the media, the term ['Mod'] was applied to anything new or quirky, as diverse as fashion designer Mary Quant or *The Avengers* TV series. [It] came to represent much more than the 'in' movement of the Sixties. It stood for a particular style and taste. It had come a long way from its early days inspired by the coolness of modern jazz and the chic of Continental fashion. It had produced its own graphic images – Pop Art targets and chevrons – and for many it came to represent more than clothes and music. Its values were applied, among other things, to architecture, design, furniture, graphic, novels etc. and the term is still used today.[20]

I want to show that it was largely through Britain's first youth culture that pre-war modernism was popularised and disseminated in late twentieth-century Britain.

A DREAM OF IDEALISED MODERNITY

'Modernism was an adversarial outcry against predictability, convention and stifling notions of duty and responsibility', the historian Modris Eksteins has written. 'Modernism, with its countercultural essence, embraced surprise. It pointed to the rot within the time-honoured and it in fact feted that rot. Indeed, modernism and the culture of youth have gone hand in hand . . . Thus a history of youth must perforce be in large part a history of modernism.'[21]

When critics have tried to find a link between high modernism and contemporary youth culture they have done so through the prism of punk. The angry nihilism that punk paraded – its insistence that 1976 was Year Zero, a radical break with the past – has appealed to armchair revolutionaries of all ages, and the revolt was given intellectual ballast by Greil Marcus's erratically brilliant *Lipstick Traces* (1989). While I acknowledge the radical antecedents of punk and join its champions Jon Savage and Simon Reynolds in celebrating the influence it has exercised since the mid-1970s on music, design and politics, I don't believe punk was the pivotal moment in the evolution of British post-war youth culture. I would also dispute that punk is where the main intersection of modernism and youth culture can be found.

Mod was the first British youth culture to celebrate technology, art and design, cosmopolitanism, racial integration, sexual ambiguity and social mobility. Mod was in thrall to the consumer society but it did not celebrate shopping for its own sake; rather it formed part of a democratisation of culture in the twentieth century, aspiring to empower lives through the acquisition of taste. Even when it failed to achieve real social mobility for its followers, Mod still created what Sarah Thornton calls 'subcultural capital' – that is a simulacrum of wealth gained through knowledge, discernment and creativity that was accessible to men and women from different backgrounds.[22]

Like many of the original Mods who disliked their authentic street style being swept up by 'Swinging London', sociological studies too often dismiss the significance of Mod's diffusion into mainstream commercial culture. Yet as Christine Feldman has argued in *'We Are the Mods': A Transnational History of a Youth Subculture*, it was precisely the mainstreaming of Mod that gave it both domestic and global reach:

In its later phase, Mod style became more fun-loving and less regulatory, global versus regional, and open to young women as well as men. It is in this progressive spirit that Mod became historicized as a radically ebullient cultural phenomenon. Due to this transformation the word *Mod* became synonymous with the youth culture impulse of the times. What started as a sartorial rebellion by predominantly working-class, male teens in London during the early 60s had transformed mid-decade into an international youth movement of streamlined style and forward-thinking idealism.[23]

Feldman concludes that 'as the culture evolved into various youth phenomena through the late 60s into the 70s and beyond, various elements could be found and adopted by anyone desiring to carry on Mod's dream of idealized modernity'. That dream is what set it apart from forms of youth culture that romanticised an Arcadian rural past, or a fantasy world.

Punk's historian, Jon Savage, has acknowledged that the mid-1960s were 'the very height of pop modernism', after which popular culture started to repeat itself, with punk merely the most influential collage of styles that appeared after the high tide of those years.[24] Simon Reynolds agrees: 'Was 1965 the absolute pinnacle of Newness and Nowness? That certainly seemed to be the case with fashion. After that high point, post-modernist-like techniques of pastiche and re-cycling began to take effect in fashion many years before they would appear in pop music.'[25]

Yet even when the modernist artists of the early twentieth century were at their most rigidly progressive and flushed with arrogance in their belief that tomorrow's world was here today, they still referenced the past: there was never a moment of aesthetic purity when the continuum of history was smashed. Similarly in the 1960s, musicians, artists and designers were conscious of acting within certain traditions. Mary Quant was as openly influenced by the 'Flapper Girl' fashions of the 1920s as she was by the Op Art of her friend Bridget Riley. The Beatles, the Kinks and the Small Faces, with their albums *Sgt. Pepper*, *The Village Green Preservation Society* and *Ogden's Nut Gone Flake*, refer-enced the music and popular culture of the early twentieth century. Interviewed by the *Daily Telegraph* in 1966, another of Quant's friends, Barbara Hulanicki, the designer and founder of BIBA, explained her use of art deco style alongside elements of Victoriana: 'I love old things. Modern things are so *cold*. I need things that have lived.'[26]

There is a tendency to associate modernism too closely with the avant-garde and its excesses. When it comes to British architecture, for example, it is usually the Brutalist style that springs to mind, which ravaged so many British towns from the 1950s to the 1980s in the name of progress; few people would cite the penguin pool at London Zoo created by Berthold Lubetkin, a Russian refugee and member of the Bauhaus school, which continued to delight families while concrete tower blocks were taking them into the sky. In terms of furniture design, critics point to David Bartlett's disposable (and less than sturdy) paper chair of 1966 rather than Marcel Breuer's 1926 tubular steel chair that became one of Habitat's best-sellers in the 1970s. In short, the modernist movement had always been a broad church.

As a youth culture, Mod was similarly diffuse, evolving into different congregations across time and space which shaped styles as seemingly disparate as skinhead, glam, punk and rave, while retaining a distinctive core that first borrowed from and then popularised various forms of twentieth-century art and design. Mod's enduring appeal to subsequent generations of Britons, as well as to Anglophile youth in Germany, Japan and America, rests on its image as a youth culture that celebrates post-Victorian, post-imperial modernity. Commenting on the perpetuation of Mod style through numerous youth cults, adult lifestyles and public habitats, the historian Bill Osgerby has argued that 'retro-chic cannot be dismissed as merely a depthless, postmodern imitation of dead styles, but instead should be recognised as an active cultural enterprise in which media forms of the past are commandeered and mobilised in meaningful ways in the lived cultures of the present.'[27]

Simon Reynolds has argued that, ironically, it has been the perception of the 1960s as a decade of perpetual innovation that has helped to make the period the source of longing for a golden age. 'Where pop nostalgia gets interesting,' he writes, 'is in that peculiar nostalgia you can feel for the glory days of "living in the now" that you didn't . . . actually . . . *live* through. Punk and the rock 'n' roll fifties both stir feelings of this kind, but the Swinging Sixties beats all comers when it comes to triggering vicarious nostalgia. Ironically, it's the absence of revivalism and nostalgia during the sixties itself that partly accounts for why there have been endless sixties revivals ever since.'[28] Some adherents of Mod have been guilty of perpetuating this paradoxical form of nostalgia; they have used the 1960s as a refuge from what they see as a barren and confusing present.

Mod! may therefore offend purists seeking a book that illustrates and reaffirms the strict codes they adhere to, or which uncritically celebrates the 1960s as a golden age. Many more readers, I hope, will see that this book pays Mod a far greater compliment by viewing it not as a set of rules to be obeyed but as the DNA of British youth culture for almost half a century, providing it with a template from which it is still evolving, and through which it still influences British society today.

NOT THE PRODUCT, BUT MAN, IS THE END IN VIEW

Since the subject of this book is potentially so wide-ranging that it can easily spiral out of control, a few caveats are necessary before we can jump on our metaphorical scooters. Although the book focuses on the half-century from the late 1950s to the present day, I am not suggesting that youth culture did not exist in some form before that. Yet what we understand today by the term is that confluence of trends within the developed world in the age of mass democracy after 1945: the baby boom, mass affluence, advances in media and communication technologies, wider access to higher education, civil rights for women and ethnic minorities, and a liberalisation of sexual mores. These changes, which took place in a relatively short space of time, made young people more numerous than before; they also made them richer, more connected to each other, more sceptical of the status quo and freer to indulge and articulate their desires and tastes. What they chose to do with that freedom sometimes shocked, scared and angered people – including the young themselves.

'Youth', as Oscar Wilde, famously observed, 'is wasted on the young.' Yet, however shallow, pretentious and antisocial youth culture has been in its many incarnations, I do not agree with historians and critics who regard it as a silly, immature expression of ourselves – for example, buying a pair of trousers that makes you look more like Norman Wisdom than Jim Morrison. Youth culture is not a sideshow to the serious business of historical agency such as voting in general elections, fighting wars or inventing machines; it is an integral part of the way that men and women in the Western world have lived in an era of unprecedented peace and prosperity.

Whether people view their youth with nostalgia, bitterness or (like most) take a rounded view of it as 'difficult but fun' and see it as an important phase in their development, youth lives long in the memory. It survives the receding of hairlines and the expansion of waistlines. Both as an individual experience and as a collective culture, it continues to shape lives in a variety of ways, ranging from how people dress and decorate their homes to how they relate to their colleagues, neighbours, lovers, friends and, above all, to their own children. Youth culture lives on, across generations, not simply in commercially exploitative revivals or in smart 'post-modern' references to a digital archive of pop culture, but in the daily choices and interactions that people make.

The generation gap, at its widest between the 1950s and 1970s, narrowed considerably thereafter as youth culture became something that most people had experienced. Even during moral panics about oversexed, out-of-it, effeminate or violent youth, relationships between parents and children rarely broke down because of teenagers' involvement in a youth culture. Different tastes in music, fashion and lifestyle, or different political views, could be lasting but they were usually safely managed until the worst tumults of adolescence were over. Generational conflict became more of a dissonance in family life than a rupture.

The possibilities for dialogue between the generations increased from the 1970s onwards as a variety of fashion, music and design associated with youth shared a cultural platform where each generation defined and experienced its own patterns of consumption, leisure and taste. When youth culture established an archive and with that a sense of heritage, cross-generational correspondence became even easier. This was not as creepy or stultifying as it seemed. Style was connected to patterns of consumption, to wider social change and to specific ideas of modernity, and those connections remained in people's minds long after they discarded specific fads and possessions, settled into careers and started their own families. So when they became parents and shared memories of their youth with offspring, they were doing more than indulging in nostalgia or using moral tales of misspent youth to teach salutary lessons: parents also employed those memories to transmit ideas and values which they associated with the youth culture they had been part of. Mod had important things to say about class, race, sexuality and nationality. And it was the style that more than any other in British youth culture made connections between consumption and modernity over time.

To some extent Mods epitomised the limitations of Western youth culture in the second half of the twentieth century. Their obsession with style, in particular the vagaries of clothing fashion, made them eager participants in an emergent consumer society. Indeed, these working-class dandies helped to create that society, providing a model of how the aspirations of newly affluent young Britons could be commercially shaped and exploited. As an editor of the *NME* once snidely remarked to the author and music journalist Paolo Hewitt: 'Modernism is just about shopping.'[29] Yet perhaps one of the reasons why Mod has attracted so much nostalgia is that it has come to stand for a certain measure of discernment in the acquisition and enjoyment of consumer goods: not shopping for its own sake but shopping with taste in pursuit of a more creative life. 'Mod was not just buying for the hell of it', as Patrick Uden once put it.[30] For original Mods like Uden, and for many of those that came later, the words of the modernist designer László Moholy-Nagy, resonate: 'Not the product, but man, is the end in view.'[31]

As in all forms of artistic and commercial endeavour, relatively few people are innovators, entrepreneurs or agents provocateurs. But that doesn't mean that 1960s youth culture barely touched the lives of people outside the *jeunesse dorée* in the capital, as some historians claim. To argue that no one beyond the North Circular was affected by Swinging London is rather like saying that the English Civil War had no impact on the country as a whole because relatively few people fought at Naseby or witnessed the Putney Debates.

Such a view displays a metropolitan condescension towards the 'provinces': even a cursory study of British youth culture shows that Manchester, Bristol, Birmingham, Sheffield, Coventry, Glasgow, Edinburgh, Newcastle, Leeds, Cardiff and of course Liverpool – not to mention numerous smaller towns from Wigan to Woking – have all produced influential artists. And although most of them gravitated towards London in search of fame and fortune, the majority came from a vibrant artistic milieu and continued to reference their regional origins in their work. Indeed, a key part of the Britishness of the country's popular music since the 1960s has been the way that artists have looked back at 'home' – both as a place to escape from and as a source of belonging and identity.

Youth culture has usually been taken either too seriously or not seriously enough by scholars. Early sociological studies of subcultures ascribed to Mods a radical purpose that was not always present in a movement whose main purpose was to have fun. Sociologists have also preferred an original subculture that was artistically innovative and an agent of social change, while disdaining its wider commercial popularity through which that change was often effected. More recent historical revisionism tends to regard youth as a phase of life in which regrettable moral and consumer choices are made by hormonally and mentally challenged teenagers, which are then largely forgotten about once adult life begins. Standing between these two approaches, I see youth culture as a lived and shared experience that resonates throughout most people's life. It is freighted with rich meanings, reflects the temper of society and can be in the vanguard of changing it – though not always for the better.

This then is the story of how a cult became a culture. It is also about the relationship between Britain, Europe and America in the first age of mass democracy and mass affluence, refracted through the eyes of young British men and women over several generations. Like youth itself, the story is littered with false hopes and broken dreams, arrogance and insecurity, vanity and at times downright stupidity. But it is also a story of the creativity and friendship, positive social and technological change which have created the world that young and old alike inhabit in the twenty-first century.

The story begins in Soho, a bohemian district in the centre of London, which since the eighteenth century has been the home, workplace and playground of artists, intellectuals, bon viveurs and *flâneurs*. It is where in 1926, above the legendary Bar Italia in Frith Street, television was first demonstrated by its Scottish inventor to an official from the Royal Institute and a reporter from *The Times*. And in 1959, in nearby Gerrard Street, a small group of sharply dressed art students calling themselves 'Modernists' gathered at Ronnie Scott's nightclub to see the stars of American bebop, the 'modern' jazz that gave Britain's first youth culture its name.

Part One

Dandyism appears especially in the transitory periods when democracy is not yet all-powerful, and when aristocracy is only partially unsettled and depreciated. In the confusion of such periods, some few men who are out of their sphere, disgusted and unoccupied, but are all rich in natural force, may conceive the project of founding a new kind of aristocracy.

Charles Baudelaire, Paris, 1836

1

CLEAN LIVING UNDER DIFFICULT CIRCUMSTANCES
The Birth of Modernism

As individuals they were nothing. They were England's lowest common denominators. They had to submit to the middle class way of dressing and way of speaking and way of acting in order to get the very jobs which kept them alive. They had to do everything in terms of what existed already around them. That made their way of getting something across that much more latently effective, the fact that they were hip and yet still, as far as Granddad was concerned, exactly the same.

Pete Townshend, 1968[1]

Even though you were an oik at heart, you wanted to be classy. It was the original wannabe culture. Wannabe boys and girls, wanna create, wannabe rich, wannabe famous, wannabe loved, wannabe known.

Jeff Dexter, original Mod, c.1990[2]

MODERNISTIC KNICK-KNACKS

The bohemian quarter of England's capital city sprang to life in the late seventeenth century after King Charles II gave some land on a hill just north of Westminster to his illegitimate and equally dissolute son, the Duke of Monmouth. Britain's first nightclubs started there a century later and Soho became home to writers, painters, actors, composers, pimps, whores, drug dealers, bohemians and hedonists of every kind. Perhaps because of its outré nature, Soho was also a place where immigrants felt comfortable, its famous residents including

Mozart, Karl Marx and Casanova. During the Second World War, European émigrés were joined by black and white American GIs who could escape their segregated military units and party together in an area where almost anything goes.

When today's sex industry emerged in the 1950s it made Soho its headquarters, adding strip clubs, sex shops and cinemas to the brothels that had been there for centuries. The presence of the media helped to draw entrepreneurs and artists to the district, from pornographers such as Paul Raymond to jazz musicians like Ronnie Scott. It was home to the British music industry from the 1920s until the 1980s and much of the advertising, film, broadcasting and publishing industries too. Until 2011, Soho also embraced Central St Martin's School of Art, one of the powerhouses of British design, and the London College of Fashion is not far away, in Oxford Street.

Into this effervescently louche, tolerant and creative place stepped waves of immigrants from Europe, Africa and the Caribbean. Italian immigrants made a mark on Soho by opening restaurants and coffee bars. Coffee's role as a lubricant of eighteenth-century London life had been eroded by the Victorians' preference for tea, but the coffee house revival began after the first Gaggia machine arrived from Italy in 1952. Coffee bars became a hang-out for teenagers unable to get into pubs, and places like the Bar Italia and the 2i's were also a meeting point for musicians and talent spotters, giving unsigned acts the opportunity to play.

Soho at this time was the haunt of the Australian-born writer Colin MacInnes – one of the first celebrants of post-imperial Britain, a champion of its multiracial society and an analyst of its embryonic youth culture. Stylistically influenced by the American beat writer Jack Kerouac, MacInnes's 1959 novel *Absolute Beginners*, about a nameless 19-year-old freelance photographer, captured the atmosphere of Soho at just the moment when it became the incubus of British youth culture:

In this Soho, the headquarters of the adult mafia, you could everywhere see the signs of the un-silent teenage revolution. The disc shops with those lovely sleeves set in their windows, the most original thing to come out in our lifetime, and the kids inside them purchasing guitars or spending fortunes on the songs of the Top Twenty. The shirt-stores and bra-stores with cine-star photos in the window, selling all the exclusive teenage drag I've been describing. The hair-style salons where they inflict the blow-wave torture on the kids for hours on end. The cosmetic shops, to make girls of seventeen, fifteen, even thirteen, look like pale, rinsed-out sophisticates. Scooters and bubble cars driven madly down the roads by kids who, a few years ago, were pushing toys on the pavement. And everywhere you go the narrow coffee bars and darkened cellars with the kids packed tight, just whispering, like bees inside the hive waiting for a glorious queen bee to appear.[3]

Rock 'n' roll was the sound blaring out from most of the disc shops, and the godfathers of this teenage mafia – from Chuck Berry to Elvis Presley – were all American. Since the 1920s American mass culture, its music, films and fashions, had appealed to millions of Britons as the emblems of a more democratic society. That was especially true for the working class, who had most to gain by embracing a nation that promised social mobility and believed that where you came from mattered less than where you wished to go.

Meeting real Americans during the Second World War had not tarnished the glamorous image of the United States which Britons had previously consumed second-hand; on the contrary, a government official informed Winston Churchill in 1945 that 'an unmistakeable interest in America has been aroused among the young'.[4] Three years earlier, George Orwell had observed that 'cultivated' people often saw the United States as 'the vulgarizer of England and Europe' while 'the ordinary patriotic middle class' saw Americans as 'boastful, bad mannered and worshippers of money'. In contrast, 'English working class people . . . have no preconceived cultural hostility'. Consequently, wrote Orwell, 'In the big towns they are being more and more Americanised in speech through the medium of cinema.'[5]

What made rock 'n' roll more explosive than previous American imports were the social conditions in which the fusion of music, commerce and media took place in the 1950s. There were more young people, for a start. The number of people under the age of 20 grew from around three million in 1951 to four million in 1966, while in America the teen population rose from 10 to 15 million in the 1950s.[6] They also had more money to spend than previous generations. Teenage incomes in Britain had already risen substantially between the wars, but after 1945 they increased against a backdrop of greater access to secondary and higher education (the school leaving age was

raised to 15 in 1947).[7] An oft-cited market research survey in 1959 estimated that youngsters' real earnings had risen by 50 per cent since
1945, double the increase for adults. Their estimated annual expenditure
of £830 million was largely concentrated on clothes, motorcycles and
music, with records accounting for over 40 per cent of spending;
British record sales consequently rose from 4.5 million singles a year
in 1955 to over 61 million in 1963.[8] All of which, the report stated,
marked the emergence of a 'distinctive teenage spending for distinctive teenage ends in a distinctive teenage world'.[9] In addition, the
advent of television in the 1950s created a powerful medium which
instantaneously transmitted youth style to a national audience of
teenagers for the first time.

The term 'teenager', which first appeared in print in 1941, became
common currency in the American advertising industry in the early
1950s, but there were marked differences between Britain and the
United States.[10] Although music of black origin became ever more
popular on both sides of the Atlantic, the US teen market 'was pre-
eminently white and middle class', according to Bill Osgerby, whereas
in Britain 'it was understood as a more working class phenomenon'.
The 1959 survey concluded that 'not far short of 90 per cent of all
teenage spending was conditioned by working class taste and values'.[11]
That may have been an exaggeration but there can be no doubt that
the different class politics of Britain profoundly shaped the country's
youth cultures, from rockers to ravers; and as we will see, Mod exemplified that difference between Britain and the United States.

Throughout the twentieth century both the demonisation and the
celebration of youth culture in Britain revolved to a great extent
around its perceived relationship to America. In 1950s Europe as a
whole, the hostile reaction to rock 'n' roll was so intense because,
aside from concerns about sex and drugs, it was seen as the most
threatening form of Americanisation, targeting as it did the citizens
of the future. In Britain the threat was even greater because there
was no language barrier, which offered some protection to other
European cultures. What added to this anxiety was the fact that rock
'n' roll emerged at a time when America was replacing Britain as the
Western superpower: Elvis's first hit, 'Heartbreak Hotel', entered the
British charts in May 1956; later that year the United States forced
the humiliating withdrawal of French and British forces from the Suez

Canal. As political and economic supremacy was grudgingly conceded, the struggle to prevent American cultural domination intensified.

Liberals disdained America as much as conservatives. In the 1930s the playwright J. B. Priestley castigated what he called 'Admass' (and what the German émigré Theodor Adorno in the 1940s called 'the culture industry'): an inauthentic mass culture artificially created by advertisers and other manipulators of taste that created conformity under the pretence of individualism. Published in 1957, Richard Hoggart's *The Uses of Literacy* painted a bleak picture of English teenagers listening to American rock 'n' roll on a jukebox in the 'milk bars' that had sprung up in the Yorkshire towns where the author had grown up in the 1920s and 30s:

Most of the customers are boys aged between fifteen and twenty, with drape suits, picture ties and an American slouch. The young men waggle or stare, as desperately as Humphrey Bogart, across the tubular chairs. Compared even with the pub around the corner, this is all a peculiarly thin and pallid form of dissipation, a sort of spiritual dry rot amid the odour of boiled milk. Many of the customers – their clothes, their hair styles, their facial expressions all indicate – are living to a large extent a myth world compounded of a few simple elements which they take to be those of American life.[12]

Hoggart correctly observed that the rockers embraced a second-hand ersatz version of America – something that Mods would also oppose in the coming years. But what really annoyed the 39-year-old professor of literature was that the world of the jukebox was replacing the traditional working-class culture of his own youth which, although it may have been tasteless, was at least authentic. 'In the nastiness of their modernistic knick-knacks, their glaring showiness', Hoggart observed 'an aesthetic breakdown so complete that, in comparison with them, the layout of the living rooms in some of the poor homes from which the customers come seems to speak of a tradition as balanced and civilized as an eighteenth-century town house.'[13]

Americanisation was not just the concern of intellectuals. Following the French example, both Labour and Conservative governments tried to legislate America away with a haphazard system of cultural protectionism that began in the 1940s and lasted until the 1970s. Limits were placed on the number of Hollywood films that cinemas could show and the amount of American comics that retailers could distribute. The number of commercials that could be shown on TV was also curtailed, a ruling that means the British still watch fewer ads than Americans. Television's potential to be a conduit of Americana, piping it direct into the family home, was the main reason that commercial TV was not launched in Britain until 1955, a decade after it became available in the United States.[14] In *The American Invasion*, published in 1962 and a typical polemic of the time, the journalist Francis Williams asked, 'Need alliance involve occupation? Must we become Americans to save Western Civilisation?'[15] That the word 'invasion' should be used in that context, so soon after the British had been faced with a real invasion by Nazi Germany from which the United States had helped save them, is a measure of how strong anti-American feeling was among Britain's elites in the mid-twentieth century.

IT IS DEPLORABLE. IT IS TRIBAL. AND IT IS FROM AMERICA

Rock 'n' roll, the revolutionary fusion of black and white American music, had captivated Britain's working-class youth since its arrival in the early 1950s. 'Teddy Boys' first came to national attention in the summer of 1953 after a south London gang fight that ended in murder.[16] *The Wild One*, released later that year, starring Marlon Brando, captured the classic American rocker look of black leather jackets, denim jeans and T-shirts; Colin MacInnes memorably described it as the look of 'an urban, motorised cowboy'.[17] The film was banned in Britain until 1968 because of government fears that it would incite juvenile delinquency, but it had British imitators, notably *The Damned* (1963), starring Oliver Reed and directed by Joseph Losey, an American exile blacklisted in Hollywood during the McCarthy era. The film opens with its theme song:

Black leather, black leather, rock, rock, rock
Black leather, black leather, smash, smash, smash,
Black leather, black leather, kill, kill, kill,
You know leather love is way out of line.[18]

But rock 'n' roll was more than 'a contemporary incitement to mindless fucking and arbitrary vandalism: screw and smash music', as George Melly once described it.[19] Those who embraced rock 'n' roll at its peak between 1953 and 1959 were the first to experience modern youth culture as a hedonistic revolt against authority that used music, style and sex to assert a distinctive generational identity. Like the Mods later, the early Teddy Boys subverted the social order with their appearance, combining the greased American rocker hair-style with a crisp mimicry of British upper-class Edwardian dress, wearing long, velvet-collared 'drape' coats and tight, 'drainpipe' jeans. Yet Britain's rock 'n' rollers generally aped the music, language and styles of the United States, rather than creatively borrowing from America to produce something distinctively British, as most subsequent youth cultures have done; British rockers such as Cliff Richard and Tommy Steele were mere imitations of their more potent heroes.

In Britain the emergence of youth culture coincided with the first large-scale African, Caribbean and Asian immigration, as people from former colonies made use of their British citizenship to migrate to the United Kingdom in search of a better life. In the long run, this influx helped Britain develop its own, distinctively hybrid, youth culture which challenged that of America without taking refuge in indigenous folk traditions as other European countries tended to do. In the short term, however, black immigration heightened hostility to rock 'n' roll. Alarmed by the creation of 'ROCK AND ROLL BABIES', the *Daily Mail* declared in 1956: 'It is deplorable. It is tribal. And it is from America. It follows ragtime, blues, Dixie, hot cha-cha and the boogie-woogie, which surely originated in the jungle. We sometimes wonder whether this is the Negro's revenge.' As in America, rock 'n' roll's overt sexuality was the main source of concern. The *Mail* article continued: 'Rock and roll is sexy music. It can make the blood race. It has something of the African tom-tom and voodoo dance.'[20]

Yet those who welcomed decolonisation and deplored racism also lamented that American popular music had eclipsed that of Britain. One sign of it was the closure of the nation's music halls, a staple of working-class entertainment since the mid-nineteenth century. The playwright John Osborne employed a fading music hall star, Archie Rice, as a metaphor for the end of empire in *The Entertainer* (1957) – one of the reasons why he was attacked as 'an intellectual Teddy Boy' at the time.[21] Although comedy and other types of vaudeville survived by transferring to television, music faced tougher competition from the United States. Colin MacInnes's essay, 'England, Half English', captured his regret about the Americanisation of the nation's youth:

Until some forty years ago, the English song about English life resounded boisterously in the Music Halls. Since then, new American musical idioms, potently diffused by the cinema, radio, gramophone and now TV have swamped our own ditties with the help, above all, of the shared language of the lyrics . . . Even the skiffle singers – a thoroughly English phenomenon – use mostly transatlantic ballads. The battle for a place among the top twenty has been won by British singers at the cost of splitting their person-alities and becoming bi-lingual: speaking American at the recording session, and English in the pub around the corner afterwards . . . With this odd duality teenage fans seem quite at ease . . . rather as the congregation might wish the sermon to be delivered in the vernacular, and the plainsong chanted in mysterious Latin.[22]

'Will [song-writers] begin to write songs in an English idiom,' MacInnes asked, 'about English life, that the performers can sing as Englishmen not only in body, but in voice as well? Can teenagers, in short, take songs about *themselves*?' His answer, written in 1961, at a time when rock 'n' roll had lost its original impetus, was cautious:

It's certain that if English pop songs, as well as singers, do appear, they'll be profoundly influenced by America. It's a question of measure though: of an influence not becoming, as it has done in the pop world, an eclipse. Song after all, is the simplest, most instinctive way by which a people expresses its own ideas about itself; and if a people – like the English – sings about another people – the Americans – then this may be a sign that it is ceasing to be a people in any real sense at all. Perhaps this is happening: perhaps it has to. Yet who, ten years ago, could have foreseen the sensational rise of professional jazz artistry in Britain?[23]

It would, as MacInnes thought, be a question of 'measure' rather than a transatlantic battle for the nation's soul won by one side or the other. And, as he guessed, it was another strand of American music that incubated popular Modernism in Britain during the early 1960s.

BIRTH OF THE COOL

The origins of Mod lay in two countries whose political revolutions in the eighteenth century the British had violently rejected: America and France. And the midwife that slapped it into life was not rock 'n' roll but jazz. The movement got its name from a nucleus of around two hundred founding 'faces' who emerged in Soho around the summer of 1958, calling themselves 'Modernists' after their love of modern jazz, or bebop. Led by saxophonist Charlie Parker, bebop fizzed in New York just after the war then exploded at the same time that Elvis Presley took to the stage, with the release of Miles Davis's *Birth of the Cool* in 1957.

The term 'cool', now so often a lazy expression of approval, originally meant a taught state of mind in which you harnessed your anger against injustice. It sprang from the earlier Jazz Age – coined, it is thought, by the Harlem Renaissance author Langston Hughes in the 1930s. 'I play it cool', Hughes wrote, 'and dig all jive / That's the reason / I stay alive.'[24] Modern jazz was not just a musical reaction to the easier, more tuneful, sounds of traditional ('trad') jazz that had originated in New Orleans; it was also a political reaction to a segregated America in which black musicians were harassed by the police, exploited by the music industry and seen as entertainers rather than artists. 'Beboppers refused to accept racism, poverty or economic exploitation,' explained drummer Kenny Clarke. 'If America wouldn't honour its constitution and respect us as men, we couldn't give a shit about the American way.'[25]

Beboppers embraced Europe, performing and sojourning in Continental cities where they were feted and found sanctuary from segregation. Paris was a favoured destination, as it had been for Americans in the 1920s and 30s. But whereas performers of that era like Josephine Baker had often perpetuated stereotypes of black people in shows like the Revue Nègre, the stars of modern jazz rejected caricature in favour of a creative dialogue with Europe. The French Existentialist movement influenced some. Jean-Paul Sartre's famous dictum that 'one must act to be free' appealed to the more educated and politicised generation of black musicians that emerged after the Second World War – a generation personified by Miles Davis, who met Sartre when he and Charlie Parker played the Paris Jazz Festival in 1949. At that time, Davis also fell in love with the singer Juliette Greco, beginning a passionate three-year relationship that has been called 'the marriage of bebop and existentialism'.[26] Greco was the epitome of Left Bank cool: tall, with straight black hair, she wore a black beret and raincoat with the collar turned up, singing the songs of her husband, the poet Boris Vian, in Paris jazz clubs with studied ennui. Bebop stars soon adopted elements of Left Bank style. Pianist Thelonious Monk and trumpeter Dizzy Gillespie took to wearing berets, goatee beards, horn-rimmed glasses and plenty of black, while Davis made sharp Italian suits one of his early trademarks.[27] His favoured make, adopted by jazz fans on both continents, was Brioni, founded in Rome in 1945 then launched in Britain and America in 1954. The first retailer to import Brioni to the UK was Cecil Gee's shop in the Charing Cross Road, which became an early Mod haunt.

Modernists fused this look with American style, especially the so-called Ivy League look, which was popular with middle- and upper-class American youth from the mid-1950s to the mid-1960s, and which later enjoyed a revival thanks to the TV drama *Mad Men* about the advertising world in that period. The style is epitomised by the suits and shirts of the Brooks Brothers clothing company. Founded in New York in 1818, it had invented the button-down collar on dress shirts in 1896, after its owner had noticed English polo players using buttons to stop collars flapping in their faces. Brooks Brothers' controversial use of colours like turquoise and mauve had livened up the urban American man's wardrobe. To these were added Bass Weejun loafers, introduced by the Bass company of Maine in 1934 and based on moccasins worn by Norwegian farmers (hence the name 'weejun').

A more casual version of the Ivy look included Sta-Prest trousers and desert boots, introduced by Clarks in 1949 and based on the comfortable suede boot worn by off-duty British army officers in the Second World War. This was complemented by the Baracuta G9 jacket with its distinctive tartan lining, popularly known as the 'Harrington' after the clothes retailer John Simons (the main importer of Ivy clothes in Britain) noticed the character Rodney Harrington wearing it in the TV series *Peyton Place*.[28] The look was completed by the neatly cropped 'college boy' hairstyle made famous by John F. Kennedy. It all became known as 'Jivy Ivy' when jazz artists adapted the style, notably Miles

Davis on the cover of *Milestones* and his 1959 release *Kind of Blue*, still the best-selling jazz album of all time.

Like a number of black figureheads of the time, Miles Davis came from a middle-class background – he was a dentist's son educated at the elite Juilliard School of Music – but that didn't stop him getting almost beaten to death by police outside New York's Birdland jazz club just after the release of *Kind of Blue*. At that time, fashion was not just a form of conspicuous consumption driven by vanity and a desire to conform; it could be a subtle political statement, designed to unnerve the powerful, and sometimes it succeeded with violent effect. The author and lifelong Mod, Paolo Hewitt believes that Davis's 'use of the Ivy League look remains one of the great fashion statements of all time. By dressing in the clothing of those who fiercely resent their culture, their music, the colour of their skin, Miles and his peers are playing the enemy beautifully, walking amongst them whilst changing the landscape forever. You think he's a bank manager, in fact Miles is a revolutionary in silk and mohair.'[29]

Before the mass media and high street retailers noticed their style, Mods had to be devoted enough to seek out the small independent shops that sold their favourite clothes or records. Former Mod Nick Logan, who founded the influential British style magazines *The Face* and *Arena* in the 1980s, remembered how much harder it was in the early 60s: 'There were no style sections in newspapers to help you, just the obscure corners of the weekly music press at a time when the music editors were clueless as to what was really going on.'[30] One of the ways that 'Jivy Ivy' was transmitted was by studying the album covers of bebop stars, especially those for the record company Blue Note. A pioneering independent jazz label, Blue Note was set up in 1939 by two Jewish refugees to the United States from Nazi Germany, Alfred Lion and Francis Wolff. Committed to bebop even when it wasn't making them much money, Blue Note did more to promote modern jazz than any other label; it also had a huge influence on fashion. In 1956, Lion and Wolff employed a young Californian called Reid Miles to design their covers and over the next decade his artworks were a style template for fans on both sides of the Atlantic. As well as crisp black and white photographs of artists like Sonny Clark, Lee Morgan and Herbie Hancock, Miles's work employed the graphic principles of the Bauhaus.[31]

It was that fusion of American and European fashion and design, married to the musical and political dynamism of modern jazz, that captivated young Modernists wanting to escape the cloying traditions of British working-class culture without becoming ersatz Americans. Some studied at Central St Martin's Art College and others worked in the media in Soho, but whatever their occupation, they gathered there from all over inner London. Other Mods came from suburbs and satellite towns around the city, like Croydon and Woking, where in the early 1960s bars and dance halls began to cater for them. Still hardly known outside the south of England, Modernism gestated for approximately three years in the capital and its outskirts, where it spread organically from district to district.[32] During this gestation period, its style codes were haphazardly developed through random encounters on streets or in bars and clubs, with no clear figureheads in the world of music or fashion, still less a manifesto, until a national magazine took notice of it in 1962.

It should also be remembered that in this period the followers of trad jazz far outnumbered the Modernists. At its most commercial, the British trad revival of 1945–65 rivalled rock 'n' roll for mass appeal. It was epitomised by the Bill Haley of jazz: clarinettist Acker Bilk who, though younger than Miles Davis, appeared to be from another age with his chubby figure, beard, bowler hat and his sanitised version of the Dixieland sound. In 1962 Bilk had a No. 1 hit in the United States with 'Stranger on the Shore', and that same year he appeared in the film It's Trad, Dad!, directed by the American Dick Lester, who would later work with the Beatles. More purist than bebop, trad was popular among middle-class youths, especially Left-leaning bohemian types, which the media called beatniks. Many were at the same time followers of the Anglo-American folk revival, and the bastard child it conceived with jazz and blues, skiffle.

None of that appealed to the Modernists. They regarded parent-friendly trad as merely retrograde; and folk music was beyond the pale, since it tended to romanticise rural, pre-industrial society and therefore held little attraction for these self-consciously urban, cosmopolitan teen-agers. Those Mods who grew up in the suburbs looked beyond their parents' privet hedges to the fast, neon-lit world of the city for their kicks and not to the peripheral fields on which their homes had been built. The British folk revival of the 1950s and 60s – led by Ewan MacColl and Peggy Seeger – was more politically radical than previous incarnations of the genre, but if it engaged more with urban life it usually did so by celebrating the struggles of the shipbuilder or the miner – traditional working-class worlds that Mods were desperate to escape from.

The other reason why the Modernists of Soho disliked trad and folk music was their followers' apparent indifference to style. As Graham Hughes, one of the first Mods and a student at St Martin's, remembered: 'We looked different because modern jazz we felt was always a bit more stylish and we responded to that. We would go to the allnighter dressed in these box jackets that Cecil Gee imported . . . It was to look different from the others in the jazz crowd, which was all very studenty, scruffy. We simply didn't want to wear long woolly jumpers and jeans covered in paint.'[33] Terry Rawlings concluded that Mods were 'teenage dandies reacting against all that had come before – the Fifties yobbos and, even worse, the scruffy, cider-drinking ex-students who grew beards, wore loose sweaters and liked watered-down Trad Jazz.'[34]

For those Mods about to storm the music industry, modern jazz was a revelation. As Ian McLagan, future keyboardist for the Small Faces, recalled: 'When I first went to art school, Dixieland, or "Trad" as we all knew it, was all the rage. It was loose and rowdy and it went well with cheap cider and stomping about on the dance floor like an idiot.' Then one night McLagan heard bebop while listening to trumpeter Humphrey Lyttelton's radio show, *Jazz Club*:

He played 'I'm Your Hoochie Coochie Man' from *Muddy Waters at Newport*, and Thelonious Monk's 'Blue Monk' from *Monk's Moods* and I couldn't believe my ears . . . Although I didn't know anything about modern jazz, and still don't, I knew straight away that Monk was someone very special . . . in very different ways they were both playing the blues . . . I went to all three record stores that we had in Hounslow High Street the next Saturday morning, eagerly expecting to hear and buy both records, but not only were they not in stock, the salesman thought I'd made the names up. In England in 1963, there was no one called Thelonious or Muddy. Ian was about as exotic as it got back then.[35]

It is here, rather than during the Mod/rocker riots of 1964–65, that the first fault-line in British youth culture appeared. Fights broke out between followers of traditional and modern jazz at the Beaulieu Jazz Festival in 1960, just before Acker Bilk was due to come on as the headline act, prompting the BBC to take its TV coverage off the air. Beaulieu was the first festival of popular music in Britain – a cultural phenomenon which, like so many in the country, owes its existence to an enterprising aristocrat. Lord Edward Montagu had staged the event on his Hampshire country estate since 1956, conceiving it as 'a British version of the Newport Jazz Festival' in America 'and, ideally, as the Glyndebourne of Jazz'.[36] Pre-dating Glastonbury by fourteen years, it was the first such event to provide on-site camping, a car park, toilets and fast-food stalls. Yet complaints by locals about the disturbances forced Montagu to terminate the festival in 1961.

The poet and jazz critic Philip Larkin saw these skirmishes as part of a struggle for the future of civilisation. A trad fan, Larkin believed that Charlie Parker and his followers were part of international modernism, which had already corrupted art and literature:

This is my essential criticism of modernism, whether perpetuated by Parker, Pound, or Picasso: it helps us neither to enjoy nor endure. It will divert us as long as we are prepared to be mystified or outraged, but maintains its hold only by being more mystifying and more outrageous: it has no lasting power. Hence the compulsion on every modernist to wade deeper and deeper into violence and obscenity: hence the succession of Parker by Rollins and Coltrane and Coltrane by Coleman, Ayler and Shepp. In a way it's a relief: if jazz records are to be one long screech, if painting is to be a blank canvas, if a play is two hours of sexual intercourse performed *coram populo*, then let's get it over, the sooner the better, in the hope that human values reassert themselves.[37]

The young British fans of Coltrane et al. found an unlikely champion in the trad singer and author George Melly, who had performed at the first Beaulieu Festival. In his seminal study of 'the pop arts in Britain', published in 1970, Melly argued that modern jazz was the crucible of British youth culture. Although it was 'less popular and more esoteric . . . it was based on a contemporary form and had none of the archaic romanticism of the revivialists'. Bebop's stars, wrote Melly:

had no interest in using their music as an in to success in a white world; on the contrary they used it as a wall; its very inaccessibility an expression of their contempt for a society which offered them a living only in exchange for the mugging acknowledgement of racial inferiority . . . The early British modernists based their lives and art on the same premises. They too affected dark glasses and the hip stance of their heroes . . . Being both white and British they were as far removed from their idols as the revivalist was from his . . . This is not to doubt their sincerity. They understood not only the musical complexity of bop but the spirit that created it and, within their emotional means, they tried to play it. Yet they remained what Norman Mailer called 'white negroes'. They chose to reject society; it didn't automatically reject them. It's this voluntary choice that they share in common with the recent spirit in pop music.[38]

Melly was a regular at Britain's most famous jazz club, Ronnie Scott's. A descendant of Jewish émigrés from Russia, Scott opened his club in Soho in 1959, booking the best bebop musicians to perform for their British devotees. The author Len Deighton, then a Soho habitué, remembered that within a 'class-system [that] was far more disruptive than race or religion, jazz was the great leveller and we were all devoted to jazz music'.[39] Another regular at Scott's club was Colin MacInnes, who described the music's integrative potential in *Absolute Beginners*:

The great thing about the jazz world, and all the kids that enter into it, is that no one, not a soul, cares what your class is, or what your race is, or what your income, or if you're a boy, or girl, or bent, or versatile, or what you are – so long as you dig the scene and can behave yourself, and have left all that crap behind you, too, when you come in the jazz club door.[40]

Unlike either trad or rock 'n' roll, British bebop did not fall for hero worship or imitation. While Bilk mimicked Beiderbecke and Cliff Richard aped Elvis Presley, modern jazz virtuosi like pianist Stan Tracey and saxophonist Tubby Hayes developed their own sound, Hayes touring successfully in America and presenting his own TV show in Britain. Caribbean artists added to the mix of British and American styles to produce something even richer. A decade before calypso, ska and reggae influenced British youth culture, West Indian jazz musicians were helping to lay its foundations. The greatest of them was the saxophonist Joe Harriott, who came to Britain from Jamaica in 1951 and whose 1960 album for Blue Note, *Free Form*, was hugely influential on both sides of the Atlantic. He died prematurely in 1973, at the age of 45. Most American beboppers were also dead by then, ravaged by heroin addiction and the struggle to make money from a form of music that rarely made it into the charts.

Their fame had ebbed a decade before their health did. The more commercial bebop classics like Lee Morgan's 'Sidewinder' remained dance-floor favourites at Mod clubs, and the Hammond organ sound of Jimmy Smith influenced countless British artists from Steve Winwood to Paul Weller. But once Beatlemania exploded, jazz would never again have the impact that it briefly did in the mid-twentieth century. When John Coltrane died of cancer in July 1967, one of his biggest English fans, Pete Townshend, was completing the Who's first concept album, *Sell Out*. By that time, Mod had become a global movement of millions thanks partly to the Who and to the British rhythm and blues explosion which they were part of.

RAGE FROM THE UNDERGROUND

To some extent Mod's obsession with black American music was based on its raw sexuality, absent from so much white popular music, which had drawn young whites to it since the early twentieth century. But black music was not all about sex and many Mods identified with the substance as well as the sound of music that expressed the struggle of living in one of the most racist and segregated societies on earth. They were smart enough to know that being raised on a sharecropper's farm in Alabama or in the ghettos of Chicago was a harsher existence than any social apartheid caused by class prejudice in Shepherd's Bush or Hackney. Still, the redemptive aspect of rhythm and blues chimed with white working-class Britons. 'R&B emanated from struggle and the English working class totally identified with black America', explained the Who's Roger Daltrey. 'The Blues had that element of rage from the underground.'[41] As John Lee Hooker and Otis Redding began to replace John Coltrane and Miles Davis as the soundtrack to Mod lives, the man responsible for the transition was not a hip young Svengali from London but a modest, 50-year-old accountant from Merseyside called Harold Pendleton.

A jazz devotee, Pendleton had moved to London in 1948 and given up his career in finance to set up the National Jazz Federation, before launching the Marquee Club in Oxford Street as a bebop venue in 1958. Sensing changing tastes, in 1962 he started a rhythm and blues night at the club. 'The entrance is murky, and the air inside is hot, damp and salty', reported one female journalist later in the decade. 'If you really like pop music and can survive in unconditioned air you should investigate this place.'[42] Pendleton brought over American stars like Muddy Waters and showcased British acts, such as Alexis Korner's Blues Incorporated, which included a young Brian Jones. Jones had been a bebop fan since his teens and had run his own jazz club in his hometown of Cheltenham. But he disliked the way that some in the jazz world, Pendleton included, looked down on R&B, complaining in a letter to *Jazz News* about 'the pseudo-intellectual snobbery that unfortunately contaminates the jazz scene'.[43]

It was at the Marquee that Jones's second band, the Rolling Stones, performed their first professional concert on 12 July 1962 in front of an audience of Mods, with the band dressed like them in sharp suits. Their 19-year-old manager, Andrew Loog Oldham, was another bebop fan who had been a Mod since he was a schoolboy. He remembered having his dove-grey mohair suit confiscated because it did not conform to school standards: 'As he took my suit away, Mr Oughton, the housemaster, said, "I don't know why you bother, you only wore it for a day." "Yeah," I thought, "but what a day."'[44] Having left school at 16, Oldham worked as a waiter at Ronnie Scott's club in Soho and as an assistant to Mary Quant at her Chelsea boutique before joining the music industry as the manager and producer of the Rolling Stones.[45] He shared an office with a fellow Mod on the Stones' payroll, the graphic designer Pete Meaden, who worked in advertising. 'Peter and I bonded on the look of American jazz style . . .', remembered Oldham. 'We found each other's anger and reinforced our ambitions.'[46] Meaden went on to become the Who's manager, and two years after the Stones' debut at the Marquee the band got a residency at the club. The monochrome posters that the band had designed for their act – showing Pete Townshend's arm aloft, ready to crash down on his Rickenbacker guitar, with the slogan 'Maximum R&B' – became one of the iconic images of the Mod movement.

Harold Pendleton's influence didn't end there. In 1961, when the Beaulieu Jazz Festival folded, he founded the National Jazz & Blues Festival in the verdant west London suburb of Richmond. As at Beaulieu, there were soon complaints about the noise and improper goings-on, with the local paper describing the festival-goers as 'people of all ages with a penchant for vagrancy and little use for all the conventional paraphernalia of beds, changes of clothing, soap, razors and so on'.[47] Jazz acts gradually gave way to R&B performers. In 1965, when the Rolling Stones played in front of 33,000 screaming fans, there were more R&B than jazz bands; by 1971, when the event moved site to become the Reading Rock Festival, jazz musicians had virtually disappeared from the line-up.

R&B and soul also began to sweep through the nation's nightclubs, creating the club culture we know today: a tautly hedonistic subter-ranean world where people from all backgrounds collided and congre-gated, driven by confidence-building, energy-boosting drugs that enabled them to dance, talk and grind all night. Clubs, drugs and youth were not a new cocktail, of course: all three had been shaken together in the new Jazz Age. The first drug raid on a British nightclub had taken place in 1950, when police entered Soho's Club Eleven to find that the two hundred black and white bebop fans dancing together were in possession of marijuana, cocaine and a small amount of opium. Among those arrested that night was Ronnie Scott.

What made these clubs different was that they fostered the cult of the DJ, a phenomenon imported from France in the late 1950s – together with the word *discothèque*, literally a library of records.[48] Le Discotheque and the Flamingo Club (which had also opened as a jazz venue in the 1950s), both in Wardour Street, were early Mod haunts. But their temple was the former Club Eleven, now called the Scene Club, in Ham Yard. Every weekend hundreds of Mods packed its floors until 6 a.m., fuelled by their drug of choice, 'French Blues' – blue-coloured amphetamines imported from France. Andrew Loog Oldham remembered the place as 'a loud, smoky haven for the disenfranchised working class ... posing more than dancing, jaws frantically chewing the night away. Three-legged, legless Mod monsters, pilled to the walls of aurafide stress, bound and bonded by sound and dread of the job on Monday.'[49]

The Scene was run by Irishman Ronan O'Rahilly, a maverick entre-preneur like Pendleton, who had once managed Alexis Korner's Blues Incorporated and who in 1964 founded Radio Caroline, Britain's first pirate radio station. With padded walls and cushions strewn around the edge of the dance floor for overheated dancers to relax, it pre-dated the style of the psychedelic clubs in the late 1960s and the chill-out rooms of ambient and trance clubs in the 1990s. The club's resident DJ was Guy Stevens, who would go on to produce Mott the Hoople and The Clash. O'Rahilly described Stevens as the 'Lenin of British club culture', the man who led the dance revolution: 'Everyone would come to hear Guy. The Stones, the Beatles, Eric Clapton – all the major stars. People would come from all over the country and from France and Holland too. He used to carry his records around in a huge trunk and he was so protective of them that he used to sit on it while he DJed. I've seen him sleep on it. It was like a religion to him.'[50]

Live music thrived too. 'Everything is exploding', one band manager told *Melody Maker* in 1965. That year, within a 40-mile radius of central London, an estimated 300,000 people were paying to hear R&B bands every week. There were 140 groups in that area and a further 160 nationwide, creating a live music business thought to be worth £1 million a week.[51] The cult's following had grown to approximately 500,000 by this time, with many more on the periphery, derided as 'mids' or 'tickets' because they had metaphorically bought a ticket to join the movement.[52]

As the cult grew it also spread out of London and the south of England. *Mod* magazine received letters from followers in Scotland and the North protesting about the arrogance of Londoners, and prompting an apology from the editor: 'We're always inclined to think that the girls and guys up there walk about in kilts saying "haggis" or "och" with every other word. It's not true. Seeing some of the photographs that they have been sending I'd say that in some parts they are in fact just as fashion mad and go-ahead as we are in London.'[53] 'There are many places in the North and Midlands that are as mod – if not moddier – than London', confirmed Steve Marriott of the Small Faces.[54] Yet Britain's capital city remained Mod's spiritual home-land. Ian Hebditch remembers 'the strange inferiority complex' at his club the Birdcage, in Portsmouth: 'The Mods from London were admired and yet feared. Any visitor from London to the Birdcage earned instant respect. There was a big hole in the ceiling over the stage where Pete Townshend stuck his guitar through it, it was never repaired because it was a kind of status symbol for the club, "Ah, Townshend did that, what a night."'[55] Britain's first youth cult was not only the cradle of today's nightclubs and music festivals; Mod had also given the world its first rock group.

THAT'S ELGAR ON SPEED

One of the reasons for Mod's enduring popularity is that it was never too closely associated with one genre of music or a particular set of artists. But acquiring figureheads between 1964 and 1966, who in their music, dress and interviews articulated Mods' outlook, turned a local style cult into a national youth movement when the Who formed a triumvirate with the Kinks and the Small Faces.

The Small Faces were regarded as the most authentic of the big three because they came from the East End. The cockney has had an iconic place in English culture since the late nineteenth century, romanticised in song, film and on TV as the epitome of working-class grit, wit and streetwise ambition; in the 1960s the cockney became the poster boy for an era when it seemed that working-class pop stars, actors and designers were creating a more meritocratic Britain. 'They bring into the world of Soho and Mayfair a fresh honesty, a cockney sense of humour, and the ability to stand outside themselves and laugh', concluded one female journalist in an early interview with the Small Faces' Steve Marriott. 'Listen, luv,' Marriott told her, 'we don't know a flat from a sharp, on paper. Our whole success has been a giggle to the rest of the lads and me. It was a gay, phenomenal accident.'[56] It was true that no one from the music industry had groomed Marriott, Ronnie Lane, Kenney Jones and Ian McLagan. They were four short men who had been 'faces' on the Mod scene long before their ruthless manager, Don Arden, persuaded them to sign a contract at his Carnaby Street office with their disapproving parents looking on.

Recalling why he became a Mod, Marriott was vague: 'I liked the attitude. It was certainly a lot different than my mum's, that's as blatant as I can put it. I was starting to turn Mod when I was living at home, trying to be an individual and having terrible rows with my Dad for looking like a poof.'[57] Of the group he said, 'We had a lot of energy, a lot of push and a little bit of flair which was missing off the scene at the time.'[58] The Small Faces released their first single, 'Whatcha Gonna Do About It?', in the summer of 1965 after playing together for only five months. One of the song's co-writers was also responsible for Cliff Richard's 'Move It' – a fact which showed that even the most devout little Mods could sometimes play the industry to their advantage.

However authentic these East End teenagers were, it was their four friends from west London – Pete Townshend, Keith Moon, Roger Daltrey and John Entwistle – who drew together key strands of contemporary art, fashion and music, allied them with social change and stamped 'Modernist' over it all. As 'Irish' Jack Lyons, another original 'face', remembered: 'Nobody spoke to Mods until Pete Townshend wrote "I Can't Explain". "I feel hot and cold down in my soul" – that's Elgar on speed.'[59] The Who's first single, released in January 1965, was barely noticed in America but reached No. 8 in the British charts. The group's biographer Dave Marsh described it as 'an exceptional expression of the mod ethos', because it dramatised the inability of its adherents verbally to articulate sexual and social frustration. Far more than the anthemic grandstanding of 'My Generation' the song expressed a sense of what it was to be young and from an ordinary background at that time. 'I Can't Explain' opens with short, sharp R&B power chords reminiscent of the Kinks, whose producer the Who shared at the time. At the end of the second verse, Daltrey pauses in mid-line and the music fades; then come a few rapid drum shots from Keith Moon – which to the ears of the critic Greil Marcus were 'hard as two cracks from a rifle'– before Daltrey finishes the line and the song reaches a climax of unresolved frustration.[60]

Mods thought that Pete Townshend's song really expressed how they felt. Although the Who was formed five years after the movement began in Soho and the group were frank about the fact that they had adopted it for their own ends, Townshend became a believer in the cult. In an interview given to the American readers of *Rolling Stone* in 1968 he summed up what it meant to him and his fans:

One of the things that has impressed me most in life was the Mod movement in England . . . It was a movement of young people, much bigger than the hippie thing. It was an army, a powerful aggressive army of teenagers with transport. Man, with these scooters and with their own way of dressing . . . it was hip, it was fashionable, it was clean, it was groovy. You could be a bank clerk, man, it was acceptable . . . To be a mod you had to have short hair, money enough to buy a real smart suit, good shoes, good shirt; you had to be able to dance like a madman. You had to always be pilled up . . . You had to have like an army anourak [sic] to wear on the scooter.[61]

Happier than some to assume the mantle of a youth spokesman, Townshend explained that 'My Generation' was his expression of feeling part of that 'aggressive army of teenagers'. In the same interview he declared that 'most mods were lower-class garbagemen', not 'the sort of people that could play the guitar, and it was just groovy for them to have a group'.[62] Yet Townshend did more than recruit people to the cause in the 1960s; over the following thirty years, the Who would inspire subsequent generations to play for the 'garbagemen' and so regenerate Mod in a way that completely undermined the longing for death expressed in 'My Generation'.

Ironically, the group most responsible for exporting Mod style around the world was the band that some Mods affected to despise: the Beatles. They rejected the Fab Four for three reasons: first, because the leather outfits and covers of American rock 'n' roll in their early years made them suspect; second, because purists regarded their music as too poppy and therefore 'girls' music' (illustrating just how laughably sexist Mods could be); and thirdly because the Beatles' music later embraced psychedelia, bringing an end to the golden age of R&B.

The Beatles didn't care. When they appeared on Mods' favourite TV show, *Ready, Steady, Go!* on 20 March 1964, the host Cathy McGowan asked the four Liverpudlians: 'Are you Mods or Rockers?' 'I'm a mocker', Ringo replied, his witty ambivalence expressing the group's reluctance to be categorised.[63] Yet the Beatles were sympathetic to the Mod movement. Like the Rolling Stones they appropriated its style and their phenomenal success helped to popularise it. As the American author Jonathan Gould concluded:

The Beatles, who would be instrumental in sending Mod style around the world, were already a little old, by 1962, to qualify as Mods per se. Yet for several years they had been assimilating many of the same influences and cultivating many of the same fine distinctions of taste. Though they had convinced their fans in Liverpool and Hamburg with their swaggering imper- sonation of Rocker nihilism, under the leather, under the skin, the Beatles were quintessential Mods: young men who had rejected the sanctioned avenues of advancement as too narrow, too compromised, and simply too boring to pursue.[64]

Years after their manager Brian Epstein decided to smarten up what he called his 'four ill-presented youths' in 1962,[65] Lennon claimed to have objected, saying that 'my little rebellion was to have my tie loose with the top button of my shirt undone, but Paul'd always come up to me and put it straight.'[66] That should be taken with a pinch of salt, as part of Lennon's attempt to present himself as the group's avant- garde conscience; actually, for most of the 1960s he embraced different aspects of Mod style both formal and casual. The Beatles' first, and most Mod-inspired look – the collarless Bavarian-style jackets and round-collared shirts – was created by the Soho tailor Dougie Millings and inspired by the French designer Pierre Cardin. Millings was a Glaswegian who had been dressing stars since moving to London in the 1950s, fusing American and Continental styles to great effect (another client was Michael Caine). The Scotsman continued to work for the Beatles until the late 1960s. As he remembered:

Hardly a day passed without seeing or hearing from them. In fact, they called me Dad. The phone used to go and there'd be a voice asking for ridiculous things in a foreign accent. Usually it was John messing around. Once I had somebody telling me that 'His Excellency' would be with me shortly, and I said, 'Oh, right, John.' Then this great big car pulled up with a flag on the front. It was Haile Selassie's grandson, the Crown Prince of Ethiopia. I said, 'I thought you were John Lennon.' He said, 'Who's John Lennon?'[67]

Faces without Shadows

Lennon may have been unknown to East African princes, but news of popular Modernism began to reach the rest of Britain a month before the release of 'Love Me Do'. In September 1962, three Jewish

Mods from Stoke Newington in north London gave an interview to a men's magazine called *Town*. Originally called *Man about Town*, it had been bought up and relaunched in 1960 by Clive Labovitch and a young entrepreneur called Michael Heseltine, who would become a controversial star of the British Conservative Party in the 1980s. Under the editorship of Nicholas Tomalin and the future chat show host Michael Parkinson, *Town* appealed to its target audience of smart, professional young men out to have a good time, by using modern graphics, photographs by Terence Donovan and David Bailey, and features by Shirley Conran and Kingsley Amis. This was not only the moment when the insular little world of London Mods entered the national media; it was also the point when a section of bourgeois Britain saw a new reflection of itself in working-class life – an image that was reassuringly familiar and yet slightly distorted in a strange, and what turned out to be a rather compelling, parody of middle- and upper-class life.

The feature, called 'Faces without Shadows', reproduced interviews with three aspirational working-class men: 20-year-old Peter Sugar, whose Polish family owned the hairdresser's salon he worked in; 20-year-old Michael Simmonds, who worked in another hairdresser's; and 15-year-old Marc Feld, the son of a market trader and still at school, who had fallen in love with French style while on holiday in Paris with his parents. The photos for the feature were taken by Don McCullin, who later earned fame for his coverage of the Vietnam War. The chief 'face' that McCullin shot for *Town* was Marc Feld who would eventually transform himself into the glam rock star Marc Bolan. Feld said that his heroes were Beau Brummell, the upper-class dandy of Regency England, and John Stephen, the working-class Scottish clothes retailer who had recently set up shop in Carnaby Street and who would soon dress thousands of modern dandies like Feld.

Expecting to find naive rebels against the status quo, *Town* instead discovered three young men whose aim was wealth and social mobility, and whose status symbols were clothes (of which they had many) and hairstyles (they cut one another's hair). And while they expressed support for the 'Ban the Bomb' movement, their politics were firmly to the right:

'I'm a Conservative,' said Sugar. 'I mean, Conservatives are for the rich, aren't they, and everyone wants to be rich, really, don't they?'

'They've been in a long time and they done alright,' said Simmonds.

'Yeah, like he says, they're for the rich, really, so I'm for them,' says Feld.

'Of course I don't know much about it,' says Sugar.[68]

The interviewer detected in this strange young trio 'a general lack of mercy towards the rest of the world'. Were they harbingers of the thrusting Thatcherites that Michael Heseltine fought twenty years later as a guardian of moderate Conservatism? Certainly this would not be the last time that Mods publicly expressed support for the Conservative Party; in the 1970s and 80s some would also be associated with the Far Right, thereby dashing hopes invested by the postwar Left in the radical potential of youth culture. Little Thatcherites or not, what motivated the trio in *Town* was a desire to get rich without conforming, an urge of ambitious young men in any age. In that context, the theatre critic Kenneth Tynan's definition of a dandy sheds light on Marc Feld's love of Beau Brummell. 'A dandy', Tynan once said, 'is a rebel who wants to be accepted by society but on his terms.'[69]

One of the first 'faces', Steve Sparks, saw the *Town* interview in 1962 as the beginning of the end of the movement he had helped to found:

Mod before it was commercialised was essentially an extension of the beatniks . . . It was to do with modern jazz and Sartre. It was to do with existentialism. Marc Feld was an early example of what was the downfall of Mod, which was the attraction of people who didn't understand what it was about, to the clothes. Marc Feld was only interested in the clothes, he was not involved in thinking. Mind you it's quite hard to think on twenty Smith Kline and French Drinamyl.[70]

Throughout its history, Mod was regularly pronounced dead by participants and observers. Some pointed to its periodic association with violence, from the Mod/rocker riots of 1964–65, through to the more organised and routine gang violence of football hooliganism that skinheads and Casuals were associated with in the 1970s and 80s, all of which undermined the movement's claim to be subverting working-class stereotypes. Other critics pronounced death when Mod was taken up by middle- and upper-class youth, particularly in the 'Dandy Mod' period of *c.1966–c.1971* when its flamboyant style precepts became associated with the 'Chelsea Set' of the King's Road and with prohibitively expensive boutiques. Others felt Mod's pulse fading in the mid-1960s when mass retailers commercially exploited it, providing cheap copies of clothes and accessories for poorer teenagers and, worse still, attaching the movement to a generic concept of modern lifestyle.

Commercialisation vexed Mods and sociologists alike. The so-called Birmingham School of subcultural theorists, which attributed to youth cultures a ritualised form of working-class resistance to capitalist society, tended to see the reappropriation of Mod by middle-class participants, and its diffusion into mainstream commercial culture, as a neutering of its original, subversive parody of that world. Later sociologists have taken a more expansive view of the movement's history. Addressing the supposed death of Mod, in the 1960s, Christine Feldman wrote: 'This post-mortem was premature, as Mod's existence has transcended both the 1960s and Britain', adding that sociologists 'did not recognise how this diffusion into mass culture liberalised Mod'.[71]

Participants who shared academics' contempt for commercialisation also announced the many deaths of Mod in the half-century after 1962. However, their antipathy to the 'sell- out' was rather different; after all, hadn't they once celebrated the liberating potential of the consumer society? Part of the explanation for that paradox lies in the valid distinction that the original Modernists made between consumption based on taste and consumption for its own sake. Mods like Steve Sparks watched aghast as teenagers with no interest in Jean-Paul Sartre or Thelonious Monk donned parkas and popped pills until there was nothing left to explain.

But there is another, simpler reason for Modernists' disapproval, which is that the creators of any youth culture often despise camp followers, preferring purist obscurity to corrupted popularity. Some of the founding 'faces' were not really interested in the democratisation of taste that they appeared to champion. What they really wanted was to challenge established elites by creating an elite of their own, a kind of secret society for which they set the terms of entry – one based on what you wore, listened to or read rather than where you had gone to school or who your father knew on the company board – a society where they could be noblemen and not serfs, at least for the weekend.

That helps to explain the hostility of some Mods to the growth of their movement after 1962 when the media began to amplify it: because once the music and fashion industries, high street retailers, film and TV companies got hold of Mod, 'faces' lost control of the perfectly formed little world they had created; and they lost control of it to commercial giants like Granada, EMI and C&A over which few of them had any influence beyond a job in the post room or the typing pool. The commercial exploitation of Mod may have been the predictable fate of a youth cult that celebrated consumerism more than any other; but for some its popularity undermined the emotional reason for belonging to the movement in the first place. However, for millions more, Mod was about to define what it meant to be young and British in the post-imperial age.

2

I'M A MOCKER
Class, Consumerism and the Triumph of Mod

We all wanted to be different, to get away from the council estates, the pits and the factories, all that cloth-capped bullshit. Spending two weeks' wages on a made-to-measure shirt or an import LP seemed to do it.
  Mick Taylor, Doncaster Mod[1]

More boys are wanting to know themselves.
  Rave magazine, December 1965

ALL THAT CLOTH-CAPPED BULLSHIT

Mods shimmered on to the horizon at a time when affluence seemed to be the quickest route to a more equal society and youths the outriders of social change. But Mods were not as unique in British life as they often pretended to be. Like many Britons in the mid-twentieth century, including their own parents, they were seeking a different way of being working class, one that resembled middle-class lifestyle but in which they retained a working-class identity and maintained valued social links with older relatives and communities. Mods were also the product of big changes in the British economy, which had been developing since the 1920s but accelerated in the 1950s: a shift away from heavy industry towards lighter manufacturing and service industries, resulting in a rising number of men and women entering white-collar employment (between 1931 and 1985 the number of people working in offices more than doubled, from 23 per cent of the workforce to 54 per cent).[2] This was accompanied by a population drift away from Scotland, Wales and the north of England towards the Midlands, London and the south-east, so it is perhaps not surprising that popular Modernism should have originated in London and spread out from the south. These changes, together with an overall rise in the standard of living, formed the concrete backdrop to the rapid development of Modernism into a national youth culture between 1962 and 1967.

Mods represented a society in transition after the Second World War, one in which opportunity and affluence had begun to blur class boundaries while simultaneously heightening class-consciousness and expectations, a compound that would lead to growing frustration and anger in the 1970s and 80s, which later generations of Mods would address in different ways. In the 1960s, however, the promises of mass consumption had yet to be tested and found wanting. Shopping was still a novel, exciting, even subversive act, especially for men. Mods' fastidious and hedonistic consumption of clothes and music was not simply an escape from the reality of drab, thwarted lives; it was also an expression of hope that they could improve their living standards and social status.

The early Modernists' preoccupation with quality over quantity continued into the 1960s, with the result that specific forms of clothing and brands became associated with Mod culture. One example is sportswear. Commonly associated with the global influence of the United States, the connection between sport fashion and youth was actually established by Mods in the 1950s, long before the mass consumption of American brands like Nike in the 1970s. The use of sportswear to assert social status goes back to the birth of modern spectator sport in Britain in the late nineteenth century, when men and women from private schools and elite universities wore cricket, rugby or hockey shirts and jerseys to social events. And it was precisely this antecedent that attracted Mods.

The brand most replete with meaning was Fred Perry. The last Briton to win Wimbledon, in 1936, Perry personified the aspirational spirit of Mod as well as highlighting the country's recent sporting failures. His father had been a left-wing Lancashire cotton spinner who moved the family to London when he became a Member of Parliament for the Co-operative Party. Perry attended a grammar school – that hothouse of working-class talent in the mid-twentieth century – before his ascendancy on the courts (and off them too: one of his film-star girlfriends was Marlene Dietrich). Yet in Britain, unlike the situation in America, sporting talent was still shackled by an anti-professional ethos that viewed the amateur gentleman as a socio-athletic ideal. Disgusted with the snobbery of the tennis establishment, Perry took American citizenship and settled in the United States where he spent most of his time until his death at the age of 85 in 1995. But his ultimate revenge on the 'blazerati' who looked down their noses at him was to launch a white cotton pique polo shirt at Wimbledon in 1952. Its design was taken from the French company, Lacoste, while the famous laurel wreath was the original logo of the All England Lawn Tennis Association. Mods made the shirt fashionable and it was only after they demanded a dizzying range of colours (the company obliged) that the Fred Perry polo shirt became a British style icon, worn by all manner of Mods since. Originating in a sport associated with well-off Britons, the story of the Perry shirt illustrates how Mods' shopping appropriated the symbols of middle- and upper-class life.

WE SAVED STRING

But how much shopping could they acually do? Despite the post-war improvements in living standards, the historian David Fowler has argued that the affluence of Mods has been exaggerated:

they could not afford to drive cars, to take foreign holidays, or to visit many of London's 'swinging' discotheques. In effect, they could not transmit their Mod culture across Britain themselves. Moreover it should not be forgotten that the overwhelming majority of Mods lived with their parents. In other words, they could not even afford to live independently in lodgings. In this sense, their lifestyle was essentially no different from those lifestyles of interwar teenage consumers of the Northern cities such as Manchester, who visited cinemas and dance halls as habitually during the 1930s as Mods visited dance halls like The Tottenham Royal in the 1960s.[3]

Although there is no accurate statistical data on their incomes, education and occupation, there is plenty of oral evidence to suggest that some Mods entered white-collar professions and even went on to succeed in them at a senior level. Robert Hall recalled that 'A lot of these boys went off and did jobs like bank clerks, and their managers thought they were fantastic. They'd never seen anything like it because you would be better dressed than your boss . . . I was better dressed than my boss by a long way. It was a great way to be different.'[4] Mods were different from their 1930s predecessors in one crucial respect: aspiration. Although ambition and social mobility did not start in the 1960s, oral testimony overwhelmingly demonstrates that Mods' expectations were far greater than those of interwar teenagers and of the 50s rockers they defined themselves against. Mods expected to have more fun, sex and money – also better education, job satisfaction and homes, and a more reflective life in which material consumption was a matter of taste and not merely the acquisition of a few consumables to sate the senses or acquire a little status in working-class communities.

Aspiration doesn't equal sense of entitlement, or even expectation. Most working-class Mods had a realistic grasp of how little youth culture could transform the power structures that shaped and determined their lives. But that didn't usually reduce its value. When desires were inevitably thwarted by prejudice and lack of opportunity (or by their own individual inadequacies) Mods often found solace in their chosen culture rather than rejecting it for raising unrealistic expectations of what life offered. This difference between appearance and reality was at the heart of the quintessential Mod anthem, 'Substitute' by the Who, which reached No. 5 in the UK charts in 1966 (and went to No. 7 when it was re-released a decade later after being covered by the Sex Pistols):

> You think we look pretty good together
> You think my shoes are made of leather
> But I'm a substitute for another guy
> I look pretty tall but my heels are high
> The simple things you see are all complicated
> I look pretty young but I'm just backdated, yeah
>
> Substitute your lies for fact
> I can see right through your plastic mac
> I look all white, but my dad was black
> My fine looking suit is really made out of sack

The song continues with this rebuke to anyone who might pity the man or woman dressed in disappointment:

> I was born with a plastic spoon in my mouth
> The north side of my town faced east and the east was facing south
> And now you dare to look me in the eye
> Those crocodile tears are what you cry
> If there's a genuine problem you won't try
> To work it out at all, just pass it by, pass it by

For many Mods, the exotic panorama of cosmopolitan taste and good living continued to act as a substitute for the real thing. Thus, Mod was simultaneously aspirational, realistic and consoling.

Those Mods for whom money was tight developed strategies to stretch their budgets, but their spending still marked a generational difference in many families.[5] Anne Filer remembers that:

There was always this sense from people who were older that . . . 'We saved string, why are you throwing it away?' They had gone through austerity problems . . . they had gone through wartime. But we didn't have that, so how could they have understood us? They saw us as frivolous and we were completely frivolous.[6]

Mods would save up for more expensive items and services, from a new suit to a scooter or an occasional haircut at Vidal Sassoon and, like other Britons who benefited from the consumer boom of the time, they took advantage of hire purchase.

Customising cheap clothes was another Mod strategy that was linked to their urge for individual expression. Some had relatives in tailoring; those less fortunate bought cheaply from traditional menswear chains like Burtons and employed local tailors to make the necessary adjustments. Interviewed in *Rave* magazine, 18-year-old Mick Tanner, a tailor's cutter from Stepney, explained: 'Before, tailors used to invent styles and everyone bought them. Now we invent them and the tailors are going out of their mind trying to keep up. I started wearing crepe, nylon cycling jumpers because they were cool for dancing. All the tickets wanted to know where I got it – but if I told them they'd all be down the shop tomorrow.'[7]

'From my perspective Mod was very much about working-class lads doing something very upper class, which was having suits made to order', remembers the designer Paul Smith. 'Burtons the tailors had 2,000 shops across England, so it was normal to have a suit made, but these lads had to really save up to have a suit made. And then instead of just going into Burtons and them saying "this is the suit you're having" – which is what most guys did – these boys went in and "designed" their suits.'[8] Mod's own designs ranged from a whole look that lasted for years to the smallest short-lived fad: they were the creators of modern street style, displaying an eclectic DIY aesthetic where almost anything was possible. Johnny Moke, who later became a shoe designer and retailer, recalled how a craze would take off:

We went to a bowling alley wearing old plimsolls. We hired a brand new pair of bowling shoes and afterwards I walked out with mine. That weekend we went to Clacton. It was the weekend of the first trouble. I'd taken off the big number 8 that was stuck on the back and was the only guy walking around Clacton with bowling shoes on. When I went to Brighton about six weeks later, half the kids had bowling shoes.[9]

Customising was a way of maintaining one's individuality within the tribe, even though half the pleasure was, as Johnny Moke suggests, watching the rest of the tribe copy you. That tension between individual identity and group solidarity gave Mod a creative edge that enabled it to regenerate over time, as well as offering the risible sight of teenagers rebelling by conforming.

Whether they were 'faces' or 'tickets', customisers or mere customers, Mod style is best understood as a subtle parody of middle- to upper-class American and European sartorial conventions, a hybrid of styles and practices that subverted those conventions by being a little too fastidious and self-conscious. One of the best summaries of Mod has been provided by the author and jazz musician Jonathan Gould in his study of the Beatles:

By the early 1960s the Mods had evolved into a kind of living parody of the expectations and aspirations of post-war British life. Finding jobs in shops and offices, they adopted a mode of dress that satisfied the white-collar requirement to 'make a good impresson' with a vehemence that turned the markers of class identity upside down. Away from the workplace they cultivated a demeanour as preoccupied and self-important as a City financier. Mods had destinations, rounds and appointments to keep. Restlessness was a creed with them, and what they lacked in social mobility, they made up for by being mobile in the literal sense of the word . . .

The special privilege of parody . . . is that it allows its authors to participate in the very set of conventions they mean to debunk or transcend. Mods *were* eager, well-dressed young men on the go. (And in its formative stage, it was primarily a male fashion.) That they weren't really going anywhere, most of them – that there wasn't anywhere in Britain for them to go – was rendered momentarily insignificant by the satisfaction of suggesting that success was merely a function of *style* to begin with.[10]

Mods' parody of middle-class style was accompanied by a subversion of time management, so that life was geared not to hard work and the steady accumulation of professional advancement but to unadulterated pleasure. As the sociologist Dick Hebdige observed:

More firmly embedded than either the Teds or the rockers in a variety of jobs which made fairly stringent demands on their appearance, dress and 'general demeanour' as well as their time, the mods placed a correspondingly greater emphasis on the week-end. They lived in between the leaves of the commercial calendar, as it were (hence the Bank Holiday occasions, the week-end events, the 'all-niters'), in the pockets of free time which alone made work meaningful. During these leisure periods there was real 'work' to be done: scooters to be polished, records to be bought, trousers to be pressed, tapered or fetched from the cleaners, hair to be washed and blow dried . . . Here, beneath the world's contempt, there were different priorities: work was insignificant, irrelevant; vanity and arrogance were permissible, even desirable qualities, and a more furtive and ambiguous sense of masculinity could be seen to operate.[11]

Of course this was not the first time that young people had put pleasure before work; nor were they the only ones to do that in the 1960s. Furthermore, as they entered their twenties and thirties, even the most wired Mods settled into family life and the demands of the work that was necessary to finance it. But it was its ability to subvert educational and professional expectations that made Mod culture, far more than hippie counter-culture, attractive to middle-class youth. Mod became a national movement in the 1960s partly because it offered hedonism without political radicalism, or the pressure to 'drop out'. But there was another aspect of the cult that made it unthreateningly familiar and attractive to middle-class youth: Mods' attitude to Continental Europe, their adoption of its fashion and embrace of its lifestyle.

A PACKAGE TOUR OF THE SOUL

Mods' adoption of Continental styles and products – from French haircuts to Italian scooters – expressed their desire to enjoy a cosmopolitan, middle-class life. As we have seen, one of the reasons that Mods disdained rockers was that they mimicked American popular culture without creating anything original. Mods venerated Europe just as much, and it was their amalgam of the two continents that created the template for a new British youth culture.

One of the first to observe this aspect of Mod was Colin MacInnes. In 1959, in an essay for the journal *Twentieth Century* entitled 'Sharp Schmutter' (after the Yiddish term for clothing used by Londoners), he described the 'aggressively elegant silhouette of any sharp working class boy today' characterised by 'some variation of the *Italian* style – which, first appearing in the summer of 1958, has now swept the land'.[12] This led MacInnes to a broader conclusion about Britain's post-war relationship with America and Europe:

US influence has declined somewhat from its initial supremacy . . . because the American 'hero' has been increasingly replaced by European models . . . The explanations here may be cheaper travel, the increased prestige of Continental films – and of course the astute promotion, by the Shaftesbury Avenue Svengalis, exploiting (or perhaps, to be fair, creating) the teenage market. But it may also go deeper, and hint at a certain degree not of 'anti-Americanism' so much as growing indifference to America – to which may also bear witness the abrupt emergence, in the past few years in England, of native-born singing, motor-racing and athletic heroes, and in general of a more aggressively confident 'European' spirit.[13]

It was premature to detect indifference to America among the young but MacInnes was right to sense a fresh engagement with Continental Europe that was not an anti-American impulse, as it so often was among the moneyed and educated elites of Britain. For young, self-styled Modernists who wanted more fulfilment, money and sex, America remained a land of opportunity. But to that American dream they added a European one.

Later familiarity with Mediterranean beaches and cynicism about the European Union make it easy to forget just how attractive Continental Europe seemed to aspirational young people in mid-twentieth-century Britain. Out of the reach of most teenagers, Europe was then as exotic as America. Few working-class families could afford to leave the British seaside resort and venture abroad in the early 1960s: cheap air travel was still a decade away. Fathers of working-class Mods who had taken part in the D-Day landings and the advance on Germany rarely spoke about their experiences; this experiential divide – between Britons who had been to Europe in war, and those who yearned to go in peace – widened the already large generation gap. Moreover, the Continent was still viewed by many with dislike and suspicion as a result of the struggle against Nazi Germany. The xeno-phobia generated by the war found its way into popular films and comics that perpetuated Continental stereotypes well into the 1990s. When Prime Minister Harold Macmillan led the first attempt to take Britain into the Common Market in 1961, he declared: 'We in Britain are Europeans . . . This is no time to bury our heads in the sands of the past and take the kind of parochial view which regards Europe with distrust and suspicion.'[14] Few voters agreed, and although the French veto of Britain's application provoked some anger, there was little actual disappointment at the result.

Mods were the first working-class youths to straddle this divide in British culture: the first to see Europe as much as America as conti-nents of style and opportunity, and the first, as Mary Quant remarked, 'not [to] think in terms of "us" against foreigners'.[15] It helped that young people no longer had to go into the armed forces after National Service was abolished in 1957. As early Mod Paul Stagg recalled:

Ours was the first generation that hadn't been obsessed by the war. It didn't matter to us at all, yet I looked at my older brothers and they were all fucking shell-shocked – they knew their place, we didn't give a shit. We were the first to miss out on national service. Even the Teds got caught up in that one . . . Mods never grew up and I still don't think they have, they're all still eighteen at heart.[16]

The places that held the greatest allure for Mods, as they did for the middle classes they emulated, were the Mediterranean countries of Western Europe, especially France and Italy. To them, France was not a nation of cowardly Nazi collaborators with funny voices and even funnier food but a land of cool, epitomised by Existentialist writers and film stars of the *nouvelle vague*. If Marlon Brando provided a template of rebellion for rockers in Elia Kazan's *The Wild One*, then Jean Paul Belmondo became a role model for Mods in Jean-Luc Godard's *A Bout de Souffle* (1960), a Gallic homage to the American gangster movie replete with a bebop soundtrack by the king of modern French jazz, Martial Solal.

Belmondo's slackened lower lip – known to Mods as 'throwing a noodle' – was imitated just as Elvis Presley's arched upper lip was copied by rockers. The main inspiration that French film provided was not attitudinal, however, but sartorial. Early Mod Dicky Dodson remembered:

The girls started cutting their hair like Jean Seberg and we all wanted to be Jean Paul Belmondo, he was the hero . . . We wanted that lifestyle, we wanted a girlfriend that looked like Jean Seberg and [to] live the way they did in those films and from that came wanting to know everything about it. We moved totally away from the American stuff, which we now considered too showy and wanted to be French.

The girls looked like boys and the guys were ultra cool, smoking Gitanes out of the corners of their mouths. Alain Delon had a scooter, he was in Paris, and he had a girl on the back. Fuck me, what more could you want? Our behaviour was obsessive and completely took us over. It got so bad that the film didn't matter. What mattered was seeing what Belmondo or Delon was wearing and knowing we couldn't get it so we would have to improvise.

We would actually sit in the cinema in the dark with sketch pads and try to draw the clothes, what the collar was like on the shirts, how far away the lapel was from the shoulder and so on. Luckily we were art students so the drawings weren't too bad in the daylight![17]

Hairstyles were also copied. The 'French Crew', a longer version of the American 'College Boy', was a favourite. Launched by Fernand Gautier of the Syndicat de la Haute Coiffure Masculine in 1963, it was popularised by the Small Faces and by Rod Stewart – then known as 'Rod the Mod' – and became the male equivalent of Sassoon's five-point bob, which characterised the female Mod look. Of course France had influenced British fashion for two centuries: in 1911, Herbert Asquith had invited Paul Poiret to 10 Downing Street, but the cheapest dress on show was double the annual salary of a scullery maid working there at the time. When Dior introduced the New Look in 1947, cheaper copies became available in Britain, but this was a period of austerity with rationing more severe than during the war, so until the mid-1950s the style was affordable mainly for middle-class women, by which time it seemed stale in comparison with American teen fashion.

Mods' immersion in French style could be superficial more than baptismal, as Johnny Moke recalled:

We used to go to see French movies as much as we could. Mostly I couldn't understand a bloody word of it. Next day I'd tell everybody, 'Hey, I saw a great French film, you should go and see it, it's absolutely wonderful' . . . We never smoked but would light up a Gauloise just to be seen with it. We all got into the French films and magazines, but Les went beserk. He used to wear a striped jumper and a beret and eat garlic and everything. He started to learn French. We saw him once sitting in Aldgate Wimpy holding up a copy of *Le Soir*. When we went in and joined him we saw that he was really reading the *Sunday Pictorial* which he had concealed in the middle pages. It was all a pose.[18]

For others, however, Francophilia was the genuine expression of a more cosmopolitan and aspirant working-class identity. Mancunian Steve Plant was one of those Mods for whom the cult opened up new horizons. His friends 'started to read . . . they started to look at art . . .We started to see ourselves not only dressing smart, listening to great music, but we viewed ourselves as being intellectual.'[19]

Few young Britons had the opportunity to actually go to the Continent until the mid-1970s, but for those able to afford it, *Rave* magazine provided handy features on Continental travel that were geared to the young – advice that was in tone and attitude a world away from the Baedeker or Michelin guidebooks. In 1967, for example, it ran a series of features on European capitals, starting with Paris and Madrid, and ending in Moscow. 'Join the Rave team as they take a fabulous BEA jet flight across the channel to have a Rave-up in Paris', announced the magazine, promising 'everything you need to know to have a swinging time.'[20] These articles pre-dated by several years the creation of travel guides like the *Lonely Planet* series (founded in 1972) and the *Rough Guides* (1982) which would initially cater to the more middle-class, backpacking traveller embarking on the so-called 'Hippie Trail' through Asia.

For the majority who were unable to jump on a BEA plane, Mods romanticised Continental Europe as much as hippies idealised Asia, or as young Britons had once adored the United States. Yet Mods' vision of Western Europe was different to that sketched by Elizabeth David, author of *French Provincial Cooking* (1960). She and other British writers with a bohemian bent offered an exotic pastorale that tempted thousands of upper-middle-class Britons to move to the Dordogne and Provence after the 1960s, in search of English country life with added herbs. In contrast, Mods' Europe was urban, secular and cosmopolitan. What they yearned for was a seat in a cafe on a busy street, enjoying the sunshine and the good food – not the harvesting of olives alongside peasants in picturesque villages: that sounded too much like the manual labour which they were trying to escape. The European lifestyle Mods were drawn to was, in the words of Paolo Hewitt, 'a mix of intellectualism and casual living'.[21] As Julie Burchill explained in her study *Damaged Gods*: 'Mod represented the raised expectations of the most intelligent and metropolitan of working class youth. Mod was the gap between full employment and unfulfilled aspirations, the missing link between bomb sites and Bacardi ads. The earliest Mods were besotted with all things Continental – to them Modernism was a package tour of the soul.'[22]

It was not until the 1970s and 1980s that it would also become a package tour of the body. But Mods were the harbingers of the mass engagement with Continental life that would gradually transform Britain. It revolved around consumption – food, clothes, cinema and foreign holidays – but as we shall see, its very materiality connected the youth cult to the broader modernist project that so influenced Western living in the twentieth century.

I SAT TIGHT AND EDGED INTO THE STRUDEL

Michael Caine epitomised the Continental taste that accompanied aspiration, in a role he made his own, when he played Harry Palmer in the films *The Ipcress File* and *Funeral in Berlin*, based on Len Deighton's best-selling novels, published between 1962 and 1966. Deighton had a similar background to Caine and the sort of career that Mods dreamed of. Born in London in 1929 to working-class parents, after National Service he studied design at Central St Martin's in Soho before getting a scholarship to the Royal College of Art. After a number of glamorous jobs, he became art director at a London advertising agency before writing made him famous.

It has often been remarked that unlike James Bond, Harry Palmer was a cynically insubordinate working-class man with no time for the Old Etonian head of MI5, Colonel Ross. Palmer was *Saturday Night and Sunday Morning*'s Arthur Seaton in glasses and an Aquascutum raincoat (a favoured Mod brand), and the glasses (Caine's idea) deliberately rebuked the idea that a man of his background had no brains. Less remarked upon is the fact that the upward mobility of the sharp-suited Palmer was expressed less in despatching Soviet spies and more in the Continental lifestyle he avidly pursues outside work. Palmer greets a pay rise with the words, 'Oh thank you, sir, now I can get that new infrared grill.' The key scene in *The Ipcress File* takes place in a new American-style supermarket where he wheels his trolley around the aisles in search of the good life. The bowler-hatted Colonel Ross appears suddenly, slams his trolley into Palmer's and contemptuously reprimands the young spy for having his hands on a tin of expensive French mushrooms:

PALMER: Oh, good morning, sir.
ROSS: *Champignons*? You're paying ten pence more for a fancy French label. If you want button mushrooms you'd get better value on the next shelf.
PALMER: It's not just the label; these do have a better flavour.
ROSS: Of course, you're quite a gourmet aren't you, Palmer?[23]

With a wry smile and a steady voice Caine captures the insolence of choice. Labels and brands are more than a way for companies to exploit Palmer's aspirations; he knows that products chosen well can literally improve his quality of life. Deighton's meaning is not only that his hero can afford the more expensive French mushrooms but also that he *knows* they taste better. That was a metaphor for a whole generation asserting their ability to exercise cultural taste, and not just mining their affluence to sate their senses.

Deighton's hero knows how to do that too, for when Palmer seduces a beautiful middle-class colleague in his small apartment, he does so with music and *champignons*. Serving wine to the accompaniment of Mozart and modern jazz, Caine announces: 'Courtney, I am going to cook you the best meal you've ever eaten.' Intrigued, she replies, 'You like girls but you're not the tearaway [Ross] thinks you are. You also like books, music, cooking.' Here is a man who has read his Elizabeth David; he is subverting the idea that cooking is women's work, which was then so prevalent as to be not worth commenting on.

Deighton was quite a gourmet himself (the close-up of the hands cooking in the seduction scene are actually his). 'My mother was a professional cook [and] I learned a great deal from her', he explained. 'At that time, few women worked in the kitchens of top ranking restaurants so I didn't see anything unusual in the idea of men who could cook. But looking back, I can see that for some people, husbands and boyfriends who could cook were a revolution. Michael personified it.'[24] Deighton also wrote the first cookbook that was successfully marketed to British men. The cover of his *Action Cookbook* (1965) had a sprig of parsley coming out of the barrel of Harry Palmer's pistol to reassure its readers that cooking was not effeminate; in his memoirs Michael Caine described this as 'butch cooking'.[25]

The *Action Cookbook* became a landmark in the reformation of British masculinity that Mods championed in the same period. Including recipes such as 'Eels across Europe' and 'Veal Chop *En Papillote*', as well as the once exotic 'Chicken Korma', it cautioned against fast food and instant coffee: for all the speed of urban life that Mods celebrated, theirs was a culture of leisure, of time out well spent. As in other cookbooks, some of the dishes on offer were more a symbol of aspiration than an affordable recipe. Deighton advised his readers that 'crushed ice as a bed under a large plate of oysters, or in a bucket with a couple of bottles of Chablis, will work more efficiently than an overcrowded fridge and will be appetizing on the table.' Image counted as much as flavour but Deighton took care to demystify foreign cuisine. He scraped off the intimidating layer of class associations that had grown like mould on simple ingredients like mozzarella because of their scarcity and prohibitive price. 'Take a good look at items that attract you in the delicatessen,' he advised, 'it's a good way to learn professional garnishings and presentation.'[26]

The sexy European dimension of Harry Palmer's world swept readers along in the four successful novels he appeared in. This too came from Deighton's personal experience. 'In my six years of studying I went to many places in Europe', he recalled. 'I suppose I am a xenophile. After leaving the RCA I became an airline steward for BOAC and had long stopovers in such places as Tokyo, Cairo, Sydney, Calcutta and Beirut. Later I became the travel editor of *Playboy* magazine with all the necessary travelling. As a writer I have seriously researched the places mentioned in my fiction books and history books. It has provided endless pleasure (along with flashes of pain and the occasional dull ache).'[27] Like Colin MacInnes, Deighton's literary style is American but the setting and sensibility of his novels were European. Early in *The Ipcress File*, Palmer *flâners* with friends and colleagues around Soho, much as his creator had done as a design student in the 1950s:

I walked down Charlotte Street towards Soho. It was that sort of January sunshine to point up the dirt without raising the temperature. I was probably seeking excuses to delay. I bought two packets of Gauloises, sank a quick grappa with Mario and Franco at the Terrazza, bought a *Statesman*, some Normandy butter and garlic sausage. The girl in the delicatessen was small, dark and rather delicious. We had been flirting across the mozzarella for years.[28]

Passages like this pepper the Palmer novels, deliberately suggesting that this is not a holiday from reality but the start of a new way of life for many. It's a world where food, drink and sex are never far apart, but it's not always the shiny world of the Ideal Home Exhibition. As Palmer waits for an agent to appear in a Soho cafe he decides to have a snack: Russian tea and a little taste of Austria. 'I sat tight and edged into the strudel', he reports, before going to a Soho revue bar, where 'in the cardboard proscenium a fat girl in black underwear was singing a song with the mad abandon that fitted 2.10pm on a Tuesday afternoon.'[29]

From the delis and strip joints of Soho Deighton transported his readers to the Continent with his third Harry Palmer novel, *Funeral in Berlin*. Both book and film set the contemporary image of Germany as the Arctic of the Cold War. But amid the subterfuge and misty checkpoints, Deighton essayed the bright new liberal capitalist Germany of Adenauer and Adidas that was beginning to attract young Britons less hung up than their parents about the war. Spies draw up to meetings in sleek BMWs and Mercedes; 'two girls with silver hair were eating Bockwurst' and drinking coffee in the 'Quick Café' where Palmer encounters the West German agent Johnny Vulkan – a man 'who could deliver a bomb or a baby and smile while he was doing it'. Out of the rubble rise buildings as sleek as the cars, one of them 'with its slick modern tower, like a tricky sort of h-fi speaker cabinet'.[30] Surveying West Berlin, Palmer says to himself: 'Brassieres and beer; whiskies and worsted; great words carved out of coloured electricity and plastered along the walls of the Ku-damm. This was the theatre-in-the-round of western prosperity . . . "Today I've joined the cast," I thought. "Now they've got an illusionist."'[31]

Like the most astute Mods, Palmer senses how much of the West's moneyed freedom is an illusion. But though he knows the ennui of lonely evenings with an infrared grill, he is still seduced by the tran-sient comforts of consumption, which form part of his identity as a modern urban man. Sociologist Dick Hebdige has observed that 'Harry Palmer is a fictional extension of Mod' and has connected the aesthetic and material choices of Mods to the broader modernist project:

What is so remarkable here . . . is the defection of a man like Harry Palmer not to Russia – still less to America – but to Italy, to the Continent. It is perhaps the final irony that when it did occur the most startling and spec-tacular revolution in British 'popular' taste in the early 1960s involved the domestication not of the brash and 'vulgar' hinterland of American design but of the subtle, 'cool', Continental style which had for so many years impressed the British champions of the modern movement.[32]

The cover of the paperback edition of *The Ipcress File* was pure Bauhaus for exactly that reason, having been designed by Raymond Hawkey,

Deighton's friend from their RCA days. As art editor first on the *Express* and then the *Observer*, Hawkey played a major part in popularising modernist design by shaping the look of colour supplements and magazines in the 1960s and 70s. In Britain, those magazines promoted a more Continental lifestyle for young people, one associated with leisure and pleasure rather than war and famine, and in the process they established a subtle, often subliminal, link between modernism and good living.

The more committed Mods also absorbed that lifestyle through Continental films. Here the influence of Italy was as important as that of France, not least because a number of the original Mods were children of Italian immigrants. The film star Marcello Mastroianni was as much of a Mod hero as Belmondo. Coming from peasant stock and having escaped Fascist imprisonment during the war, the suave and beautifully dressed Mastroianni embodied the modern, urban European male in films like Fellini's *La Dolce Vita* (1960) and Antonioni's *La Notte* (1961). And while the Italian coffee bar was the Mods' preferred hang-out – the Bar Italia in Soho being the most legendary of all – cycle racing was another form of Continental influence on Mods at a time when the sport was dominated by the French and Italians.

Early Mod teenagers cycled to school and college on Tremelli bikes rather than British makes like Holdsworth, and the preference spawned a fashion for the colourful, tight cycle jerseys and cropped haircuts favoured by the foreign cycling stars of the day. Graham Hughes, a design student from west London in the late 1950s, recalled why he and his friends loved the sport:

Cycling was so influential on the first Mods, terrifically so . . . You followed the Tour de France and all our heroes were Italian cyclists, basically because they were foreign. Our sporting heroes ranked alongside our cinema heroes. Not English footballers or cricketers like most other teenagers were into, we adopted cyclists. Instead of Stanley Matthews, I had Louie Jean Balvet and Fausto Cockpee. It was just to be different and because they looked good. You'd buy all the Italian newspapers from Solosisis in Charing Cross Road, an Italian newsagent that would have papers and sports papers imported for the Italian community that stretched up from Clerkenwell in to the West End. Enormous, great broadsheets that had pages and pages of cycling and racing. The haircuts came from Pete's, an Italian hairdresser at the back of

Rathbone Place. You would go there and he had all these pictures of cyclists right round the wall, with these great haircuts . . . Mods wore berets because these papers had pictures of cyclists racing in the winter and training out of racing jerseys. Wonderful roll collar jumpers with a beret and dark glasses. We had to adapt the look to get the best results and because we all had a graphics background, we came at cycling with the graphic in mind.[33]

Those who were lucky enough to obtain a Tremelli and original Italian cycle-wear usually did so at a cycle shop on the Fulham Road, partly owned by the restaurateur Bertorelli family. Yet for later Mods the symbol of their mobility was not the Tremelli but two other Italian imports: the Vespa and Lambretta.

YOUR FIRST-CLASS TICKET TO INDEPENDENCE

Mods fetishised technology that accelerated physical mobility, often as a substitute for the social mobility they craved and couldn't always attain. Yet ironically, the scooter was far slower than the Harley-Davidsons and Triumphs preferred by the rockers they mocked for being primitive.

Scooters were a French invention of 1902 but fell out of fashion in the 1920s. Then, in 1945, at Piaggio's aircraft factory, the Italian engineer Corradino d'Ascanio built a prototype of what became the Vespa: an open-framed machine with flat footboard, enclosed engine and small wheels, on which the rider sat upright. Launched at a Roman golf club in April 1946, the project was capitalised by American aid, which had poured into Western Europe after the Second World War to finance reconstruction and dent the appeal of communism, in Italy a serious political force. By the mid-1950s, Vespas, and their main imitator the Lambretta, were exported in their millions, and had become an icon of European youth, sold as 'your first-class ticket to independence'.

Small, neat and manoeuvrable, the scooter was designed to zip around town rather than do a 'ton' up a motorway. The emphasis was on style and convenience rather than the speed and power which drew rockers to the larger, more macho motorbike. For all their curves, scooters were less aerodynamic. Not only did the design make you sit up straight, but Mods deemed it correct to sit with knees and feet sticking out at a 45°-angle to the body. Slowing the vehicle down in this way enabled every detail of the owner's look to be seen as he glided past – and prevented carefully coiffured hair from being blown out of place.

The scooter's cleanliness augmented its appeal. Because the engines of Vespas and Lambrettas were covered, it was easier for machine and rider to stay spotless. Mods no more wanted oil on their jackets than wind in their hair and to protect smart suits and dresses from the weather and scooter dirt they made use of the parka. Few things are more closely associated with Mod than this particular item of clothing. Although the word comes from northern Russia (meaning animal skin), it was the M-51 'fishtail parka', an American military jacket first used in the Korean War, that was adopted by some early Mods. Acquiring it from army surplus stores after it was withdrawn in 1956, the parka became associated with Mod in the public mind during the seaside disturbances of 1964–5 when many of those involved were photographed wearing one. The jacket would remain a key signifier of the movement and never entirely lost its appeal to young recruits. Originally embellished with Pop Art symbols, later Mods added patches to signify different phases of the movement's development, from Northern Soul, through to punk and Britpop.

Whereas rockers took a masculine pride in the greasy business of servicing their bikes, just as their fathers serviced their cars, Mods disliked rolling up their carefully pressed sleeves and opening a toolbox. Remarking on that fact, one of the main British scooter dealers, Eddy Grimshaw, said that his vehicles were preferred because 'The boys feel it's not a dirty great machine. It's not *working class*, the way bikes are.'[34] Not all Mods were strangers to the spanner, however. Scooter clubs for enthusiasts were started in the 1950s and still exist today, together with magazines like *Scooter & Three Wheeler* catering to those with a more mechanical bent. But if a Mod needed work doing on his Vespa or Lambretta, he usually took it to a garage, many of which offered package deals that included servicing and customising.

Customising stamped an individual mark on machines that were factory produced, just as it did on mass-produced suits. Mods calibrated the look as much as the power of their machines. The craze for clusters of spotlights and mirrors, which took hold in the winter months of 1963, made the scooter even less aerodynamic but it became one of the most recognised features of the cult's look.[35] Electrical tape was used to put the name of the owner on the windshield (a trend that was carried over into car ownership in the 1970s). Above all, Mods loved colour: the monotonous black, white and chrome in which most bikes left the factory was sprayed with blues, reds, mauves and a range of other pastel shades, often in two tones. Some would respray their scooters as often as they would buy a new suit. This was made easier by the commercial introduction of aerosols – a tool which by the 1970s became synonymous with graffiti and the vandalism of public spaces.

The scooter was a means of pulling women – and most women knew their Vespa Sportiques from their Lambretta TV 200s, as Ken Browne recalled:

If you met a girl in a club you fancied . . . you were basically interested in taking her home, so you'd ask if she wanted a lift and she would actually ask you 'What kind of scooter have you got?' You'd have to say you had a GS or a GT 200, because they were the ones to have. Boy, if you said it was an LD 150 or whatever you had no chance. There were scooters that were totally passé, like the LD and the Sportique, you just didn't want one of those . . . Girls knew about it, if they were up on it. They'd turn to their mates after and say 'I'm going home with him, he's got a GS' and that would be it. You'd get them on the back and drive some place, bonk them down an alley, if you were lucky. It was a bit difficult bonking on a scooter . . . but I tell you they actually knew what was what.[36]

For the most fastidious Mods, bonking on a scooter, or anywhere else, came second to preserving the cut of their cloth. As writer Nik Cohn remembered, 'In Newcastle-Upon-Tyne, I knew a boy called Thomas Baines, who refused to have sex at parties unless there was a shoe tree available and a press for his trousers.'[37] '[We were] not too heavily into chicks,' remembered the Who's manager, Pete Meaden: 'no, because chicks you got to remember are emotional, distressful situations for a man, and we were totally free because your sex drives, your libido, I think it's called your libido, was turned right down low by Drynamil . . . Chicks, or "sorts" as they were called were similarly not into sex, they were very matriarchal.'[38] Meaden ended his days living with his parents.

FIFTY PER CENT OF THE MOD SCENE IS MOD BIRDS!

Perhaps the greatest inadequacy of a movement that celebrated modernity was that women usually played a subordinate role in it. Clinging on to men's waists and widely referred to as 'pillion fodder', Mod girls (just like rockers before them) were, says Angela McRobbie, 'ritualistically installed on the back seat . . . Few girls ever penetrated to the symbolic heart of the culture.'[39] Ironically, therefore, Mod emerged when the British state was beginning to grant women more control over their personal and public lives.

Oral and photographic evidence from around the world suggests that millions of women were involved in Mod culture at one time or another. Yet in fashion terms, they were rarely acknowledged as 'faces', with a few celebrity exceptions like Mary Quant and Cathy McGowan, while in music the occasional black American soul singer, or their white imitators like Julie Driscoll, were accorded a kind of honorary status. Pop and Op Artists Pauline Boty and Bridget Riley were revered but that too didn't translate into a respect for the ordinary Mod female. As one devotee, Val Palmer, put it, '50 per cent of the mod scene is mod birds! Unfortunately the record playing side of it has always been male dominated', adding: 'Mod girls were wearing A-line dresses and long socks and it was a very, almost librarian look . . . it's always been very tame, the women's fashions. It wasn't glamorous . . . they didn't wear suits.'[40] The idea that Quant's designs were not glamorous is debatable, but it's worth noting Palmer's point about the importance of the suit to the politics of Mod style. The more androgynous femininity of Mod women drew the media's attention to them as the counterpoint to the feminised appearance of the Mod male, although it wasn't as shocking to parents and employers, since it was based on 1920s style and because rising hemlines raised fewer questions about female sexuality than longer hair did for male sexuality.

Androgynous femininity was part of the Mods' move away from mere imitation of American style, as Richard Barnes remembered: 'The Fifties teenage fashions that emerged for girls were American college campus stuff, bobby sox, pedal pusher pants, hoop skirts and ponytails';

but female Mods 'got away from the Doris-Day-and-freckles-look. It was more Juliette Greco and smoky French nightclubs.'[41] More importantly perhaps, the gamine Mod style in hair and clothing appealed to women because it was more comfortable and manageable, giving the wearer a sense of freedom that corresponded with wider social trends. This was a period when more women were entering the white-collar world of the office, a trend that had begun before the Second World War but which accelerated in the 1960s. It is the practicality of Quant's clothing, more than her pronouncements on the reputed classlessness of Mod culture, that made her a heroine to so many young women in the 1960s.

In the course of the decade Mod fashion attracted millions of women to the periphery of the movement, but what drew them to become socially involved in it? Evidence suggests that the usual combination of teenage boredom and a vague search for excitement were motives, but also a rejection of the traditional female path from school to marriage. In 1964, *Boyfriend* magazine (its title spelling out the parameters of so many girls' lives) ran a feature that gave voice to the healthy scepticism of one 18-year-old:

I've been called a mod. I'm supposed to dress like a mod. It's another label in a world full of labels. I'm not really interested in wearing a 'uniform' and belonging to a group in that sense. But there is something I agree with the mods about, and that is – what is all the excitement about life? Some girls have one long ball . . . getting dressed up like a painting on the front of a chocolate box to go to some dance with a chinless wonder who spills drinks all over you! . . . These are the highlights of their dull little lives. They stagger breathlessly from one peak of enjoyment (someone's engagement) to the next (an actual marriage!) and their eyes become all shiny as they tell you about it . . . What are we looking for? I wish we knew. Something really exciting. Something really thrilling. We'll know when it comes.[42]

Even if they were relegated to the back seat of the scooter, Angela McRobbie believes that women were partially liberated by the less aggressive, more self-obsessed Mod male:

The fluidity and ambiguity of the subculture meant that a girl could be a 'face' without necessarily being attached to a boy. Participation was almost wholly reliant on wearing the right clothes, having the right hairstyle and going to the right clubs. With this combination right, the girl was a mod. Like her male counterpart, the mod girl demonstrated the same fussiness for detail in clothes . . . facial styles emphasized huge, darkened eyes and body style demanded thinness.[43]

Evidence from Mods and contemporary observers, however, suggests that little had changed in the way young men related to young women in the public domain since the 1950s. Ian Hebditch remembered which sort of Mod female he and his friends preferred:

The focus wasn't on picking up girls, but that didn't mean there was no interest in them . . . I'd divide them into two categories. There was a group of girls I'd call no-hopers and they would effect what I'd call a loosely masculine style. They'd have short hair, long suede coats, Hush Puppies, ski pants, probably a crewneck jumper. Got on with them fine but didn't think of them as girls. Then there was another group who were much more stylish. You would get the white lipstick, really severe hair cut and they would wear polka dots, white stockings, big plastic jewellery and a very short skirt with a big wide belt on it, like a pelmet skirt. They'd wear shoes with hour-glass heels and lot of them were totally unavailable. They really were, in their own way, very stylish and part of the scene.[44]

An eyewitness account of local Mod clubs by a female journalist in 1967 found that 'ballrooms in South London differ from the West End clubs in that conversation is possible'. But it was not conversation with girls that male Mods were after: 'A lot of the boys go simply to talk, and drink at the Revolving Lager Bar with each other', she observed. 'Any pairing off or picking up is done very late – in the last half hour – or outside afterwards.'[45]

One of the reasons for the subordinate role of women in the move-ment is that the fruits of feminism had not ripened when Mod peaked. The concept of equal opportunity in sex, education, employment and marriage that was enshrined in the reforming legislation of the period 1966–76 came too late for the early Mods. In fact, gender equality was not widely accepted in British society until the 1980s and 90s and even then it remained contested. Writing in 1976, Angela McRobbie concluded her study of the Mod female with caution:

The presence of 'girls' in the urban panoramas of trendy fashion photography, the new found autonomy and sexual freedom, have got to be set alongside other material factors which still determined their lives . . . The jobs which provided the extra cash afforded immediate access to consumer goods, but few opportunities for promotion or further training. There is nothing to suggest that participation in the mod subculture changed the social expectations of girls.[46]

Mods' attitudes to women were little more modern than that of their fathers, or for that matter of the young French and Italian men whose style they so admired. Here too, then, the Mod movement reflected the social limits of the time rather than being an outrider of modernity.

The female Mod would remain a subordinate figure even in the post-punk era when women gained a more central role in youth culture as artists and entrepreneurs as well as discerning consumers. That anomaly points to another reason for male domination of the movement: the perceived effeminacy of the Mod male (coupled with the movement's aesthetic and social links with gay subculture) led many of its male followers to anxiously reassert traditional masculine attitudes and behaviour. Hence the fact that even when the preening, homosocial aspect of Mod was openly acknowledged and enjoyed, it could still be accompanied by misogyny, homophobia and even gang violence. However, for all these traditional restrictions that male Mods continued to impose on women, when the vain, self-regarding young peacocks that led the movement spread their feathers, thrust out their chests and screeched their creed in the urban parklands of mid-60s Britain, they transformed the nation's masculinity.

HELLO DARLING

Mod changed how most British men looked, felt and smelt. As the cult grew in size and influence, its obsession with style made them better dressed and better groomed. It also made men more sexually ambiguous, both in appearance and attitude, eventually helping to break down barriers between the sexes and those that men had erected between themselves. The Mods' reformation of British masculinity distinguished them from Americans, and male fashion remains one of the striking differences between men on either side of the Atlantic today.

Since the Americans invented mass-produced, ready-to-wear fashion in the early twentieth century, a conservative approach to male clothing had been handed down from fashion house to chain store. As the Small Faces' Ian McLagan remembers: 'Burtons had three styles: small, medium and large.'[47] It also had three colours: black, brown and navy. In 1913, Giacomo Balla's 'Futurist Manifesto of Men's Clothing' had declared 'WE MUST DESTORY ALL PASSEIST CLOTHES and every-thing about them which is colourless, funereal, decadent, boring and unhygienic.'[48] Mods were to make that modernist manifesto a reality: they introduced colour to male clothing for the first time since the Regency era of the early nineteenth century. It was fitting, therefore, that the most flamboyant Mod style was known as the Regency, displayed by the Kinks in March 1966 in publicity for 'Dedicated Follower of Fashion', their affectionate satire of a Carnaby Street dandy.

Colourful clothing was a self-conscious escape from the drabness of early post-war Britain – not only from the economic dolour of the times but also from the conformity that good citizenship seemed to demand. As a girl in the early 1950s Val Wilmer remembers looking at a photograph of Clement Attlee wearing a suit and thinking, 'He's the Prime Minister and look how badly cut his suit is.'[49] A decade later Alfredo Marcantonio remembered 'buying a scarlet shirt and my Dad saying to me, "Where are you going? Bullfighting?" He'd never seen a scarlet shirt before.'[50] Bullfighting was the most favour-able jibe a straight man could expect for wearing colourful clothes which were associated with homosexuality.   Exceptions were permitted in certain circumstances – such as the brightly coloured waistcoat worn by young, upper-class men like the prefects of Eton College, which was mimicked by Teddy Boys. But Teddy Boys main-tained an outward code of strict heterosexuality and their dislike of the more ambiguous Mod male was another cause of the conflict between the two tribes, as one young woman testified in 1964: 'I'd hate to marry a Mod, they're not men at all really. When there's a punch-up they fight like girls . . . They say the Rockers are scruffy; that we don't wash. I'd rather not wash than be mistook for a prissy little Mod girl. You know what Mod stands for – Moderation in all things. What a way to carry on.'[51] Some Mod girls agreed that 'Mod boys are getting too feminine',[52] but by the mid-1960s most young women had embraced the new masculinity driven by male vanity and ego, and were playing a role in its evolution by encouraging the recalcitrant and faint-hearted.

Attitudes to the new masculinity varied around Britain and high-lighted deeper regional differences. Since the nineteenth century, the industrial north had stood in the national imagination for plain speaking and a robust masculinity inherited from generations of shipbuilders, miners and factory workers. The south, on the other hand – home to the media, banking, Parliament, and generally associated with elites – was paradigmatic of an effete bourgeois English masculinity: all brains and no trousers. To many people in the north, therefore, Mods looked like typical southerners. Nik Cohn observed that 'When Mod caught on, there were many teenagers who refused to go along with it. Especially in the north, and in rural districts, they found it soft and creepy.'[53] But letters to the magazine *Mod Monthly* from northern fans tartly reminded readers that Mod was not just a London cult. With some pride, these fans conceded that it was harder to dress flamboy-antly the further north you lived, requiring a toughness of mind and body to withstand public mockery; one woman told readers of what her boyfriend went through in order to wear tight white jeans in Leeds.[54] Ironically, therefore, northern Mods helped to perpetuate regional stereotypes by regarding themselves as tougher than the cult's followers in the south – if only because they had to face higher levels of abuse.

But the Mod wardrobe also exposed generational differences, as Carlo Manzi discovered:

I bought a big pink shirt from a shop called Gay Lord. It had a giraffe collar and a tab front. I put it in the wash. The next day I went to get it and I couldn't find it. I said to my mum, 'Where's that pink shirt?' She said, 'I've torn it up. It's a duster now.' I couldn't believe it. I said, 'Why?' She said, 'Because everyone will think you're a poof. I'll give you money to buy a new shirt. But please, don't buy pink.'[55]

Many didn't heed the warning, such as Mark Timlin, a roadie for the Who and later a crime novelist:

I remember one Friday lunch time you got paid in cash those days and me and a friend went down to Austins and we both bought pink shirts. My mate took his back. Got a white one because people were calling him a poof. But I thought bollocks. I'm not taking mine back so I wore mine on the Monday morning on the train to work. I was sweating, so many people were looking at me. I wore it with a blue knitted tie, a blue suit, Annello and Davide shoes. And I looked the business.[56]

Some were prepared to suffer violence in pursuit of the pleasure principle, as Kay Marriott, mother of the Small Faces' front man, remembered: 'My Steve, the first time he wore white trousers he was beaten up.'[57]

This was an era when anyone thought to be gay risked derision, ostracism or violence. Homosexual acts between men over 21 were legalised in 1967, but then only in England and Wales. While there was a British vaudeville tradition of camp comedy which had made a successful move to film and TV, notably in the shape of Kenneth Williams in the *Carry On* series, Britain was still a deeply homophobic country that regarded actively gay men as effeminate, predatory, immoral and a threat to the social order. Wearing pink was therefore not simply a lifestyle choice but an act of defiance, and Mods cut a path that British men have strutted down ever since. This was no campaign for gay rights but Mod was the first youth movement to engage directly with gay culture, something acknowledged even by those who insist that all scooter boys were straight. According to Ken Browne:

There was a definite gay influence involved with the early Mods. The London clubs would have a lot of gays in them wearing outrageous white suits with big high heels. Mods took that influence, it became a case of looking as pretty as possible, as nice as possible. I never knew any gay Mods. Every single one I met was very heterosexual, even though they weren't that interested in girls. They were so wrapped up in themselves, interested in their scooters, clothes and pills. I had a few girlfriends but on the whole they weren't into the scene. The clubs were just full of blokes.[58]

Recalling gay life in London during the early 1960s, Peter Burton remembered how close Mods were to the world he moved in:

The premiere Mod club – the Scene in Ham Yard behind Shaftesbury Avenue – was basically a straight version of [the gay] Le Duce. Economically, those who frequented the Scene and Le Duce both came from the same working-class – South and East London – backgrounds. Both groups paid the same attention to clothes; both groups looked much alike. Not surprising, really, as their clothes came from the same shops – initially Vince in Carnaby Street (whose catalogue of swim- and underwear could *almost* be classified as an early gay magazine) and eventually from the John Stephen shops in the same street . . . Both groups took the same drug and shared the same music.[59]

Dialogue between the gay and straight worlds was spearheaded by key figures in the arts and entertainment industry, which traditionally offered sanctuary to deviants of various kinds. One of them was the manager Larry Parnes, who capitalised on the growing profitability of pop by building a stable of stars in the early 1960s. Parnes ruthlessly shaped and sold their images, and among the young, gay managers inspired by him were Kit Lambert, Simon Napier-Bell and Brian Epstein. Napier-Bell, whose clients have included the Yardbirds, Marc Bolan and Wham! attributes the 'sensational success' of British pop to the 'fusion of working-class youth and middle-class homosexual'. As well as the shared pursuit of money and sex, what these managers and artists had in common was a strong sense of being outsiders. According to Napier-Bell:

An upper-middle-class public school background was still the principal key to success for the behind the scenes people in the music business. Record company executives were nearly all of that background and found difficulty in communicating with the new generation of young artists. However, young men in their early twenties with a public school education plus a modicum of unconventionality could cross the divide between the two cultures. And the most frequently found 'modicum of unconventionality' was a touch of homosexuality . . . It was gay managers and their friends in fashion and media, who were chiefly responsible for creating the image of British youth culture that was being sold around the world.[60]

Pete Townshend agreed: 'Gays were different. They didn't behave like other adults; they were scornful of conventional behaviour; they mixed more easily with young people, and seemed to understand them.'[61]

When it came to openly discussing sexuality with their fans, however, pop stars were reminded how much British society lagged behind the more tolerant world they inhabited. The Kinks' 1965 song 'See My Friends' tackled bisexuality, a subject close to the hearts of the Davies brothers. Ray Davies recalled:

I know there was resistance to it . . . I remember that Keith Altham of the *New Musical Express* hated the record. I talked to him about duality and people, bisexuality and things like that, and the *NME* wouldn't print that sort of thing. They wanted us to be really normal, go-ahead 'all day and all of the night' boys you know, have a pint and piss off. But I wasn't like that.[62]

In the world of fashion it was John Stephen, the so-called 'King of Carnaby Street', who facilitated the dialogue between the gay and straight worlds. Stephen worked at Vince's, a boutique selling 'Exclusive Continental Styles for Men' and quietly frequented by homosexuals and artists since the mid-1950s. Pablo Picasso once bought a pair of suede trousers there, while the former 'Mr Scotland' muscleman and future James Bond actor, Sean Connery, appeared in the adverts that Vince's owner placed in *Town* magazine. Stephen built his fame and fortune on making the flamboyant colours, textures and designs of Vince's more widely available and socially acceptable.

A gay working-class Glaswegian, Stephen was the sixth of nine children and had arrived in London at the age of 18 to work in the military department of Moss Bros. After the spell at Vince's, he began making and selling his own clothes, opening his first store in Soho in 1956. A year later he moved to Carnaby Street, eventually turning it into the epicentre of London fashion. Stephen dressed classically all his life, in dark suit, white shirt and tie, and he had only two extravagances: his Rolls-Royce (at 20, he became the youngest person ever to own one) and Prince, the white German shepherd dog who regularly dined with him at the Ivy.[63]   But Stephen believed that men 'should be able to wear whatever they like',[64] and sold a range of dazzling, innovative clothes, from luminous orange hipsters to the less successful 'mini-kilt', a homage to his native land.

Irvine Sellar, Stephen's main rival in Carnaby Street, created the first unisex shop, selling clothes for both men and women following

Stephen's success with the boutique Mod Male. But Stephen was the first to employ young shop assistants wearing his own clothes instead of a company uniform. As a result, the barriers between store assistants and customers came down in the new boutiques of London. 'Nobody approaches the customer to ask them what they want', said Stephen. 'The assistants are all in casual clothes – in the case of the Mod Male in very Mod clothes. They just smoke and lean against the wall and put records on . . . it's all very casual.'[65] Stephen also understood how important it was to have stars of pop, cinema and sport buy his creations. It was John Stephen, as a designer, retailer and consummate publicist, who was responsible for mass-marketing gay style to straight youth.

The very act of shopping subverted masculine norms in the mid-twentieth century. 'What lack ye? What lack ye? Madam, will you buy?' was a common cry of pedlars in seventeenth-century English street markets. Since then, from the shopping arcade of the eighteenth century to the emergence of the department store in the nineteenth, the shopping experience had been largely designed around women. The same was true for those who could not afford a visit to Selfridges: shopping for life's essentials was seen as the woman's sphere, directly connected to her role as homemaker and unpaid domestic servant. This was especially true in working-class culture, where physical strength was valued more than mental agility and the cultivation of taste; man's dignity stemmed from his ability to hew and manufacture.

As Shari Benstock and Suzanne Ferris have written, by 'worshipping leisure and money' Mods were 'scorning the masculine world of hard work and honest labour'.[66] 'They were dandies, aesthetes', observed Paolo Hewitt. 'For the first time young working-class men were displaying an obsession with clothes that had only been previously noted in the gay movement . . . Modernism has longevity because there will always be someone wanting to dress up to fuck off a world that constantly wants to put you down.'[67]

Clothes were not the only way that Mods transgressed gender boundaries. Mod was the first youth cult in which it was acceptable for men to dance with each other. It was also the first to sanction the wearing of male make-up, mainly eyeliner and mascara which was quietly taken from sisters and girlfriends or bought for them by more understanding ones. Those using make-up were few in number but widely admired. Alex Miller, an electrician, told *Rave* magazine: 'Only one mod boy in hundreds wears powder. And it doesn't mean he's funny. He just does it to be different.'[68] Funny or not, it was a dangerous business. Ken Browne remembers going to a club in Essex in search of a girl with his friend John:

I had this bloody bright multi-coloured striped blazer and red shoes on, my hair all bouffanted up . . . She was right down the front and there were about five or six Mod girls there. We walked up to them looking totally outrageous. John even had eye make-up on . . . We were talking to these Mod girls and the place literally filled up with Rockers. About a hundred of them walked in almost in one hit and there was just us two down the front. I was absolutely shitting myself . . . I couldn't see a side exit, so we had to walk through all these guys, the whole lot of them and they all parted. It was all 'Hello Darling' and tripping you up and the rest of it. I thought we'd made it because we got as far as the door, John was much smaller than me so they didn't pick on him but they decided I would do and I got absolutely hammered.[69]

Mods frequented women's hairdressers because the traditional British barber was unable to cut the required styles, especially the backcombed, bouffant known as 'the French', which required a blow-dryer rather than a tub of greasy hair cream.[70] 'We thought it was very French, it probably wasn't though,' remembered Johnny Moke. 'I used to go to bed every night in hair rollers to keep my hair in.'[71] Those not wanting to be seen in women's salons arranged special times to have their hair done once the female clientele had left, usually entering from the rear of the shop.

Grooming began to become an accepted part of masculine behaviour in the 1960s and Mods were at the forefront of that revolution, wearing aftershave and deodorant and using moisturiser. Products such as Brylcreem had been advertised regularly in magazines since the 1930s, but it was Mods who turned grooming from a necessary routine into a fetish that proclaimed the importance of male beauty as an aesthetic end in itself. In 1965, *Rave* – one of the first unisex style magazines and a house journal of the Mod movement – launched its 'Fashion and Beauty for Boys' section. 'It's a new RAVE idea!'

proclaimed the magazine. 'More girls are wanting to know the latest on the boys' scene, and more boys are wanting to know themselves too!'[72]

Wanting to 'know themselves' suggested a journey into deeper, uncharted waters. In fact, advertising remained unambiguously hetero-sexual to reassure men that looking and smelling nice did not mean you were entertaining thoughts of other men beyond competing with them for the attention of the opposite sex. Then as now, from Old Spice to Lynx, companies sold their products by promising men sexual conquest as a reward for submitting to what were still seen as innately feminine practices. However, Mods' grooming did mark the beginning of a more relaxed British masculinity, which improved the daily dialogue between the sexes, not least because men were encouraged to take women's advice on the subject. 'Quite a few boys suffer from troublesome skins', reported *Rave*. 'Soap and water can be hard on skin in this condition. Most boys take a few hints from their girlfriends on this subject and don't object one bit to using preparations aimed at the female market like Pond's skin cleansers. It'll do your skin good!'[73]

Girlfriends and sisters encouraged this reformation of masculinity and anecdotal evidence suggests that it made Mod attractive to young women. Market researchers discovered that women drove the accept-ance of male grooming in the 1960s and 70s by demanding personal hygiene as a condition of dating and mating; and advertisers often directed their wares at the 'modern' woman who was demanding a better man. As we shall see, this feminine calibration of the British male had a long-term effect on national life, as teenage Mods matured and entered the world of marriage and domesticity better equipped to appreciate spheres of life previously ignored or derided as intrinsi-cally female.

In the meantime, Mod remained a male-dominated movement in which heterosexual men were seen to be the arbiters of taste and the stage directors of social interaction, be it with homosexuals or women; yet attitudes towards the latter were based more on narcissism than on misogyny. 'Some of our clothes are a bit effeminate but they have to be. I mean you have to be a bit camp', said the future Marc Bolan in the 1962 interview in *Town* magazine. Speaking in 1967 as a 19-year-old he recalled:

I'd say that Mod was mentally a very homosexual thing, though not in any physical sense. I was too hung up on myself to be interested in anyone else . . . I didn't think at all. The only thought I ever had was, 'Oh, I just bought one suit this week and I should have bought three.' That was all. I was completely knocked out by my own image, by the idea of Mark Feld.'[74]

It was not until former Mods like Bolan and David Bowie developed gender-bending glam rock in the early 1970s that these homosexual tendencies became more overt and subversive. In the meantime, Mods' embrace of R&B and soul highlighted another thing that seemed to put them ahead of their time: attitudes to race.

INTO THE STEEPLE OF BEAUTIFUL PEOPLE

Music and fashion were zones where multiracial Britain was not only visible on the surfaces of style, but where an underlying social dialogue took place between black and white that marked progress towards a racially integrated society. Mods claimed to be the first youths on either side of the Atlantic collectively to make a moral connection between their consumption of black culture and their attitudes to black people.

As with attitudes to class, there was certainly a difference between Mods and rockers. Not all rockers were racists but they were notorious protagonists in the Notting Hill riots of 1958, leading attacks by white gangs on the area's black population. Like the white American youth they admired and copied, most rockers were able to consume music that originated in black America while simultaneously holding racist views, which they expressed to the black people they encountered in Britain. A 1964 survey for the Institute of Race Relations concluded that

The Rockers (as opposed to the Mods) represent good old roast-beef English values. One of these is hostility to foreigners. It goes with the cult of maleness and a proper contempt for fancy clothes. I know one Rocker gang in South London for whom chasing blacks is an accepted way to pass an evening. 'I wish there was a war' said one, 'and I'd join up in the marines to fight for old Queen-and-country. The first thing I'd do would be: go to the stores, draw out a machine-gun and shoot down every nigger I could see.' His mates gave nods of assent.[75]

In contrast, Mods were rarely involved in violence or intimidation and most prided themselves on their lack of prejudice.[76] Yet the evidence suggests that here, too, Mods' claims to be in the vanguard of modernity were exaggerated.

As we saw in Chapter One, Mods adored black American music. But of all the genres they sampled – from bebop in the 1950s to House in the 1990s – the most consistent influence on Mod-related youth cultures was soul music. Like bebop, soul was rooted in the American civil rights struggle, a fact that is often forgotten when the melodies of Motown swirl around a party; yet in the 1960s the politics of soul music were as clear to most Mods as the politics of the Continental suit. Alongside the raw celebration of sex with which soul took gospel onto a secular level, there were many songs on the Mod DJ's playlist that spoke of claiming equal opportunity in a society that despised or patronised you. One favourite was Curtis Mayfield's 'Move On Up' (1970). Mayfield was born in the projects of Chicago, and this song, though popular among black activists, didn't register in the mainstream US *Billboard* charts. In Britain, on the other hand, it spent ten weeks in the charts in 1971, its mixture of hedonistic optimism and stony realism strongly appealing to Mods whose dream was their only scheme:

> Hush now child and don't you cry
> Your folks might understand you by and by
> So in the meantime, move on up towards your destination
> Though you may find from time to time complications
>
> Bite your lip and take a trip
> Though there may be wet road ahead
> And you cannot slip so what you wanna do
> Just move on up for peace you will find
> Into the steeple of beautiful people where there's only one kind . . .
>
> Take nothing less than the supreme best
> Do not obey for most people say 'cause you can past the test
> So what we have to do is move on up and keep on wishing
> Remember your dream is your only scheme so keep on pushing.

No one affected a southern black accent quite like Mick Jagger, and as Paolo Hewitt has written, 'Everyone who formed a band in the early 60s wanted to sing like a black American . . . There were no exceptions.'[77] A childlike awe is visible in the facial expressions of the Small Faces when they met Diana Ross and the Supremes on the set of *Ready, Steady, Go*, the TV show on which soul stars from across the Atlantic regularly performed. When the 1967 Stax tour reached Britain, its stars, led by Otis Redding, Eddie Floyd and Booker T. & the MGs, were swept away by the reception they got. 'They treated us like the Beatles', remembered Booker T. guitarist Steve Cropper.[78] In fact, the Beatles sent limos to collect them on their arrival at Heathrow airport and take them to an exclusive gig attended by the British pop aristocracy. Black American stars would often combine TV appearances with performances at Mod clubs, where they attracted huge crowds. Soul legend Geno Washington recalled: 'I got out of the US Air Force and came back to England in 1965 to start a band . . . We didn't really know anything about the Mods at that point but suddenly these kids started showing up wearing sharp Italian suits and long leather coats. Everyone got real sharp man. Soon we were pulling big crowds . . . We had an army of Mods following us around. Man, it was a really exciting time.'[79]

The Spencer Davis Group disliked the term R&B because it didn't catch the force of black influence on their work. 'Definitions have gone to pot', Davis told *Melody Maker*. 'We much prefer to call it younger generation Negro pop . . . It has been made popular by disc jockeys and they have done a lot to change public taste. We don't play any white stuff, and we don't say that in a derogatory way. It's just that we prefer Negro stuff. There are so many new names to hear, undiscovered artists, and it's so exciting. The Beatles paved the way for American Negro pop here, by liking the Supremes.'[80] Fortunately, the term 'Negro pop' did not catch on.

When the Beatles invited Motown singer Mary Wells to tour Britain with them in 1964, performing cover versions made John Lennon uncomfortable. 'I hate singing "Twist and Shout" when there's a coloured artist on the bill', he told journalist Ray Coleman. 'It doesn't seem right, you know. It seems to be their music and I feel sort of embarrassed. Makes me curl up . . . they can do these songs much better than us.'[81] But when George Melly met Lennon at the launch of his book *In His Own Write* that same year, a drunken fight nearly broke out when Melly suggested the Beatles were derivative. 'You must feel', he told Lennon, 'that one's real debt is to black singers like Muddy Waters and Chuck Berry, who invented the idiom in which we both sing.' 'I could eat 'em for breakfast . . .' an angry Lennon replied, 'they don't make anything like I make.' Later he said: 'Look, we copied nobody. I am not a Negro so I can't copy a Negro singer. We've got our own style based on the music we grew up with, and it annoys me a lot to find groups getting on the wagon by copying sounds we were playing two years ago.'[82] Steve Marriott too insisted that the Small Faces were not just mimicking their black American heroes: 'Everyone's got soul, but as far as Negro soul singing goes only they can do it. But white artists can interpret coloured soul into their own. You don't have to be born on the wrong side of the tracks.'[83]

Yet both adoration and interpretation went hand in hand with plagiarism, as all white British artists, like their American counterparts, stole from their musical mentors. Mods chastised those who did it too brazenly. One night after the Rolling Stones played in Manchester they visited the city's legendary Mod club, the Twisted Wheel (later home to its spin-off cult, Northern Soul). Seeing them enter, the club's resident DJ, Roger Eagle, decided to play the original version of every blues song on their first album in corresponding order; embarrassed and angry, the band left soon after. Pete Meaden, who cared less about making money than most managers, wrote the Who's first songs (when they were still the High Numbers), 'I'm the Face' and 'Zoot Suit', by ripping off the chords of Slim Harpo's 'Got Love If You Want It' and the Showmen's 'Country Girl'. It didn't matter to black musicians like Jimmy James and the Vagabonds, the band Meaden managed after being sacked by the Who. 'I came over to England from Jamaica in 1964', James remembered, 'and started off by playing to the West Indian community . . . The mod kids picked up on us because we played with energy. We pitched our sound more and more to this new scene, so much so that when we put out our first album it was called *The New Religion* . . . Mod meant a mode of living . . . It was an era of invention, everything looked new and seemed new.'[84]

But Mods didn't just consume black music and fashion: in bars and nightclubs across the country they sometimes socialised with West

Indian immigrants. Mod exploded at a time when Parliament passed the first Race Relations Acts, in 1965 and 1968, to legally prohibit discrimination in civil society. More importantly, Mod rose to prominence when the first generation of children born to black immigrants were entering adolescence. These young men and women were forging a new identity that welded the cultural heritage of their parents with that of the country into which they had been born. And this painful process coincided with white working-class youths attempting to create a new identity for themselves within Britain's more affluent society. Mod was therefore driven by the relationship between these two sets of young people; it was a relationship that would remain unsteady and volatile over the next half-century but which would become one of the defining features of British youth culture, setting it apart from America's more segregated society.

In the early 1960s West Indians made up Britain's largest non-white population with around half a million, most settling in the south and Midlands of England. They brought with them ska, a Caribbean form of R&B, and rocksteady, its more laid-back cousin and the precursor of reggae. West Indians also imported the associated character of the 'Rude Boy' – an archetypal Jamaican man-about-town-cum-hustler, similar to the white British 'wide boy'. His porkpie hat, tight-fitting suits, Fred Perry polo shirt and loafers soon augmented the already eclectic Mod look. In addition, the bold display of colour by West Indian men in everything from hats to socks helped to get colourful clothing accepted, not least because Caribbean culture – highly macho and homophobic – offered reassurance, to those who needed it, that being a peacock did not mean you were gay. It was not just what Rude Boys wore, but how they wore it that captivated white Mods, as Ian Hebditch recalled: 'They wore their trousers shorter than we would wear them, with socks showing. Also, they brought in the idea of never doing your tie up. You always had a button undone. The influence was seen in the way they wore their clothes which was with a kind of arrogance that the Mods had as well.'[85]

Yet we should be careful not to romanticise these embryonic relationships between black and white. Few blacks actually called themselves Mods in the 1950s and 60s. That was because, unlike the much older and larger black population of America, most were immigrants. It was not until the 1970s, when enough children of those immigrants were in their teens and twenties, that there existed a body of British born Afro-Caribbean or Asian youth large enough to create their own, indigenous cultures that had an impact on British life. As we shall see in Chapter Eight, no longer content to be flattered as an exotic foreign influence, it was that generation which truly developed British youth culture, utilizing it as a way of locating itself within, and beyond, national life. So while young black men and women can be spotted dancing comfortably in most editions of *Ready, Steady, Go!* and *Top of the Pops,* black youths were a small physical presence in the movement.

From 1961 onwards, the headquarters of the Mod/ska nexus was Rik Gunnell's Flamingo Club in Wardour Street and the Roaring Twenties in Carnaby Street, where Count Suckle DJed and Prince Buster, the 'Godfather of Ska', played. British artists who were influenced by ska included Pete Townshend, jazzman Georgie Fame, who played with Buster for a time, and John Paul Jones, who performed in a ska band before becoming Led Zeppelin's bass player. 'All the Mod style was from Jamaica, stingy brims and high buttons', recalled Jones.[86]

When Buster embarked on his 1964 tour of the country, Mods gave him a scooter escort out of every town he played, riding in formation alongside his car as a semi-official motorcade.[87] He first encountered them at the start of the tour when he got out of the car to buy a snack from a roadside cafe. Seeing a large group of white youths standing around, his entourage advised against it. 'I don't see why I can't walk anywhere', remembered Buster. 'I got out, these guys look me up and down, and tell me I must be all right because I've got on the same narrow-foot pants they have! Everywhere I went they would go and make sure everything was all right. They'd be round me like bodyguards, they'd ride along all around my cars on their scooters, like I was royalty.'[88]

'We're hero-worshipping the Spades,' one Mod told interviewers, 'they can dance and sing and they've got style. I often go to a West Indian club, where everyone makes their own clothes. It's fantastic, everyone is individual, everyone is showing themselves as they really want to be'.[89] 'Hero-worshipping Spades' for their style, be they visiting stars, resident West Indians or black British Mods, indicates that Mods' veneration lacked a political dimension. Desmond Dekker was surprised that his song '007 (Shanty Town)' became a hit in Britain in 1967: 'It was actually about the troubles that were happening in Jamaica at the time. There'd been student riots and the police and soldiers had been called in to break them up . . . I think people [in Britain] liked the tune even if they didn't understand what the song was about.'[90] When Dekker got to No. 1 in the UK charts a year later with 'Israelites', he was hailed by the *NME* as 'a man from the land of sunshine and sugar cane . . . [with] his beautiful West Indian accent'.[91] Nonetheless, Mods laid important foundations in the mid-1960s for the closer engagement of later generations of black and white.

Patrick Uden, who later became a TV executive, attests to the mood of the time: 'There was an off-shoot of Modernism which was West Indianism, put in simple terms. And there was a merging. Many of the clubs were run by West Indians.'[92] Simply going to black clubs was transgressive; so too was welcoming blacks to white clubs, and what may have started as a rebellious gesture did lead to friendships and relationships. Multiracial groups also began to emerge with a corresponding fan base, like the appropriately named Anglo-West Indian soul outfit the Foundations.

The British government noticed the emergence of a multiracial youth culture. Indeed, there was so much concern about the extent of integration at Mod venues that the Home Office sent officials on undercover missions to find out why it was happening. After visits to the Flamingo Club, a report submitted to the Home Secretary in 1964 concluded:

There is traffic in 'pep-pills' and there is a great deal of necking, especially with coloured people. In this atmosphere any young person is obviously in serious moral danger . . . It requires a strong character and a secure home background with understanding parents to avoid contamination once the young person has entered the 'club world'.[93]

It was during this period that the association between youth culture and recreational drug use became embedded in the public mind, leading to more draconian narcotics legislation from 1964 onwards, when amphetamines were banned precisely because of their wide-spread use by Mods. In 1950, the British government proscribed 33 narcotics, in 1960 the figure was 65 and by 1970 it had risen to 106. Blacks became more stigmatised as they were perceived as being disproportionately involved in drug dealing and drug use.[94] In the 1979 film *Quadrophenia*, for example, the sole black character was a drug dealer on the fringes of the Mod gang; and although a controversial element of the film at the time, it reflected the marginal role of black youth in the movement during the 1960s.

It was also at the height of mid-60s Mod that a splinter of violent teenagers grabbed headlines with the Mod–Rocker battles on England's south coast. The confrontations (of which more in Chapter Six) showed that taste and testosterone often went hand in hand, fostering a tribal hooliganism similar in effect to that of earlier youth movements. The Mods involved in the disturbances of 1964–5 were not just an embarrassment to the early Modernists trying to escape working-class stereotypes; those arraigned in Brighton's courtrooms were also the precursors of the skinheads who would show how much Mod's multi-racial ethos was a pretty thin veneer on a class culture still shot through with the prejudices of pre-war Britain.

In the meantime, Mod made its first Atlantic crossing. The figure-heads of the so-called British Invasion discovered a more racially divided country than their own, one in which the African American parentage of popular music was largely denied or reviled before the Beatles arrived to remind white Americans where most of it came from. 'I look all white but my Dad was black', sang the Who in 'Substitute', acknowledging their musical influences, but for the single's US release the group were forced to record another version of the song where the offensive line was changed to 'I try going forward but my feet walk back'.

3

I TOOK THE MI

Mod and the Reclamation of British Pop Culture

The Mods were, for me, the revolution . . . There's a North Vietnamese Army who are stolid troops, and there's the Vietcong who are like Mods, who are the ones who've been fighting all the time. They've never let down the side, they've always been fighting in a minority group, against the vast armour of the American army.

    Pete Meaden, 1978[1]

Some people pick up their guitars and take Route 66. I took the MI.

    Ray Davies, 1995[2]

WE NOW LEAD THE WORLD IN POP MUSIC!

'It is now 6.30 a.m., Beatle time. They left London 30 minutes ago. They're out over the Atlantic Ocean headed for New York. The temperature is 32 Beatle degrees', one American DJ informed his listeners as they rose for another day's work on 7 February 1964.[3] The American people were largely unaware of the Mod phenomenon when the Beatles touched down at Kennedy Airport a few hours later. The music and fashion industries in the United States had been slow to realise what was going on in Britain, and even when they caught on, from 1964 to 1967, the mediation of Mod-related music and fashion to young Americans reflected how conservative the United States was compared to the country that generated this peculiar form of popular

Modernism. The British Invasion brought the youth of Europe and America closer together than at any time in their history; but the invasion also showed how far apart they remained in their attitudes to issues of masculinity, race, religion and class, all of which Mod carried with it as freight on its Atlantic crossing.

It was not the first time that British figures had made an impact on America. Charlie Chaplin had moved there in 1913 and, before being expelled as a suspected communist in 1952, had developed Hollywood's global reach with his internationally popular clown. Alfred Hitchcock had followed in 1939 and done the same with his development of the thriller in the 1950s. Yet it was America and not Britain that had been the making of both men, and it was America that had mediated their work to the rest of the world. Now here instead was a cultural product accepted as uniquely British. As Bill Osgerby explained:

The explosion of Beatlemania as an international phenomenon in 1964 . . . is at odds with simple concepts of American dominance of popular media. Admittedly, the British pop 'invasion' of the US during the early 60s could be seen, in some respects, as a by-product of 'Americanisation' with the British media re-making and re-marketing music genres that had initially been imported from the States. In Britain, however, these genres had been appropriated, re-interpreted and synthesized with local cultural elements, so that the end product was recognisable as a distinctly British cultural form that fed back into the development of popular music and youth style in America.[4]

The speed with which Beatlemania captured the United States confounded scepticism about the quality of British pop. Forty-eight hours after landing in New York, the Beatles performed on *The Ed Sullivan Show* in front of an audience of 70 million, 60 per cent of all American viewers. In 1964 alone, American stores sold an estimated $50 million worth of Beatles merchandise.[5] Among the thousands of fan letters the group received was this one from Karen Fondly of Massachusetts: 'Dear Ones, Yesterday, to show my loyalty, I bought a Beatle wig, a Beatle sweatshirt and four Beatle dolls. I spent $24.79. I adore you. Take my heart. It is all I have left.'[6]

Such devotion impressed the king of merchandise, 'Colonel' Tom

Parker and the young man who had made him rich. The Colonel sent a message of congratulations from himself and Elvis Presley that was read out by Ed Sullivan just before the Beatles performed. In private, 'Elvis saw the Beatles and the whole British invasion as a threat and it galled him to be widely perceived as passé', wrote his biographer.[7] When the Beatles visited Elvis at Graceland a year later, Lennon and McCartney jammed with their hero once the small talk ran out, while the Colonel and Brian Epstein gambled at a roulette table and Harrison sat by the pool explaining Hinduism to one of Elvis's entourage over a joint. The group left with 'a prickly mix of anger and disillusion', and Elvis later told the FBI that he blamed them for 'many of the problems we are having with young people by their filthy unkempt appearances and suggestive music'.[8]

Still, that telegram read out on the Ed Sullivan show in 1964 didn't just make the King appear magnanimous. For a moment it seemed to erase the humiliation Britain had suffered during the Suez Crisis in 1956, for it said to the British: 'We still matter in the world.' It mattered to Mods that they, and not Americans, were influencing global youth style for a change. As one teenager told *Rave* magazine in 1964, 'I think it's great that British Mods are setting the trends throughout the rest of the world. It seems to me the Americans resent us for it.'[9] The British generally didn't resent it; indeed people of all ages came to value their pop culture quite overtly as a consolation for the loss of political and economic power to the United States. In 1965, the *New Musical Express* celebrated the award of MBEs to the Beatles thus:

Did the Beatles deserve to be honoured by the Queen? The answer must be irrevocably and unquestioningly – Yeah! Yeah! Yeah! Where the Beatles deserve their awards is in the field of prestige. Their efforts to keep the Union Jack fluttering proudly have been far more successful than a regiment of diplomats and statesmen . . . We now lead the world in pop music![10]

NME readers agreed that the Fab Four deserved the award they got from the Queen. 'In three years they have done more than a stuffy civil servant could hope to achieve in 100 years', wrote one.[11]

Actually, stuffy civil servants and diplomats recognised the value of this new popular culture. It was partly a question of trade because the music and fashion industries were worth considerably more to the national economy than before. For example, by 1969 the annual value of British fashion exports was estimated to be £84 million, up from £11 million twenty years earlier.[12] But its cultural value was also recognized by officials, and from 1964 onwards the Foreign Office used fashion to promote the United Kingdom abroad in the hope of rebranding the country's stuffy imperial image. One government film declared that Britain had become 'the fashion centre of the world' by 'flaunting convention, designing clothes to suit a modern woman's life and whims . . . If she wants to she can play it cool as a Carnaby Street mod' – a British style that, thanks to export networks, 'girls from Sydney to Sarasota' could enjoy.[13] Some blamed diplomats rather than pop stars if something went wrong with this strategy. After a reception at the Washington Embassy for the Beatles during their 1964 tour, young Foreign Office aides pinned down Ringo while one of their wives cut a lock of his hair, leading the *Sunday Express* to remark, 'The Beatles haven't let their country down in the US, but some British diplomats have done so . . . [men who are] still apparently in the juvenile delinquent stage. If that's the type we are sending to Washington, it doesn't seem a very good advertisement for Britain. Indeed, if we brought them home and left the Beatles there in their place, our diplomacy in America might be considerably improved.'[14]

The Rolling Stones' manager remembers the full force of the British Invasion at its height: 'Everything just mushroomed. It was like Englandmania. The English won that war; even crappy acts became successful.'[15] The success of Mod-related music and fashion in America was partly due to the familiarity that existed between the two countries, as the author and counter-culture activist Barry Miles observed in his study of the British Invasion:

Sometimes it takes an outsider to show you the obvious. The music might have originated in the American South, the industrial cities of America's North, and the honky tonks of the Midwest, but it was finessed and played by the British; the movies may have taken their lead from Hollywood and Paris, but they were made in England. The attitude and accents, at least, were all British. And it was acceptable because it was coming from Britain, the country with which the USA has its greatest historical ties. Millions of

Americans have British ancestors; it is the home of the language and much of the legal system; innumerable place names east of the Mississippi have British origins; and less than 20 years before the Beatles arrived, Brits had fought alongside Americans in the Second World War. So, it was more like cousins coming to visit than a real invasion.[16]

The American critic and godfather of music journalism Lester Bangs was critical of British pop but acknowledged its wider significance. He told *Rolling Stone* readers:

This elevation of our mood had to come from outside America's own musical culture, if only because the folk music which then dominated American pop was so tied to the crushed dreams of the New Frontier . . . it took the influx of the Beatles and a thousand trashy imitators to bring us together. The British accomplished this by resurrecting music we had ignored, forgotten or discarded, recycling it in a shinier, more feckless, and yet more raucous form . . . So the British Invasion was more important as an event, as a mood than as music.'[17]

Many American bands in the mid-1960s were brazen imitations of British groups in sound and style, just as British rock 'n' roll had mimicked American music between 1954 and 1964. The Monkees, invented in 1966 for an American TV series about four boys longing to be the Beatles, were merely the most visible of the imitators, and the show playfully captured American jealousy about the British Invasion with Micky Dolenz and the other Monkees regularly throwing darts at a picture of the Fab Four. Tribute bands sprang up in small towns all over the United States, devoted to playing covers of the various British artists who had stormed the American charts in the Beatles' wake.

But the British Invasion also exposed differences between the two countries. A large part of its appeal was that for the first time British music and fashion seemed more dangerous and fun than its American counterpart. The academic John Dougan, raised by Irish immigrants to the United States, remembers his youth as a Who fan:

Rock and roll now had a British accent – and it sounded hipper, smarter, and funnier to my pre-adolescent ears than Elvis's down-home drawl. I didn't abandon American rock bands but après the Beatles came the deluge – bands creating new rules for an emerging hipoisie exuding a continental cool that made everything else obsolete . . . It was through rock and roll that England, London in particular, revealed itself to me like Oz to Dorothy. The London of my imagination was the Technicolor opposite of my tiny, black and white Massachusetts hometown. . . . Somewhere in the world, there was a city run by young people, where rock and roll wasn't treated with disdain, long hair was mandatory, blindingly colourful sartorial psychedelia (nothing like the drab shirts and slacks my parents bought from Sears) was standard dress, and British accents, regardless of region or class affiliation, made everyone sound smart and hip.[18]

Dougan's view of London was just as romantic as the vision that British teenagers once had of the United States. But the fact that young Americans now took British pop seriously marked a change in the American perception of Britain, and it was based on a certain amount of truth. The cheeky confidence and ironic humour with which the Beatles and other groups despatched the patronising questions of the media were a refreshing change from the supine deference which American stars usually employed to maintain their pop careers.

The United Kingdom became a more liberal country than the United States during the 1960s, and this in part explains the attraction and credibility of British youth culture among young Americans. On top of the public healthcare system created by Labour in 1948 the party's next period of office in the 1960s saw the abolition of capital punishment, the decriminalising of homosexuality and abortion, and the Pill becoming freely available on the NHS even for unmarried women. This tranche of liberal reform was underpinned by the retreat of religion from public life, in sharp contrast to the continuing power of the religious Right in America. And while Britain adopted America's more draconian drug prohibition policy in 1964, the minimum legal drinking age remained at 18, whereas in America it was 21 in over half the states until the 1970s, before further restrictions were imposed so that by 1988 it was 21 in every state – which meant that it was legal for millions of young Americans to vote, have sex and die for their country but not have a beer.[19] On balance, therefore, the average British youth enjoyed more freedom than his or her American counterpart even though their incomes were generally lower. Moreover, British teenagers, already free of National Service after 1963, didn't have to fight in Vietnam between 1965 and 1973. Indeed, the real significance of Vietnam for British youths was not the flag-burning leftist demos outside the American Embassy in London but the fact that the Labour government of Harold Wilson prevented the trauma and death of countless young men by keeping Britain out of America's neocolonial war.

In the United States, youth culture was at best tolerated by government, and at worst met the sort of violent resistance from small town bigots that was dramatised in Dennis Hopper's hippie road movie *Easy Rider* (1969), a reworking of the Western for freewheeling Baby Boomers. Despite being adept at utilising American culture for propaganda purposes during the Cold War, it is telling that, unlike the British Foreign Office, the State Department did not employ music and fashion in that way during the 1960s and 70s.

The concept of Swinging London may have been a simulacrum of Mod culture but in the United States it came to denote not cheeky fun but a moral revolt, and some Americans looked with envy at the freedom with which young Britons expressed their desires and paraded their lifestyles. Yet Britain remained a more class-conscious, less mobile nation. That difference helps to explain why the popularity of Mod style in the United States would fade by the late 1960s, whereas in Britain it maintained its appeal sufficiently to foster a lineage of interconnected subcultures, which in their different ways used style to rebuke class stereotypes.

THEY WERE DICTATING CULTURE TO THE REST OF THE WORLD

Mod-related groups created a distinctive musical style by fusing American rhythm and blues with the cadences of the British music hall; they also sang about British life, sometimes in native accents that hadn't been heard in popular music for a generation. The use of vaudeville tunes and imagery in albums like the Small Faces' *Ogden's Nut Gone Flake* and the Beatles' *Sgt. Pepper* – the song 'Being for the Benefit of Mr Kite', replete with fairground organ, was adapted by John Lennon from a Victorian circus poster[20] – was a fitting tribute to that tradition, given that one reason why music halls had closed from the 1930s was the dominance of American mass culture. In December 1964 *The Times*'s music critic hailed a renaissance:

For several decades, in fact since the decline of the music hall, England has taken her popular songs from the United States, either directly or by mimicry. But the songs of Lennon and McCartney are distinctly indigenous in character, the most imaginative and inventive examples of a style that has been developing on Merseyside during the past few years. And there is a nice, rather flattering irony in the news that the Beatles have become prime favourites in America too.'[21]

In Pete Townshend's view, the Kinks were the most distinctive and influential of the Mod groups, although they had the least success in America. 'The Kinks were much more quintessentially English', he said. 'I always think that Ray Davies should one day be Poet Laureate. He invented a new kind of poetry and a new kind of language for pop writing that influenced me from the very beginning.'[22] Davies explained that on 'Sunny Afternoon' he mimicked an aristocratic accent because 'I didn't want to sound American. I was very conscious of sounding English.'[23] While prevented from performing in America from 1965 to 1969, the Kinks produced three albums that cemented their reputation as the most English band of this era: *Something Else* (1967), *The Kinks Are the Village Green Preservation Society* (1968) and *Arthur (Or the Decline and Fall of the British Empire)* (1969). *Village Green* was a homage to rural England, which celebrated village life while condemning skyscrapers. *Arthur*, meanwhile, produced the single 'Victoria', a sardonically affectionate tribute to the British queen who had presided over the empire at its zenith. (In 2004 Davies was rewarded by her great-great-granddaughter for 'services to music' with the anachronistic title Commander of the British Empire.) As the music critic Charlie Gillett later wrote: 'The records stood the test of time and served to inspire and influence other British writers to deal with the British way of life, sung and played in an English manner.'[24]

The native nuances of this music were often lost on foreign ears. But that didn't stop the creative dialogue between Britain and America intensifying as the competition between the two nations' artists spurred them on to new heights. One showcase was the rivalry between the Beatles and the Beach Boys. At the Waldorf Hotel,

London, in June 1966 a meeting took place between Keith Moon, John Lennon, Paul McCartney and Bruce Johnston of the Beach Boys. Just before their album *Pet Sounds* was released, Johnston had flown to London with an advance copy eager to get the opinion of his British peers. Moon, a long-standing Beach Boys fan, showed him round the city, then called Lennon and McCartney over to Johnston's hotel suite. After sinking a few beers, playing cards and chatting, the four men sat around a portable mono record player and listened in silence. McCartney was blown away, calling it 'the album of all time'.[25] A commercial flop in the United States, *Pet Sounds* was a direct influence on the creation of *Sgt. Pepper's Lonely Hearts Club Band* (though it only hastened the drug-addled mental breakdown of the Beach Boys leader, Brian Wilson, as he failed to compete with his British friends).

Released on 1 and 2 June 1967 in Britain and the United States respectively, the Beatles had begun recording *Sgt. Pepper* after their last live performance in San Francisco on 29 August 1966, when they withdrew to create what arguably marked the high point of Britain's post-war influence on American culture. Some critics described the album as a landmark of Western civilisation, calling 'A Day in the Life' the *Waste Land* of its time. But amid all the hyperbole and LSD rumours, beat poet Allen Ginsberg made an important point when he argued that in the fusion of classical, vaudeville and modern pop music, the Beatles had created a multi-generational work of art that helped to 'defuse the tensions of the generation gap', as well as transcending the barriers of class culture.[26] Unusually for pop music at this time, 'When I'm Sixty-Four' even imagined life in old age.

Ginsberg's point is less surprising if we remember that pop figureheads usually stayed close to the families that raised them.[27] The main difference between these family relationships in the 1960s and those of later periods is that they were usually played down by stars in order to maintain the subversive image that made them appealing to rebellious youth. Some stars, like Pete Townshend and Ray Davies, grew up in professional musical families that nurtured their talent and connected them to earlier forms of popular music. Townshend's parents drank, argued and were unfaithful to each other, but the Who guitarist acknowledged the support of his father, a saxophone player in the RAF Dance Orchestra, which after the war became the Squadronaires and played in seaside holiday resorts. Townshend remembered that his dad was 'immensely proud that I was successful at anything. He really didn't like that it was rock because it wasn't really decent in his view; he hated the drugs. But he was an absolutely sterling supporter of anything I did.' He added: 'I just wanted to be like my dad; you know, I worshipped him. He was a magnificent player and a fantastic man.'[28]

Nick Hornby observed that this 'generation was not afraid of the past, nor of popular culture outside the rock and blues tradition (compare the Beatles or the Kinks to just about any American band of the same era, and you can only conclude that our bands liked their parents more).'[29] Whatever the accuracy of that comparison, it was certainly ironic that the art and music of Britain's most powerful former colony should inspire a cultural renaissance that helped to forge Britain's post-imperial identity. Some American commentators wondered if the surge of creativity was a result of Britain shedding its empire. As one Washington journalist remarked in 1965: 'Talent is getting to be Britain's export commodity . . . England, shorn of its world-wide responsibilities for keeping the peace, has turned its energies, previously dissipated in running the colonies, inward towards personal self-expression.'[30]

Music had served British national identity before. There is a parallel between the pride triggered by the revival of British popular music in the 1960s and that generated during the heyday of British classical music in the 1890s. In both cases, anxiety about the nation's declining economic and political power drove the quest for a cultural renewal.[31] In the late nineteenth century, the main challenge to Britain came from Germany rather than the United States, and before the First World War it resulted in an attempt to match Germany's cultural dominance as well as her military might: for Elvis, hear Brahms. Then, as in the 1960s, the Establishment backed an emerging cultural movement, resulting, for instance, in the creation of the Royal College of Music in London. The compositions of Gilbert and Sullivan and Edward Elgar won audiences well beyond the usual reach of such composers. And, like the British groups of the 1960s, their work is still thought to express a quintessential Englishness (even though Elgar was heavily influenced by German music). It is fitting, therefore, that Elgar had recorded his compositions with the London Symphony Orchestra at Abbey Road studios, where the Beatles recorded theirs.

Commercially, the results of this second musical renaissance were impressive: from 1963 to 1968 record sales in the UK quadrupled and for the first time the majority of records were the work of British artists; by 1968 their share had risen to 72 per cent, having previously not exceeded 53 per cent.[32] In the wake of the British Invasion, they made a similar impact on America. From 1960 to 1963, only ten records by British artists got into the *Billboard* 100; between 1964 and 1967 there were 173.[33] (It would be 2002 before there was no British presence in the *Billboard* Top 40.)[34] And by the mid-1960s the *NME* had become one of the world's best-selling music papers, notching up weekly sales of over 300,000 copies.[35]

Continental European record companies also took advantage of the British Invasion. Europeans now began selling Britain to America. Polydor, the pop branch of the classical music label Deutsche Grammophon, and the Dutch company Philips, set up offices in London in the early 1960s when it became clear that British pop was overtaking America's. Polydor's blond-haired, middle-aged Horst Schmolzi 'came at the English with all the subtlety of a Porsche overtaking a Morris Minor in the inside lane', recalls the American impresario Joe Boyd.[36] Within months Schmolzi had lured the Who away from Decca (their punk-era progeny, the Jam, would later sign to the German label too); he also signed Cream and an unknown American who had just arrived in London, called Jimi Hendrix.

Emboldened by this success, Polydor set up an office in New York. At the press launch in 1969, a German executive told shocked American reporters that he had wanted to live in Long Island ever since he'd seen its skyline through the periscope of his U-boat in 1943. His story was probably apocryphal, but the audacity of the speech epitomised the confidence with which Europeans sold America a more developed form of the youth culture it had invented.[37] Marshall Aid had reconstructed Western Europe, and America would cast a spell over the Continent's youth for the rest of the century. But the Old World was not simply remade in the image of the New. The Polydor press conference showed that a cultural deficit was being repaid – and it was Mod that made that moment possible.

For a time, it seemed that for America the pop war was over. From 1964 all manner of Americans were consuming British popular culture, rather than the fine arts that the educated classes of the United States had traditionally imported from Europe. And for the first time British popular culture was judged to be emblematic of a modernity previously ascribed to the New World and not the Old. This was not the passing enthusiasm of screaming teens but a lasting recalibration of American views of Britain. The actor, director and figurehead of American counter-culture, Dennis Hopper, journeyed across the Atlantic several times in the mid-60s to experience the zeitgeist. As he remembered:

The fashion and art and everything was just exploding. Music. It was just amazing. The dance clubs and the jazz and these packed places, it was just incredible. I've never been anywhere that had that kind of impact on me, culturally. You can think of the hippie thing later, but this was more of a cultural explosion. It wasn't the anti-, drop out, tune-in whatever thing we did. It was really about culture, painting, music, sculpture, fashion, clothes. I'd say for about five years, no one could touch them. They were dictating culture to the rest of the world.[38]

THEY WERE A LITTLE BIT IN THE DARK AGES

Mod fashions accompanied music across the Atlantic but with less long-term effect. When the Beatles arrived in America they were surprised to find that the country they had admired from afar was actually rather 'old-fashioned' in its social attitudes and style, as Paul McCartney put it. 'We felt it was a little bit backward,' he said, 'it hadn't kinda had the youth revolution that we'd had in the UK and Europe . . . We were some exotic beast to them, nobody had seen people with their hair all down, all the gear and the clothes and the sort of Mod look, you know, they were a little bit in the dark ages.'[39] As Jonathan Gould has noted, in the period 1963–67 the Beatles were 'instrumental in sending Mod style around the world'.[40] *Look* magazine reported that, 'From Maine to California, teen-agers have gone mad for mod. Credit for the quick catch-on of mod is due to those pied pipers of fashion – the rock 'n' roll combos. Their unsquare outfits mesmerized youthful followers as much as their far-out rhythms.'[41]

British fashion designers, who had previously played second fiddle to their French and Italian counterparts, now stormed America. Banks

of reporters awaited Mary Quant when she and her partner Alexander
Plunket Greene touched down in New York in 1964. Quant believed
that going to the United States was 'the greatest thing that has ever
happened to me professionally'.[42] She strongly resisted parochialism:
'World markets must be the aim of every British fashion designer
today,' she wrote in her 1967 memoir, 'style now has to be truly international, to be as acceptable to the girl in Birmingham as it is in
Bangkok, to look as right on the girl in Boston as it does on the girl
in Brighton.'[43]

Quant was promoted in the United States through her association
with Mod culture, a link she not only encouraged for commercial
reasons but of which she was genuinely proud. The paperback cover
for the American edition of her memoirs depicted her cutting up a
Union Jack into an outfit and promised to tell the story of 'Britain's
Mod girl . . . the gay, outrageous, wildly successful career of Mary
Quant – Britain's top designer of Mod gear'. The blurb continued:
'Her Chelsea shop stayed open until midnight and became a nonstop
cocktail party where kooky models displayed her creations against a
background of jazz.'[44] The bible of the American fashion industry,
Women's Wear Daily, proclaimed: 'These Britishers have a massive
onslaught of talent, charm, and mint-new ideas. English chic is fiercely
NOW, by the young for the young – cocky not kooky . . . Where is
English chic going? How high is the moon?'[45] Quant had arrived to
sign a deal with J. C. Penney, the Marks & Spencer of the United
States: it was the first time that the clothes of a named British designer
were sold in an American chain store. 'We were made to feel we
owned New York', Quant remembered.[46] The couple were photographed wherever they went for *Life* magazine, including at a Harlem
club where Plunket Greene (like Quant a lifelong jazz fan) played
trumpet with Dizzy Gillespie.

Mod style initially spread beyond cosmopolitan New York thanks
to the huge coverage it received in the American media – a campaign
for Jayson's 'authentic Mod look from England' in the autumn of
1966 pictured five sharply dressed young men arriving in a rowing
boat flying a Union Jack. The style was successfully marketed to
those Americans who had helped to create it in the first place: middle-
class 'preppy', professional, white youth in the suburbs, and their
aspirational black counterparts, especially on the east coast, which

felt more connected to Europe. It was a way of offending parents
and it liberated young people who felt trapped by the codes and
expectations of Middle America – a deliverance embodied shockingly
by David Bowie in later years. Yet even at the peak of its popularity,
the style was opposed on the grounds that it made men too effeminate and women too boyish. One magazine article on 'The
Minneapolis Mods' (a city where John Stephen opened a store)
observed that the world of Carnaby Street had 'hit America's theor-
etically ultraconservative farmland', leading to 'a creeping feminiza-
tion' of its previously robust young men. Another magazine blamed
women for exacting a subtle form of revenge on America's male
population. Because of their failure 'to gain total entry into the man's
world', women were 'forcing men to worry about things like fashion
and dancing, art [and] pop movements', all things that were essentially
'a woman's world'.[47]

The Mod icon responsible for the gamine female aesthetic that
some found threatening was the first global supermodel, Twiggy. The
Neasden teenager arrived at JFK in 1967, her image splashed over
magazines including a one-off special called *Twiggy: Her Mod, Mod
Teen World*, which announced: 'She's doing for Mod fashions what the
Beatles did for the Mod sound in music.' It made the joke by now
common to reports of the British Invasion, winking that 'Twiggy has
claimed the colonies for the Crown.'[48] Among the countless Twiggy
products on sale to American teens was a Barbie doll produced in her
image. The Mattel toy company had already produced Francie –
'Barbie's Mod Cousin' – and an African American version was also
created to cater for black girls who wanted to be Mods.

Christine Feldman's study of readers' letters to magazines from
all over the United States shows a clear generational divide, in which
young people were more receptive to Mod. A Pittsburgh reader
reported on how he felt on wearing his first hip-hugging trousers:
'The difference in comfort amazed me. So whoopee for John Stephen
and Pierre Cardin – the revolution is here to stay.'[49] In a sense it was.
The second half of the 1960s was a boom time for the American
menswear industry as millions of aspirational Americans in their
twenties and thirties began to take more interest in style and
grooming. In 1968, *Newsweek* observed, 'Now, no longer afraid of
criticism, the American male is submitting his body to perfumes and

his hair to stylists; wrapping himself in form-fitting suits of every shade and fabric . . . adorning his feet with brightly buckled shoes, and generally carrying on like a dandy straight out of the days of Beau Brummell.'[50]

But some Mod pioneers encountered American conservatism when they crossed the Atlantic. In 1966 Vidal Sassoon opened a salon in New York, bringing with him from London a team of young stylists. The launch party was a success – the guests were served fish and chips with beer on one floor, lobster and champagne on another – but fashion editors soon told him that his look was 'too angular for America', and suggested that he soften it to look more like Jackie Kennedy's. Sassoon was also forced to take a hairdressing exam by the State of New York in order to receive a licence to practise. Contemptuous of English effeminacy, the state judge ruled: 'We're not going to be told what to do by these damn foreigners, especially those limeys. Over there you can't tell the difference between the boys and the girls.'[51] Although Sassoon walked out of the test – 'I looked around the room, truly aghast at what I saw – the sheer absence of style, the lack of any form of modernism', he remembered[52] – within a decade his hair products, books and a TV show had made him a Californian resident and a lifestyle guru.

While British men became more sharply dressed and more adventurous with their appearance during the 1960s, the majority of American men continued to wear looser-fitting, more casual clothing, a difference that outlasted the century. In 1964, a 55-year-old Hardy Amies wrote a pocket book, the *ABC of Men's Fashion*. His entry for 'American Styling' contained this observation:

The American will not be uncomfortable. This has led him to an insistence on lightweight cloths which in their turn can be used successfully in suits the lines of which are more loose than restricting . . . Whilst this conservatism is often admirable for the middle-aged it can be criticised as being completely unadventurous. The American seems to have a horror of being different; except in play clothes where he is quite happy to be a horror.[53]

Mike Leander, an executive for the record label Decca, which distributed the Who's recordings in the United States, regretted that Mod fashion had not made an Atlantic crossing in 1964: 'Generally, most young people in the States have no idea how to dress', he remarked. 'They still go for lightweight suits, conventional white shirts and slim ties. Or else they go to the other extreme and wear jeans and sweat-shirts. To dress casually and smartly in the United States is very expensive. Besides there are no smart menswear shops there – most of their fashionable casual wear is imported from Europe.'[54] Moreover, the reality for young American men was that colourful and flamboyant clothing remained a sign of effeminacy and homosexuality, the social consequences of which deterred dandies and homophobes alike.

On the other hand, the 'Regency' Mod style that the Who sported when they toured the United States in 1967 did not put off their American fans because their music – by then called rock – seemed to convey a reassuringly macho heterosexual message in both its lyrics and stage style. As feminist authors have argued in their critique of 'Cock Rock', the idealised image of the rock star in the late 1960s and early 1970s was common to both America and Britain: a drug-taking, hotel-smashing, groupie-devouring hyper male for whom the micro-phone and guitar were penis extensions, while amplifiers that went up to 'eleven' provided a roar of sound that mimicked the Dionysian góds of ancient Greece as well as the perceived potency of the black male.[55] Nonetheless, Mod culture highlighted conflicting sartorial parameters that represented deep transatlantic differences.

Mod style took a firmer grasp of the European male than of his American counterpart for a number of reasons. Since the Revolutionary Wars, the supposed effeteness of the Redcoats had been set against the hardy American rebel, an image cemented in the nineteeth century by the life and legends of the Wild West. Despite the closing of the American frontier in the 1890s and the rise of white-collar office work in the early twentieth century 'urbanites, who favoured a more debonair style, were not seen as sufficiently American but somehow sissified', according to Christine Feldman.[56] Sharp-suited gangsters and tuxedoed playboys, not to mention the casual world of the Californian surfer celebrated by the Beach Boys, all offered varieties of the same American masculinity. It was a template that owed much to the ideal of the rugged pioneer, dominating nature, natives and women as he moved westward on his civilising mission. In 1960s America, the cowboy himself remained a feature of national life, dramatised by Hollywood (albeit in a more complex way than before) and present in advertising and country music.

At the same time, the corresponding British ideal of the imperial hero was retreating from the national imagination just as real-life colonial administrators were packing their bags in offices all over the world. By the 1960s the stiff-upper-lipped derring-do of the colonial 'chap' had virtually disappeared from British popular culture, his exit hastened by the onset of modern youth culture with its more liberal views of race, women and sexuality. Of course, the British macho lived on in genres such as the war film, but whenever the colonial hero made a reappearance – for example in the film *Charge of the Light Brigade* (1968), in the Mod taste for colourful military jackets, or in songs like the Kinks' 'Victoria' – Empire was sent up with lashings of irony as young Britons slowly developed a post-imperial identity.

Ironically, the running joke of the British Invasion, replayed in American magazine articles, TV shows and advertising, was that Redcoats had returned to reclaim their colony. When Britain's super-model, Twiggy, arrived in the United States, *Life* magazine commented that 'any hopes chauvinistic Americans have nourished that swinging London was slowing down a bit as a trend-setter have been soundly squashed by Britain's latest export . . . she has in two short weeks almost converted this colony for the British Empire.'[57]

WE DIDN'T CARE A MONKEY'S ABOUT THE AMERICAN DREAM

Contrasting attitudes to masculinity were not the only differences that the British Invasion exposed. The musical essence of British pop and rock was a reworking of rhythm and blues by white men less hung up on race than their American counterparts. Because the United States was historically more segregated than Britain, millions of white Americans were unfamiliar with black music until it was repackaged and sold back to them with a British twist and a reassuringly white face by musicians under the spell of Miles Davis, Chuck Berry and Otis Redding. Until the British arrived, American attempts to use black music (with the possible exception of Elvis) had usually involved forms of minstrelsy littered, in the words of Craig Werner, with 'visions of comic dandies, childlike Uncles and sex-crazed apemen'. In contrast, writes Werner in his study of soul and racial politics, 'every British group with a harder edge than Herman's Hermits traced its roots to *modern* black American music' and unlike most white American artists they paid homage to them on their tours of the United States:

While Dylan was changing the way musicians were thinking about rock, the British bands that invaded the United States in 1964 and 1965 played an equally crucial role in preparing the audience for the new take on the blues. Much more consciously immersed in the Chicago blues and Southern soul than their contemporaries in the colonies, the Animals, Rolling Stones and Yardbirds introduced black music to multitudes of white Americans who didn't know their John Lee Hooker from John Hope Franklin . . . Their songs hit hardest in the vanilla suburbs and cream-of-wheat heartland, where American teens lacked exposure to the real thing.

The welcome given to the British Invasion by black artists was due to more than the money and status they acquired from it: they also saw the British as a foreign ally in the war on American racism. James Brown described the Rolling Stones as 'brothers' rather than 'competitors' and acknowledged that the Kinks and the Animals 'had a real appreciation for where the music came from and knew more about R&B and blues than most Americans'.[58] Robert Fields, a black teenager from Chicago, told an interviewer:

One of the things the British Invasion did for me was opening my mind to the fact that a white artist's 'cover' version of an R&B tune could be more than passable . . . When I heard the Beatles' 'Please Mr Postman' and the Rolling Stones' version of Willie Dixon's 'I Just Want to Make Love To You' in 1964, I realised that I actually liked cover versions of American Soul . . . This piqued my curiosity about other groups emanating from England.[59]

R&B, joked Little Richard, stood for 'Real Black' because the American *Billboard* charts and radio stations were more segregated than their British counterparts, even though in number they offered more choice than Britain's more state-controlled broadcasting system. But so great did white America's consumption of black music become in the wake of the British Invasion that *Billboard* integrated its chart in 1965, a move attributed to the success of Motown and to Mod-related music. But it was a temporary move and, as Craig Werner concluded, the

British Invasion 'illuminated some shadowy corners of America's multi-racial culture' that showed how easy it was simultaneously to love black music and hate black people.[60] During the Animals' tour of the States in 1965, for example, Eric Burdon met a southern white girl who liked the same black singers as he did; but when he asked if she'd been to see Otis Redding in town the night before, she replied, 'Did I see him? You got to be joking, man, the place was full of niggers.'[61] On the Beatles' first tour of the United States, they refused to perform at Gator Bowl in Jackson, Florida without a guarantee that the audience would be unsegregated.

While black American artists were happy to meet the Englishmen whose work owed so much to them, white entertainers – their age and artistic limitations more cruelly exposed by the British Invasion – reacted badly. Dean Martin did his best to humiliate the Rolling Stones when they appeared on his TV show, and *The Les Crane Show* even made them miss the stuffiness of British television. It was hosted, their manager remembered, 'by some stagger-brained, lacquered pimp with a smile and demeanour so fake we felt like we'd stopped off on the wrong set . . . God, suddenly old Auntie Beeb seemed far-seeing in comparison . . . It's OK to have your home kind question and ridicule you, but I took this . . . as a personal violation of all that was dear to me.'[62] The violation was sharply felt because the reality of American conservatism clashed with the artistic inspiration that America had provided on vinyl: this was not a question of art imitating life but a question of life exposing the limitations of art. When the Stones toured the United States for the first time in 1964, they were met at the airport by police and whisked straight to half-empty venues. As Keith Richards recalled: 'I've never been hated by so many people I've never met as in Nebraska in the mid-Sixties. Everyone looked at you with a look that could kill. You could tell that they just wanted to beat the shit out of you.'[63] Andrew Loog Oldham remembers them playing at a state fair in Texas:

Wood-panelled station wagons manned by off-duty good ol' boys greeted us with surly what-the-heel-kinda-freaks-we-got-here? disdain. Some mellowed out when they realised we weren't 'contagious or queer' . . . [Other] menfolk chewed gum, cud or baccy. While scuffing their heels in the sand, they eyed us like bulls in heat at the idea of some pansy-quiffed matador for dinner.

The more enthusiastic girls, well . . . They wanted to poke, squeal and see if we were real. The mood was tense. This was not turning out to be the America of anybody's dreams.[64]

On the Beatles' first trip to America, George Harrison told a journalist from the *Liverpool Echo*, 'They've got everything over there. What do they want *us* for?'[65] Yet within a year British artists and their managers had become less awestruck and more realistic about the United States. In 1965 Mick Jagger told American reporters: 'I wouldn't live in America. I don't like the country enough. I prefer England', adding that 'all the food tastes pre-packed', as if it were a metaphor for the nation.[66] Jagger's view was reiterated by other touring British artists in later decades.

When the wisecracking primetime American comedian Tommy Smothers told Keith Moon he had 'sloppy drums' just before the group performed 'My Generation' on *The Smothers Brothers Comedy Hour* in 1967, a visibly riled Moon went off script and told the presenter, 'my friends call me Keith but you can call me John'. He then destroyed his drum kit with greater venom than usual while Townshend smashed his guitar and the set collapsed around them, to the dismay of their host and the evident delight of the young studio audience.[67] In an interview for British TV a few years later, Pete Townshend commented: 'What made us first want to go to America and conquer it was being English. We didn't care a monkey's about the American dream or about the American drug situation or about the dollars. It was 'cos we were English and we wanted to go to America and be English.'[68]

From memoirs and contemporary interviews with artists touring the United States at that time a clear pattern emerges in which the awe and excitement of transatlantic discovery were replaced by the realisation that America was a more flawed civilisation than their youthful idealism and discontent with Britain had led them to believe. Dave Davies remembered the Kinks' first tour of America:

The States were fun, just like I had imagined. Cowboys and Indians in Reno. Big-titted glamour girls in Hollywood. Hamburgers to go, Coke and fries. The land of *I Love Lucy*, John Wayne and Frank Sinatra. The place where most of my heroes were born: Eddie Cochran, Buddy Holly, Big Bill Broonzy, Chuck Berry, Hank Williams. Twenty Flight Rock, Kentucky Fried Chicken, and pizza. Yeah, you couldn't get real pizza in England then. An incredible experience.

But the country he had admired since he was a boy soon disappointed Davies:

I felt that after the novelty had worn off the Americans didn't really understand our music or our culture. Coming from a country where having central heating was considered posh and a refrigerator a luxury, Americans seemed to me to be strangely spoiled and 'old-fashioned'. They seemed lost in the forties and fifties. I expected to find Americans more forward and progressive but I was surprised to find many very set in their ways, just like their English counterparts. The sixties' cultural revolution was instigated by the English youth, and the Americans soon followed. We were resented by an older generation of Americans during the British Invasion because, after all, the Yanks invented rock 'n' roll, and here were some cheeky Limeys showing them how to do it.[69]

The British Invasion showed the extent to which Britain was becoming a more secular country than the United States in a way that allowed (and possibly encouraged) a search for meaning in alternative music and fashion and a sense of belonging through the youth movements they defined. Devotional fan mail, bedroom posters, lapel badges and later public shrines to dead pop stars testified to the quasi-religious features of youth culture, and for the most devoted teenagers on each side of the Atlantic pop truly was an alternative to Christianity or Judaism. 'It's a way of dressing and a way of walking, a world where the solidarity of your friends has replaced religious feeling', commented a French documentary on British Mods in 1965.[70]

The secularisation of British society in the second half of the twentieth century, which culminated in Charles Darwin gracing the back of the £10 banknote from the year 2000, enabled the legal reforms and moral shifts of the 1960s to be implemented and accepted. Far more than in America, in Britain established religion retreated from the public sphere, where once it had framed social policy and national identity, into the private sphere, where its influence was confined to individual conscience and personal networks. Although around 80 per cent of the British continued to believe in God (and 70 per cent of them were of Christian origin), churchgoing declined by 20 per cent in the 1960s, down to 10 per cent of the population.[71] In America on the other hand, church attendance fell by a mere 3.9 per cent between 1964 and 1980, by which time 60.5 per cent of the American

complex phenomenon. The present renaissance, the article argued, had begun following the Suez Crisis of 1956 and reflected a post-imperial identity built on a fragile post-war economy and a rejection of 'Victorianism': 'Britain has lost an Empire and lightened a pound [and] in the process it has also recovered a lightness of heart lost during the weighty centuries of world leadership.'

The article noted that the phenomenon extended from music and fashion into art, architecture, theatre and film: 'The London that emerges is swinging but in a far more profound sense than the colourful and ebullient pop culture by itself would suggest.' It compared the British capital with *fin-de-siècle* Vienna, Paris in the 1920s and inter-war Berlin (which had 'briefly erupted with the savage icono-clasm of Brecht and the Bauhaus'), the New York of bebop and Expressionism in the 1940s and the Rome of *La Dolce Vita* in the 1950s. *Time* concluded that (like Mod) this cultural renaissance was a trans-continental phenomenon – it was 'a blend of flash American, polished Continental and robust old English influence that mixes and merges in London today'.[77]

Time's 'Swinging London' issue was a map of taste, offering Americans wealthy enough to travel there a map of the city and all its style hotspots (just as *Rave* offered British Mods advice about where to hang out in Continental cities). After a vacation in England, one female American Mod told the readers of *Teen* magazine that Englishmen were not all effete; in fact by expressing themselves through fashion they were more comfortable with their masculinity and therefore more fun to be with. 'English males', she wrote, '[are] infinitely superior to their American counterparts. English boys are much more masculine and also more mature.'[78]

Not everyone wanted to alter the stereotypical image of Britain. Older Americans in particular, who had fought alongside the British in the war, disliked the new version of the 'special relationship' that youth culture was transmitting. Objecting to the role of women in this less martial alliance, one reader told *Life* magazine: 'History shows that you can measure a nation's strength by the principles of its females. Britain and France, once great, are now noted for nothing but unkempt hair and short skirts.'[79]

The traditional image of Britain did not disappear from view in the United States – notably, Americans continued to believe that the monarchy remained central to British life – but that image, at least in regions on the east and west coasts more engaged with the outside world, was now contested by the youth culture created by Mod. Sure, in America the movement had been adapted as a marketing cliché in order to cash in on all things British, just as it did back home to the consternation of purists. But the fact that the elision of Mod with British modernity could be made at all was not just testament to the power of advertising and the gullibility of adolescents, but revealed that British music and fashion in the mid-1960s caught a wave of discontent in America. Moreover, this transformation of Britain's image in the United States was a long-term one that survived the waning of the United Kingdom's cultural influence in the punk era, and the subsequent divergence in the musical tastes of British and American youth in the 1980s and 90s.

AMERICAN ORIENTED FROM THE CRADLE TO THE GRAVE

'For a while in '66 everything British was best: sex, drugs and rock 'n' roll,' remembered Chris Farlowe, whose single 'Buzz with the Fuzz' was a Mod anthem.[80] But behind the patriotic pride in British pop lay some harsh economic realities and more softly spoken insecurities about American influence that within a few years would make Mod seem irrelevant to many of its original followers on the other side of the Atlantic.

Time's Swinging London feature became part of the mythology of the 1960s. (At the height of Britpop it would be reprised by *Vanity Fair* in a 1997 issue that claimed 'London Swings Again!' and paid homage to the continuing influence of Mod on British pop culture.) Reasonably accurate though the article was as a portrait of Britain's cultural renaissance, the iconic status it later acquired suggested that the British needed their pop culture to be validated by the United States. Put simply, mattering to the Americans still mattered to the British, whereas the opposite was not true. Pete Townshend may not have 'cared a monkey's about the American dream' but cracking America remained the benchmark of success for most artists.

Back in Britain, the United States had launched an invasion of its own, taking over the boardrooms and plants of British companies as surely as beat groups had taken over the concert halls and record players of America, though with more tact and less publicity. In the year Mod first emerged, the Conservative government of Harold Macmillan had made it easier for foreign companies to invest in the UK and by 1963 a thousand American businesses had set up there with a total value of $6 billion, twice the amount they invested in West Germany in the same period. Like good captains of industry, the Beatles won their MBEs (according to the official citation) for exports. Yet by the time 'Paperback Writer' was blaring out of transistor radios in 1966, there were 1,600 US subsidiaries in the UK, accounting for a tenth of all goods produced in British factories, including half the cars, domestic appliances and office machinery.[81] Heinz, Kodak and Ford were household names; and American inventions, from the tampon to the tea bag, were part of everyday life. James Macmillan and Bernard Harris, in *The American Takeover of Britain*, concluded in 1968 that 'from the moment an English baby is weaned on American-owned baby food, until he is carted away in an American-owned funeral car, he is to that extent American oriented from the cradle to the grave'.[82]

American retail techniques continued to change the way goods were sold. Britain's first supermarket opened in Croydon in 1950; between 1960 and 1966, the number of supermarkets rose from 367 to 2,500. The nation's first shopping mall opened in Birmingham in 1965. A few months later, as the Rolling Stones prepared to release '(I Can't Get No) Satisfaction', the Elephant & Castle shopping centre opened in London, near the childhood homes of two British exports to America, Charlie Chaplin and Michael Caine. *The Times* welcomed the bracing modernist design of this concrete-and-glass import from America, erected in an area that had been heavily bombed by German planes in the Second World War: 'To be able to stroll around the shops without fear of passing cars, to pause without the inevitable jostling, even to make a casual remark to one's wife without need of an ungallant brawl: such luxuries are not unique in Britain, but they are still a novelty in the age of the affluent society.'[83] The nation's youth loved these new spaces, flocking there to shop, meet, drink, flirt, and sometimes to enjoy the ungallant brawls that have always been a feature of gang culture. By the 1970s, shopping centres were being condemned not only for destroying traditional family stores but also for hosting juvenile delinquency. They were, therefore, symbolic of the way that optimism about youth and consumption turned into abject pessimism about both.

In the meantime, a sense that the British had reclaimed their popular culture was behind the BBC's decision to finally embrace it in 1963. Executives' distaste for what they saw as the corrosive American influence of youth culture had limited the Corporation's output of pop shows and allowed commercial TV to steal a march on them since its introduction in 1955. Belatedly, the Corporation's Head of Light Entertainment, Bill Cotton, told the Controller of BBC1 that 'after years of US domination, enough of the Top Twenty [is] British to make it a possibility'.[84] The result of this change of mind was the launch, on New Year's Day 1964, of the longest-running British pop show, Top of the Pops. In a symbol of British secularism, the show was first broadcast from a disused church in Rusholme, Manchester, with the Beatles singing 'I Want to Hold Your Hand' and the Stones (first on the programme) 'I Wanna Be Your Man'. Facing less media competition in a smaller country than the United States, TOTP collected the nation's youth around family TV sets in a weekly act of communion.

The British renaissance that TOTP aimed to showcase relied on the investment of American corporations as much as any other sector. Music, art, cinema, publishing, fashion and music were all subject to British innovation but like the computing industry, in which America led the Western world in the late twentieth century, the commercial heartland of pop culture remained the United States. Yet it was precisely the power of modern capitalism that enabled Mod to be transmitted and commercialised for a mass audience in Britain between 1964 and 1967. Furthermore, the continuing lure of the American Dream for British youth, with its promise of a more mobile society, enabled Mod tacitly to present itself as a British version of that dream. It may have been Beatle time and Beatle temperature for a moment at JFK airport in 1964; but in another sense, it was America that transformed Mod from the incestuous obsession of a few working-class youths into a mass movement and a style globally associated with being young and British.

Before we fly back across the Atlantic to see how that happened, perhaps the best expression of the Mod attitude to America is to be found in the following dialogue from Colin MacInnes's *Absolute Beginners*, when its photographer hero explains to his young neighbour, 'the Fabulous Hoplite', why being proudly English did not mean being 'anti-Yank':

'Because I want English kids to be English kids, not West Ken Yanks and bogus imitation Americans, that doesn't mean I'm *anti* the whole US thing. On the contrary, I'm starting up an anti-anti-American movement, because I just despise the hatred and jealousy of Yanks there is around, and I think it's a sure sign of defeat and weakness.'

'Well that's a relief,' said Fabulous, a bit sarcastically . . .

'The thing is,' I said, 'to support the local product. America launched the teenage movement . . . but we've got to produce our own variety, and not imitate the Americans – or the Ruskis, or anybody for that matter.'[85]

4

NEVER LET THE MUSIC GET IN THE WAY OF THE ACT
The Marketing of Modernism

Being Mod is a frame of mind. You can't just buy it off some geezer in a shop.
   Harry Matthews, 19-year-old Mod from Pimlico, 1964[1]

Modernism seemed to offer a chance to reshape the world in an exciting way.
   Sir Terence Conran, 2001[2]

WE LIVE POP ART

The architect of the so-called Special Relationship with the United States died just as Mod was renewing the cultural foundations of that relationship for a younger generation. Asked what he thought about Winston Churchill by a French TV crew in 1965 a young Mod from London replied, 'I suppose he was all right; people say he was a great man but to me he was just like anyone else.' The documentary, *Les Mods*, made shortly after Churchill's death in January of that year, told viewers that 'for a lot of French people Mod is what English youth is about', estimating the size of the movement to be '*seize millions de jeunes*'. 'Mod means modern,' the programme began, 'it's a movement that recruits its members from the working class, a new kind of dandyism found in the big cities.' The most loquacious interviewee was the Who's manager Kit Lambert who tried to put this new dandyism into context. Drawing languidly on a cigarette and speaking in fluent French Lambert explained: 'The Mods were influenced by bourgeois and aristocratic style and they imitated it – they're more lively and have more spiritual and intellectual energy', but, he added, 'I regret that the origins of the Mod movement are perhaps bourgeois. Their working-class milieu is the result of post-war prosperity.'[3]

Lambert's reservations about the youth movement his band represented and profited from were shared by some of the original Modernists, who watched in horror as their cult was commercialised by forces beyond their control. By the time Winston Churchill died, Carnaby Street had become the most famous British thoroughfare in the world. For Britons, it was second only to *Coronation Street* and just as mythical. If the cobblestoned Manchester setting of the nation's favourite soap opera cherished a close-knit, working-class community, London's tarmacked shopping emporium celebrated the erosion of that way of life by mass affluence. Carnaby Street came to symbolise the commercialisation of Mod, and the optimism and disillusionment this simultaneously generated. Lynda Lee Potter told *Daily Mail* readers that the street 'has proved to be the best thing to hit Britain's tourist trade since they built Buckingham Palace. Shoppers all over the world are grabbing at anything with a Union Jack on it.'[4]

For some Mods, Carnaby Street's appearance in tourist guidebooks proved that a once vibrant movement had become a heritage monument, its merchandise no more liberating than the Winston Churchill plates sold on tacky tourist stalls. Seventeen-year-old Mod Margaret McFadyen, a typist from Chelsea, had her say in *Rave* magazine: 'Manufacturers put out trash to youngsters of 12, telling them it was mod. I don't want to look the same as a lot of little kids in mass-produced gear.'[5]

Cinema's portrayal of British youth in the 1960s was another form of mass-produced horror for the original Mods who idolised Belmondo and Mastroianni, or Caine at a push. Although the trilogy of Harry Palmer features captured the movement's ethos, most films failed to explore the specific origins and nuanced impact of Mod-related youth culture, geared as they were to exploiting the legends of Swinging London (and usually funded by American studios with a transatlantic audience in mind). The thoughtful 'kitchen sink' dramas of the early 60s were made before Mod appeared on the nation's radar – although in that genre the angry, sharp-suited and fun-loving Arthur Seaton in *Saturday Night and Sunday Morning* did capture something of the male Mod's style and ambivalence towards consumerism when it was released in 1960.

Smashing Time (1967) is one example of the other tendency. Despite a script by George Melly and a star cast it was – like the more sophisticated *Darling* (1965) – a morality tale about the vacuity of celebrity life. Brenda and Yvonne (Rita Tushingham and Lynn Redgrave) are two northern women who arrive in Carnaby Street in search of fame. Yvonne is spotted by a photographer (Michael York); after she records a trashy song called 'I'm So Young' the two women head to a swanky party on top of the Post Office Tower, at which they realize the shallowness of Swinging London and decide to return north to a more authentic life. Brenda and Yvonne became *Private Eye*'s hip nicknames for the Queen and Princess Margaret, but Melly's story was a trope borrowed from earlier films about youth's disillusionment with the metropolis. Even the more innovative pop-related features, like John Boorman's vehicle for the Dave Clark Five, *Catch Us If You Can* (1965), had the group travelling around the country disillusioned with stardom. With the exception of the sketchy, low budget and rarely seen *Bronco Bullfrog* (1970), set in London's East End, it was not until the Who's *Quadrophenia* (1979) brought the perspective of time to bear on Mod that the movement acquired a film that portrayed its regular followers without demonizing or romanticizing them.

There has been no shortage of critics willing to affirm the disillusionment that many Mods felt when the cult became more popular. Writing about the Who, the American academic John Dougan concluded that 'when The Who released their maximum R&B, proto-punk album *My Generation* in December 1965, mod was, for all practical purposes, drawing its last breath. Thoroughly co-opted by the mainstream culture industry, it had gone from subcultural phenomenon to marketing strategy, a fashion impulse sold to those who could afford the look.'[6] And according to the journalist Nik Cohn:

Mod had been discovered by the media and, from here on, the movement began to go backwards. Up till now, Mods had been something quite specific, a distinct style and approach; but now the press and TV began to use the word indiscriminately. Because Mods had once shopped in Carnaby Street, the whole Carnaby Street ballyhoo was now called Mod. After that it was only a matter of time that anything young, anything remotely new or fashionable, was pigeon-holed Mod, and therefore made instantly comprehensible to the general public. The Beatles were Mod, Mary Quant was Mod, and so were Mario & Franco's restaurants, and David Bailey; Anthony Armstrong-Jones was very Mod indeed. In the hands of admen it became an all-purpose instant adjective, like Fab or Gear, to be used for pop groups or cornflakes, or dog biscuits alike. By 1965 it had lost all meaning.[7]

In fact, it was in this period that Mod became a permanent feature of Britain's social and cultural landscape. A Mod aesthetic was developed across all media, through advertising, television, cinema, art, design and photography, its signs and symbols forming the basis of a visual culture that reached out to a mass audience: in the mid-1960s, Mod became embedded in the mainstream of British life. Yet even in the full pomp and circumstance of that decade, popular Modernism was not just a creature of the media and big business or a conceit of fashionable artists and architects. One of the links between modernism and the youth culture that bore its name was formed by Pop and Op Art, which swept Britain's more experimental art schools in the 1950s and had a commercial impact beyond their walls, in the clothes people wore, the TV shows they watched and the shops they spent their money in.

Pop and Op Art resulted from a blurring of boundaries between high and low cultures that reflected the more permeable class divide of the period. Both tried to democratise art while referencing avant-garde art movements of the early twentieth century. Pop Art sought to challenge the studio and gallery as privileged sites of production and distribution, while engaging with modern technology, consumerism and popular culture as subject matter. The work of the British artists Peter Blake, Pauline Boty and Richard Hamilton were showcased in the 1962 BBC documentary 'Pop Goes the Easel'. Their experiments were pursued to more dramatic ends in New York at Andy Warhol's 'Factory'. Warhol's collaborative, serial model of art production ostensibly displaced the figure of the artist as a solitary purveyor of artisanal skills. Although in his case it made a celebrity of the artist, Warhol's sponsoring of the Velvet Underground also suggested a deeper engagement with youth culture.

Op Art owed more to the legacy of Constructivism, particularly Rodchenko's graphical experiments with industrial forms, and to the Bauhaus, where one of Op Art's leaders, Josef Albers, was based for a time. Artists such as Albers, Victor Vasarely and, in Britain, Bridget Riley aimed to make work that was immediately comprehensible, enabling many more people to experience it regardless of education, social standing or class. Both movements' belief in the exciting and potentially liberating effects of affluence complemented Mods' own belief in cash-register democracy. Richard Hamilton's famous dictum that art should be 'Popular, transient, expendable, low cost, mass produced, young, witty, sexy, gimmicky, glamorous, big business' could have been a Mod manifesto.[8]

Of course, this was not the first time that culture in Britain was experienced in a less class-conscious way. At Shakespeare's Globe theatre in the sixteenth century, at the Pleasure Gardens of Vauxhall in the eighteenth or at Dickens's public readings in the nineteenth, poorer and less educated citizens enjoyed the best drama, literature and music that England had to offer. Earlier in the twentieth century, the success of the Everyman Library and Penguin Books demonstrated that state education and rising literacy rates had produced a significant working- and lower-middle-class appetite for literary classics. The commercial success of music halls and then cinema owed much to a corresponding middle-class desire for entertainment (and the oppor- tunity for sexual liaisons those venues offered). However, the 1960s was the first decade when the young working classes were seen to be in the vanguard of creating this more democratic culture, not merely as consumers but also as producers.

More than in America, art schools were an engine room of youth culture. 'During the 1960s, British art colleges acquired a reputation for being the most experimental public-funded educational institutes in the world', wrote the critic Nigel Whiteley in his study, *Pop Design: Modernism to Mod*. 'They became the focal points for those who sought change, excitement and an alternative culture.'[9] At Central St Martin's in the 1950s, Len Deighton recalls, 'It wasn't very "arty" or in any way student directed. There were many ex-servicemen studying – some of them supporting wife and chil- dren – and everyone worked very hard, with a view to subsequently getting a job. The only student demos I remember were two in which students urged longer hours for study. Both demos failed.' Later, however, says Deighton, 'they provided a launching pad for actors, musicians, composers and writers in a way that the universities failed to do.'[10]

Art schools became more innovative after reforms introduced by Sir William Coldstream in 1961, which brought in a new multi-disciplinary Diploma in Art and Design, the DipAD, which gave students the chance to range across four subject areas: fine art, graphics, three-dimensional design, and textiles and fashion – an approach pioneered at the Bauhaus in the 1920s. This encouraged design students to adopt more of 'a fine art attitude' to their work, and inspired painters and sculptors to borrow from popular culture.[11] As a result art schools produced several generations of designers whose work shaped the visual culture of Britain, from Michael English in the 60s through to Jamie Reid in the 70s and Barney Bubbles and Neville Brody in the 80s. Influenced by various streams of modernism, they designed album covers, posters and promotional films for musical artists, while also working in the wider world of advertising, shop, restaurant and product design.

As Deighton indicated, Coldstream's reforms also turned Britain's art schools into schools of rock. Among the musicians who began their careers as art students in the 1960s and 70s were John Lennon, Ray Davies, Keith Richards, Eric Clapton, Ian McLagan, Eric Burdon, Ian Dury, Bryan Ferry and Pete Townshend. Those who attended in later generations included Britpop artists like Jarvis Cocker and Damon Albarn. 'Without the bridge of art college, I don't think the rest would have happened', remarked Ray Davies who attended one of the more radical colleges, Hornsey, in north London.[12] 'When I went to art college that changed everything because we saw bands playing in the college hall and that's where music really kicked in. I wanted to be an artist . . . I just changed my palette if you like, left the drawing board and went to music.'[13]

At Ealing Art College with Pete Townshend in 1961 were Ron Wood of the Faces (and later the Rolling Stones) and fellow Mod and author Richard Barnes, who became Townshend's flatmate. Course director Roy Ascott constantly reminded them that 'art is more than just old apples on tables'.[14] As Townshend recalled:

There would be lessons where you listened to jazz. Or listened to classical music. Or explored minimalism. We had jazz musicians, film writers, play-wrights as well as artists to come and lecture. It was a clearing house, and music was something that was very much considered to be okay and not something that you only did after hours. It was part of life. You could sit in a classroom with people painting *and* playing. I used to do it.[15]

According to rock legend, the Who's stage act was inspired by a lecture Townshend attended by Gustav Metzger, during which the auto-destructive Dadaist smashed a double bass. According to Townshend it was an accident that became a spectacle. While playing a gig at the Railway Tavern in Harrow & Wealdstone in September 1964, he cracked his guitar against the ceiling while 'getting into feedback', and when the audience started laughing he hid his embar-rassment by pretending to have meant it and proceeding to destroy the guitar. The next day the place was packed. Kit Lambert seized on the spectacle to promote the band and before long fans routinely demanded it as a visual expression of their energy and frustration. 'Never let the music get in the way of the act', Lambert used to tell the Who before they went on stage.[16] However much of a rock cliché the guitar-smashing became, for Townshend it was also a commen-tary on what artist Richard Hamilton called the 'transient, expend-able' nature of mass culture. When one of the Bee Gees asked Townshend whether he would break a Stradivarius, he replied, 'Of course I wouldn't, but a Gibson guitar that came off a production line – fuck it!'[17]

Pop Artists like Roy Ascott and the American Ron Kitaj, another of Townshend's tutors at Ealing, had an even greater influence on him than Metzger. The flat he lived in after graduating was covered with Pop Art images torn from a book he had stolen from the college library. These included the chevrons, targets, flags and geometric shapes that the Who later sewed on to their clothes and stuck on their equipment with electrician's tape, symbols that became an enduring part of Mod style. One of the cult's best-known icons – the red, white and blue target – was taken from the Royal Air Force roundel and conceived as an ironic play on the military institutions which the Mod generation had escaped serving in. It first appeared in Peter Blake's painting *The First Real Target* in 1961 before making its way into clothing fashion via art students and rock musicians like Townshend. Not surprisingly, the Who's management team, Kit Lambert and Chris Stamp, describe them as 'the first pop art band'.[18]

Another Mod group, the Creation, from Enfield in Middlesex, could also claim that accolade. Their lead singer, Kenny Pickett, would make 'action paintings' during their performance, using aerosol cans to spray canvases (as well as amps and naked women) with bright colours. At the climax of the act he would set light to the cans and use them as flame-throwers to destroy his finished work. Remarking that 'our music is red – with purple flashes', the Creation showed back-projected film during their stage shows and they were the first to play guitar with a violin bow (a technique later adopted by Led Zeppelin's Jimmy Page). Such inventiveness secured them a large following in Continental Europe and a five-album multimillion-dollar deal with United Artists. But the band disintegrated in 1968 due to in-fighting, after recording only one album; lead guitarist Eddie Phillips turned down an invitation to join the Who and became a bus driver.

Chris Stamp's father was an east London tugboat captain. His co-manager of the Who, Kit Lambert, was the son of the composer Constant Lambert, who had shocked the classical world in the 1920s and 30s by incorporating jazz idioms into works like *The Rio Grande*. Interviewed in 1970 about the significance of Britain's new youth culture, Kit said:

My father brought me up to distrust musical snobbery of any kind . . . When his music was played at the Albert Hall, people were shocked. They couldn't understand how someone of his talents could hang around with such as Louis Armstrong rather than with the classical musicians and the whole establishment BBC crowd. Fortunately the musical frontiers are now beginning to disappear; classical influences are being absorbed by pop and pop by classical. And I really think there is more valid new creative music being made at the pop end. I don't see any good classical composers emerging at the moment. I certainly haven't heard a decent new symphony or a decent new opera in the last eighteen months and I think the whole impetus has passed to the younger generation and the excitement that is generated in pop.[19]

It was this unification of popular and avant-garde interests across the class divide that angered critics of youth culture like Christopher

Booker. In his 1969 polemic *The Neophiliacs*, Booker attacked the 'sudden vogue among teenagers and the avant-garde middle class for visual images pillaged indiscriminately from a century of industrialised culture', which were just 'titillatory' and had led to a 'disintegration of any rigorous intellectual standards'.[20] Yet Lambert's view was so widely shared and frequently repeated that it became orthodoxy in the late twentieth century. It is what Paul McCartney meant when he told an interviewer in 1968 that pop was 'the classical music of now'. The so-called 'pop aristocracy' was therefore not merely emblematic of softening attitudes to class; it also spearheaded a democratisation of culture.

That change became less dependent on the concept of youth, but at the height of their confidence in the 1960s some pop stars claimed to be an alternative intelligentsia. George Melly told readers of the *Observer* that Pete Townshend 'looks like the art student he once was and talks vividly and rapidly in the classless Cockney of the young intellectual'.[21] It was soon apparent that even pop stars who had been to art school were ill equipped for their new role in society. Interviewed for Jonathan Aitken's study of Britain's new 'classless' elite, *The Young Meteors*, Townshend, then 22, said, 'Being a modern pop star is a sort of way of being intellectual without being intellectual. Intelligence is useful but you can easily get snowed under by the lava of publicity, hysteria and screaming women. It's so easy too, I've fulfilled my wildest dreams already, but it's a bit of a hollow triumph. I make a lot of money, but I'm not all that happy, and I don't read anything like as much as I would really like to. In fact a pop singer's life is murder, but it's well-paid murder.'[22]

Whatever the human limitations of figureheads like Townshend, the significance of Pop Art and its relationship with Mod culture helped to establish the aesthetic influence of both movements in Britain. Reviewing 'The New Generation' exhibition at the Whitechapel Gallery in east London in May 1964, the satirist Jonathan Miller linked art, music and design under the banner of Britain's foremost youth movement:

Mod, of course, is the word one is groping for since it gets, better than the over-used 'pop', the emotionally indifferent swish of these paintings, so many of which are decorative in a camp sort of way. There is now a curious cultural community, breathlessly *a la Mod*, where Lord Snowdon and other desperadoes of grainy blow-ups and bled-off lay-out jostle with commercial art-school Mersey stars, window dressers and Carnaby pants-peddlers. Style is the thing here – Taste 64 – a cool line and the witty insolence of youth.[23]

A year later, George Melly wrote, 'The Who have lately been playing "real pop art music". Is this just a gimmick? Actually there was something in it, because pop art borrowed from real pop and they were taking it back again.'[24] For a time in the mid-1960s Pop Art was discussed as avidly in the fashion and music press as it was in serious newspapers and art journals by the likes of Jonathan Miller, and not only because Mod groups plundered its symbols for their clothes, instruments and record covers but also because the democratic precepts of Pop Art made a direct appeal to young people who wanted to challenge the relationship between class and culture.

The black and white geometric paintings of Bridget Riley were one of the influences on Mary Quant. Quant was born in south London, the daughter of Welsh teachers originally from mining families. She had studied art and design at nearby Goldsmiths College, one of Britain's leading schools and a cradle of young British artists into the 1990s. In the summer of 1965 *Rave* ran a special feature on clothes inspired by Pop Art, including a dress commissioned from Barbara Hulanicki. 'Everybody's talking Pop Art!' it excitedly announced. 'Suddenly it's "in" to be Pop Art minded, wear Pop Art clothes, visit a Pop Art club and listen to Pop Art music!' 'The general idea of Pop Art', it explained helpfully, 'is to place something out of context (wear a camouflage jacket to look conspicuous, a Union Jack when you're not the slightest bit patriotic!). In fact the Beatles' current military jackets are hardly what you'd expect – no four boys could be less regimental!'[25]

That same summer *Melody Maker* asked, 'Well, What Is Pop Art?' Pete Townshend had the answer for its young readers:

It is re-presenting something the public is familiar with in a different form. Like clothes. Union Jacks are supposed to be flown, we have a jacket made of one. Keith Moon, our drummer, has a jersey with the RAF insignia on it. I have a white jacket, covered in medals. We stand for pop art clothes, pop art music and pop art behaviour. This is what people seem to forget – we don't change offstage. We live pop art.[26]

Yet if anyone lived Pop Art, it was the millions who consumed it (knowingly or not) as Mod exploded into the national consciousness between 1964 and 1967. New style magazines like *Fabulous* and *Rave* joined the established music press to herald the modern world, the former selling 900,000 copies a week, the latter 250,000, alongside a host of smaller titles like *Mod*. The Pop Art sets and sharply dressed maverick heroes of cult TV dramas like *The Avengers* (1961–69), *The Saint* (1962–69) and *The Prisoner* (1967–68) augmented Mod's following still further, with Mary Quant, John Stephen and Pierre Cardin among those working on them. But nothing matched the influence of the Mod-related TV show *Ready, Steady, Go!* which premiered the movement's anthem, ''My Generation', on Guy Fawkes night in 1965.

'SMASHING', SHE SAID

Ready, Steady, Go! was launched by ITV on Friday 9 August 1963, announcing temporary release from the routines of school and work with its catchphrase 'The weekend starts here!' Watched every week by over three million people, the show ran until 1966 and remained a model for youth programming until the end of the century. *Oh Boy!* (1958–59) had been the first TV show to devote itself to teen music but it mostly presented the leather-clad imitations of American rock 'n' roll like Marty Wilde, Billy Fury and Cliff Richard.[27] *RSG* not only announced the arrival of the weekend: it proclaimed the advent of popular Modernism. 'It has identified itself with teenage modernists, it sets trends', the programme's editor announced a year into its run.[28]

The historian David Fowler has argued that *RSG* 'is probably the key to understanding how the Mods became a national movement'.[29] The show helped to change the relationship between media, music and fashion because, as an instant visual, TV could disseminate trends more quickly than the radio or cinema had done before the Second World War. In his 1970 study of British pop, George Melly made a similar point:

In the McLuhanesque sense *RSG* was an important breakthrough. It plugged in direct to the centre of the scene and only a week later transmitted information as to clothes, dances and gestures, even slang to the whole teenage British Isles. When I was touring in the 50s, fashions took an almost incredible time to get spread. Even the large provincial centres like Liverpool and Manchester were at least six months behind, while in small Yorkshire mining communities as late as 1960 it was still possible to find Teddy Boy suits . . . As for the borders of Scotland the girls' dresses had hardly changed since the middle 30s. *RSG* changed all that. It made pop music and fashion work on a truly national scale . . . It was almost possible to feel a tremor of pubescent excitement from Land's End to John O'Groats.[30]

The music industry was well aware of the show's influence and Dave Clark attributed the success of his group the Dave Clark Five to *RSG*: 'A lot of well-meaning people used to tell me that you had to get about the country on one night stands in order to get a record in the charts. Although this might have been true once it isn't true today. Up to now my group hasn't done any touring – we've spread our musical message through our television appearances.'[31]

As well as all the leading British groups of the time, the show had visiting Americans like John Lee Hooker, Otis Redding, Jimi Hendrix and every significant Motown artist – line-ups that were a reflection of Mods' musical tastes and of the extent to which the youth culture they generated was taken seriously by American artists, few of whom had previously crossed the Atlantic to appear on British TV. There were also interviews with taste shapers like Michael Caine, David Bailey, George Best and Muhammad Ali – 'anyone interesting who had the look', as the show's producer Vicki Wickham put it.[32]

Its host, Cathy McGowan was a 19-year-old secretary from Streatham, south London, who had been plucked from obscurity as a 'typical teenager' by TV executives and dubbed 'Queen of the Mods' by the press. In 1965, she claimed the show had nationalised the cult: 'We started the mod craze. It all started with the idea of our show being for Young Moderns, so we just called them Mods.' This was a self-aggrandising claim, from which historian David Fowler has concluded that 'What actually happened is that her programme hijacked the term "Mods", and used it to describe all young people who shared an interest in pop music . . . It is thus more accurate to say that *Ready, Steady, Go!* made pop music as a whole, rather than mod culture, a national movement.'[33]

According to Fowler, McGowan 'seemed to cultivate a rather witless persona' by using 'teen words like "fab" and "smashing" with no sense of irony'.[34] Yet her teen argot actually reflected the way that teenagers perennially invented and appropriated language to assert generational difference. 'Coy and breathy yes, hopelessly amateur perhaps, but she *was* RSG, the bridge between pop and its audience', wrote George Melly. 'Her clothes, her *jolie-laide* sex-appeal totally transformed the girls of Britain . . . She destroyed the class basis of fashion, gesture and speech. "Smashing" she said.'[35]

For thousands more, Cathy McGowan was an authentic spokes-woman who proved that women were playing a greater part in youth culture and were not merely sex objects, hysterical teenagers, or the passive adorers of male stars. As well as writing articles for *Mod's Monthly*, she influenced British fashion by what she wore on *RSG* and the advice she gave viewers, with whom she continued to mix in nightclubs. In an interview in 1964, McGowan explained:

They got me on the programme so that I could tell them what was going on in the teenage fashion world. They wanted to make *Ready, Steady, Go!* into a programme which starts fashion trends instead of following them.
By fashion, I don't meant the 'Paris Couture' kind – I mean the sort of fashions that teenagers invent for themselves . . . the great thing now is that wherever we go, to clubs and shows, people come up and tell us about any places they know, where we can see some new fashion craze that has started up in their particular area.[36]

'We all wanted to look like Cathy McGowan', remembers barrister Liz Woodcraft.[37] The model Twiggy admitted, 'I'd sit and drool over her clothes. She was a heroine to us because she was one of us.'[38] Every week, several thousand Mods queued up to be one of the 180 people chosen to dance for the cameras and display their latest hair-styles and customised clothes. Even though these were auditions in which the decision to admit rested with the production team, the show gave working-class youth a rare opportunity to influence national taste. 'You get on the show and you find nobody's ordering you about.

You just dance and chat like you would normally', a hairdresser from Balham told *Rave*.[39]

For some Mods, *RSG* typified the media's corruption of Modernism in the same way that Carnaby Street typified its commercialisation. Fans could buy Cathy McGowan jeans, stockings, record players and dolls. According to one of the original 'faces': 'By the time Cathy McGowan came on TV it was all over. You might as well have drawn the curtains. If that was the date, 1963, then that was when it died. I think the original Mods were quite happy to see themselves emulated on television but when that spread nationally it was finished.'[40] Others drew the opposite conclusion and accused the show of elitism. *Melody Maker* declared: 'It is the TV stronghold of mods, the frighteningly clean, sharply-dressed arbiters of tomorrow's tastes in practically everything. They consider themselves a cut above everyone who does not conform to their cult . . . Their attitude smacks of social prejudice instilled in too-young minds.'[41]

Both sets of critics missed the point. By popularising and developing Mod style the show actually tempered the movement's self-absorbed elitism. 'Mod fashions spread all through England over-night', remembered Pete Townshend, 'and it wasn't the same any more, because in the real Mod scene no one would tell you [anything] . . . It was incestuous and secretive. Difficult to be an up-to-the-minute Mod 'cause no cunt would tell you where to get the clothes.'[42] *RSG* showed that the media had identified Mod as the first authentic British youth culture; by amplifying and visualising the music, fashion and design associated with it, and by turning it from a cult into a culture, *RSG* accelerated the process by which Mod became associated with the broader cultural renaissance of the 1960s.

RSG connected the art and music of the era through the show's bold Pop and Op Art sets, designed by Nicholas Ferguson, who took ideas directly from artists of the day, a style then copied by the BBC's rival show *Top of the Pops*. As George Melly recalled:

The two cultures were moving closer. I remember going to a live *RSG* at the Wembley Studios to hear James Brown and meeting the British pop artist Derek Boshier. He, a keen pop music fan, was starry-eyed. 'I've just met the designer', he said, 'and he *knew* me' . . . They'd done him last week. Copied his striped barber's-pole-shaped pictures as a framework for the groups and he was knocked out. It was very different from when Pears Soap had used *Bubbles* as a poster – Millais was furious.[43]

What Melly described as 'two cultures moving closer together' was even more apparent if you stepped outside the TV studios and into the high street, where the marketing of Mod reached its peak after America's most famous magazine heralded the arrival of Swinging London.

SHOPPING IS MY HOBBY

Swinging London was not the invention of *Time* or of a metropolitan elite flattered by American approval. The origins of the renaissance that the magazine identified lay in the world of art and design and the commercial impact they had thanks to youth culture. As the critic David Mellor observed, 'The foundations for the visual mythology of Swinging London were laid early on [in the 1950s] and it was the artists and photographers who first formulated its particular brand of metropolitan romance and modernity.'[44]

It could have been any Mod talking when the artist Richard Smith told an American interviewer: 'I find, er, shopping is my hobby, it's what I do when I'm not working.'[45] The link between art and shopping extended beyond the manifestos of Britain's art schools. In 1959, Robyn Denny was commissioned to construct a mural for the flagship store of the men's tailor Austin Reed in Regent Street. According to Denny, the company wanted 'to change their image, which had been a very conservative one. Instead they were going to try to address a younger customer who might buy clothes with greater regularity.'[46] Denny, the press noticed with interest, liked to paint to the sound of pop music. A bold, colourful collage of posters on hardboard with exclamatory letters in bold red, white, blue and yellow, the mural spelled out the words GREAT, BIG, WIDE, LONDON and, according to the critic David Mellor, 'it epitomised the euphoria of London in the process of redevelopment – at the height of the office building explosion [and] it spoke the language of the new promotional culture' of the consumer boom.[47]

The mural was deemed significant enough for the Beatles to be photographed standing in front of it in 1963, after buying from the store the pointed, Cuban-heeled boots that subsequently became known as Beatle boots. A few minutes' walk from Austin Reed, in Carnaby Street, other Pop Artists could be found creating shopfronts and interiors. After graduating from the Royal College of Art, Michael Davies was commissioned by John Stephen to decorate one of his first boutiques, Domino Male. There, Davies established a visual lexicon creating, in the words of one critic, 'a synthesis of the immaculate technique and discipline of Continental modernist graphics with the energy of American mass media imagery'.[48]

Soon modernist design was everywhere, spreading from London throughout the country. Whether or not you drove a fashionable Mini Cooper, the typeface, chevrons and arrows of Britain's road signs helping you to find your way were designed for the Ministry of Transport in 1963 under the influence of Pop Art style, by Margaret Calvert and Jock Kinneir at the RCA, and are still in use today. And it was at the RCA that the British flag was reconfigured from a symbol of state denoting order, tradition and conquest, into a fashion icon of post-imperial Britain. It began when students marked the wedding of the Queen's sister, Princess Margaret, to the photographer Anthony Armstrong-Jones in May 1960 – a match that led to Margaret being dubbed 'the Mod Princess' in the popular press.[49] Textile student Geoff Reeve first painted his friend Philip Harrison's sunglasses with a Union Jack and then exhibited a huge red, white and blue silkscreen that broke up the geometry of the flag's design. Later that year another student, Peter Phillips, showed his seminal painting, *Purple Flag*, which turned the Union Jack into a colour usually associated with decadence (a move that got him expelled). Michael English, who had studied with Pete Townshend, designed a range of Union Jack merchandise for the Carnaby Street boutique Gear, and it was thanks mainly to the Who that the British flag became a fashion item when Townshend appeared on the cover of the *Observer* colour magazine wearing a jacket stitched out of a real flag.[50]

It was a daring statement at the time. Interviewed in 2000, Roger Daltrey remembered: 'Kit came up with the idea for that jacket – he should be posthumously knighted for it. Prior to that, the Union Jack had only ever been flown on buildings as the national flag. When we walked into a Savile Row tailor and said "Will you make a jacket out of this?" they said, "No". They thought they'd go to jail.'[51] The Union Jack has never been as revered in Britain quite as the Stars and Stripes has been in America. Designed in the early eighteenth century to represent the new United Kingdom (inadequately, given that Wales remains unrepresented on it) the British flag became widely associated with imperial conquest. For most Americans, by comparison, the Stars and Stripes unequivocally symbolises democracy and freedom – not least from Britain itself. In Britain it is more common to see a version of the Union Jack on a teenager's clothing and accessories than on a flagpole outside their parents' house.

Mods wore it with two aims in mind: to affront the British Establishment and to proclaim the fact that they were still proudly and distinctively British. The sociologist Dick Hebdige put the appropriation of the British flag into a wider context:

The Mods could be said to be functioning as *bricoleurs* when they appropriated another range of commodities by placing them in a symbolic ensemble which served to erase or subvert their original straight meanings. Thus pills medically prescribed for the treatment of neuroses were used as ends-in-themselves, and the motor scooter, originally an ultra-respectable means of transport, was turned into a menacing symbol of group solidarity. In the same improvisatory manner, metal combs, honed to a razor-like sharpness, turned narcissism into an offensive weapon. Union Jacks were emblazoned on the backs of grubby parka anoraks or cut up and converted into smartly tailored jackets. More subtly, the conventional insignia of the business world – the suit, collar and tie, short hair, etc. – were stripped of their original connotations – efficiency, ambition, compliance with authority – and transformed into 'empty' fetishes, objects to be desired, fondled and valued in their own right.[52]

On the cover of the *Observer* on 20 March 1966 Pete Townshend stood moodily in the foreground with another British flag draped behind the band. It was an image that marked the high point of Mod's initial impact, as Jon Savage observed years later in the same magazine:

Here, attitude meets aesthetics, business practice and the state of British youth culture in 1966. The image is dominated by the perceptual tricks of Op Art – almost a Bridget Riley painting come to life . . . The Who embody that classic British pop cult paradox: foppish violence . . . The Union Jack backdrop and jacket represent both a punky subversion of a national symbol and a serious statement about the rebranding of a fusty, static, class-ridden country as the international centre of a synaesthetic youth culture. The photo says it all. This is Pop Island.[53]

Sensing a commercial opportunity, manufacturers were quick to plaster the flag over a range of merchandise targeted at young consumers, and it became a symbol of Mod's ubiquity. Yet the retailing of Mod style did not mean the dissolution of it. Few of those who became Mods in the mid-1960s customised clothes bought from retailers like Burtons as the early Modernists had done, but that was mainly because there were now more retailers to create and supply dizzying variations of Mod style off the peg. The so-called boutique revolution was a significant moment in the history of British youth culture that paralleled the heyday of the independent record label between the foundation of Immediate Records by the Rolling Stones' manager Andrew Loog Oldham in 1965 and the end of Stiff Records in 1985.

The (slight) power shift within the music industry towards young artists and entrepreneurs was mirrored in the fashion world in the way that independent designers and their boutiques briefly challenged the dominance of the haute couture fashion houses and the big high street retailers. According to one young woman, the new boutiques 'were shops my mother couldn't have bought things in. They understood completely how we wanted to look. They understood we wanted music belting out and blaring in our ears the whole time.'[54] Another remembers that in her local boutique 'you could just amble around the racks of clothes. It was very dark and mystical, and the music, the way the assistants were dressed had a sort of . . . well, it didn't have a sort of commercial feeling to it.'[55]

Boutiques catered for the craze for military jackets, started in 1966 when Mick Jagger wore one on *RSG*. It became an enduring feature of British menswear, but like the RAF roundel it originally both rebuked military service and assaulted class conventions since the favourite type were colourful officers' tunics. 'A girl assistant was wearing a full dress jacket of the old Hertfordshire Regiment over skin-coloured tights, another customer was strutting around in black and gold "diplomatic gear"', one TV reporter noted at I Was Lord Kitchener's Valet which first stocked them. Wearers were sometimes stopped in the street by irate military veterans and in September 1966, *The Times* reported that 'a Muswell Hill youth' had been conditionally discharged after being stopped wearing a Scots Guards tunic. 'I think it looked fashionable and smart', he said in his defence. The Carnaby Street branch of Lord Kitchener's got into trouble with the Lord Chamberlain for selling leftovers from the 1953 coronation ceremony, including replicas of the royal coat of arms, over 3,000 flags and 2,200 yards of bunting, all of which sold out before they could be impounded.[56]

By 1967 there were 2,000 shops describing themselves as boutiques in the Greater London area. Three years later the *Daily Mail* estimated that there were some 15,000 boutiques across Britain, catering for the under-25 age group.[57] They spread all over the country, even to parts of it where the old industrial economy was ailing. In Newcastle-upon-Tyne, home of the Animals and the city where Richard Hamilton first taught, retail turnover in the central shopping area rose from £56 million in 1951 to £121 million in 1971. 'Newcastle, like other cities in Britain, began to develop a distinct retailing infrastructure,' the design historian Cheryl Buckley has concluded, 'based on youth cultures, particularly small independent boutiques.'[58]

'This was the huge breakthrough that really democratized fashion,' remembered Mary Quant, 'because before that time anything new came from couturiers from the top, and they designed for a tiny minority, a couple of thousand people altogether, who were incredibly rich and they lived a completely different life to everybody else. Whereas I was an art student, I was making and designing really for other art students, I mean that's how I started.'[59] With dresses on sale for between £6 and £9, her poorer customers had to save up (and often did) until her launch of the Ginger Group in 1963 put her designs into mass production and made them more affordable. Placed in the centre of her boutique as a sentinel of modernism was Quant's chaise longue designed by Le Corbusier.[60]

The road that led to the metaphorical summit of Pop Island was built by Quant's friend John Stephen. Once a shabby little road situated behind the wealthy elegance of John Nash's Regent Street, Carnaby Street became synonymous with Mod fashion between 1964 and 1966 and with British youth culture as a whole. By then

Stephen owned twenty-two shops in Greater London. His clientele, even more than that of Quant's Bazaar on the King's Road and Barbara Hulanicki's BIBA on Kensington High Street, was a mixture of working- and middle-class customers ranging from teenagers to men and women in their late twenties. Charging £7–10 for a jacket and £3–5 for a shirt in 1964, his clothes weren't cheap but within the reach of Mods willing to spend a large proportion of their weekly wages (on average £20 at the time) trying to dress their way out of class stereotypes. Welcoming 'Dandy Days' in the *New Statesman* in 1966, the old critic of consumerism and 'Americanisation', J. B. Priestley, celebrated the wave of working-class dandies that Mod had spawned: 'A lad who lives in a dingy back street and does a boring stupid job all day is surely entitled to change into some colour and do a little swaggering. He is in a sense defiantly wearing his uniform, that of his individual male youth, turning himself from a world unit, herded to and from a factory, into a unique Jimmy Brown or Ted Smith.'[61]

Stephen's boutique Lord John and his moniker 'the King of Carnaby Street' suggested an awareness of the class politics that made his cash registers ring as loudly as the pop music that his shop assistants played to attract customers (in some, he employed teenage 'faces' on the Mod scene to add authenticity).[62] Yet to describe Stephen, as one historian has done, as 'an opportunist rather than a prime mover in the Mod culture' is to misunderstand both the genesis and development of the movement with which he became so closely associated.[63] It is true that Stephen was not himself a Mod. His personal taste for sharp but sober suits and ties was at odds with his flamboyant designs and accorded more with a shy and nervous personality that, together with a fierce work ethic, left him reliant on sleeping pills and alcohol to get four hours' rest each day. However, like Mary Quant, Stephen was associated with the creative and commercial milieux out of which Mod grew in 1950s London. Although he was not part of the art school, modern jazz set like Quant or Townshend, he emerged from the gay subculture to which some of the early Modernists were closely linked.

In 1966, *Boyfriend* magazine profiled Stephen as the man 'responsible for the gear that flows through the neon-lit mod paradise'. He was photographed for the magazine looking pensive, sitting in a dressing gown on the sofa of the Jermyn Street flat he shared with his lifelong partner Bill Franks. *Boyfriend* drew a fairly accurate picture of the Gorbals boy who had swapped shipbuilding for fashion. 'Quiet and unassuming, he appears more of a courtier than a King', the magazine told its female readers. 'He's got a funny, spluttery laugh that's infectious, and bites his fingernails. His best features are grey/blue eyes that are very direct . . . John Stephen, tailor-made for success in a 1966 world where you buy and live off the peg.'[64]

Like other retailers, Stephen incorporated more pattern into his designs in the late 1960s to appease the lust for paisley, but he retained the clean, Modernist cut of his early designs, sensing correctly that not all young people thought a kaftan a good idea. As his biographer has noted, Mod 'was still making a consolidated stand' in music and fashion when Stephen launched two publicity stunts. In 1967, at the Hilton Hotel, Steve Marriott presented the Miss Mod award to Jayne Harries, a blonde dancer spotted on *Top of the Pops* wearing 'second-skin' black velvet hipsters and a white silk blouse: her reward was a clothes voucher worth £500 and backstage passes for a forthcoming Small Faces tour. This was followed by the Beau Brummell award for the best-dressed man of the year – given to Barry Gibb in 1968 – who received a 12-inch silver statuette of the Mods' Regency hero.[65]

There is no doubt Stephen colluded in making Carnaby Street as much of a tourist attraction as Piccadilly Circus. He supported the move, by Westminster Council between 1967 and 1973, to pedestrianise the area, which prevented Mods from gathering on their scooters outside his stores, but which increased the foot traffic to a peak of 15,000 people a day and triple that at weekends.[66] In 1968, he succumbed to the council's Christmas decorations: fourteen pairs of illuminated legs in micro-miniskirts erected over the street, the middle pair flashing Union Jack panties to complete the display. However much some Mods looked on with distaste, Britain had come a long way in the fifteen years since 1953, when Conservative MPs had complained to Winston Churchill in the House of Commons about the sale of Union Jack underwear to celebrate the coronation.

More than anyone else, Stephen was responsible for mainstreaming the reformation of British masculinity. Taking his knowledge of subterranean camp style and applying it to Mod's heterosexual dandyism, he utilised a thawing in attitudes to homosexuality in order to redraw what it was permissible for men to wear at work and play. By taking Mod to market Stephen disseminated it to a national audience but was then blamed for helping to destroy it: he was attacked on one side by some of his working-class clientele for commercialising Mod, and on the other by high-end Chelsea designers of vulgarising the dandy aesthetic. By 1966, high street chains and department stores from C&A to Selfridges began to incorporate the work of designers like Quant and Stephen and by the mid-1970s had bought most of them out.[67]

Yet the commercial explosion of Mod was not simply a journey from super-cool Soho to cheesy Carnaby Street, in which a few cultivated, trend-setting 'faces' found themselves outnumbered by copycats who didn't know their *nouvelle vague* from their Lord John. Mod's extraordinary popularity in this period, coupled with the movement's ability to allow stylistic developments, marked its transition from cult to culture.

IT IS ACROSS THE CHANNEL THAT ONE FINDS TRUTH

As so much of Mod culture sprang from Continental Europe, the acid test was whether Europeans would embrace this strange hybrid of two continents created by the island that sat between them. Celebrating Swinging London in 1966, *Time* magazine had claimed that a city once famous for global trade was now famous for global culture. That view was shared throughout Western Europe. In 1966, the conservative French newspaper *L'Express* declared that Britain 'is the country where the wind of today blows most strongly', adding, 'Thanks to the Beatles and the Rolling Stones, Britain rules over international pop music.'[68] Just as it took British artists to make multiracial popular music acceptable to white America, it was these same artists who made music of American origin more acceptable to the notoriously anti-American French.

French youth embraced Anglo-American youth culture as a way of defining themselves against parents who had lived through the Occupation, many of whom were carrying the stigma of collaboration. When in January 1965 the magazine *Salut les copains* asked its readers 'French Rock or Anglo-Saxon Rock?' the following reply from a 15-year-old was typical: 'No one can equal the Rolling Stones, the Beatles, the Animals, the Kinks and all the English groups. I find them better than the Americans, for since Elvis Presley has taken to singing with violins and the greats (Buddy Holly and Eddie Cochran) have gone, it is across the Channel that one finds truth.'[69]

Artists like Serge Gainsbourg and Johnny Hallyday remained hugely popular in France, respectively performing French jazz-folk and a Gallic pastiche of American rock 'n' roll. Indigenous music still made up 90 per cent of French record sales in the late 60s; and although *Salut les Copains* had a readership of 900,000, sales of British rock remained relatively low, with *Tommy*, a huge transatlantic success, selling only 17,000 copies in 1969. Rock concerts also remained a minor activity compared to Britain and America, with 92 per cent of French people stating that they had never been to one as late as 1974.[70] Nonetheless, as a direct result of Mod-driven youth culture French artists had to compete with British musicians for the first time and the cross-Channel traffic was mostly one-way. A rare exception to this was Gainsbourg's 'Je t'aime . . . moi non plus', a 1969 duet with his English lover, Jane Birkin, replete with explicit lyrics and a simulated female orgasm; conveniently banned by radio stations in the UK and across Europe, it was a huge hit in Britain. (So too was Jean-Michel Jarre's 'Oxygène' in 1976, which briefly gave Germany's Kraftwerk a run for their money when electronic music became popular in the next decade.)

As in the United States, a nuanced awareness of Mod and its mutations did not survive the 1960s. However, the French image of Britain was permanently changed as a result of the movement's heyday in this period. For the first time since the eighteenth century, London outshone Paris, and this is one of the reasons why Britain's new youth culture became a source of patriotic pride far beyond its original teenage constituency. In their history of Anglo–French relations, Robert and Isabelle Tombs sum up how this shifting balance of power highlighted a broader acceptance of popular culture in the Western world:

London replaced Paris as the cultural centre of Europe, and England became, for the first time for nearly two centuries, the epitome of cultural modernity. Certain areas of French cultural life, combining impressive intellectualism with fashionable chic, enjoyed international prestige, not least among British intellectuals. The experimental French cinema was the universal reference. Philosophical plays and novels, the Annales school of history, and reinterpretations of German philosophy applied to literature and the humanities attained unparalleled influence in Anglophone university departments. But in mass youth culture, especially that associated with music, clothes and morals, London and Liverpool – that exotic imagined city – had a global impact, in comparison with a Paris where fashion and entertainment were elegantly middle-aged and middle class.[71]

In the world of fashion Mod style challenged centuries of French dominance. When Dior's elegant New Look had arrived in 1947, its widespread influence was seen to emanate from an *ancien régime* of style. The British now became associated with a more classless fashion industry in which the 'street styles' of youth culture set trends as much as the catwalks of the haute couture houses. *In Gear*, one of the Look at Life series of short documentaries made for cinema by the Rank Organisation in 1967 to explain contemporary youth culture to older Britons, captured the sense of patriotism with which Swinging London was sold:

These soft, music-loud caverns of the avant-garde can be misleading for they are the work cells of revolution: once upon a time, just a year or two ago to be precise, fashion originated in the haute couture salons of Paris, then spread downwards through society in ever-cheapening copies with one predominant theme. Shops such as this would have interpreted the mode. But no more. Now they originate, and so do a dozen others in a dozen different styles, owing nothing to Paris or anyone else.[72]

When London Fashion Week was launched in 1961, the capital began to rival both Paris and Milan. Mary Quant travelled to Rome in 1966 to collect a fashion award. She landed in a helicopter on the Spanish Steps before entering a department store selling her collection, where she was greeted by hundreds of young Italians chanting 'Ave Maria'.[73] 'CARNABY A MILANO' screamed the Italian magazine *Ciao Amico* when British stands were opened in the city's Standa department store a year later: 'You enter and have the real impression of finding yourself in London . . . Here you can dress yourself exactly like our friends from across the Channel . . . The sales girls are pretty and, needless to say, dressed in miniskirts.'[74]

The French media grumbled that Courrèges and not Quant was the real inventor of the miniskirt and *Paris Match* thought that British style was too 'kooky' and 'dandy'.[75] But the fashion houses of Paris and Milan were forced to absorb the style of Britain's boutique revolution, later employing British designers to head up their operations, and in the spring of 1971 British fashion won the ultimate accolade: the work of Quant, Hulanicki and Ossie Clark was exhibited at the Louvre in Paris alongside some of the greatest European art.

Gushing guides to Carnaby Street appeared in Continental magazines, the effect of which is remembered by BIBA's founder Barbara Hulanicki: 'Tourists from all over Europe were pouring into London for cheap weekends. They would buy suitcases full of clothes for virtually nothing as the exchange rate was so good. London was vibrating with French, Italians, Germans and Swedes coming to listen to the music, see the shops and gawp at the beautiful girls. We were selling mounds.'[76] Selling mounds abroad was not always so easy. When a consortium, led by Quant, Stephen and the Beatles, opened six boutiques in Rome, the shops met with stiff resistance from local retailers and closed within three years.

The success of British music and fashion on the Continent was celebrated partly because it came at a time when President de Gaulle was freezing the United Kingdom out of Europe because he regarded Britain as the Trojan horse of American mass culture as well as a threat to France's political independence. But de Gaulle could not stop British pop sweeping the Continent and undermining his attempts to preserve French culture from *les rosbifs*. During the Beatles' first tour of France the band spurned French cuisine and ordered steak and chips every day. The *NME* commented that 'the Queen herself would have been proud of the Beatles if she could have seen these thousands of happy French folk stamping, cheering and shouting for the four little Englishmen'.[77]

From 1964 to 1967 Mod was at its peak in West Germany, where it was popular in urban areas from Hamburg to Munich. Here it was not just a contemporary dressing up of teenage hedonism but a deliberate rebuke to parents, and formed part of the post-war creation of

and on their return a relieved Manfred told the British music press: 'I came back thinking England was a good scene – and I was just that little bit more Union Jack conscious.'[86]

VINGT SECONDES POUR FAIRE UN LIT!

Visiting London in 1959 the author Nancy Mitford, one of the Bright Young Things of the inter-war years, noticed that:

working class girls and boys are incomparably smarter than the others . . . Compare the publics in Oxford Street and Bond Street of now and of however far your memory goes back, and the present superiority of Oxford Street is startling. You will also observe there – as in any proletarian district of the capital – the lavish, colourful eruption of gay stores selling 'separates' to the girls, and sharp schmutter to the kids: shining, enticing shops like candy floss. But the transformation of the working class to power and relative affluence means that these styles . . . are no longer 'working class' in the old sense at all.[87]

That democratisation of taste did not begin in the 1960s but it was accelerated by youth culture and its 'colourful eruption' decorated homes as well as bodies. The late Victorian era had produced the modern advertising, retail, leisure and entertainment industries, and a middle class which created domestic interiors that conferred status not only through the acquisition and display of material objects but through interior design and the idea that even the humblest home could be a canvas on which the individual expressed their personality.

According to Christopher Breward, 'in its harnessing of "art" to the chariot of retail and publicity . . . the Aesthetic movement antici-pated and hastened the consumerist idea of the "lifestyle".'[88] The Arts and Crafts style was the first to be marketed commercially and influenced the middle-class domestic interior via department stores like Liberty's, where the designers of window displays were known as 'curators'. As early as 1883, the *Furniture Gazette* claimed that 'Decorative Art is really the only art that is within the means of the largest proportion of people . . . the home is the fit altar at which to offer up our artistic efforts.'[89] More people were creating those altars of taste in the second half of the twentieth century, and at an earlier age. According to a 1961 government report on 'Homes for Today and Tomorrow', the 'basic requirements' of warmth and shelter for working people were giving way to the view that a home 'must be something of which they can be proud; and in which they must be able to express the fullness of their lives'.[90]

'Social habits are changing. Youth is more independent and free-wheeling', the *Sunday Times* magazine remarked in 1964 when profiling technology in the home. Noting their fondness for 'sliced bread, pre-scrubbed carrots and launderettes', the architect and interior designer Sir Hugh Casson rightly observed that what worried the young was not that new gadgets might 'undermine some traditional way of life – but that there are not more of them, and they are not yet good enough, either in looks or performance, nor cheap enough.' Casson cautioned that 'a house should not be just an exhibition of technical devices – it is a work of art and art (we are always told) is a matter of selection.'[91] It was this twin vision of the British interior – as a laboratory of well-designed, entertaining technology *and* as an artistic palette for creative spirits – that was sold to young Britons in the 1960s, with more money and education than their parents, as a way of expressing their own sense of modernity.

The man who did more than anyone to bring Mod to market, and into the home, was a former protégé of Casson's, Terence Conran. Having previously designed the interior of Mary Quant's King's Road boutique, he opened his first Habitat furniture store nearby, on 11 May 1964, at the age of 33. By making contemporary design affordable to millions, it helped to shape the nation's taste a generation before Ingvar Kamprad brought the first IKEA store to Britain in 1987. Launching Habitat as a 'shop for switched-on people', Conran combined the aesthetic and political vision of twentieth-century European modernism with the attitude and style of Britain's emerging pop culture. Conran was influenced by Pop Art, having been taught by one of its leading exponents, Eduardo Paolozzi, at Central St Martin's. But most of all, he was a follower of the Bauhaus school of design.

The most humanistic branch of the modern movement on the Continent, Bauhaus was founded in Germany in 1919 by Walter Gropius with the aim of marrying technological change with aesthetic innovation to create a more ordered, just and beautiful world. It drew some of Europe's most creative minds, from architects to textile designers, to live, study and work together in the belief that our habitat shapes how we think, feel and interact with each other. When the Nazis shut the school down in 1933, Gropius and most of his staff dispersed to Britain and America from where they continued to leave their mark on the aesthetics of Western life in the late twentieth century. Among the influential works they produced were Josef Albers' Stacking Tables (1927), Club Chair (the Wassily Chair, 1925) by Marcel Breuer, and Marianne Brandt's Teapot (1924). In graphic design there was Herbert Bayer's pioneering Universal typeface (1925), versions of which fostered the twentieth-century taste for 'clean', unfussy, sans serif lettering, with which Mod became associated in the 1960s through record, magazine, film and poster design. In architecture key works included the Bauhaus building in Dessau (1919–25) and the Fagus Factory (1911–13), both designed by Gropius. While teaching architecture at Harvard's Graduate School of Design, Gropius was responsible for projects including the US Embassy in Athens (1959–61). Committed to breaking down artistic and social barriers, in the Bauhaus manifesto of 1919 Walter Gropius had declared:

Let us then create a new guild of craftsmen without the class distinctions that raise an arrogant barrier between craftsman and artist! Together let us . . . create the new structure of the future, which will embrace architecture and sculpture and painting in one unity, and which will one day rise toward heaven from the hands of a million workers like the crystal symbol of a new faith.[92]

These ideals went on display in 1968 at the Royal Academy in London at the first post-war retrospective of the movement in Britain. Few workers adopted those 'crystal symbols' as a direct result of the show, but Bauhaus did not just influence designers like Conran. As Mary Quant told an interviewer years later: 'I love Bauhaus . . . The Bauhaus ideal is about making modern design accessible and design being about the way you live; about everything you do, and the importance of the detail. And why not make all the details as beautiful as the design of the whole?'[93]

The ghost of Gropius could even be found in the most popular female Mod hairstyle, created by the Jewish West Londoner Vidal

Sassoon for Mary Quant in 1963, then immortalised by Terence Donovan in *Vogue* and, in another version, by Mia Farrow in Roman Polanski's *Rosemary's Baby* (1968). The five-point bob was inspired by the 1920s bob and by Sassoon's study of Bauhaus architecture, which had been stimulated by meeting Mies van der Rohe in New York in the early 1960s and by observing the modernist architecture rising all around him. 'When I looked at the architecture, the structure of buildings that were going up worldwide,' Sassoon later recalled, 'you saw a whole different look . . . Great architects was where I came from, that was my inspiration – the Bauhaus! For me hair meant geometry.'[94] This meant eliminating the superfluous but in line with the natural structure of the face. As he told Quant: 'I'm going to cut the hair like you cut material. No fuss, no ornamentation. Just a neat, clean, swinging line.'[95]

Quant's friend Terence Conran believed that the alliance between the creative talents of Britain's youth culture was the means by which modernism was finally embraced by the British people: it 'fitted in perfectly with the democratic spirit of the times; people didn't want to go back to the old elitism. We felt that we were in the perfect position to put the Bauhaus ideals into practice . . . Habitat did for the home what designers like Mary Quant, Barbara Hulanicki and Ossie Clark were doing for clothes. We were part of a minor revolution in taste instigated by young people.'[96] Based in an old jam factory in Camberwell, Conran set out to combat what he called 'the paternalistic, elitist nature of British design' that reflected 1950s Britain.[97] 'The whole design world seemed to consist of a lot of frightfully nice chaps who belonged to the best clubs and were all terribly concerned about the "appalling" taste of the working class', he remembered.[98]

Conran believed that most people recognised good design when they saw it and that it simply needed to be 'put under their noses at a price they can afford'.[99] Cutting costs through technical innovation, primarily by introducing flat-pack furniture in 1962, Conran understood how education and affluence had grown aspirations and changed attitudes. In the past, most young people had moved from the family home straight to the marital home and they inherited furniture or bought it second-hand. Now, with a growing number of young people beginning to live independently, either on their own or with friends, there was an expanding market for innovative design.

The style of Conran's products, from kitchenware to furniture, was self-consciously international. Like the clothing designers who mixed epauletted Victorian military jackets with A-line Op Art dresses, Conran fused traditional, sometimes rustic, materials with twentieth-century American, European and global design, creating a world where raffia mats and stripped pine sat reassuringly next to white plastic and chrome, often in the same object. 'I've never really thought of myself as a retailer of Continental style . . .' Conran remarked, 'it's an eclectic British style, made up of products culled from every corner of the world.'[100]

The classic example of Conran's eclecticism is the duvet, seen as a curiosity by eighteenth-century English gentlemen on their Grand Tour of Europe. Yet what the British used to sniffily call the 'continental quilt' actually became ubiquitous on the Continent thanks to British enterprise. Conran mass-marketed duvets to the French when the first foreign Habitat opened in Paris in 1973, with the promotion 'Vingt secondes pour faire un lit!' 'It was symbolic of social change', remembered Conran, 'and undoubtedly changed the sex life of Europe.'[101] Whether or not he single-handedly improved the sex life of millions, Conran did help to get modernist design accepted in Britain, where previously it had been viewed with suspicion. The journalist Yvonne Roberts recalls that:

A visit to Habitat was a step into the future. It allowed a working class girl to leap from the dark brown world of her mother's fake oak, heavy-duty sideboard, floral carpet, chintz three-piece suite into an uber-Scandinavian land of very yellow pine and a plethora of plastic . . . The first Habitat was a work of Pop Art, crowded with items you didn't realise you desired because you'd never heard of them before . . . storage cubes and the ubiquitous Japanese paper lantern that turned many a grotty bedsit into a grotto of good taste. Even the Habitat catalogue was a work of modernista art (35p in 1975). For the posh, Habitat was probably nasty and vulgar. For a large group of baby boomers, however, raised in terraced rooms . . . the shop did the trick. They were aspirational and socially mobile but many also wanted to inhabit a different kind of middle class from that which had gone before.[102]

For TV executive and lifelong Mod, Patrick Uden, Habitat was 'a revelation. Terence Conran was, in a sense, an early Mod . . . he brought into Britain things that we had never, ever seen in England before and that Elizabeth David had described in her cookery books. And they were suddenly available in Habitat and they just walked out of the shops.'[103] Or they were delivered on Conran's pale green Vespa, which he had bought in the 1950s. '[Its] design seemed to encapsulate the whole flavour of the time', he recalled. As well as being 'perfect for taking girls around London it doubled up as a delivery vehicle in the early years of my business'. He credited the Vespa with the introduction of flat-pack furniture, because its small frame forced him to compress what he delivered by scooter.[104]

The privately educated, thirty-something Conran may not have been a Mod in a way that an amphetamine-fuelled cockney teenager at the Scene Club would have recognised, but the sharp-suited, scooter-riding furniture designer did epitomise the way that Mod became 'more than the "in" movement of the Sixties'. It stood, as Richard Barnes observed, 'for a particular style and taste',[105] which over the next thirty years was embraced by most Britons in one form or another. Mod not only regenerated their music and fashion; it transformed their living environment, at home and beyond, in bars, restaurants, shops and offices. It is not the lava lamp and other glorious kitsch that stamped the 1960s' mark on the nation. It is the primary colours, clean strong lines, and laminated floors that fill the metropolitan, suburban, and even country homes of the twenty-first century – an accessible amalgam of modernism that in Britain was first successfully packaged by Habitat, which Conran correctly described as 'one of the first lifestyle shops'.[106]

PSYCHEDELIC SHACK

Most working-class Mods in the 1960s did not have 'pads' where they were able to apply their aesthetic tenets to interior decoration beyond sticking a poster, an album cover or a few press clippings on their bedroom walls. And even the more middle-class ones still relied on their parents for food, shelter and other comforts until they entered their twenties. Still, pop culture reached into the interior lives of the young emotionally and materially, even when they had little money.

Oral evidence suggests that when teenage Mods brought their style

Absolute Beginners

Colin MacInnes

Colin MacInnes' 1959 novel, regarded as the first literary expression of the Mod movement. The cover image, by the influential photojournalist Roger Mayne, was shot in the Southam Street area of Notting Hill where the novel was set. A decade later the area was bulldozed, partly to make way for the modernist housing block Trellick Tower.

Top: A New Perspective (1963) by the bebop and funk trumpeter Donald Byrd: one of the many Blue Note record covers by Reid Miles that were a graphic template of taste for early Mods.

Bottom left: Birth of the Cool: Miles Davis in Germany in 1959, performing his innovative modern jazz in one of the sharp suits that helped to make him a Mod hero.

Bottom right: Dancing in a Soho backstreet in 1956 – the cradle of British youth culture where, in *Absolute Beginners*, Colin MacInnes noted 'the un-silent teenage revolution' stirring.

Top: The weekend starts here! An exhausted Mod couple take a break from dancing inside the Flamingo.

Bottom left: The legendary Flamingo Club in Soho, a jazz, R&B and ska venue where a multiracial crowd defied convention and won the attention of government snoopers who in 1964 warned against the 'serious moral danger' of the 'club world'.

Bottom right: A teenage Marc Feld (the future Marc Bolan), photographed by Don McCullin for 'Faces without Shadows: Young Men Who Live for Clothes and Pleasure', *Town* magazine, September 1962.

Top: 'I look pretty tall but my heels are high': the Who stand imperiously across the tracks in Paris in 1965, wearing the 'Pop Art' clothes that helped to make them Mod icons.

Bottom left: 'Queen of the Mods' and *Ready, Steady, Go!* presenter Cathy McGowan in 1965, modelling one of the dresses she designed.

Bottom right: Like the Vespa, Lambretta scooters were originally marketed to the young of both sexes; but most female Mods had to be content with being 'pillion fodder' on the back of scooters ridden by men.

Top: 'Into the steeple of beautiful people': the Small Faces perform with the American Soul singer P. P. Arnold who sang on their 1967 hit 'Tin Soldier'. She and Steve Marriott (*second left*) had a brief, unpublicized romance that year.

Bottom left: Music hall meets R&B and Op Art: the Kinks perform on *Ready, Steady, Go!* in 1964.

Bottom right: 'A fictional extension of Mod': Raymond Hawkey's 1965 design for the Harry Palmer novel *Horse Under Water*, which framed Michael Caine's face above Bauhaus graphics.

Top left: The Beatles wearing the collarless 'Bavarian' jackets, adapted by Soho tailor Dougie Millings from a Pierre Cardin design in 1963, with which they helped to export Mod style around the world.

Top right: Mod goes to America: the 1966 US edition of Mary Quant's memoirs, showing how she accompanied the 'British Invasion' led by the Beatles.

Above: Mod goes to France: French men bring English fashion to the cafes of Paris in 1966.

Above right: Bauhaus in London: this riverside building was redesigned by the Conran Group in homage to the crucible of modernism, and was opened as the Design Museum in 1989.

Above: 'Football mini dress' by Mary Quant's Ginger Group, 1967, showing the influence of pre-war British sports clothing and of Bauhaus design.

Top right: 'A minor revolution in taste instigated by young people': the scooter-riding Terence Conran, friend of Mary Quant and fellow admirer of the Bauhaus, who made modern design more affordable in the 1960s.

Bottom right: The 'King of Carnaby Street', John Stephen, chats with a 'recruit' to the Mod movement, fellow Scot Angus Young. Young went on to form the Australian hard rock group AC/DC.

Above: Mods and rockers clash at Margate in 1964, laying waste to family picnics on the beaches that Churchill swore to defend from foreign invasion in 1940.

Below: Mod invades village-England: Giles' Grandma disturbs the peace with her transistor radio at a cricket match in 1964. Giles was responding to the Mod–rocker clashes in Brighton and Margate that began on 16 May that year.

"Excuse me while I have a word with this Mod about transistor radios."

Sunday Express, May 17, 1964

home it was often accommodated by parents wise enough not to reject their offspring's taste out of hand. Moureen Nolan attended a Catholic convent grammar school in Liverpool while being a teenage 'face' on the Merseybeat club scene, escaping to the Cavern club with her friends, dressed in black polo necks and PVC jackets. She not only had a love of Twiggy make-up, Sassoon hairstyle and BIBA clothes but also an embryonic love of interior decor, which she used to make a statement in the family's modest suburban home in the year *Sgt. Pepper* was released:

My sister and I turned our creative talents to interior décor, which was also going through a revolution at the time. We attacked the magnolia gloss of our bedroom door and wrote PSYCHEDELIC SHACK in big wobbly letters (to give the effect of an LSD hallucination) and coloured them in poster paint – lime green, purple and orange. My sister tore up the lino and carpet, scrubbed the floorboards and gave them five coats of yellow gloss paint. The walls were emulsioned orange and green and we dutifully hung our posters of David Bailey and Warren Beatty.[107]

Teenage experiments in decor, assisted or not by parents, had some commercial value. By 1967, the 15–19 age group not only accounted for half of all clothing sales in Britain; they were also 'having an impact on the sale of household goods' according to one study.[108] In her analysis of female Mods, Angela McRobbie observed that 'Because mod style was in a sense quietly imperceptible to those unaware of its fine nuances, involvement was more easily accommodated into the normal routines of home, school and work. There was less likelihood of provoking an angry parental reaction since the dominant look was neat, tidy, and apparently unthreatening.'[109] Youngsters who had jobs and still lived at home had more financial independence but that didn't make them more of a handful. A *New Society* survey in 1964 reported that three-quarters of those involved in the cult gave half their take-home pay to their parents and that 'Mods usually tell their parents about their worries, and they quite often tell them what they are doing when they are asked. Parents rarely complain about their behaviour.'[110] A literal example of parental accommodation was that the concept of a specially designed, unisex teenage bedroom began to be marketed by retailers in this period. Displayed at the Ideal Home Exhibition and at an official show staged by the Design Council in 1969 this room was highly modernist in style, and in that respect anticipated the more affordable teenage bedrooms sold by IKEA twenty years later. Like dolls and pets with which children practised parenting, the teenagers who acquired one of these rooms were effectively given a modernist template in which to exercise their taste, albeit with mixed results.

Public awareness and approval of modernity in the 1960s and 70s therefore extended beyond national icons like the Post Office Tower or Concorde (opened and launched in 1965 and 1969 respectively), which both Harold Wilson and Ted Heath variously celebrated as symbols of technological progress. The public's taste for modernity even survived the much maligned Brutalist architecture that became such a feature of the urban landscape in this period. Popular Modernism had a more subtle, pervasive and long-term influence through the reshaping of domestic space, through the furniture, fittings and gadgets with which young Britons created a room, and ultimately a home, of their own.

Newspaper colour supplements promoted the idea of modern life-style to a younger, more unisex, and expanding middle-class readership from the 1960s onwards. Features on home interiors were combined with those on travel destinations and with restaurant reviews, in which the taste of the restaurant's design was critiqued with almost as much seriousness as the taste of the food. The *Sunday Times* colour supplement launched in 1962, the *Daily Telegraph* and the *Observer* followed in 1964. As the design historian Penny Sparke has shown, this coincided with the heyday of the post-war British design movement, which had begun in the late 1940s and reached a peak in the 1960s with a plethora of 'elegant neo-modernist furniture' that 'extended the modernist programme' of the interwar years by using newer materials like aluminium and plastic.[111]

Pop-Art inspired furniture attracted media attention because it was sold as disposable fashion objects for freewheeling homes. Peter Murdoch's 1964 bucket-shaped paper and resin chair decorated in polka dots and the transparent inflatable plastic Blow Chair of 1967, each with a life expectancy of six months, had commensurately little impact on the average British home beyond 'a proliferation of bean-bags and blow up chairs' in student flats.[112] Pop Art furniture therefore became a symbol of the transient superficiality of the 1960s, and the way that an obsession with youth had allowed fashion to intrude into every area of life. Sparke thinks that 'the engagement of the British public with modernity' was limited, because 'the impact of the Pop revolution and the cultural influence of youth were manifested predominantly in the public sphere of music and fashion and not in the home'.[113] In reality the two spheres were not completely separate. As Mod culture spread outside London, it increased the taste among young adults for modern design that went beyond the gimmicky and disposable. Manufacturers and retailers of household goods, like clothing chains before them, adapted to the new trends to meet demand.

One of the icons of Swinging London was the Cockney fashion photographer David Bailey, a poster boy in teenage bedrooms like Moureen Nolan's, who was fictively immortalised in *Blow-Up* (1966). Antonioni's Oscar-nominated critical portrait of London's hip elite was a visual smorgasbord of Mod style and sensibility with its Op Art sets, Herbie Hancock soundtrack, live performance by the Yardbirds and spacy Courrèges-dressed models (one of whom was played by Jane Birkin). The inscrutable opening scene, with mime artists appearing in a concrete modernist plaza, was shot at a Piccadilly complex created in 1964 for the *Financial Times* by the architects Alison and Peter Smithson, who as part of the Independent Group had exhibited at the 'This Is Tomorrow' exhibition in 1956. Critics agreed that the film showed how superficial pop modernism was; the *Daily Express* said that it exposed 'the scene' like 'an eggshell gently tapped to disclose the emptiness inside without disturbing the finish'.[114] Still, the film acquired cult status in Europe and America and lent its name to Paul Tunkin's Blow Up, one of the most popular Mod clubs of the Britpop era.

Photographers like Bailey who became associated with Swinging London were not just celebrity ciphers of aspiration; like artists and architects of the time they influenced the visual culture of Britain in the 1960s and 70s through their photojournalism in mass circulation magazines like *Town*, *Nova* and *Queen*.[115] Rising to prominence between 1957 and 1965, they were led by Terence Donovan, Roger Mayne (whose work included the first cover of *Absolute Beginners*), Don McCullin (who had photographed Marc Feld and his fellow Mods for *Town* in 1962, as well as being the set photographer on *Blow-Up*), and Robert Freeman (who's work included 'Changing Faces', a *Sunday Times* feature on Mods in 1964). Their photography focused on the changing urban landscapes of Britain; it was characterised not by a superficial obsession with celebrity but was rooted in the social realism of the late 1950s and early 60s.

The magazines and colour supplements in which their work appeared, alongside that of foreign photographers like Henri Cartier-Bresson, were shaped by modernist aesthetics. The editors and artists who designed these magazines were heavily influenced by the giants of modernism, in particular by Lásló Moholy-Nagy, the Jewish Hungarian and Bauhaus exile whose *Vision in Motion* was a designers' handbook. Influenced by Constructivism, *Vision in Motion* was his account of setting up a 'New Bauhaus' in the United States. Despite important work on London Transport posters in the 1930s, Nagy had been rejected by the art establishment and moved to America; but in the 1950s he had a belated influence in Britain through young followers there, especially those who trained at the Central School of Arts. As Martin Harrison noted in his study of British photography, 'the modernist syllabus at Central School produced a high proportion of the graphic designers whose collaborations with photographers resulted in the most impressive advertising and magazine imagery of the 1960s.'[116]

Some designers overtly celebrated the links between modernism and the youth movement that bore its name. Placing a Mod target next to pictures of contemporary products in 1966, *Design* magazine noted approvingly that retailers all over the country now gave more emphasis to modern design for their interiors and product packaging because 'they have realised that their young customers will respond to surroundings which are as colourful and modern as the clothes'. 'As with Golden Egg restaurants' (a favoured hang-out of Mods because of their cheap food and glaringly modern interiors), wrote the authors, 'the starting point [of boutique] design is a desire to escape from the dreariness of predominantly drab and depressing surroundings into something that comes much nearer to the dream world promised by twentieth century technology.' The feature concluded that

one day 'Carnaby Street' could rank with 'Bauhaus' as a descriptive phrase for a design style and a design legend . . . the young are behind the movement away from dowdy good taste. The Carnaby Street approach which started with clothes is now spilling over into other areas, and what has happened is of great significance for design as a whole . . . Can any enduring design standards survive a close association with high speed changes of fashion? We think the evidence shows that it can.[117]

People were given more time and space to be young from the 1960s onwards. The growth of the university population not only expanded career opportunities; it also fostered the kind of semi-independent life, at arm's length from bill-paying parents, which had once been the privilege of young people from wealthy backgrounds. Whether living on campus or off it, in receipt of a student grant or not, higher education allowed a relatively carefree lifestyle to be prolonged before entry into the workplace. It also sharply enhanced female independence: while women made up just 23 per cent of the university population in the early 1960s, by 1985 the figure would rise to 45 per cent.[118] For those who didn't make it to university, or those who had recently graduated, flat and house sharing became more common and permissible than it was before the war, when a woman was thought to be morally suspect if she entered the bedsit world. From the mid-1960s onwards there was a steady rise in the number of young people who could afford to live alone, or with friends and partners, in rented accommodation prior to setting up a marital home. London Mod Pamela Talbot recalls that 'Everyone came to London . . . there was more accommodation to be had in those days, so you rented flats, you shared flats . . . there were lots of youngsters, particularly young girls who would be firmly chaperoned at home, who were running loose in the West End and Soho . . . they all had jobs, they used to work in offices or they worked in coffee bars . . . you could make enough money to live on.'[119] An *Observer* report on 'Bedsit World' in 1966 found that 'Bursting upon London from the provinces and overseas are the 20–25 year olds . . . for them the big city spells severance from over protective mothers and fathers and new breaks in journalism, teaching, art, design, publishing.' It also noted that landlords were becoming 'unrestrictive about times and visitors . . . and about their efforts to decorate their rooms if they choose.'[120] The BBC television series *Take Three Girls* (1969–71) followed the fortunes of three young, single girls sharing a London flat.

The cohabiting of young men and women did not become a conventional, morally acceptable part of British life until the 1980s, and nor did home ownership rise substantially until then, but the foundations for both were laid in this period as young Britons surveyed the possibilities that opened up for adulthood. Flat-sharing didn't just mean that young people had the space to party, have sex and do drugs; it also meant that a growing number could exercise taste in their choice of interior decoration and furnishings, even in the rented accommodation upon which most had to rely. This could be as pointed a way of proclaiming their modernity as their choice of clothing or music. Patterns of taste formed in adolescence continued into adulthood in adapted forms, with fond memories, style choices and social attitudes creating a framework for consumption well into middle age.

Advertisers and companies were keenly aware of this and by the mid-1960s when Mod was at its peak, they milked the teenage market not as a fickle cash cow but with the long-term aim of targeting people in their twenties and thirties as they began to graze on the richer pastures of adult affluence. In 1966 the marketing division of the Pearl & Dean Group produced a report called 'Cinema and the Teenagers', which noted that there were six million people in Britain between the ages of 15 and 24, 4.6 million of whom were employed, with a disposable income of £1,500 million, which they estimated to be a sixth of all consumer spending in the UK. The conclusion of the report was that 'by 1970 half of the total population will be under 35, so the importance of reaching the teenage market is obvious. The expendable income of teenagers is large, but what is more important is their potential spending power over the next ten years and to tap this future spending it is essential to influence the teenagers now.'[121]

The notable development of this period, therefore, was not a superficial obsession with passing teenage trends but the fact that the parameters of youth were now expanding as Britain's youth culture became an established feature of national life. Teenage Mods became adult consumers with much of their taste intact; but what was the connection between those ordinary domestic lives and the celebrity culture of Swinging London?

IT IS GOING TO BE TERRIBLY POSH

Historians who question the social impact of British youth culture in the 1960s point to the fact that most Mods did not go to the same parties, clubs and restaurants as the figureheads of Swinging London.[122] That is true in a strictly physical sense, but it fails to capture the emotional relationship that Mods had with them. Just as their parents had been captivated by the music hall and movie stars of the pre-war era, so teenagers of the 1960s obsessed over the artists and celebrities directly or indirectly associated with Mod culture. From Marriott and McGowan to Sassoon and Stephen, all were living proof of what it was possible to achieve, or at least offered the chance to experience success vicariously by following their lives through the media.

Even London Mods could not afford to go to the expensive night-clubs where the stars hung out in the West End and Mayfair, the Scotch of St James's or the Ad Lib, or even mid-range clubs like Tiles, near Oxford Street. Exploring the world of the teenager for Len Deighton's *London Dossier*, a 1967 snapshot of metropolitan life he edited for Penguin, the 28-year-old journalist Jane Wilson also noted that Mods at cheaper venues on the fringes of the city could be far from cosmopolitan in their attitude to strangers. 'The central London locations where mods congregate in large numbers . . . are worth investigating, and nobody minds so long as you don't behave as if you're in a zoo', she advised readers. However, 'Mod clubs and beat ballrooms in the suburbs are something else. Here there is some xenophobia, and a definitely *local* feeling, so it is as well to have a talent for merging with the woodwork.'[123] Clearly, self-contained local cultures, whether working or middle class, as well as Scottish, Welsh, Northern Irish and regional ones, were not eradicated by the sense of belonging to a national youth culture.

However, if Swinging London did not routinely bridge social divisions except at an elite level among stars and their retinues, more people from working-class backgrounds became national figureheads in the 1960s than in previous eras, and more were directly connected to youth culture than before. Older, more tradi-tional role models did not all lose their appeal. In a 1968 poll on the subject, the Duke of Edinburgh made it into the top eight,

behind the Beatles, Quant, Issigonis and Twiggy but just ahead of
Mick Jagger, Peter Blake and John Stephen.[124] And the figureheads
of youth became more not less popular when they appeared to gain
the respect of the Establishment.

When the monarchy and politicians began doling out awards to
musicians and fashion designers in 1965 it was a popular move among
young Britons, which augmented the reputation both of the stars who
received them and the Queen who handed them over. Beyond
Buckingham Palace, it was only the most conservative members of
extant elites who felt the awards had been devalued by association
with pop culture, and it was only the most radical recusants within
pop who regarded it as a sell-out. The royal patronage of pop should
also be seen in historical context. Throughout the twentieth century
British monarchs and prime ministers had curried favour with the
public by engaging with popular culture, from George V's appearances
at the FA Cup Final to Elizabeth II's attendance at the Royal Variety
Performance. The difference – apparent when the Beatles appeared
at the latter in 1963 and John Lennon advised titled guests to 'rattle
your jewellery' – was that the youth culture generated by Mod was
a less deferential one that required careful handling.

The cross-class relationships between stars at awards ceremonies,
in expensive nightclubs or in bed with each other were not therefore
some parallel universe for Mods but were emblematic of their own
aspirations and arguably set an example that made it a little easier for
cross-class relationships to be achieved within the rest of society. As
Jonathan Gould wrote in his study of the Beatles:

Britain's traditional working-class culture had been governed by a preference
for well-defined boundaries . . . that succumbed to the satisfying logic of Us
and Them. Beginning with their dandified rejection of an aggressively masculine style, and continuing with their openness to the influence of such unlikely
objects of working-class toleration as blacks, foreigners, and homosexuals
(who were seen as fashion leaders), the early Mods were a striking exception
to this rule . . . The most important result of the Mods' connoisseurship
and cosmopolitanism involved the way that their cool, chic style appealed
to middle-class youth as well. In the early 1960s this allowed the Mod subculture to serve as a bridge across which middle-class and working-class talent
and ambition could commune.[125]

It was partly because Mods resembled middle-class people in style but seemed to behave in a subversively hedonistic way, which affronted social convention, that their subculture grew into a national and international phenomenon between 1964 and 1967. For 1960s Mod Richard Williams, who would become editor of *Melody Maker*, Mod 'did have a middle-class thing to it':

The multi-class aspect of it is often overlooked, it's quite hard to talk about in a way, as the English class system always was . . . The marvellous thing about it was that everyone got swept up in it so that people who were reading Camus were carried along by the same people who were going to tailors in Whitechapel. I used to love that. I was going to public school and my friends were working in chip shops and we used to meet up on a Saturday night. We had in common that we responded to all those influences in unison even though we came from different social bands. There was no problem in that at all as there would have been two or three years later; for those years in between, I would say, '62 and '66, none of that mattered . . . It was very exhilarating. It felt very different from what your parents had done.[126]

By being both reassuringly bourgeois in outlook and taste yet excitingly working class and multiracial in origin, Mod captivated millions of middle-class teenagers in Britain. This helps to explain the last phase of Mod culture in the 1960s, the so-called 'Peacock Revolution' or Dandy Mod, at its peak between 1966 and 1969.

In one sense it epitomised the remoteness of Swinging London from the youth culture that cradled it. Residing mostly in the smarter neighbourhoods of inner London, Dandy Mods tended to be a little older, in their twenties and thirties, more affluent, successful and, it's fair to say, more middle to upper middle class. The designers and boutiques associated with the trend, like Blades and Mr Fish, catered to a wealthier clientele in the arts and media who liked to dress up without necessarily being gay or bisexual (although many openly were). Mr Fish, situated in Clifford Street, between Savile Row and Bond Street, offered a white brocade jacket for £35, at a time when the average weekly salary was £25. Even Mods who lived on baked beans and withheld rent struggled to acquire such extravagant clothing. In 1969 *The Times* approvingly reported that:

Mr Fish is a phenomenon of our age. He is a product of the 1960s sartorial revolution. His shop is probably the axle around which spins that particular, exclusive type of fashion associated with the swinging aristocracy – the suave velvet suits and incredible lace shirts . . . the shop is in fact a way of life, an equivalent to a Pall Mall Club where the assistants have names and the clients sign bills.[127]

As Geoffrey Aquilina Ross noted in his study *The Day of the Peacock*, these stores and their clients deliberately sought to distance themselves from Carnaby Street, in much the same way that wealthy holiday-makers in the 1970s sought out more exotic destinations as affluent working-class Britons began to invade once-exclusive resorts in the Mediterranean.

One of the instigators of the trend, John Michael Ingram, 'had no plans to attract Carnaby Street Mods', and when interviewed by Ross on the matter Ingram said, 'Carnaby Street is a different social phenomenon entirely . . . it caters for a type who was working class [and it] has not so much to do with fashion as [with] the social revolution.'[128] Cilla Black financially backed the launch of another tailor of this ilk, the 26-year-old Tommy Nutter in 1969, a humbly born Savile Row apprentice. An excited Cilla told the *Sunday Express*, 'It is going to be terribly posh. There will be none of the common gimmicks of Carnaby Street, and no gaudy décor . . . I particularly want to have something made for Lord Snowdon.'[129]

The clothiers beloved by Mods like Cecil Gee and John Stephen were looked down on by the likes of Ingram: 'Gee was fun and important but basically bad taste', Ingham said. 'I tried to get the same excitement but without the vulgarity.'[130] But the two groups were linked. Favoured Mod groups like the Kinks and the Who were among those who adopted the Regency style after 1966 and the more daring Mods were no strangers to double-breasted velvet jackets and roll-neck shirts. Michael Fish – the owner of Mr Fish – was an Essex boy; born in 1940 he left school at 15 and his early career included a job as an assistant in one of John Stephen's stores. Fish's first love was a type of early, Ivy League Mod style, while he shared with Marc Feld an admiration of Beau Brummell. Like many boutique owners, Fish was forced to close during the recession of the 1970s, but it was this strand of Mod that would form the basis of glam rock fashion: Mr Fish's 'man's dress' was worn on stage by Mick Jagger and David Bowie.

TURN UP, SHELL OUT, GET LOST

Few people ever believed that all you need is love. But when the BBC broadcast the Beatles singing their new song on 25 June 1967 to a global live audience (estimated to be between 400 and 700 million people in thirty-one countries) even cynics could see that Britain stood on the meridian of Western popular culture. For a moment, it seemed that the nation's young meteors had defined the co-ordinates of a post-imperial age, much as the Astronomer Royal, George Airy, had created those of the Victorian age when he established the Prime Meridian at Greenwich.

Like all manifestations of the consumer society Mod fashion had built-in obsolescence. Commercialisation went too far even for some of those who had made money out of it. Pete Townshend remarked in 1966 that 'Mods were just as conformist and reactionary as anyone else'.[131] When a music magazine asked why the group were 'rarely seen wearing anything patriotic these days', he replied:

We have finished with pop art in a way. Though we are not completely departing from it. For instance we are thinking of starting one of our TV programmes by bursting in through Union Jacks. It will be to show group development, presenting The Who as they were a year ago. But that's all it amounts to now with us – group history. We've passed the stage where we used it as a great promotional idea. We don't need that now . . . What I'd like to do is to go into writing musicals and operettas.[132]

In fact Townshend hadn't finished with Pop Art. A year later he used it to explore the contradictions of the consumer society and its relationship with youth on the 1967 album *The Who Sell Out*. The first of the group's concept albums, *Sell Out* was a tribute to the illegal commercial radio stations which had helped to kick-start British youth culture by beaming British and American pop into millions of teenage bedrooms. 'It was pirate radio that made the music scene in this country', declared Townshend. The Labour government had shut down the stations by Act of Parliament in 1967 and it was not until 1972 that the next (Conservative) government licensed commercial radio. In the meantime, Britain's youth were offered consolation with BBC Radio 1, which launched on 30 September 1967. As if to reassure listeners that the Establishment was down with the kids, a psychedelic pop tune – the Move's 'Flowers in the Rain' – was the first to be played on the new station.

The Who borrowed real Radio London jingles on *Sell Out*, using them (along with fake commercials) to punctuate songs, and so create the illusion that an entire radio station had been given over to the group. Townshend was reminding fans that however much commerce and the media compromised youth culture, artists depended on both to reach their target audience. He also suggested that British capitalism was not as ruthless as that of the United States. 'We will never be so money-oriented in this country', he said, 'unlike Americans, we don't understand the business theory of *creating* demands.'[133]

Writing in *Queen* magazine, Nik Cohn described *Sell Out* as a sonic parallel to '[Claes] Oldenburg's hamburgers or Andy Warhol's soup cans'.[134] The album's Pop Art cover featured each member of the group in adverts for deodorant, spot remover, bodybuilding and baked beans, with Roger Daltrey in a bath of beans clutching a Heinz tin, a brand that symbolised American mass culture almost as much as Coca-Cola. The group had previously written music for a real Coke commercial, riffing on the *Batman* theme, and the original plan was to sell advertising space on the cover. That was abandoned when Coca-Cola were the only corporation to express interest, a reminder that rock was still considered too dangerous by some. The project was thus laced with irony in the best Pop Art tradition but there was more irony in the fact that *Sell Out* didn't sell, peaking at No. 13 in the British chart. This was largely because *Sell Out* fell between two trends. Musically the album mixed the band's trademark R&B sound with psychedelia, and although *Sell Out* contained the group's biggest US hit, 'I Can See for Miles', some fans just didn't get the concept.

Like a number of Mods Townshend embraced psychedelia, swapping amphetamines for LSD, growing his hair longer and dabbling in the counter-culture that emerged on both sides of the Atlantic in the mid-6os. Soon after the UFO club opened near Tottenham Court

Road in London in December 1966, Townshend frequented the acid-drenched shows staged there by British psychedelia's 'house orchestra', Pink Floyd.[135] 'When we read that Townshend had been seen at a Pink Floyd gig, we knew it was all over', remembers one Mod.[136] Describing psychedelic music as 'the great American comeback', *Melody Maker* warned its readers (with tongue firmly in cheek) that 'our pop weapons system might be knocked out in a decisive trans-Atlantic singles strike . . . with the use of "freaking out" and other powerful new devices'.[137]

The break was not as dramatic as it seemed to the broken-hearted. Psychedelia was shot through with the influence of Mod. The quintessential psychedelic record *Sgt. Pepper* was, like the Small Faces' *Ogden's Nut Gone Flake*, an hallucinogenic take on English music-hall culture, which affectionately marked the passing of pre-war working-class life in a way that chimed with Mod's original aspiration. Peter Blake's cover for *Sgt. Pepper* caught that intent: its collage of global icons ranging from Einstein to Chaplin, which framed the Beatles in their luminous military band tunics, was an exemplary Pop Art statement. A lifelong fan of modern jazz, in the early 1960s Blake had expressed a wish for his work to achieve the 'directness and distribution of Pop music', a wish he fulfilled over the next thirty years by designing album covers for the Who, Paul Weller, Oasis and his former pupil Ian Dury.[138]

In fashion terms, colours and patterns associated with psychedelia grew out of the flamboyant Dandy strand of Mod, whose designers employed motifs, such as paisley, without advocating revolution in the head. Stylistic continuity, as well as brazen ambition, explains why original Mod Marc Feld had no trouble mutating into elfin Marc Bolan, the trippy, Tolkien-reading, poster boy of glam (T. Rex's last album before his premature death in 1977 was called *Dandy in the Underworld*). Boutiques also paraded their links with the recent past: Granny Takes a Trip, the King's Road headquarters of British psychedelia, was co-founded by a Mod tailor, John Pearse. Musically, too, there were connections between Mod, psychedelia and glam rock. Former Mod David Bowie arrived at Ziggy Stardust via the 'Space Oddity' of Major Tom, inspired by the Apollo missions and the film of the 1969 moon landing, which entertained regulars at the UFO club as they watched Pink Floyd play 'Interstellar Overdrive'. Syd Barrett's group started out performing at the Marquee, one of the original Mod venues, and the self-consciously English folk-whimsy of their early work had much in common with the Kinks.

Curious Mods venturing into UFO stood in tense, suspicious groups while Joe Boyd's swirling lights melted walls and bodies, and Manfred, the club's resident German acid dealer, moved among the shadows in search of open minds. One UFO regular, Chris Rowley, remembered a night when 'the Mods were standing there pilled up, chewing, looking around them, semi-freaked out. The girls, noting that this Mod group were hostile, almost lashing out at the hippies around them, descended on them semi-naked and began caressing them. These guys did not know what hit them, but they soon calmed down and later were seen to be holding flowers and talking to Manfred.'[139] Even when sex and drugs weren't on offer, the differences in style and social background between Mods and hippies rarely descended into violence as the rivalry between Mods and rockers once had. As Simon Reynolds and Joy Press have pointed out:

While mod had looked to the spotless formica future, hippie rock harked back to lost golden ages: hence its love of Edwardiana and medievalism. Perhaps it's no coincidence that the mods were obsessed with streamlined style, from suits to mopeds. After all, the Italian futurists despised tranquillity, resisted slumber and worshipped speed. In contrast, Psychedelia revived the concerns of Romanticism . . . Like these ancestors Psychedelia mistrusted masculine logic, proposed the cultivation of 'feminine flow' and receptivity, and believed that industrial, urban existence was synonymous with living death.[140]

The hippie movement, with its taste for alternative spirituality and its anti-capitalist ethic, had political roots in the folk revival that Mods had rejected as retrogressively anti-modern.

But, for many Mods, changing what you wore and listened to was a development that reflected the course the movement was taking, just as they had previously switched from jazz to R&B – much as a voter can remain loyal to a political party without endorsing every item in its manifesto at general elections. Charles Shaar Murray, who started out at *Oz* magazine before making his name in the 1970s at the *NME*, recalls:

Mod was a way into so many other things . . . the jazz thing, the R&B thing, the blues thing . . . it was not a narrow movement. If you were a Mod you could listen to anything from Charlie Mingus to Dusty Springfield and it would all fit in. And then, around about the third quarter of 1966, acid came into the mix and you got into the Regency jackets and the paisley shirts and the permed hair. As far as I can tell, psychedelia came out of Mod . . . it was Mods who took acid.[141]

Each fashion choice left traces of its previous incarnation. 'For me the turning point from mod to hippie occurred one '67 Saturday afternoon', remembers Murray, 'during a town centre encounter with the schoolmate who had been Ace Face mod of the year above me. Previously renowned for his crisp haircut, tab-collar shirts and immaculate taste in shoes, he was now sporting a hip-length kaftan with a bell around his neck (though still sporting the white loafers).'[142]

Whether your white loafers survived or went to the local charity shop for stylistic recycling, dressing up in psychedelic clothing did not mean a straightforward choice between dropping out or conforming. Most young people chose to inhabit a world in between those two extremes where they continued to hold down studies, jobs, monogamous relationships and even family responsibilities while simultaneously buying into the idea of youthful freedom and nonconformity, using music, fashion and design to express their aspirations and frustrations. Foot soldiers of the Carnabetian Army needed steady jobs in order to afford their epauletted military tunics from Granny Takes a Trip just as they had needed money to buy suits from Mod Male. And while it is convenient to associate certain youth cults with particular drugs, the reality was that sustained recreational drug use of any kind was rarely compatible with maintaining a job, a career or a personal relationship (or even a university place); for those Mods who ventured into the UFO club and sampled LSD, the experience usually remained tied to weekend leisure time, as amphetamine consumption had been.

Most manufacturers, retailers and advertisers understood that for the majority who were unable or unwilling to drop out, fashion was not a crude adolescent rebellion against authority but a more subtle expression of individuality that placed the wearer in the vanguard of contemporary lifestyles, and the perennial quest for sex and success. As Bill Osgerby notes, 'The iconography of radical youth served as an emblem of non-conforming individualism, as affirmation of a masculine identity that eschewed stodgy conservatism in favour of fashionable leisure, stylistic display and the pleasures of commodity consumption.'[143] Not all retailers comprehended these nuances. When scooter sales fell sharply in 1967, east London scooter dealer Eddy Grimstead resorted to selling 'psychedelic' Vespas and Lambrettas decorated with paisley patterns and fairground motifs from *Sgt. Pepper*. But few customers of 'Hippy Eddy' – as he now called himself – responded to his call to 'Get Flower Power.'[144]

When Pink Floyd's first album, *The Piper at the Gates of Dawn*, was released in the summer of 1967, the group were simultaneously delighted with its success and concerned that the psychedelic movement was losing credibility as it emerged from the dark, multicoloured underground into the bright white light of the media's glare. According to the group's drummer, Nick Mason:

The business community had latched on to the new craze for psychedelia and every pop show, dance and sing-song was now being advertised as a freak-out . . . The original concept of everyone making their own entertainment had already gone to the wall in favour of a commodity that could be sold . . . The audiences the gigs were attracting were now turning up to observe the phenomenon rather than participate.[145]

In response, the group placed a spoof ad for one of their gigs, calling it 'Freak Out, Schmeak Out', and subverting Timothy Leary's dictum 'Turn on, tune in, drop out' by inviting punters to 'Turn up, shell out, get lost'. Few got the joke.

WE'RE NOT BUSINESS FREAKS, WE'RE ARTISTS

On a visit to London in 1968 the American journalist and critic, Tom Wolfe, observed: 'There is no more contest between "mod" and "rocker" styles. The Mod style and style of life have won completely . . . It is the style of life that makes them unique, not money, power, position, talent, intelligence.'[146] Wolfe correctly saw that Mod's ubiquity was a victory – but for whom? The transformation of Mod from style into lifestyle did not create a meritocratic Britain, still less a classless society. After visiting the Scene Club, where people were dancing at lunchtime, Wolfe concluded:

There is hardly a kid in all of England who harbors any sincere hopes of advancing himself in any very striking way by success at work. Englishmen at an early age begin to sense that the fix is in, and all that work does is keep you afloat at the place you were born into . . . All the articles about 'Swinging London' assume that the class system is breaking down and all these great vital young proles from the East End are taking over . . . Actually, the whole 'with it' 'switched on' set of young Londoners is almost totally removed from the working class Mods. It is made up chiefly of bourgeois men and women in photography, fashion, show business, advertising and journalism. Aside from the four Beatles, two actors, Terence Stamp and Michael Caine, and two photographers, David Bailey and Terence Donovan, there are no working class boys in the New Boy Network.[147]

In the music and fashion industries, which had been the cockpit of Britain's flight of fancy, reality was visible to the most clouded eyes. The story of the Beatles' Apple Boutique was a warning of where creative freedom and too much optimism could lead. Opened on Baker Street in London on 7 December 1967, the boutique was run by a trio of Dutch 'Provocateurs' who called themselves The Fool. George Harrison had got them to decorate his Mini Cooper and his home in Esher with psychedelic patterns. The store itself had a three-storey mural of an Indian goddess. Inside, most of the stock was 'shonky, pretty awful garments', according to Apple's director, Tony Bramwell: 'people used to come in, and it was quite crowded at times, but not many bought stuff – it was more of a tourist attraction'.[148] The shop's manager, Pete Shotton, who had been in Lennon's first band, the Quarry Men, tried to bring the Beatles down to retail earth. But when he pointed out that silk labels with the Apple logo on each garment would double their cost, Lennon snapped back, 'We're not business freaks, we're artists.'[149] The store closed seven months later, having lost the Beatles £100,000 (the equivalent of around £1 million today).

Naivety only partly explains their failure. The end of such dreams was also due to the fact that the business freaks were still in charge of the media, music and fashion industries. The Beatles' producer, George Martin, who had been at the centre of the music industry's transformation, observed that despite a grudging acceptance that artists now had to be respected and indulged, executive attitudes hadn't changed very much. 'It bothered me that record companies should behave as part of the establishment', he recalled. 'They saw pop artists, and the young people who bought their music, as a source of profit and nothing else. Despite the success of the Beatles, there was still a lot of class snobbery.'[150] Most artists, including the Beatles, continued to be exploited by music industry bosses – and by their own managers.

Don Arden represented the Small Faces and later the Electric Light Orchestra and Black Sabbath. A Jewish Mancunian from a poor background he had begun his career as a music-hall performer before moving into management. By the 1960s he managed a roster of stars, assisted by gun-toting heavies and later his teenage daughter Sharon, who to his horror married one of their clients, the former Black Sabbath singer Ozzy Osbourne. Arden became known as 'the Al Capone of pop'. When Robert Stigwood made a bid for the Small Faces, Arden paid his fellow entrepreneur a visit, dangling Stigwood by the ankles from the fourth-floor balcony of his office until the Australian promised to back off. Arden had obtained the Small Faces' first hit by chart-fixing, spending £12,000 on bribes. But when the band, who were paid a weekly salary of £20, demanded to see their royalty statements in 1966 Arden told their parents they were junkies and had spent all their money on drugs. They were eventually sold to the Stones' manager Andrew Loog Oldham for £25,000 cash, delivered in a brown paper bag. The group saw little of their vast earnings until a court settlement with Arden in 1996.

Although few executives and managers were as brutal as Sharon Osbourne's father, most had no more time for artists' complaints than he did. Steve Marriott was notorious for speaking his mind, an attitude that sprang from a pronounced class-consciousness and a belief that talent would be enough to see him through. In 1966, it got the Small Faces excluded from *Top of the Pops*. Believing that the show's producer was retiring, Marriott strode up to him after miming their latest single, 'My Mind's Eye', and announced, 'I'm glad you're leaving. I always thought you were a major cunt.' The BBC producer calmly informed him that it was another member of the crew who was leaving, then showed Marriott the studio door and told him not to return.[151] The singer discovered the hard way that a refusal to play the game was just as costly in the music industry after the artists' revolt of the 1960s as it had been in the days of Tin Pan Alley. In short, it had become acceptable to drop your Hs, but if you didn't mind your Ps and Qs you could still get into a lot of trouble.

The relationships forged between the pop aristocracy and members of the older elites, who were charmed and excited by it, gave the British Establishment a veneer of sexy fashionability that arguably shored up traditional power structures and accelerated the development of celebrity culture. The few who found room at the top mimicked the *ancien régime* more than they mocked it. Buying a country mansion became the ultimate symbol of success for the pop star with dropped aitches, as well as providing an escape from the obsessive attention of fans. Beyond their security gates, industrial unrest and student protest increased in the late 1960s but few Mod figureheads got involved in politics. 'I don't know which side I'm on,' said Ray Davies in 1967, 'I'm a rock 'n' roll singer. There's left, and there's right, and there's rock 'n' roll.'[152]

John Lennon was never afraid of taking sides, but as he became more politically active and spoke out on global issues, some fans questioned whether he still cared about them and their ordinary lives. In December 1971, *Melody Maker* published the following open letter:

Dear John and Yoko,

We love you very much and if all rock stars save one were to be lined up against a wall tomorrow and shot, you would be the one we'd save . . . [But] do you like being a 'product'? Apple may be a wonderful company but all we notice is that its records get steadily more expensive . . . Power to the people, yeah – but which people? We were the Beatles' people all right but we don't know if we're yours. We're T. Rex's and Slade's – there they are on *Top of the Pops* (it might be rubbish but it's all we've got) and at St. George's Hall, Bradford (at sixty pence a bit cheaper than a super album of your Fillmore gig). Are you one of us? So please, dear John and Yoko, give us a break from your public nasties on Paul (we're not very interested in your tax situation) and start explaining what rock liberation can mean when art and money get so mixed up. There aren't many people who can explain it. Pete Townshend has had a go; now it's your turn. Happy Christmas. Love,

Simon and Gill Frith, Keighley, Yorkshire[153]

Lennon's reply tried to justify the way art and money had got so mixed up, echoing the point Townshend had artfully made on *Sell Out*:

Dear Simon and Gill,

Apple was/is a capitalist concern . . . <u>You</u> may not worry about our tax-scene, but if we don't, your fab four will end up like Mickey Rooney, Joe Louis, etc. – performing for the rest of their lives to pay back the tax man . . . I personally have had enough of Apple/Ascot and all other properties which tie me down, mentally and physically. I intend to cash in my chips as soon as I can – and be FREE . . . Until we find an alternative, the Apples, EMIs, etc., are the only way of getting our product to the people – if you know of any other way – don't keep it a secret! Power to the People,

John and Yoko[154]

When Lennon and Yoko Ono left London for New York on 3 September 1971, the public reaction was more muted because few realised that the move would be a permanent one. When this became apparent it seemed to echo W. H. Auden's move to America on the eve of war in 1939. Auden, the left-leaning light of British poetry, had been accused of betraying his fellow artists and his country at a time of crisis. The writer Norman Mailer later made the comparison when he took the stand during Lennon's struggle to get a Green Card, telling the judge that Lennon was 'a great artist who has made an enormous contribution to popular culture. We lost T. S. Eliot to England and only got Auden back.'[155]

As the clever hopes of the 1960s expired, John Lennon explained why he had left Britain: 'In the States we're treated like artists. Which we are! But here [in Britain] I'm like the lad who knew Paul, got a lucky break, won the pools and married the actress. It's like 1940 here, it's really the sticks you know . . . [New York] is the Rome of today, a bit like a together Liverpool. I'd always like to be where the action is. In olden times I'd like to have lived in Rome or Paris.' 'The Seventies', he later declared, 'are gonna be America's.'[156]

ALL THE WORLD HAS BECOME MOD

'Of all the teenage movements', wrote Nik Cohn in 1971, 'Mod is the best example of the process by which pop cults rise up out of the undergrowth and spread and escalate into mass-media terms, and are softened up, and then disintegrate.'[157] But had Mod really disintegrated? By the mid-1960s the movement had become associated with all the creative dynamism and social change of that era, embracing a range of icons from Michael Caine to the Mini; and although few of them had been part of the original cult they were successfully grouped together to form a generic Mod brand, through which a vision of British modernity was sold to the world.

It was the extent of Mod's success that appeared to have killed it in the late 1960s. As early as 1965 one of the movement's magazines asked: 'Where have all the Mods gone?' The answer was decisive: 'What's happened is that all the world has become "Mod".'[158]

There was a great rebellion against the existing styles available for those between twelve and twenty. It was coupled with the complete capture of show business by young artistes who brought a great raw, rough, almost amateurish talent which suddenly made the established entertainers seem old-fashioned. This happened not only in Pop but in films and the theatre and art and literature. The English love the amateur whether it be in showbiz, sport, or even politics. They also get tired of the amateur very quickly if he doesn't prove to be the equal of the professional. This upsurge caught hold of almost everybody young in mind and the whole world has gone Mod. Now everyone between six and sixty is trying to think young. We see women in their fifties wearing the latest 'Mod' gear. City stockbrokers in suits that would not be out of place in Carnaby Street. Young executives in big corporations with hair styles that would have got them shown the door but a year or two ago.

Strangely enough, the people who resent it most are not the old squares . . . but the people who started it all – the teenagers. For some reason they think it slightly obscene that old people (anyone over twenty-five) should be interested in the Mod scene and disgusting that they should try and take part in it. This seems to show that it is not the attainment of the rebels' aims that gives satisfaction but the fun is in the rebellion itself.[159]

It was an astute observation about what would become a growing dilemma for young people: what happens when older generations don't condemn your way of life but embrace it? The optimistic midcentury claim that generation was now a more important category than class was not only undermined by the intensification of class conflict in the 1970s and 80s. What also challenged the supremacy of generational identity was the fact that youth culture outlived the 1960s, creating a new form of common experience that blurred conventional age boundaries, without ever destroying the healthy divide necessary for each generation to express its singular life and times. The man who wrote 'My Generation' told an interviewer in 1968, 'Pop is more than short skirts. The effect pop music has on society is incredible . . . It concerns far more than the twenty-year-olds. It concerns everybody now. It's lasted too long.'[160] That common experience gave birth to a canon of music, fashion and design the best of which claimed parity with art and literature, and which over the next half-century help construct the identities of people from all backgrounds and articulate their desires.

In 1965, *Mod* magazine implored its readers to embrace their success and look to the future: 'So darling Mods, it seems you are right back where you started, not out on a limb but following the same fashïons as everyone else. Having turned the fashion world upside down you now have nothing you can call your own, the only advantage is that you can follow the fashions a little faster because you have more money and are not tied down with such things as mortgages and babies . . . Is there a new revolution brewing up?'[161] There was – and it would prove John Lennon wrong: the 1970s would not, as he thought, belong entirely to America.

Britain continued to produce innovative youth cultures, and it did so while simultaneously forging links between the generations. When asked in 1965 if Mod would last, Kit Lambert replied, 'We can't tell if it's going to have a profound effect on English society. Personally I doubt it.' But he concluded, 'It's going to renew itself with other young people.'[162] In southern England and the Midlands, skinheads would strip Mod down into a macho, nationalistic cult that retained elements of its clothing styles while rejecting consumerism and, eventually, cosmopolitanism in order to recreate a cohesive white working-class community. Simultaneously in the north of England, Northern Soul was created by other working-class ex-Mods who retained Mods' engagement with black music. But rather than rejecting consumerism outright, Northern Soulers sidestepped it by having a party, and in the process they helped to invent modern club culture.

From its earliest days, Mod had been strictly hierarchical. The 'faces' who sat on the movement's self-appointed, informal style councils acted as alternative arbiters of taste, attempting to police what and who were 'in' or 'out' at any given time. But as a result of Mod's commercial exploitation and enormous popularity in the 1960s, the movement was transformed. Over the next decades, fresh and innovative manifestations of Mod style were developed by successive generations in subcultural milieux similar to those in which Mod had begun; some of these, like glam rock, also became national youth movements with a mass audience, celebrity figureheads and a wider influence on British culture that extended from domestic interiors to civic life.

Accompanying those new incarnations of the movement was a more conservative Mod elite with a power base in scooter clubs, fanzines, independent boutiques and record labels. Operating from within those micro-economies of taste, they periodically rejected Mod's commercialisation and were prone to nostalgia for the 1960s. But by monitoring the movement's progress over time, and by according certain trends and objects (like the Ben Sherman shirt) a permanent 'classic' status, they created a template for younger generations to begin their exploration of Mod culture, sometimes in the more innovative ways described above.

Some of this elite were ageing members of the original style councils of the early 1960s, revered by younger followers for the cultural capital they had accrued through loyalty to the movement. But what connected all these strands were the solid bonds formed between Mods of different generations. Those bonds helped to transmit and perpetuate Mod culture over the next half-century as people found it less 'disgusting' that 'old people' should be involved in the movement. A survey of London teenagers in 1967 observed that 'No one knows what happens to old mods because we haven't had a whole generation of them yet. Presumably they marry, have children, and settle down to form the backbone of England.'[163] That is exactly what most of them did – but the backbone of England was never quite the same again, for its vertebrae had been subtly realigned by the experience of Britain's first youth culture.

Part Two

Style is a unity of principle animating all the work of an epoch, the result of a state of mind which has its own special character . . . All objects of modern life create, in the long run, a modern state of mind . . . Workers and intellectuals, these people too, claim their rights to a machine for living in, which shall be in all simplicity a *human* thing.

Le Corbusier, *Towards a New Architecture*, Paris, 1923

5

ECSTATIC EXAGGERATIONS
Northern Soul, Glam Rock and the Strange Survival of Mod

Soul, like life itself, goes on and on. Because each and every one of us keeps the faith.

Dave Godin, *Blues and Soul* magazine, 1970[1]

Glam Rock is just rock 'n' roll with lipstick.

John Lennon to David Bowie, 1975[2]

A DREAM IN WHITE SPARKLE AND MIRRORS

Where did Mod go after the 1960s? The common answer from purists is that, having long been compromised by commercial forces, it survived in little subcultures of cool. Like extremist religious cells, these style elites kept Mod alive by codifying its tenets, branding heretics and by occasionally admitting new disciples who adhered sufficiently to its laws. At the same time, these style elites disdained the great mass of uncool people among whom they were forced to live until their promised land of modernity was somehow realised. The purists' teleology and their concept of 'Mod' are important, not least because they explain why people of all ages still relate to and participate in a movement that was originally supposed to be by and for the young; it also helps us to understand why the movement came to be so weighed down with nostalgia for the 1960s. However, this purism offers a limited understanding both of Mod and of British youth culture as a whole.

Mod survived largely because it was transmitted to a mass audience. Popularisation is the logical, almost inevitable outcome for every youth culture, but especially for one that celebrated consumerism as much as this one did. Yet the success of Mod devalued one of the emotional functions that it had for 'faces', which was to provide them with a substitute society over which they ruled, and which to some degree compensated them for a lack of influence in the 'real world'. This ersatz social elite was undermined by Mod culture outgrowing them and subsequently shaping a wider world, in Britain and abroad.

While 'faces' watched in horror as their kingdom of style became a sprawling empire over which they had no control, the millions of teenagers who bought into it used Mod for their own ends. This broader, more democratic, constituency adopted those aspects of Mod culture that suited their needs and desires without caring about the disapproval of purists any more than they cared about the disapproval of parents and teachers. The critic Simon Frith summed up this defiance of stylistic elitism:

Most working-class teenagers pass through groups, change identities, play their leisure roles for fun; other differences between them – sex, occupation, family – are much more significant than distinctions of style. For every youth 'stylist' committed to a cult as a full-time creative task, there are hundreds of working-class kids who grow up in a loose membership of several groups and run with a variety of gangs. There's a distinction here between a vanguard and a mass, between uses of leisure within subcultures.[3]

This tension, between the authentic subculture policed by its most devoted adherents and that which millions more enjoyed, is common to all youth cultures. The successful mass marketing of Mod style in the 1960s helps to explain why so many people were shaped by it and brought that influence to bear on subsequent, contrasting subcultures such as skinhead or glam rock, with each tribe believing that it was maintaining the true spirit of Mod.

Mod also survived because subsequent generations never completely rejected the youth culture of their predecessors, despite all the defiant poses teenagers love to strike. Children growing up in the 1960s often watched and admired older siblings who had become Mods, envious of their greater freedom, and their memories and impressions would influence them when they came to create their own youth cultures. In his memoirs, subtitled *From Soho to Spandau*, the Spandau Ballet songwriter Gary Kemp, who grew up in a music-loving, style-conscious, upwardly mobile working-class family in Islington, described such an epiphany outside his family home in the 1960s:

Once a month, local mods would converge on the pub and I'd stare out of my bedroom window, thrilled by the scooters gliding down the street, a dream in white sparkle and mirrors, reflecting the sharp, neat lines of their riders. This was certified mod country – a greased rocker wouldn't dare walk the Essex Road. Young men here took a feminine level of time in their grooming, and my cousins' boyfriends would be all slim suits [and] burned-in partings . . . The mods would reincarnate themselves here one day as soul boys and I would join them.[4]

Thus Mod survived not merely in the form of nostalgic revivals but was 'handed down' and imaginatively regenerated over time.

When a teenage Gary Kemp, sporting a 'suedehead' haircut, sought out Mod style in the early 1970s, his father took him to a Jewish tailor in east London to be measured for an electric blue-green 'tonic' suit. With money from his paper rounds and begging a little contribution from his mother, Gary and his brother Martin later went to their favourite shop, which they entered in a state of awe:

At the Angel a shop run by some tasty ex-mods was a windowless little grotto of working-class style. Oh, that giddy sensation when I first saw Brutuses and Ben Shermans, as one of the shop's oh-so-fashionable owners slipped them off the shelves and laid them out for my delectation . . . Some were gingham, others a confectionery of ice-cream colours, and all impossible to choose from. I wanted to own every one of them, collect them with the same eagerness that I'd collected World Cup coins the year before, but I had to make a choice and my eyes kept returning to a pale yellow one . . . The power of making that choice left me light headed, almost a little nauseous with excitement and I was desperate to get home . . . The smell of the fresh cotton as its lemon folds flew open and caught the light had me falling further in love . . . as I slipped it on my skin had never felt such bliss. Leaving its straight-bottomed tails hanging out over my trousers, I would be a la mode that winter, but what terrible trousers they now looked next to my new shirt. These were awful. They had to go. More begging ensued.[5]

In countless other homes style was also shared with siblings and transmitted from parents to children – a fact often ignored by sociologists, who believe that subculture is by definition a generational revolt against normative behaviour and dominant ideologies. In her critique of those preoccupations, Angela McRobbie pointed out that in the 1970s 'few writers seemed interested in what happened when a mod went home after a weekend on speed. Only what happened out there on the streets mattered.'[6]

Conservative critics too ignored the extent to which 1960s youth culture was passed on to subsequent generations. This was partly because they were keen to trivialise the consumption of music and fashion as a passing phase, and partly because they tended to see youth culture as part of a permissive society that was assaulting traditional family values. But adults continued to regard themselves as Mods long after they stopped being active participants in the movement, and they often transmitted their enthusiasm to siblings, spouses and their own children; there is ample evidence that many absorbed and adapted Mod style from their elders while suiting it to their own generational conditions.

This was not just an inheritance of taste; elder Mods also passed on moral and social attitudes to sex, class and race, which had evolved through their experience of youth culture, and which remained with them throughout their lives. Paradoxically, therefore, youth culture could operate simultaneously as a parenting tool and as a source of teenage revolt. For some parents, bequeathing this inheritance of taste and values to their children was as important as leaving them money or possessions, in much the same way that earlier British folk cultures had been handed down as valuable substitutes for material wealth.

As the hundreds of thousands of young people who had called themselves Mods in the 1960s produced families, held down jobs, pursued careers and settled into adult leisure patterns, manufacturers and advertisers targeted them as consumers who retained a sense of being modern within a more domesticated environment. Scooters were swapped for cars, for instance, as Small Faces drummer Kenney Jones recalled: 'I started out with a light blue Lambretta but the minute

I got my driving licence I got a Mini. It's the official Mod car, you know. Everyone had got a tiny bit older and the girlfriend was on at them to get a car – "I'm not getting back on a fucking scooter" and all that.'[7] But for Jones it was also state interference that triggered lifestyle changes:

I tell you what killed Mod, the crash helmet law. When they brought that law in, there was a big hoo-ha, I remember, everyone was up in arms because the Indians could wear turbans instead of the crash helmet and we said 'Well fuck it', you know, 'we can't have that'. To be honest, a Mod looks absolutely stupid with a crash helmet on. I used to have a little French beret and that would sit forward, nice, perfect. I was a bit pissed off myself . . . one of the great things was, you didn't have to wear a crash helmet, it wasn't a legal requirement, and mainly because of the Mod hairdo it was perfect. If you put a fucking crash helmet on it would kill your hairdo, wouldn't it? It kills the old Mod look stone dead.[8]

Despite the social conflicts of the 1970s and 80s, this period saw a rise in home ownership and foreign holidays. Just under a third of British homes were owner-occupied in 1951; by the end of the century this had risen to 69 per cent.[9] The subsequent crazes for DIY and furnishings, encouraged by lifestyle magazines, all stimulated an appetite for modern design. This was also the period when colour television made pop a more vivid presence in British homes. Introduced in 1969, a steady rise in the ownership of colour sets led them to surpass black and white ones in 1976. British homes increasingly became a screen on to which people projected personal identities – identities which had previously been shaped by their engagement with youth style. Mod style grew up and left home without losing touch either with its family roots or its youthful rebellion. Thus modernism continued to influence British taste in the last quarter of the twentieth century: a love of Italian design was extended from riding a scooter high on speed to boiling an Alessi kettle for a cup of coffee in a kitchen decorated in primary colours bought from the local B&Q.

At the start of the next century intergenerational correspondence led to concern that parents and children understood each other rather too well, and that consequently the moral and aesthetic territory in which young people had once marked out their identities now looked less like a battlefield and more like a public park through which all could promenade. This metaphorical park formed part of a wider landscape in which youth culture was incorporated as much by the political Establishment as by commercial interests.

The artistic innovation, political activism and consumer spending of young people that continued after the 1960s made Western politicians take them more seriously. In Britain governments of Left and Right continued to use the honours system to reward those involved in youth culture for their artistic or commercial achievement. The result was that in the UK, far more than in America, youth culture was not merely incorporated by business and media into the spectacle of mass entertainment; it also became part of the spectacle of state. Music, fashion and design were used both to make the monarchy appear more relevant to young people, and to encourage them to vote for one party or another.

However, while honouring the figureheads of youth culture became established practice, this did not mean either a surrender of the state to the vagaries of fashion or a corresponding end to youth rebellion. British governments simply continued policies that had begun in the 1930s, of fostering good citizenship among the young, to ameliorate juvenile delinquency and to encourage more productive participation in society. The clearest sign of this approach was the lowering of the voting age throughout most of the democratic world in the 1970s. Britain led the way, reducing it from 21 to 18 in 1969, followed by Germany and Canada in 1970, the United States and the Netherlands in 1971, Australia in 1973, France in 1974 and Italy in 1975. India relented in 1989, leaving only Japan with the higher age of 20 by the end of the century. Few changes demonstrated the impact of global youth revolts of the 1960s more than this extension of the franchise, however much it failed in the long run to refresh faith in democracy.

Earlier attempts to extend the franchise had been based on the idea that if young people were old enough to die for their country then they were old enough to vote. In a period of unprecedented peace in Europe, the argument now ran that teenagers were more mature as a result of their greater access to education and wealth. This was the conclusion of the 1967 Latey Committee, set up by Harold Wilson to define the age of majority, which resulted in 18-year-olds voting for the first time at the election of 1970. Business leaders with a stake in the youth market and most experts from the medical and education professions who submitted evidence to the committee agreed with Latey's conclusion that 'young people today are not what they were. They are largely literate and educated; they are far better off financially and far more independent of their parents; they are taught to think for themselves and mostly do so; and their experience of life is wider.' The press were blamed for the fact that the 'very word teenager conjures up horror images of pop fans screaming at airports, gangs roaming the street and long-haired rebels being rude to their head-masters'. Still, most of the press agreed with the report. Alongside a cartoon of Harold Wilson painting the Houses of Parliament in psyche-delic colours and shapes, the *Daily Mirror* welcomed the Latey report with the headline 'SWINGING! A Charter For Teenagers'.[10]

Juvenile delinquency and student radicalism were not ignored in these debates, and Mods were singled out by some opponents of reform as examples of the former.[11] But teenage enfranchisement was also seen by reformers as a way to temper rebellion by encouraging civic responsibility among the young. In France, where student protests had briefly threatened to topple the state in 1968, President Giscard d'Estaing's reform was supported by the Left on the grounds that it would modernise France and foster a sense of citizenship: 'It is high time to modify the rules of a society which is largely obsolete,' said France's Socialist leader, Pierre Mauroy, 'a society of the nineteenth century, a society of the bourgeoisie where one came to create the myth of youth in order the better to keep it away from active life.'[12]

However mythologised the state of youth had become since the nineteenth century, inviting 18-year-olds into voting booths did not place young feet on firmer ground any more than the introduction of civic youth clubs in 1960 had tempted teenagers away from sex and drugs by offering digestive biscuits and table tennis. As the West was plunged into the worst recession since the 1930s, young people did not engage more in conventional party politics than before. In fact, the period from 1964 to 1980 showed a decline in youth voter turnout, from a post-war high point of 88.6 per cent (of the 21–24 age group) in 1964, down to 73.1 per cent 1980 (although over the same period there was a slight rise in youth involvement in political groups of the Far Left and Right).[13]

Most young people continued to seek comfort and kicks in the subcultures they created and followed. Movements like glam rock and its younger sibling New Romanticism embraced retro or futuristic escapism while others, like skinhead and punk, tended towards nihilistic confrontation with the present. As we shall see, the strange survival of Mod in the 1970s and 80s was due to the fact that subsequent generations took different things from the 1960s template. Mod offered a variety of ways for young Britons to express themselves, while maintaining a recognisable core style and a cohesive appeal based on its idealised form of modernity. Perhaps its strangest manifestation in post-1960s youth culture, therefore, was Northern Soul, a form of nostalgic escapism that showed for the first time how Mod could become obsessed with the very thing it had once set itself against: the past.

PROTEST THROUGH STYLE

Northern Soul was the polished, sprung floor on which a generation of working-class youth from the north of England back-flipped their way into the future by dancing to the music of time past: the mid-1960s when Mods had fallen in love with the harmonies and redemptive lyrics of black American soul. In its heyday from 1967 to 1977, this cult was more exclusively influenced by American music than any movement since 1950s rock 'n' roll. Combining British style with a love of black American music Northern Soul helped to keep alive the cosmopolitan strand of Mod at a time when skinhead threatened to extinguish it; it also laid the foundations for a distinctive British dance culture, which in the 1980s would divide the young of Britain and America.

The cult was based at several nightclubs, the most popular of which were the Twisted Wheel in Manchester, the Wigan Casino and the Torch in Stoke-on-Trent. Each weekend thousands of ex-Mods travelled from all over Scotland, the north and the Midlands to dance to rare Stax, Motown and Atlantic imports. Amphetamines kept most of them going at 'all-nighters' that lasted until around seven on a Sunday morning, with late licences obtained by not serving alcohol. But police raids became common, contributing to the eventual closure of the clubs. Scooters remained the preferred mode of transport for those travelling to these venues in the 1970s. In fact, that aspect of Mod culture never really died, and continued into the twenty-first century with rallies still regularly taking place all over the country. Organisations like the Trojan Scooter Club, formed in Morecambe in 1968, were a modern version of the cycling clubs that had flourished in Edwardian England when bicycles gave working men and women an early taste of mobility.

The continued existence of scooter clubs also showed that Mod had put down roots away from London, and that regional and family ties could harbour a youth culture once it seemed to have passed out of fashion in the capital city. During the Mod revival of the late 1970s, the BBC's popular regional programme *Nationwide* interviewing young men from a scooter club in Barnsley preparing to attend a rally in Blackpool found them proud of the fact that they had maintained Mod in its original form throughout the mid-1970s. 'They [the southerners] don't look after their scooters, they're not as interested in them like us', one of them said. Struck by the age range of the club members, the *Nationwide* presenter concluded, with a touch of irony: 'Up in Yorkshire, at a safe distance from the frantic trend-setting of London, the scooter club boys are happy to ignore the waywardness of fashion. They like scooters and short hair, and they've got nephews and younger brothers coming along who seem certain to keep up the family tradition.'[14]

As for clothes, snappy suits were still worn in the early days of Northern Soul. 'When I first went to the [Twisted] Wheel I was a Mod and so were 90 per cent of the people there,' recalled Vince Peach, who travelled to the club from Liverpool.[15] The DJ Mike Pickering, who became one of the figureheads of the 'Madchester' movement in the 1980s, was also an original Mod. He believes that Northern Soul was a working-class extension of its parent culture:

For me as a teenager there were two types of people: the middle-class kids who actually dressed down – we used to call them hairies: they had beards, old checked shirts and torn old jeans – and then there was us who were the Mods. Well, I worked in a factory, and all our money would be saved to go and get a suit made by the little old Jewish tailor in Manchester, brogues, silk handkerchiefs with diamond pins put in, and your Crombie . . . it wasn't aspirational, it was [more] like self-bettering. It was a kind of protest through style . . . The music that is my favourite and still forms a part of my life is Motown and Northern Soul. They were really sneered upon and looked down upon by people who liked Led Zeppelin or white rock music.[16]

The menswear designer William Hunt grew up in Prestwich near Manchester with an older brother who was a Mod in the 1960s, and from whom he inherited a love of soul, which Hunt described as 'beautiful music about beautiful things'. This, coupled with an admiration for the fashion style of older boys at school, led to his immersion in the Northern Soul scene. By the time he became a trainee civil engineer on local building sites in the 1970s he was dancing six nights a week with a rest on Monday. Like many involved in Northern Soul, Hunt was drawn by the paradoxical combination of elitism and community that youth cultures provide: 'What was amazing about the scene was that it was exclusively inclusive. If you were in, you were in. And if you didn't know about it no one told you about it. It was very friendly, quite tribal, very regional. So the guys from Manchester would wear this and dance like this; the guys from Stoke would dress in this style and dance like that.'[17]

Dropping the restrictive suit but retaining Mods' sartorial ethos, Northern Soulers developed a simpler style that made it easier to dance, wearing high-waisted, baggy trousers with sports vests or bowling shirts and flat-soled loafers. As William Hunt remembers:

You'd have your socks showing so you could see your feet moving. You'd have high-waisted single pleat, double pleat trousers on. You'd wear the army shirts . . . the beautiful khaki and mercerised cotton shirts with the tie tucked into the front of it . . . You'd get them from army surplus places, but the nice cotton ones the American servicemen wore, with epaulettes on the shoulder and then the tie tucked in. Beautiful belts . . . and you always wore a hat.[18]

It got so sweaty in the clubs that the dancers would often carry a change of clothing in Adidas or Lonsdale shoulder bags, together with talcum powder to dust the dance floor. 'It must have been a hundred and twenty degrees,' remembers DJ Ian Levine. 'It was so hot and packed, the sweat was rising off people's bodies as condensation and dripping back on to them from the ceiling.'[19] Northern Soulers perfected their own dance style, consisting of athletic back-flips, spins and twists that prefigured break dancing by a decade. Journalist and broadcaster Stuart Maconie, who was a regular at Wigan Casino, remembers:

The music was vibrant, pulsating, irrepressible. And the dance floor was alive with energy, with individuals each performing their own variations on the classic Northern moves and steps, crossing the dance floor at speed, shuffling, sliding, occasionally breaking into a spin. At key points in the track, the whole dance floor would clap their hands in time to a certain pivotal drumbeat and the crack reverberated around the room like gunfire. It was intoxicating, not least because the place was full of girls.[20]

The man who coined the term Northern Soul was Dave Godin, a south Londoner from Peckham with anarchist beliefs, who would later become involved in the radical newspaper *Class War*. In the early 1960s Godin had been at Dartford Grammar School with Mick Jagger, where he had encouraged the future Rolling Stone's interest in black music. After studying art and design and working for a time in advertising, Godin was recruited by Berry Gordy to set up Tamla Motown's UK operation; he also opened a record store in central London called Soul City.

By the early 1970s, most of his customers were leaving 60s soul behind and getting into funk and disco. But Godin noticed a regional difference. The football fans who came to London from the north to follow their teams 'weren't at all interested in the latest developments in the black American chart . . . I devised the name as a shorthand sales term. It was just to say "if you've got customers from the north don't waste time playing them records currently in the chart, just play them what they like – Northern Soul".'[21] What started as a sales ploy became a wholehearted tribute after a visit to the Twisted Wheel in 1970, when Godin wrote in his column for the magazine *Blues and Soul*:

While Pan's People and other grotesque automatons on Top of the Pops are employed to dance to manufactured pop, the average dancer at The Wheel shows that there is still soul in these rigid and armoured Isles . . . Between records, one would hear the occasional cry of 'Right on now!' or see a clenched, gloved fist rise over the tops of the dancers. They are my kind of people, and as I went to the station to get the train back home the faint sounds of Soul music reminded me that, no matter what obstacles are placed in its way, soul, like life itself, goes on and on. Because each and every one of us keeps the faith – right on now![22]

For Paolo Hewitt, Northern Soul was 'the friendly face of Mod. Perhaps because its roots lie in the North, there was far more focus put on friendship with little time for pretension.'[23] Dave Godin too observed on his visit to the Twisted Wheel that 'There was no undercurrent of tension or aggression that one finds in London clubs, but rather a benevolent atmosphere of friendship and camaraderie.'[24] Yet others had different experiences. As Trevor Romeo ('Jazzie B'), London-born founder of 1980s group Soul II Soul, remembered: 'There wasn't a black person there! I remember triyng to go up north and be involved in these parties but you really weren't welcomed. And I think down south there was more of a melting pot.'[25] But Northern Soul attracted some black Britons at a time when race relations were volatile and when mainstream nightclubs admitted blacks, if at all, into a suspicious and testy environment. Tim Ashibende recalls the relative peace he found: 'For me as a black person, socialising during the seventies wasn't the safest thing to do. That's what I loved about the northern scene. If you were into the music that was all the credentials you needed. I don't doubt there were racists on the scene, but I've never actually had any problems.'[26]

NO PRETENCE, NO BULLSHIT, NO PLASTIC, SUGARY SMILES AND FLASH SUITS

Yet for all the friendship and inclusivity, Northern Soul's 'underground' appeal was based, like most youth cults, on the idea of belonging to an elite. As DJ Ian Dewhirst recalled: 'It was like a dream. Like suddenly knowing you're home. And this wonderful feeling of togetherness . . . All these other enthusiasts, misfits and nutters that had travelled from all over the place. It just felt like a really little, elite, very tight scene.'[27] Mick Fitzpatrick from Lancaster remembers:

The Seventies was a time when most people just shuffled around on the dancefloor, and there was this guy jumping several feet into the air landing in the splits then spinning and moving his feet at blistering speed. From that day on I was hooked. I was lucky, not only did I love the music, we belonged to an exclusive club. We turned our backs on the fashions of the day. No weird-looking seventies fashions for us. My first suit was made at Burtons the gentleman's tailors. Can you imagine it? The rest of the youth looked like some David Bowie/Marc Bolan clones and there was us. Immaculately dressed and cool.[28]

Like Merseybeat before it and 'Madchester' rave in years to come, Northern Soul was a riposte to London's dominance that amplified a perennially strong northern English identity. The cult grew up against a backdrop of economic decline in the industrial heartlands of Britain, a process that accelerated in the late 1960s and early 1970s, when Wigan lost almost 10 per cent of its workforce. Immortalised in Orwell's portrait of working-class hardship, *The Road to Wigan Pier* (1937), the town was the subject of another investigation in 1977, when Granada TV sent a team to portray Northern Soul for the series *This England*. The director, Tony Palmer, cut shots of ecstatic dancers with pictures of the town in its industrial heyday and images of the contemporary decay outside the casino, ending with one lamenting the time 'when Wigan *was* something and people cared about each other'.[29] What the programme failed to capture was the extent to which British youth culture provided an alternative community that became a substitute not only for regional and civic pride but nationally for the decline of British global power.

Of course no amount of dancing could compensate for being unemployed but in the 1980s and 90s the region would cement its reputation for dance culture by hosting the birth of the rave movement. In their history of the DJ, Bill Brewster and Frank Broughton wrote:

A full fifteen years before rave culture would whistle into existence, northern soul provided it with an almost complete blueprint. Here was a scene where working-class kids came together in large numbers, across great distances, to obscure places, to take drugs and dance to music that no one else cared about. It was a scene where togetherness and belonging were all important. It was long ignored or treated with contempt by the sophisticates of music journalism and London clubland, allowing it to develop largely undisturbed and unobserved.[30]

The cult of the DJ became more established thanks to Northern Soul. In the early 1970s British nightclubs did not have the advanced mixing techniques and sound systems that were pioneered at the

Sanctuary in New York, which turned sets into seamless aural adventures. But British DJs' encyclopaedic knowledge of obscure soul artists did earn them a status as big as the artists themselves. Club owner Peter Stringfellow remembered his early career as a DJ at the Sheffield soul club Mojo:

Mods hit Sheffield in 1964 . . .When I started, records were nothing more than fill-in music until the group played again . . . and there were no real sound systems then. I mean you could hear the ice-cream van outside better than the records . . .There's that awful gap between each record dropping from the spindle and every time it went quiet they would start fighting . . . So I took the spindle out and put on a record and then it was a case of how fast I could whip it off and put on the next before they started kicking the shit out of each other. That was how disc jockeying got started.[31]

More influential DJs like Ian Levine, Russ Winstanley and Roger Eagle sought out ever more obscure records, like Frank Wilson's 1965 single 'Do I Love You (Indeed I Do)' which became the movement's anthem and one of the most valuable discs in recording history (only two original copies survive). Competing fiercely with each other, they travelled to America, scouring stores and warehouses for nuggets of musical gold, like prospectors working in dusty creeks.

Doubling as promoters, DJs also brought artists like Edwin Starr, Brenda Holloway and Doris Troy over from America to perform in the clubs. (Troy, known as 'Mama Soul', went on to sing backing vocals on Pink Floyd's *Dark Side of the Moon*.) Like the American bluesmen adored by the British during the R&B boom of the early 1960s, these soul artists, having been largely forgotten in the United States, found their careers revived by an appreciative British audience. Among them was Brenda Holloway, the Motown singer/songwriter who had opened for the Beatles at their legendary Shea Stadium concert in 1965, and who declared of Northern Soul: 'It's an opportunity I never got in the States. It's like a second chance. When I come over here I'm a star.'[32] Setting up their own labels to reissue soul classics, Northern Soul promoters in effect also created Britain's independent music industry, preceding by several years the rash of small labels that became associated with the punk era.

One of the few things that Northern Soul fans shared with fellow ex-Mods, the skinheads, was a search for authenticity amid the apparent phoniness of a youth culture that became ever more commercialised. According to Northern Soul's historian Dave Nowell:

The Northern Soul scene is *real*. Populated by *real* people listening to *real* music. No pretence, no bullshit, no plastic, sugary smiles and flash suits. No competing against each other with personalised number plates in the car park. The moment you walk through the door into the all-nighter you are immediately accepted for what you are – a soul fan. Small, tall, black, white, male, female, wealthy, poor, it makes no difference. You are on the scene now, and the scene will look after you and treat you like a member of the family.[33]

Where Northern Soul differed from skinhead was that the search for authenticity was not a retreat into an exclusive white working-class tribe. Its followers believed that belonging to a community of youth, however elusive or transient, could be experienced by anyone.

By the mid-1970s TV crews, like Tony Palmer's, ventured north to investigate this strange cult . A few bands cashed in on this development, like Wigan's Chosen Few, who appeared on *Top of the Pops* in 1975, with young dancers brought down from Wigan Casino to appear with them on the show. This briefly gained the cult a national audience, to the dismay of most Northern Soul fans, who were fiercely protective of its regional identity.

The southern soul scene was strikingly different. According to critic and DJ Robert Elms, both scenes were 'very much the mod faith maintained, same drugs, same music, and at first the same clothes'. Yet there was a gap:

A stylistic Mason–Dixon line split the land in two. Below it London was the centre of the southern soul scene, based on new funk and jazz-funk tunes, with their own swaying dances and a very distinctive style of dress, which soon came to be boiled down to pegs and wedges. Above the line came northern soul . . . They had their own whirling dances, which soon came to be boiled down to huge baggies and vests. And the two sides, divided by a common love of dressing up and dancing to black American music, did not get on.[34]

Part of the difference was that northern English men clung on to a more traditional masculinity than their southern counterparts. A Queens Park Rangers fan, Elms remembers getting attacked by a Sheffield United fan on a foray 'up north' to follow his team:

His antipathy was not just because I was a QPR fan and therefore a soft southern bastard, but because I was dressed as 'a poof'. I had on a pair of narrow navy straight-legged cords, pointy black winklepicker shoes and a light blue (some might say baby blue) mohair jumper, with my wedge bouncing wildly as he chased me up the street . . . The ironic thing, though, is that my assailant was perhaps a soul boy too. Northern Soul that is.[35]

Open from 1973 until 1981, at its peak the Wigan Casino had a membership of 100,000. In 1978 *Billboard* magazine declared the club to be the world's best discotheque, a year before it awarded that honour to New York's Paradise Garage. But by then Northern Soul was already in decline. According to Dave Godin: 'When the scene was at its most vigorous there was this tremendous search for obscurities, and a lot of great records surfaced as a result. But after a while, the chances of discovering some old masterpiece diminish.'[36] Some DJs got fed up with the purism of their fans. Roger Eagle had broad tastes that included jazz and blues:

I started Northern Soul but I actually found the music very limiting because in the early days I'd play a Charles Mingus record, then I'd play a bluebeat disc followed by a Booker T. tune, then a Muddy Waters or Bo Diddley record. Gradually there was this blanding out to one sort of sound. When I started DJing, I could play what I wanted. But after three years I had to keep to the same tempo.[37]

Ian Levine attempted to move things on, playing the jazz-funk of Sly and the Family Stone and disco classics like 'Car Wash'. He was greeted with shouts of 'Fuck off! Get off! Play some stompers!' and a 'Levine must go' campaign forced him out. Stuart Maconie had already left the scene behind: 'I didn't know at the time but Northern Soul was about to go back underground where it belonged. 1974 was its high watermark before it evaporated in a cheesy whiff of novelty records. But it had been fun while it lasted.'[38] Containing as it did a built-in obsolescence, Northern Soul was doomed and, unlike the R&B boom that had driven Mod in the 1960s, it was never exported back to America, with the result that it failed to attract the national pride attached to its parent culture.

It took a former Mod from the south to move things forward again, a man steeped in both American soul music and European modernism, whose spectacle of idealised modernity captured the essence of Mod culture and made him one of its most influential figureheads over the next quarter of a century. As David Bowie once said of his work, 'it captured a sense of yearning for a future we all knew would never come to pass'.[39]

I AM, YOU MIGHT SAY, A COLLAGISTE

Sometimes dismissed as a self-indulgent, escapist prelude to punk's confrontation with reality, glam rock was in fact a child of Mod that helped to shape the punk era. As the critic Mark Fisher noted, 'Glam was a return to the Mod moment(um) that had been curtailed by the hippie longueur of the late 1960s.'[40] At its peak from 1971 to 1975, the movement encompassed successful artists and performers as diverse as Elton John, Gary Glitter and Freddie Mercury, but it had four creative architects: Marc Bolan, David Bowie, Bryan Ferry and Brian Eno. By fusing rock and soul with cabaret and electronica, glam further developed the Mod vision of a distinctive British youth culture that incorporated the best music and fashion of Europe and America. In 1975 Ferry described his group Roxy Music as 'a state of mind. Hollywood movies meets English art school, with a little Schopenhauer thrown in, both in the lyrics I write and the way we look. Of course, that allows for all kinds of possibilities. I am, you might say, a collagiste.'[41]

The movement came to public notice in November 1970 when another former Mod appeared on *Top of the Pops* singing 'Ride a White Swan' while wearing glitter on his face and a feather boa around his neck. 'We couldn't have pounced without Marc Bolan,' his friend David Bowie later said, 'the little imp opened the door.'[42] Earlier in the year, Bowie had played at the Roundhouse in London with his band knowingly called Hype. Bowie performed dressed in diaphanous scarves and a multicoloured cape as 'Rainbow Man', while guitarist Mick Ronson came on stage in a gold lamé suit and matching fedora as 'Gangster Man'; Bowie's future producer Tony Visconti was 'Hype Man', a comic book superhero dressed in a white leotard and wearing a pair of crocheted knickers over it. 'I think rock should be tarted up, made into a prostitute, a parody of itself', Bowie declared.[43]

David Bowie had grown up in south London and his first love had been jazz, especially the music of Charles Mingus and John Coltrane, but like most Mods of the time he moved from jazz to R&B. He played tenor sax in his first group, the Konrads, before founding the King Bees and then the Manish Boys, who toured with the Kinks in December 1964.[44] But Bowie found even the British version of R&B too American for his eclectic tastes. Interviewed by *The Times* in 1973 he said: 'I found myself in a rhythm and blues band but didn't like singing about America, I wanted to sing about my own environment.'[45] Bowie sang in his native south London accent, a deliberate statement of authenticity from a man whose career was based on artifice.

Far more than any previous youth cult, glam was about perform-ance. As *The Times* noted of Bowie, 'To watch one of his shows is to witness a performance, not a static rendition of a series of songs.'[46] He was influenced by Weimar cabaret and, nearer home, by Lindsay Kemp, a burlesque mime artist from Liverpool who lived above a strip joint in Soho, from where he ran the dance troupe which Bowie had joined in 1968. The stage personae Bowie created with Kemp's help, from Ziggy Stardust to Aladdin Sane, were alien supermen who landed on a corrupt earth to show a new generation the way forward. Bowie had developed a rather unhealthy interest in Nietzschean philosophy, evidenced for instance in the lyrics of 'The Supermen', the closing track on *The Man Who Sold the World* (1971), where he imagined a lost race of 'perfect men'. Indeed, Bowie's Ziggy – the 'Starman' who brings his message of salvation to earth's youth via the radio – bears a striking resemblance to Nietzsche's fictitious prophet Zarathustra, whose vision of a utopian future evolves around overcoming an exhausted humanity and its outdated moral codes. Yet it is Kemp's description of his own work that offers a good summary of glam: 'My lies are simply ecstatic exaggerations', he said.[47]

In fashion terms, glam rock emerged from – and in fact plundered

– the 'Dandy Mod' look of the second half of the 1960s. As Bowie remembered:

It was the Mod days, nice clothes were half the battle. I lived out of the dustbins on the back streets of Carnaby . . . The very best young designers were down there and because they were very expensive Italians, if any of the shirts had a button off the collar or anything like that, it would go in the dustbins. Me and Marc Bolan would go around at night and nick all the stuff out of the dustbins. Entire wardrobes of clothes for, well, next to nothing. All you had to do was sew a button on or stitch a sleeve. I remember when I used to steal everything, I had to look fashionable.[48]

As Peter Doggett observed in his study of Bowie and his music, by 1965 Mod 'had become an attitude and style with a dress code as strict as any English public school'; and 'if the Who's Pete Townshend was the unchallenged poet of this exclusive, near paranoid mentality', then 'Bowie presented himself as its Prince Charming, as if his entire adolescence had been the prelude to the moment when the peacock could unfurl its feathers . . . Bowie's allegiance to the Mod community was confirmed by his hair, with its pudding basin fringe and loosely enforced side parting . . . an instant symbol of affiliation that placed Bowie in the same camp as the Small Faces and the Action.'[49]

Bowie's performance of 'Starman' on *TOTP* on 6 July 1972 was a pivotal moment. For Gary Kemp, he offered a link between a Mod past and a future that didn't merely replay it:

One Thursday night while watching *Top of the Pops* on a friend's colour TV, we both agreed that we'd seen the future and it had white nail varnish and orange hair . . . A Mephistophelean messenger for the Space Age . . . the Starman Bowie threw his arm around his golden-suited buddy and I wanted to go to that planet. For a generation, a benchmark was being drawn as to how pop music should look – not the boy next door, nor the corkscrew-haired changeling, not even the hyper-lad of the Faces, but a theatre of glittering aspiration.[50]

What most interested Bowie was the way that fashion could be used to subvert notions of masculinity. When he was three, his mother Peggy found him covered in her make-up, and when told he shouldn't wear it, the puzzled little boy from Brixton replied simply, 'You do, Mummy.'[51] As a young Mod in 1964, he participated in a discussion of British youth culture on the BBC's flagship current affairs programme *Tonight*, styling himself president of the Society for the Prevention of Cruelty to Long-Haired Men. He told an amused presenter that male Mods were sick of getting abuse for their appearance: 'I think we're all fairly tolerant but for the last two years we've had comments like "Darlin '" and "Can I carry your handbag?" thrown at us, and I think it just has to stop now.'[52] It was, of course, a protest designed to get him noticed; but like many such stunts it was not devoid of meaning.

Subverting both gender norms and working-class codes of behaviour with their flamboyant clothes, Bolan, Bowie and Roxy Music took Mod's reformation of British masculinity to the far reaches of androgyny, shocking some people and liberating others. Looking back on the movement, Bowie's long-time friend, the photographer Mick Rock, summed up the shallows and depths of Mod's most colourful child:

Glam was about make-up, mirrors and androgyny. It was narcissistic, obsessive, decadent and subversive. It was bohemian, but also strangely futuristic. It was Oscar Wilde meets *A Clockwork Orange* . . . Glam was anarchy in drag. It was sexy, glamorous, on the edge. It was the moment Hippie finally died. It was absolutely Rock 'n' Roll. But it was also fashion, art, theatre, lifestyle. It was gay, straight, multisexual. It was totally titillating and absolutely naughty. Everybody held hands with everybody, kissed everybody, went home with everybody. It was an age of accelerated discovery, when all the kinks of sexual yearning were flushed out.[53]

Glam glittered in a period when gay and feminist politics, which had first been articulated in the 1960s, were becoming more militant; but it glittered in a playfully ironic, theatrical and other-worldly way that reached past militant cadres to a broader constituency bent on having fun in tough times. It was never going to usher in a futuristic sexual nirvana but glam did reflect, and in some cases progressed, men's discovery of a more rounded masculinity and their gradual acceptance of equal opportunity for women in the bedroom and in the boardroom.

The sexual revolution has been dismissed by some as chimeric, and when measured against the dissolute lives of pop stars, the sexual life of teenagers often remained one of abstinence and frustration. However, big changes did take place in the aftermath of the 1960s that glam and other youth cultures 'flushed out', or at least reflected. In 1964, 15 per cent of 16- and 17-year-old girls claimed to have had sexual intercourse; by 1974, the figure had leapt to 58 per cent.[54] Extramarital sex had become widely accepted by the 1970s, with those who believed it was immoral falling from 66 per cent of the population in 1963 to just 10 per cent in 1973. Although infidelity was still frowned on and marriage remained a popular institution, the divorce rate rose from one in ten married couples in 1950 to one in three by 1970, a change largely driven by women escaping unhappy marriages: they now had the economic independence to do so (they accounted for 73 per cent of divorce petitions by 1977).[55]

Parents continued to police the sexual behaviour of their teenage daughters more than that of boys. It was not until the 1980s that magazines for teenage girls followed *Cosmopolitan* in providing frank advice on how to obtain sexual satisfaction. However, girls' and women's participation in youth culture, like that of men, did not usually rupture family life. In her observations on Mod females of the 1960s, the sociologist Angela McRobbie concluded that 'There is nothing to suggest that participation in the mod subculture changed the social expectations of girls, or loosened the bonds between mothers and daughters, even if they were living in flats.'[56]

At the time McRobbie wrote this in 1976, the limited social expectations of many working-class girls had remained almost as intact as their relationship with Mum. That was because, while greater sexual freedom was a reality for millions, success at school and in the workplace was not. This was partly because aspiration was stunted by the low expectations of parents and teachers, partly due to the fact that the legal foundations for equality, advocated by the women's movement in the 1960s, did not start to take effect culturally until the 1980s. Despite the 1970 Equal Pay Act, in 1973 British women's earnings were still around 65 per cent of men's.[57] The 1975 Sex Discrimination Act, passed in the year that Margaret Thatcher became the first female leader of a British political party, did not begin to smash proverbial glass ceilings until the 1980s when, compared to most European countries, young British women came to enjoy more social freedom and professional opportunities.

Another strand of Mod that found its way into glam was a fascination with Europe. Glam rock's heyday coincided with Britain's entry into the European Community and with the beginning of cheap foreign travel, which made the British more receptive to Continental taste, from the cars they drove to the food they ate. That did not create much enthusiasm among the young for either Europe's politics or, initially, its popular music but a Continental sensibility continued to distinguish British youth culture from its American parent.

FANFARE FOR EUROPE

'I'm not particularly taken with life', David Bowie told *Melody Maker* in 1972. 'I'd probably be very good as just an astral spirit.'[58] Like Northern Soul, glam rock was about escape; escape not only from the perennial pressures of school, work and family life, but from the growing conflicts and crises in a nation that seemed at times to be teetering on the edge of revolution. Just a few years earlier, millions of Americans had marvelled at British creativity and artistic innovation. But in 1975 the *Wall Street Journal* declared: 'Goodbye Great Britain. It was nice knowing you.'[59]

Largely because the British refused to join the United States in Vietnam and the country did not experience a political scandal of Watergate proportions, Britain had avoided the same level of generational conflict that affected America in the early 1970s. However, by the time Bowie released *The Rise and Fall of Ziggy Stardust and the Spiders from Mars* in 1972, civil war was raging in Northern Ireland and strikes led by militant trade unions were disrupting daily life and damaging an already ailing British economy. That year, the Cabinet formally discussed the possibility that Britain was facing a challenge to the very existence of parliamentary democracy. At a dinner party at the end of 1973 the Cabinet minister Geoffrey Rippon told friends: 'We are on the same course as the Weimar government, with runaway inflation and ultra-high unemployment at the end.'[60] David Bowie's employment of German cabaret style of the 1920s as part of his wardrobe of escape was therefore apt.

Glam rock differed from Northern Soul in being less reliant on the music and wardrobe of the past; its escapist impulse was based just as much on a futuristic, space-age vision. Bowie in particular would come to admire the pioneering work of German electronic producers and artists, such as the legendary Konrad 'Conny' Plank (who had begun his career as a sound engineer for Marlene Dietrich) and the group Kraftwerk, who between them laid the foundations for the synthesiser sound that would later form the basis of British dance music, from disco to grime. In 1976, Bowie moved to Berlin, sharing an apartment with Iggy Pop and recording the 'Berlin trilogy' of albums on which he collaborated with a fellow admirer of Plank and Kraftwerk, Roxy Music's Brian Eno: *Low* (1977), *Heroes* (1977) and *Lodger* (1979). It was time 'to experiment . . . to evolve a new musical language', Bowie later explained.[61]

Until the reunification of Germany and the advent of budget airline travel in the 1990s, Berlin was as remote for young Britons as it had been for those who had read Len Deighton's books in the 1960s. However, while the wartime generation maintained their distrust of Germans, younger Britons came to admire their technical ingenuity and avidly bought their consumer goods. When in 1960 Gallup had asked which countries produced the highest quality goods, the United States came top with 62 per cent; by 1975 it had slumped to tenth place, with 25 per cent, while West Germany, previously in third position, now occupied the top rank.[62] Young and old alike began to envy West Germany's post-war recovery: between 1950 and 1970, the average disposable income of West German households rose by 400 per cent, almost double that of Britain. It was the desire to enjoy a similar standard of living, and avoid the slide into Weimaresque chaos that Geoffrey Rippon feared, which persuaded many British people to override their xenophobia and accept the United Kingdom's joining the European Economic Community in 1973. Rippon was the minister in charge of the negotiations that sealed the deal.

To mark Britain's entry into the EEC, the government staged 'Fanfare for Europe', a programme of cultural events that included concerts by the Kinks, the glam rock band Slade, Eric Clapton and Status Quo. The concert was organised by David Ormsby-Gore (Lord Harlech), who had consistently championed Britain's youth culture as a source of patriotism and profit. A distant relation of the Kennedys (he was a pallbearer at Bobby Kennedy's funeral in 1968), Ormsby-Gore had been ambassador to the United States during the British Invasion and hosted the lavish receptions for the Beatles and Mary Quant at the Washington Embassy in 1964. At the time of Fanfare for Europe, Ormsby-Gore's youngest daughter was engaged to Eric Clapton, which probably helped persuade the guitarist to perform at two government-sponsored rock concerts, held at the Rainbow Theatre in January 1973.

The Conservative government didn't simply see the concerts as a way of selling the European ideal to the long-haired, platform-heeled youths of Britain: pop music was regarded as a product of which the whole nation should be proud. Amid the political instability of the early 1970s, pop was deemed good for morale, almost as songs had served that purpose during two world wars. The press release announcing the concerts declared: 'Britain has led the world in pop music for a decade. Export earnings from record sales have totalled millions of pounds and, perhaps more importantly, our dominance in this field has played a major part in regenerating the image of Britain as a young and energetic nation . . . The Rainbow concerts will bring together many of the talented musicians who have created the legend of British pop.'[63]

Yet some lamented that so few British youths realised how important were the Continental influences on the music and fashion they consumed. Asking, 'Can Eurorock replace the Merseybeat?' *Melody Maker* editor Richard Williams criticised the 'unconscious xenophobia of the British pop audience', concluding: 'We're just beginning to realise what a wrong-headed attitude it is that no Europeans have anything whatsoever to contribute in the sphere of pop music.'[64] But the Fanfare for Europe concerts did little to correct that imbalance, largely because the artists on stage were all British, and their musical influences were more American than European.

For many British people European pop was epitomised by the Eurovision Song Contest, which in 1974 was won by the Swedish group Abba with their glam-influenced song 'Waterloo'; for the rest of the 1970s, Abba's infectious disco tunes, over-dubbed vocal harmonies and simple English lyrics made them the most successful Continental pop act in the UK. The competition, created in 1956 in order to unite European youth, was still watched by over 500 million people into the next century. Some patriotism attended the five British victories between 1967 and 1997, but the contest was generally seen to epitomise the kitsch and soulless nature of Continental pop music. In 1975, *The Times* spoke for many about the poor quality of music on offer from Britain's economic partners: 'One objects to the Eurovision Song Contest because the music is so bad. In Orwell's *1984* there is a computer which composes pop songs for the Proles; a comparison of Orwell's computer song and the Eurovision song contest entries is absolutely frightening – the Orwell song is better!'[65] And describing 'Krautrock' at the other end of the spectrum, the critic Peter York wrote in 1977:

It was quite literally avant-garde. A succession of humourless German experimental groups with names like Can and Tangerine Dream produced a succession of odd and undanceable records that sold mainly to highbrow hippie dippy whites in America . . . it had no star network, no charisma and no corruption. It did not rely on live performance. It was recorded music of the most experimental kind.[66]

Whether or not all this was unconscious xenophobia or a fair assessment of Continental music, the fact is that few British youths took any notice of the 'fanfare for Europe' programme staged to mark the UK's entry to the EEC in 1973, and those who attended the concerts were not impressed. The *NME* pointed out that government-sponsored rock would always have a credibility problem: 'Exactly what it had to do with going into Europe, few knew and less seemed to care. Slade played just one encore, "Mama Weer All Crazee Now". That pretty well summed up what was going on around the auditorium.'[67]

To make matters worse, Britain's new partners in Europe were no longer in thrall to British pop culture. In 1974, the German magazine *Der Spiegel* declared that 'The Swinging London of the 60s has given way to a London as gloomy as the city described by Charles Dickens, with the once imperial streets of the capital of a vast Empire now sparsely lighted like the slummy streets of a former British colonial township.'[68] *Der Spiegel*'s dystopian vision of slummy London had replaced *Time*'s optimistic portrait of the swinging city eight years earlier. But for millions of young men and women in mid-70s Britain life was not all Dickensian gloom, as they followed Bowie on what felt like a gravity-defying space age dance above a corrupt and decaying adult world.

Glam became a mass movement that offered young men and women the chance to express the ambiguities of sexuality to an unprecedented degree – hitherto an opportunity afforded only to a few Bright Young Things from the upper classes or vicariously experienced by working-class audiences through the music hall and seasonal pantomime. In doing so, glam added an important dimension to the construction of individual identity and the means by which young Britons negotiated their transition into adulthood. As Dick Hebdige has argued:

Not only was Bowie patently uninterested either in contemporary political and social issues or in working-class life in general, but his entire aesthetic was predicated upon a deliberate avoidance of the 'real' world . . . Bowie's meta-message was escape – from class, from sex, from personality, from obvious commitment – into a fantasy past or a science fiction future . . . and yet Bowie was responsible for opening up questions of sexual identity which had previously been repressed, ignored or merely hinted at in rock and youth culture. In glam rock, at least among those artists placed, like Bowie and Roxy Music, at the more sophisticated end of the glitter spectrum, the subversive emphasis was shifted away from class onto sexuality and gender typing . . . And they did so in singular fashion, by artfully confounding the images of men and women through which the passage from childhood to maturity was traditionally accomplished.[79]

Glam sparkled in some unlikely places, including the industrial towns of the north. As well as offering a temporary escape from drab surroundings and a way to shock parents and peers, the movement enabled working-class men and women to express facets of their personalities that previous generations had largely repressed. Looking back on his career in 2005, David Bowie wrote: 'One overriding and mischievous satisfaction that I still derive immense pleasure from is remembering how many hod-carrying brickies were encouraged to put on lurex tights and mince up and down the high street, having been assured by know-it-alls like me, that a smidgen of blusher really attracted the birds. This, of course, was true. And always has been since woad.'[80] Evidence suggests that this was not just the vanity of an insecure rock star.

The social scientist Nick Stevenson, a working-class Bowie fan from a small Midlands town, found his hero simultaneously 'confusing, alarming and appealing' when he saw him perform 'Boys Keep Swinging' on *Top of the Pops* in a dress. Other fans from the north and Midlands whom Stevenson interviewed about 'the Prince of Bohemian Pop' felt a similar mixture of emotions:

> PATRICIA: I loved watching him. I mean I was obsessed with him physically, that androgynous thing of that time when you are still growing, almost non-gender, that was for me what I really liked about him you know.
> KATIE: I think it was his ambiguous sexuality and the fact that he had different coloured eyes.

Men too were surprisingly comfortable with Bowie's sexual ambiguity:

> LEE: It was moving and connecting. It meant something to me. It was like I was meant to find him. I was sixteen and still at school. I am heterosexual but I found him very attractive. You know, like you see lots of actors in films. I just could not take my eyes off him.
> MICKY: There is nothing more embarrassing than a forty-year-old bloke fawning over him. But at a concert during 'My Death', you know the Jacques Brel song . . . when they shout 'me, me, me', well I was the first person on the front row to shout that. Got some strange looks from Dorothy [girlfriend]. Side of me she didn't know.[81]

Glam did not transform relations between men and women at a stroke. Men were not all reading *Fear of Flying* or *The Female Eunuch* in their tea break at the factory the week after a Bowie concert. Nor did most British women relish a night on the town with a man in turquoise make-up and a matching feather boa swung deftly around his neck. A decade after glam peaked, a 1985 government survey showed that despite going to work, nearly three-quarters of married women still did most of the housework, with only repairs and the management of household finances being the areas where men shared the burden of domestic duties.[82]

Yet glam rock was part of a wider process, accelerating in the 1970s, in which men and women got to know and understand themselves and each other better. Amid feminist militancy and the sexist reaction to it, a quiet revolution in lifestyle occurred. As Brian Eno remembered:

There was a whole kind of negative movement at the time saying either men were terrible or women were pathetic, and I thought, why not just be neither of them? Why not sidestep the whole argument by becoming something else, something in between? I still think that's a strong position that a lot of people have generally adopted – the New Man is a slightly feminised man, basically. A New Man is someone who doesn't think that looking after the children is humiliating, who doesn't think that showing emotions is unmasculine.[83]

The photographer and chronicler of glam, Mick Rock, agrees: 'Rock 'n' Roll is sometimes more than just music and stars. In the early seventies Lou Reed, David Bowie and Iggy Pop synthesized and reflected not only the further reaches of popular music, but also of lifestyles in general. They were sensibility purveyors.'[84] And like the original Mods, glam rockers saw Continental culture as a badge of aspiration, as Nick Stevenson explains:

It was by identifying with Bowie that I began to push away my working-class self, and started taking an interest in anything that was European rather than British. This included reading European fiction, listening to electronic music and watching avant-garde films. Above all, Bowie was a way of getting out. In identifying with Bowie I began a career in what I felt at the time to be self-improvement, passing exams and refashioning my identity. Bowie represented the possibility of becoming different. He did not create these elements within me, but entered into my world on these terms.[85]

But when glam rock, successfully challenging the conventional boundaries of British masculinity and gender relations and informed by a European sensibility, launched its assault on America, the differences between the two countries were once more thrown into relief.

A LITTLE BIT ROCK, A LITTLE BIT SNIGGER

Young Americans never took to glam rock, despite the fact that its originators had artistic links with America. Andy Warhol and the multi-media operation that he ran at the Factory in New York had influenced Bowie since the Englishman's early days with the Beckenham Arts Lab. By the time that glam was in full swing, the hedonistic, avant-garde scenes on each side of the Atlantic had danced, snorted coke and slept together, and even found the time to inspire each other, primarily through Bowie's creative friendships with Lou Reed and Iggy Pop. In the audience at New York's Radio City Hall on Bowie's second tour of the States in February 1973 were Warhol, Salvador Dali and Allen Ginsberg. 'It was a tale of two cities', according to Mick Rock: 'London and New York. I used to pop back and forth between the two. They tumbled into each other. The Warhol scene in New York fed into the Glam scene in London. There was this carnivorous interchange going on between the two factions. It was very arty, glib and bisexual.'[86]

But if glam left the confines of the world of the avant-garde and filtered into mainstream Britain, it did not penetrate America in the same way. The 'glitter kids' — as the media had dubbed the millions of young Britons who followed their heroes from the make-up counter to the dance floor — shocked even those New Yorkers who got involved in the glam movement. Bowie's producer Tony Visconti recalls his arrival in Britain in 1970:

Coming to London was pure culture shock. I was actually seeing people walking around the streets of London looking like Austin Powers, in crushed velvet jackets . . . I thought, Wow, these people actually dress like this! I mean, no men wore make-up in America apart from drag queens. Anything gay in New York was very covert. So I realised after a few days that this wasn't Kansas any more, Toto.[87]

As we have seen, when Mod had first been exported to the United States, it provoked widespread fear that British style would feminise American men; glam did little to alleviate that fear. Even those who stood to make money from selling glam to young Americans saw Mod's more outrageous progeny as another alien British style rather than 'a theatre of glittering aspiration'. American music industry executives played down Bowie's gender bending to appease the teen-agers of Kansas: the US release replaced the picture of Bowie wearing his dress on the cover of The Man Who Sold the World with a cartoon, so as not to alienate young Americans. Bowie explains why, for all his commercial success in the States, Americans did not get glam:

Yes, we loved American underground music but we really did have our own drag queens and drugs in London, thank you very much. We also had *A Clockwork Orange*, Lindsay Kemp, and Fritz Lang, George Orwell and Nietzsche, Yamamoto Kansai, Mishima's gay army and Colin Wilson to draw on . . . The Americans at heart are a pure and noble people. Things to them are in black and white. We Brits putter around in the grey area. In our minds it's 'a little bit rock, a little bit snigger'. British Glam Rock never made an impact on Middle America to any extent. Before and aft, we were bookended by Alice [Cooper] and Kiss, butch 'manly' glam with lots of guillotines and fireworks, muscle and metal. No mistaking the sexual bent of these fellas. 'Nothing ambiguous about our boys.' That's the only way Ohio could accept lipstick on males. So we Limeys all swanned sniffily off to the wings where we did make an impression. For a brief moment or two, we ruled in New York and Los Angeles.[88]

It was this eclecticism of glam, as much as its disconcerting sexual ambiguity, that limited the transatlantic impact of Britain's most innovative youth cult in the first half of the 1970s.

Roxy Music were less androgynous than Bowie or Bolan and one of the semi-naked women to grace their erotic album covers was the Texan model Jerry Hall. But Roxy Music were just as eclectic as Bowie and wore their European hearts on their sleeves. It is not that British audiences got all their smart art school references – 1972's 'Re-make/ Re-model' was titled after Derek Boshier's 1962 Pop Art painting 'Re-think/ Re-entry' – or that they necessarily warmed to a self-proclaimed 'collagiste' who in 1973 penned 'Song For Europe' with its Latin and French lyrics, but Bryan Ferry is convinced that Roxy Music's lack of success in the States was due to a difference in sensibility: 'My view of American audiences is that they are very conservative. I think that when they went through all the social changes in the sixties they seemed to create a new style which was equally as rigid as the one they had left.'[89] In addition, 'The British are more prepared to accept weirdness and complexity, and I think that's because the hard sell principle doesn't happen quite as intensely in England.'[90]

Keyboardist Eddie Jobson, who replaced Brian Eno in the group, believes that to explain Roxy Music's failure in the US 'you have to explain the difference between American and British culture':[91]

Americans like their rock music tougher . . . The British bands who made it big there in the sixties and seventies captured something Americans related to in their rock music, like drugs (Pink Floyd) or sex (Led Zeppelin) or maybe something less mainstream, like the decadence of downtown New York (Bowie). Roxy never quite hit that or any other pulse. We were viewed as effete, amateurish, tame. The black-leather Warhol crowd thought the whole gay/glam thing was decadent and cool, but the only places in Middle America that hit were the blue-collar cities of Detroit and Cleveland. Like Glasgow or Birmingham, these places needed some glamour in their lives and Roxy, T. Rex, Bowie, Mott the Hoople, and even the New York Dolls, Devo or Television provided it.[92]

While America found it harder to accept the style and sexual politics of glam, the movement's artists and their British fans continued to be influenced by American R&B and soul. And unlike Northern Soulers they didn't remain stuck in the 1960s but moved with the times as soul transmogrified into funk and disco. In appearance, the fathers of funk – such as Bootsy Collins and George Clinton, the self-styled 'Cosmic Funksters' – were just as outrageous as Bowie or Bolan. Their clothes and stage shows utilised the imagery of science fiction as much as their British counterparts did, for funk too cried out 'escape!' – escape not only from a stagnant economy and the Vietnam draft but the ghetto. As the American critic Ted Polhemus explained:

Where Glam and Funk differed from each other was in their earthly context. The socio-economic realities of the black urban ghettoes of the USA obliged Funk to focus on ostentation as a demonstration of success. Glam's roots, on the other hand, were in a Swinging London whose comparative prosperity meant that stylistic experimentation was free to serve simply as an expression of personal identity. In particular this took the form of experimentation with gender roles. Both in their appearance and in their forthright espousal of bisexuality, Glam musicians like Bowie and Bolan challenged our culture's traditional, highly restrictive, inhibiting definition of masculinity. The extent of their success in this challenge is Glam's most significant achievement.[93]

Sections of British youth would later succumb to 'bling', as the ostentation of funk found its way into the more macho style of hip hop.

Conversely, a form of glam eventually conquered main street America via the masquerade of Madonna and the spectacle of Lady Gaga. In the meantime, as glam put down deeper roots in 70s Britain than it did in America, it also contributed to the long-term shift in the way that youth was sold.

IF YOU'RE NOT BUSY BEING BORN YOU'RE BUSY BUYING

Piccadilly, 1972: taking a turn off main street, away from the cacophony and real-life relics, & into the outer spaces myriad faces & sweet deafening sounds of rock 'n' roll. And inner space . . . the mind loses its bearings. What's the date again? (It's so dark in here.) 1962? Or twenty years on? Is this a recording session or a cocktail party? On the rocks, please . . . where's the icebox? Oh! Now! That is so cool . . . musicians lie rigid & fluid in a mannerist canvas of hard-edged black-leather glinting, red-satin slashes, smokey surrounding gloom listening to the music re-sounding, cutting the air like it was glass, rock 'n' roll juggernauted into demonic electronic supersonic mo-mo momentum by a panoplic machine-pile, hifi or scifi who can tell?[94]

Simon Puxley's liner notes capture the atmosphere of a favourite hang-out for rock stars and fans alike in the early 1970s. Roxy Music were among the bands that were regularly played on the sound system of the Kensington department store BIBA, which became as associated with glam as Mary Quant's nearby Bazaar and John Stephen's Carnaby Street had been with Mod in its original incarnation.

With the now obligatory loud music, its windows blacked out and its luxurious art nouveau interior duskily lit, BIBA sold pick-and-mix glamour to a generation aching for escape on a budget, and its successful mail order business brought glam style to Britons around the country. Founded by designer Barbara Hulanicki and her husband Fitz in 1964 at the height of the boutique revolution, by the early 1970s it was attracting up to a million customers a week and was considered the place to work by young women with aspirations to make it in the fashion industry (Anna Wintour, legendary editor of American *Vogue* was one of those who began her career on the BIBA tills). 'It was a sort of Ali Baba, Casbah sort of thing', said one of the store's designers, while the *Evening Standard* commented that it was 'a place of pilgrimage for office girls seeking refuge from the dull, dreary department store offerings'.[95]

The symbolic end of glam rock was the store's closure in 1975. Hit by the economic downturn following the rise in oil prices, BIBA had been sold to the Dorothy Perkins Group in 1973, before the doors finally closed. For some observers it also marked the end of the youth-driven retail revolution of the 1960s. 'It really is the end of the dream, the final fling for the excrescences of sixties' fashion', the socialist MP Tony Benn gleefully noted in his diary.[96] The closure was described by a historian of the store as 'the retail Altamont, the moment when it became clear that the hopes of the sixties were incapable of surviving in a corporate world of oil crises and faceless chain-stores.'[97] Like most obituaries of the 1960s these were premature. Although most boutiques were swallowed up by chain stores and BIBA had no successor in mass-marketing luxury clothing to the young, the shop did form part of the long revolution of popular Modernism. Writing in 2012, Hulanicki concluded:

I strongly believe that the legacy of BIBA is not that particular style, but rather what it stood for. Style can be a way of life, of self-expression, that is available to everyone. We started with our customers, with their needs and desires, and created a framework for them to discover themselves. We never told them what to do or wear, or how to live. We simply gave them an alternative to the mainstream and invited them in to play.[98]

The concept of shopping as a leisure activity for the young, to be shared with peers in unisex environments shaped by modern music and design, was the lasting legacy of these stores. BIBA in particular specialised in marketing to women in their twenties who had children. Hulanicki was one of the first designers, along with Terence Conran, to realise that the sexiness, vivacity and style associated with youth did not necessarily stop for her customers when their lives became freighted with responsibility: instead it became lifestyle.

Following the birth of her son Hulanicki also began designing for children and launched Baby BIBA. Hating the traditional baby blue and pink 'towelling suits or those prissy looking woolly jumpers and bonnets for babies',[99] she declared that purple and black were the colours of modern children. 'The clothing on sale was simple mini-Mod', wrote fashion historian Kate McIntyre, 'but with the essential Biba retro hallmarks – high-buttoned necklines and puff sleeves.'[100] Baby BIBA was not just a smart way to extend Hulanicki's range of products; it enabled parents to turn their children into fashion accessories. Its success resulted in the first generation of kids dressed to look like miniature versions of their hip parents. (It also inadvertently contributed to the sexualisation of children, which by the end of the century led to prepubescent girls wearing miniskirts and halter-neck tops.) Generational difference remained the platform from which rebellion was launched, yet Baby BIBA, and its imitators like Gap Kids, showed that the generation gap was being further narrowed. This was happening not only because style icons like Bowie were creatively regenerating the 1960s Mod template in music and fashion, but also because the parameters of youth were extended by commercial diffusion that profited from deeper social trends. Children now had their adolescence kick-started by parents trying to prolong theirs. Having your first Baby BIBA top pulled over your head was a kind of secular baptism for the consumer society.

Hulanicki was also one of the first fashion retailers to realise the power of the brand. Everything in her store, from the tiniest accessory to the biggest outfit, carried the distinctive BIBA label of gold art nouveau lettering set on a black background. Perhaps the ultimate accessory was to be found in the food hall, where tins of Heinz baked beans were rebranded with the BIBA logo. To students of Pop Art like the members of Roxy Music this must have seemed like a smart reference to Warhol's famous screen print of multiple baked beans tins. To the Marxist terrorist Angry Brigade the sale of BIBA baked beans proved that glam was not a convention-defying, identity-creating subculture but an expression of the final stages of a corrupt and decadent capitalism.

On May Day 1971, the Angry Brigade planted a bomb in the basement of BIBA's Kensington store. No one was hurt but the attack displayed the fury that youth culture could arouse on the Left where some regarded it as the new opium of the people – not a liberating force but the latest attempt to exploit the desires of the young. To explain their actions, the Angry Brigade sent 'Communique No. 8' to *The Times*. Riffing on the Bob Dylan song 'It's Alright, Ma (I'm only

Bleeding)', it was headed 'IF YOU'RE NOT BUSY BEING BORN YOU'RE BUSY BUYING':

All the sales girls in the flash boutiques are made to dress the same and have the same make-up, representing the 1940s. In fashion as in everything else capitalism can only go backwards – they've nowhere to go – they're dead. The future is ours. Life is so boring, there is nothing to do except spend all our wages on the latest skirt or shirt. Brothers and sisters, what are your real desires? Sit in the drugstore, look distant, empty, bored, drinking some tasteless coffee? Or perhaps BLOW IT UP or BURN IT DOWN. The only thing you can do with modern slave-houses – called boutiques – is WRECK THEM. You can't reform profit capitalism and inhumanity. Just KICK IT TILL IT BREAKS. REVOLUTION.[101]

Feminists had been under investigation since they smoke-bombed the Miss World contest at London's Albert Hall a year earlier and the police blamed this attack too on 'way-out militant women on the fringes of the "Women's Lib" movement'.[102] The *Guardian* described it as 'some kind of macabre tribute' to BIBA that anarchists should single it out in order 'to protest the rising tide of capitalist female deco-decadence'.[103]

However, many customers seemed to understand the anarchist dictum 'All property is theft': shoplifting had always been a problem at BIBA, estimated to have run at 12 per cent of turnover. It continued even during the Angry Brigade attack. The security officer in charge of getting people to leave the store on the day remembers: 'There was one girl next to me having complete hysterics, flinging her arms around and saying "Oh my God, oh my God, we're all going to die." And as she was doing this big drama, she was stuffing loads of things into her bag.'[104] Hit by shoplifting as well as the recession, the store closed in the same year that the punk movement began to rumble in Britain. When Bowie looked back on what he called the 'oncoming tremors of 1975', he wrote: 'All you'll need will be a snotty nose, an abused Ziggy haircut and an ability to pronounce "anarchy". Me? I'll be fucking off to Berlin thanks.'[105]

As Bowie boarded his plane to Germany, Mod had already spawned a very different movement that set itself against the racial and sexual progressiveness that had shaped its sibling subcultures of Northern Soul and glam rock. Emerging in 1968 and lasting well into the 1980s, the skinhead movement was successfully exported to a white global diaspora where its celebration of traditional masculinity and, later, of racial purity showed that modernity in youth culture was violently contested throughout the Western world. One of David Bowie's self-styled Cavaliers described skinheads as 'a tribe of symbolically deloused Roundheads'.[106] Their civil war was fought not in the fields of England but in the football terraces and backstreets of Britain's decaying industrial landscape.

6

A PACK OF WEASELS SQUEAKING FOR BLOOD
Recession, Skinheads and Prole Mod

[Mod] was taken over by a new and more violent sector, the urban working class at the gang-forming age and this became quite sinister . . . Everything about them was neat, pretty and creepy: dark glasses, Nero hair-cuts, Chelsea boots, polo-necked sweaters worn under skinny V-necked pullovers, gleaming scooters and transistors. Even their weapons were pretty – tiny hammers and screwdrivers. *En masse* they looked like a pack of weasels squeaking for blood.

   George Melly, *Revolt into Style*, 1970[1]

Don't get me wrong. I've got a lot of coloured friends. And they're decent people. But the Spades have got their own culture and the Pakistanis have got theirs. It's thousands of years old. But where's our culture? Where's the British culture? You wear the flag and everybody slags you off for being a Nazi. But it's got nothing to do with being a Nazi as far as I'm concerned. What's wrong with being patriotic?

   Mickey, London skinhead, 1973[2]

WE SHALL FIGHT ON THE BEACHES

'What are we for? Nothing really. We are just a group of blokes. We're not *for* anything', one skinhead told an interviewer in the early 1970s. Asked what he was against, however, and an answer came: 'Long hair, pop, hippie sit-ins and the long-haired cult of non-violence.'[3]

   The first skins were teenage Mods, dissaffected with the Dandy Mod style linked to Swinging London, psychedelia and later glam rock, all of which they saw as effete deviancy from traditional working-class culture. Skinheads particularly disliked middle-class hippies, whom they regarded as hypocrites for apparently rejecting work and family life. 'You notice that a lot of rich people turns 'ippie', said one east London gang member. 'They 'ave been spoilt. It's just to be the opposite of their parents, that's all it is. Their mum's got money and . . . they say "give your money away and all that." They don't want the responsibility of life.'⁴ The movement began in the late 1960s around the docklands of south and east London from where it spread throughout urban Britain during the next decade. As with all youth cultures, the precise number of its members is not known, although in 1972 *The Times* estimated its following 'in the big cities' to be in the 'hundreds of thousands'.⁵

A hard splinter of Mod was first noticed during the Mod/rocker disturbances of the mid-6os, which came to symbolise the antisocial aspects of British youth culture. The reaction to the Brighton and Margate riots of 1964 and 1965 had been 'moral panic'.⁶ One local MP told Parliament that he arrived in his Brighton constituency 'to find a sense of horror and outrage by the people who live there. It was almost as if one had been to a city which, emotionally at least, had been recently hit by an earthquake and as if all the convictions and values of life had been completely flouted. This was deeply felt.'⁷ It was not just the sight of family picnics being destroyed by stone-throwing teenagers that so shocked the nation. The fact that the fighting took place on the very beaches that Winston Churchill had promised to defend against Nazi invasion in his legendary 'We shall never surrender' speech made the events more troubling than if they had taken place, like most gang fights, in Britain's inner cities. As one newspaper put it, the external foe of 1940 had been replaced by internal enemies 'who bring about disintegration of a nation's character'.⁸

In reality, the events were not riots but skirmishes similar to those fought a few years earlier by followers of trad and modern jazz at the Beaulieu festival. Rockers were outnumbered by Mods, for whom it was more of a rally, organised initially by word of mouth for a bit of fun; most were not involved in the fighting and the few that did take part just baited the police rather than chasing quiffs and leather jackets across the shingle. For most Mods present, this was a seaside holiday with a tribal twist when they could let their hair down after a routine week in town.

The BBC sent a *Panorama* team to interview participants in 1964. They discovered conventionally bored working-class adolescents with little ambition, for whom Mod was an excuse for dancing, fighting and having sex, at best a mere prelude to conventional adult life:

INTERVIEWER: What do you do with your time, apart from dancing and going up the West End? Are you interested in anything else?

MOD 1:   No. All I think of is the West End, dance halls and girls.

INTERVIEWER: Are you interested in reading or politics?

MOD 4:   You couldn't see me looking at a book, I read the *Beano* though!

INTERVIEWER: Is there any age where you'll stop fighting and chasing around?

MOD 1:   Yeah, when I get married, I suppose. Settle down and then I'll stop. I'll stop being a Mod, stop being every-thing, just lead a clean life.

INTERVIEWER: Do you think it'll be difficult to lead this 'clean life', as you describe it?

MOD 1:   No, I don't think it'll be difficult once you get married, I don't think. Cause you've got no time to do nothing.[9]

Some observers tried to put the events into perspective. The *Guardian* took its readers back to early modern Europe: 'To outsiders their motives must seem as inexplicable and absurd as the motives of the Montagues and Capulets whose fifteenth-century feud obsessed Verona.' The solution was not for a Mod Juliet to marry a rocker Romeo but the same measures that the Left called for nearly half a century later in response to the English youth riots of 2011. On the one hand there must be discipline: 'Whatever the sociological origins of yesterday's scenes of violence at Brighton and Margate . . . Mrs Lily T. Stott, manageress of the Margate station buffet, has a right not to be thrown to the ground and dragged round the premises by Mods.' On the other hand, those young people who joined gangs had to be given 'a real and useful community to which they can belong', with better homes and schools. For 'if they feel left out, if they feel nothing is fun, they will need to gang together . . . and make life ugly for us all.'[10]

Psychiatrists and social scientists explained that today's youth had more leisure time in which to be bored and that despite their relative affluence, most teenagers could not yet afford to live on their own. 'Away from home's dreariness, in his bright Mod clothes, the boy finds a gayer life at places like Margate', explained the *Sunday Mirror* in the argot of a travel brochure.[11] Experts dismissed the idea that juvenile delinquency necessarily sprang from poverty and broken homes. Most of those arrested lived with both parents and were in employment, although the subtle class differences between Mods and rockers were noticed, with none of the latter holding skilled jobs.[12]

Most of the media and much of the public backed the Margate magistrate, George Simpson, a family doctor in the town for over twenty years, whose florid speeches during sentencing in rowdy, packed courtrooms helped briefly to establish him as a moral figurehead – 'like Batman saving Gotham city', according to a study of the events.[13] Addressing the first of forty-four young men to appear before him charged with threatening behaviour, Simpson declared:

It is not likely that the air of this town has ever been polluted by the hordes of hooligans, male and female, such as we have seen this weekend and of whom you are an example. These long-haired, mentally unstable, petty little hoodlums, these sawdust Caesars who can only find courage like rats, in hunting in packs, came to Margate with the avowed intent of interfering with the life and property of its inhabitants . . . It will, perhaps, discourage you and others of your kidney who are infected with this vicious virus, that you will go to prison for three months.[14]

Little time was spent establishing the guilt of defendants and a typical exchange was that between Simpson and a 19-year-old plumber accused of carrying as a weapon a roll of newspaper filled with coins:

SIMPSON: I don't suppose you were using this newspaper to further your literary aspirations.

DEFENDANT: I'm sorry I don't understand.

SIMPSON: Never mind, you'll understand what I'm going to say now: £50.[15]

Those who were arrested, charged and appeared in court made up only a tiny minority of those who attended the rallies. For example, out of approximately 1,000 Mods and rockers at Brighton on the May Bank Holiday of 1964, only 75 were charged, less than 10 per cent of the total.[16] Yet media reporting followed a pattern that had been established before the war – and which would be repeated in the punk and rave eras of the 1970s and 90s – whereby the media exaggerated the scale of the event, inflaming fears of the threat that youth posed to the social order and leading some to believe that the outlook and actions of young Britons were symptomatic of a deeper national malaise. Despite this, politicians did not panic. And despite several parliamentary debates on the matter, the only result was an updating of the Malicious Damage Act in 1964, which increased fines for affray.

Moreover, magistrates and sociologists alike tended to forget that many Mods were critical of those who had fought on the beaches, not just because they had given the movement a bad name but also because they had betrayed one of its first principles – confounding working-class stereotypes. For the original Mods, these so-called Scooter Boys, with their baggy green parka jackets, had triggered a mutation in the genetic code of Mod more toxic than its commercial exploitation by record companies and Carnaby Street clothiers.

When he wrote an obituary for the Mod movement in the *Observer Magazine* in 1967 called 'Ready Steady Gone', Nik Cohn blamed the disturbances on commercialisation. 'Mod turned violent because it got too big', wrote Cohn, who estimated its size as a sixth of the nation's youth. 'The people who were making money out of it, the businessmen and record makers and so on, kept working up greater and greater hysteria and it got to the stage where thousands of kids were turning Mod each month without even knowing what Mod was about . . . as it happened, the bank holiday riots were the culmination of the whole Mod movement.'[17] The jazzman George Melly, who approved of the movement's early cosmopolitan outlook, described the rioters as 'a pack of weasels squeaking for blood', concluding that 'by 1964 the whole Mod spirit had turned sour'.[18]

Some original 'faces' agreed, not least because rolling around on the beach was not good for an Italian mohair suit, even with a protective parka over it. As Johnny Moke remembered:

From then on it wasn't Modernism anymore; it was something different. Attitudes changed within and without, it wasn't being modern. It was more towards being a member of a gang and that's not what we were about. We were about style, fashion and lifestyle and the next thing . . . We looked at them and they looked at us and we were completely different. They were just a tribe, they weren't setting themselves apart. We were always striving and setting ourselves apart, trying to move one step ahead or forward. You were never with the gang.[19]

Given such criticism from within the movement, it is therefore inaccurate to say that by 1964 Mod culture as a whole had simply become 'a culture of consolation' for youths 'who were brought together by their lack of interest in their jobs and by the sense that they were rejects educationally', as the historian David Fowler has argued.[20] Those who attended the south coast rallies amounted to a fraction of what was by then becoming a national youth movement with a broad influence far beyond its original working-class base. The disturbances of 1964–65 did reveal that there was no uniform Mod culture; rather, several branches of the movement developed simultaneously, sometimes in opposition to each other, emerging from different social backgrounds and different attitudes to class, education and taste.

Yet it is also true that the Mods who celebrated their seafront battles were saying something about the limitations of life in modern Britain. The battles in Brighton and Margate were not the straightforward mugging of a movement by those too stupid to understand its first principles; they were a sign that Mod was indeed a culture of consolation for some young people who had good reason to feel thwarted.

THERE'S A LOT OF HATE IN ME

'Sawdust Caesars' or 'a pack of weasels', theirs was a boredom made more dangerous by the fact that they came from a generation which had been encouraged to have aspirations that could rarely be fulfilled – because of individual inadequacies but also because Britain remained a deeply stratified society where accent and etiquette still counted more than income and acquisition, and where life chances were still largely determined by what sort of school you went to.

Even those Americans who had fallen in love with London and moved there in the 1960s could see the gap between expectation and reality widening as British youth culture failed to be more than a proxy of the American Dream. At the dawn of psychedelia in 1967, UFO club founder Joe Boyd told readers of *Melody Maker*:

I think England is more right for a youth revolution than America is. I think the effect will end up being more far-reaching because the majority of British kids are treated in much the same way as the American treats the American negro . . . Unless you are exceptionally academically minded, most kids never get an opportunity to do anything other than what their fathers are doing.

Boyd predicted that with growing expectations this situation would get worse. 'As communications get better and better,' he continued, 'the kids are going to hear more and more about the kinds of things they could do in the world – which is going to cause more and more unrest about the sitiuation the kids find themselves in.'[21]

Although the overall standard of living continued to rise in the last quarter of the twentieth century, social mobility in Britain slowed in the 1970s and 80s after the initial surge of the early post-war decades. Several reasons were put forward: some thought it was because egalitarian comprehensive education had failed bright working-class children where once grammar schools had offered them a leg-up; others argued that the expansion of university education had mainly benefited middle- and upper-class teenagers; and, more controversially, some blamed feminism for the increase in women gaining access to further education and careers, who in turn squeezed out many working-class men from positions they aspired to.[22]

Yet another explanation for the toxic forms of Mod that emerged in the 1970s can be found in the continuing variety of working-class cultures and the fact that many teenagers from poorer, semi-educated backgrounds never saw the point of aspiration in the first place. Take this comment by John Braden, an 18-year-old car mechanic from London who was interviewed shortly after the disturbances of 1964:

Yes I am a Mod and I was at Margate. I'm not ashamed of it – I wasn't the only one. I joined in a few of the fights, it was a laugh, I haven't enjoyed myself so much in a long time. It was great – the street was like a battlefield.

It was like we were taking over the country. You want to hit back at all the old geezers who try to tell us what to do . . . I felt part of something important instead of just being something they look down on because you haven't passed a GCE . . . It was great being in the newspapers, who doesn't? Blinkin' film stars, and debs delights and social climbers hire publicity men to get their names in the papers. We punch our way in cost free. Reading the linens [newspapers] afterwards is part of the kicks. Makes you feel you've done something, made people sit up and take notice. What these old squares don't realise is we've got far more guts than they ever had and don't talk to me about the bleedin' war. War is for ginks . . . There's a lot of hate in me, I accept that. Why be a hypocrite? Okay, sometimes I get worried about it but what can you do? The thing I hate most is people in authority, they're idiots, they deserve all they get. I could kill them. I suppose it's because I don't have a chance. I don't talk right and I haven't been to the right schools, I haven't had the education. That makes you sick, to see them preaching at you.[23]

Confused and riven with self-pity though it is, Braden's testimony captures the disillusionment that would engulf much of Britain's youth in the 1970s. It was based on the realisation that owning a few nice clothes might set you free from 'all that cloth-capped bullshit' but could not get you opportunity, still less satisfaction.

Disillusionment did not stop young people hankering after a moment of fame. As it became clear that the 'Youthquake' of the 1960s had shaken but not destroyed Britain's social structure, the idea of getting rich and respected without working too hard or breaking the law became more appealing. Modern celebrity culture had emerged in the early twentieth century with the arrival of mass media and an enduring need for idols in a secular age. Youth culture increased the demand for celebrity and raised expectations that with the right publicist you could become famous without sitting exams or sucking up to your boss. By their own admission, Scooter Boys like John Braden were launching a smash-and-grab raid on fame, 'punching their way in cost free', as he put it – and the punishment they received from the authorities only added to the status they acquired among their peers. One of the men that George Simpson sent to jail in Margate returned home to a hero's welcome, describing the party his friends threw for him as 'a Beatles reception'.[24]

Celebrities were sometimes marshalled to set an example to the nation's youth, including Paul McCartney who told readers of the *Melody Maker* that he disapproved of the Mods' behaviour.[25] The trouble was that the popularity of most rock stars rested on outrageous behaviour that set a different sort of example to the nation's youth. From the mid-1960s onwards, managers and record companies began to publicise, rather than cover up, the misdeeds of rock stars. Notoriety was honed in hotel rooms as they sought to combat boredom with sex and violence. The Who's Keith Moon probably trashed more rooms than anyone. Travelling with a personal, monogrammed axe in case the drugs and groupies failed to satisfy, he explained: 'If it's another bloody Holiday Inn and I get bored, I just take out me 'atchet and chop the room to bits – the bed, the chairs, the floor, the wardrobe, the tele, the toilet.'[26]

During the Who's 1968 tour of Australia with the Small Faces both groups were castigated in the Australian parliament for swearing at concerts and having long hair. Then, during his twenty-first-birthday party in Wellington Steve Marriott hurled his broken portable record player out of his hotel window at fans waiting for autographs below. 'Before you knew it', Marriott recalled, 'there were chairs, TVs, settees, everything was going over the balcony and through the windows – mirrors, everything, the whole fucking deal. There was quite an audience watching it all come down. It was ridiculous, I was hurting with laughter, it was so funny.'[27] The police were called and demanded that the band pay $780 for the damages or face arrest. In response, one of the roadies picked up an armchair and threw it over the balcony to join the rest of the room's contents. 'Fuck it', he said to the police, 'make it a grand.'[28] The sex, drugs and irreverent behaviour of these groups were reported with salacious gusto by the popular press; and managers and publicists staged stunts to shape their artists' rebellious image and maximise their profits.

But for original Mods there was a more sinister element involved in the disturbances at Margate and Brighton than the hooligan looking for celebrity status. As original 'face' Dicky Dodson put it: 'Those sort of Mods that went looking for trouble on Bank Holidays were the beginning of the skinheads really. It was the Fred Perry Brigade, not what I knew to be Mods, and of course there was nothing for them to do because all the shops and cafes were shut. The press wanted a story and almost willed them to start trouble and that time they did, but it wasn't much to do with Mods and Rockers.'[29] For Paul Stagg too, the riots were 'a prelude to football violence, skinheads, racism, you name it. They weren't Mods as we knew Mods, they were just gangs of kids dressed up. No real Mod wanted to roll about in the dirt, sand, pebbles or anything else for that matter. The clothes were still the most important factor, not fighting.'[30]

SKINHEADS ARE THE REAL DROP-OUTS

From the 1960s, young people in Britain would continue to be seen in two contradictory ways. On the one hand, they were vilified as the agents of social problems that were leading the nation to destruction – sexual permissiveness, alcohol and drug use, violence and antisocial behaviour, and a general lack of respect for authority. Like Joe Boyd, some officials argued that this stemmed from the greed and anxiety that the consumer society induced in the young: 'Dislike and suspicion of authority is becoming characteristic of our country', the Association of Headmistresses told the Home Office in 1965. Their memorandum on juvenile delinquency continued:

Some of the advertising agencies develop every possible means to seize their custom. So electronic musical instruments, tape-recorders, elaborate suits, shoes, hair styles, motor bikes, accessories and gadgets of innumerable sorts are pressed upon youngsters, and fashions are changed as rapidly as possible to ensure that goods are discarded and replaced long before they are worn out.

The comparative wealth of young people makes for anxiety and stress, both amongst those who feel they have less than the rest, and amongst those who feel they must spend with ostentatious liberality if they are to retain their status in their age group . . . Surely we are now caught up in a movement which makes people ever more acquisitive, even greedy, and not only for material possessions. They also crave distraction and sensation: small wonder that the children catch on to this too.[31]

And yet young people continued to be celebrated as avatars of modernity, driving forward progress by creating a more open and tolerant society, or at least by contributing to national repute and wealth as artists and entrepreneurs. These two paradigms – what Dick Hebdige has called 'youth-as-fun' and 'youth-as-trouble'[32] – sat uneasily together. The Queen was employed by the government to try and reconcile those views in her Christmas broadcast of 1964:

It is natural that the younger generation should lose patience with their elders, for their seeming failure to bring some order and security to the world. But things will not get any better if young people express themselves by indifference or by revulsion against what they regard as an out-of-date order of things. The world desperately needs their vigour, their determination and their service to their fellow men. The opportunities are there and the reward is the satisfaction of truly unselfish work.[33]

The trouble was that by the 1970s there was less work for young people to do, unselfish or otherwise. On the very same day, 20 November 1967, that Parliament debated whether to lower the age of majority to 18, it also debated the devaluation of the British pound. Belatedly undertaken by the Labour government under market pressure, devaluation was a sure and embarrassing sign that the post-war boom was faltering as Britain failed to keep pace with the technological innovations of its American, German and Japanese competitors. Britain's share of world exports of manufactured goods, which had stood at 25.5 per cent in 1950, had fallen to 13.9 per cent in 1965; in 1975 it had been reduced to 9.3 per cent. In contrast, German and Japanese exports rose from a total of 7.3 and 3.4 per cent respectively in 1950, to 20.3 and 13.6 per cent in 1975.[34] The accompanying contraction of the manufacturing industry reduced job opportunities for the millions who had not entered further education or trained for the new world of office work. The consequences for young working-class men were particularly severe as the 1970s wore on. Unemployment among the 20–24 age group rose from less than 25 per cent in 1971 to 35 per cent in 1978, before reaching an all-time high of 50 per cent in 1983.[35]

On the whole, Mod had been the source of renewed national pride in the 1960s, but the subculture it spawned at the end of the decade clearly belonged to the 'youth as trouble' category. Skinhead began to be widely recognisable in 1968 when it acquired a name, a distinctive style, and a semi-coherent outlook that contested the meanings of Mod. The style never entirely disappeared, influencing subsequent Mod-related youth cults such as Two Tone and Britpop; it was also successfully exported to America and Europe. While most shaved their heads almost bare, some of its followers were known as 'suedeheads', named after their less closely cropped hair. In clothing skinhead was a pared-down version of the more casual Mod look, consisting of Levi jeans (Wranglers if you were from the north or the Midlands) worn above the ankles and often held up by braces; a dark Fred Perry polo shirt or a short-sleeved red, white and blue check Brutus shirt, covered with a Harrington jacket or a Crombie overcoat in winter. The more sartorially minded also sported a porkpie hat, a regimental or club tie (usually worn with a plain white shirt), and brogues or loafers in black or oxblood.

Yet the item which the public most associated with the skinhead look was the Dr Martens boot, the most popular being the eight-eyelet 'AirWair'. It had been invented by Klaus Märtens, a doctor in the German army during the Second World War, to alleviate pain from an ankle injury acquired while skiing in the Alps. Launched in Britain in 1960, the boot's combination of sturdy design and light rubber soles initally made 'DMs' popular with factory workers and policemen. Skins began wearing them in late 1969, leading to the catch-all term 'Boot Boys'; and although punks' adoption of Doctor Martens enabled the company to shed some of that association the boot remained a symbol of skinhead style.

The item that connected skins both to earlier and to later Mods was the brightly coloured button-down Ben Sherman shirt, introduced in 1963 by Arthur Benjamin Sugarman. Coming from a Jewish family of Brighton shopkeepers, he changed his name to Sherman (after the American tank) and during a stay in the United States he married the daughter of a Californian shirt-maker, learned American marketing techniques, and on his return to Brighton set up his first 'Millions of Shirts Inc.' shop (named after a Rolling Stones song). Chris Difford, later a member of the New Wave band Squeeze, was a teenage skinhead and Charlton Athletic fan who remembered a 'shopping' trip to Carnaby Street in 1970, which by then was almost wholly given up to tourists: 'One day we marched on London to see [Charlton] play. En route we stopped off for some fun in Carnaby Street, terrifying locals and tourists as we went . . . suddenly a window went in, a shop lay open, in the riot I grabbed what I could, three Ben Sherman shirts. Back home I sneaked them into my room under my parents' noses. I had the biggest trophy of the day. Check, smart, thin, sexy . . . The girls always liked the shirt on your back [and] I still wear it today.'[36] Originally associated with the Ivy League look, the Ben Sherman shirt survived its adoption by skinheads and became 'a part of youth culture, crossing over generations', as Sherman once proudly observed.[37]

By the early 1970s, the skinhead movement had acquired a large following of people like Difford who were too young to have been Mods during the 1960s. This recruitment was partly due to skinheads' involvement in football hooliganism, a European phenomenon throughout the 1970s and 80s. Hooliganism gained the cult greater notoriety and appealed to teenagers disposed to gang violence. Yet football-related violence involved a variety of young people and not all skinheads participated in it. By the time hooligansm prompted a 'state of the nation' debate, skinheads were correctly seen as just one component of a problem that stemmed from inadequate education and lack of parental discipline. As *The Times* noted in a leader article in 1977, 'Football hooligans are threatening to become the cult crim-inals of the late 1970s, just as teddy boys, mods and rockers, dominated the late 1950s and skinheads were in the ascendant a decade later.'[38]

In style and outlook skinhead was an assertion of traditional working-class masculinity and a reaction to the flamboyant, sexually ambiguous aspect of Mod. It was also a punch in the face of the consumer society. In that context, skinhead represented a disillusion-ment among sections of working-class youth with the democratic impetus of Mod, as consumerism failed to generate the social mobility that the precepts of the cult had promised. Containing a strong element of the nihilism which later also became a feature of punk, skinhead was born out of the economic stagnation which hit young working-class school-leavers the hardest in the 1970s. But it also emerged at a time of growing racial tension when black and Asian immigrants and their British-born descendants were scapegoated for the failures of the consumer society. Mod's bastard child took the patriotism which the movement had generated in the mid-1960s and expunged its cosmo-politan elements to create a more restrictive tribal identity. Skinhead replaced the inclusive patriotic pride that most Britons felt towards pop culture as a result of its international reputation with a more exclusive nationalism.

Given the cult's origins in the Mod/rocker riots on the south coast, it was fitting that skinhead first came to the attention of the national media in 1968 following new disturbances in that area. The *Daily Telegraph* reported that 'hundreds of youths in hobnailed boots left Margate last night after a weekend of fights and scuffles with police. The boot brigade, successors to the mods and rockers, met police in several clashes on the seafront yesterday. One boy, dressed in hill-billy fashion in heavy brown boots, and jeans held up by braces, said, "The boots are just part of the uniform. They make us look hard."'[39]

The cult acquired more notoriety when gangs of skins began attacking hippies at political demos and music festivals; and the term 'skinhead' was first used in a *Daily Mirror* article of 1969 entitled 'No Love From Johnny'.[40] By the summer of that year the movement was troubling the leaders of Britain's counter-culture as well as the common enemy of both groups, the police. After violence broke out at a free concert by the Rolling Stones in London's Hyde Park on 6 July 1969, the hippie magazine *Oz* reported:

The Spikeys, or Brushcuts, are summer's new dumb terrorists in jeans, braces and thick leather boots. With sharpened aluminium combs to match they have already wrecked one major free concert. They maraud in large groups, and last month beat up a few long-hairs in Hyde Park, to the accompaniment of vastly out-numbering hippies [saying]: 'Wow, what a bad scene man.'[41]

As the music journalist Pete Fowler observed, 'Here were the Rolling Stones, the old Mod idols, being defended by Hell's Angels, the descendants of the old Rockers, and the whole scene was laughed at by the new Skinheads, who were the true descendants of the old Mods . . . The wheel had come full circle.'[42]

The radical magazine *Black Dwarf* tried to get to grips with this unpleasant turn in British youth culture, arguing that skinheads:

represent an assertion of working-class identity against the hippies and lefties – groups that they very reasonably consider middle-class and irrelevant to their life-situation . . . The skinheads are the real drop-outs, as opposed to the fancy drop-outs who take a few months off work to do very nicely living by their wits. These latter people aren't really drop-outs at all, they are people whose dissatisfaction with society had led them to take a long holiday from it. The skinhead is rejected *by* society. He is *dropped* out – because he is thick, because he can't cope with responsibility, because he's disorganised. He lands up in the lowest-paid job where he has to work long, boring, unrewarding, unrecognised hours before going back to a home that has blatantly missed out on the glitter of the affluent society.[43]

Black Dwarf was near the mark: these were young people whose lives were blighted by the continuation of institutionalised social inequality in Britain. While this was a period of massive expansion in British higher education that promised unprecedented opportunity for young people of all backgrounds, in reality it largely benefited the middle classes. The number of people in full-time higher education doubled between 1963 and 1971, and by 1972 almost a quarter of a million attended university, compared to under 86,000 in 1949. But after an initial surge in the 1960s, the percentage of working-class admissions continued to decline again and stood at 26 per cent in 1974. Admissions of teenagers whose parents had professional qualifications made up 34 per cent of the total, even though this social group was seven times smaller.[44]

Little wonder that for skins education was just another form of privilege to be mocked. When 30,000, mostly middle-class, young men and women demonstrated against America's war in South East Asia on the Vietnam Solidarity march in London in October 1968, they were were taunted by around two hundred shaven-headed supporters of Millwall Football Club. When the demonstrators chanted, 'Ho, Ho, Ho Chi Minh!' the skinheads replied with 'Students, students, ha, ha, ha!'[45]

If leftists thought that skins were 'thick' and 'disorganised', the conservative press expressed a similar view. 'When they leave school they will still be so illiterate they will get lost on the Underground', declared London's *Evening Standard*. 'Already they know they are fail-ures and they resent it. Knowing no other language, at twelve or thirteen they adopt the ways of the misfit: get convict haircuts and act violently. Their number grows each year, their behaviour becomes more extreme. They represent, without doubt, one of the major chal-lenges to our education system.'[46]

For the writers of *Black Dwarf*, it was the education system itself that was the problem, designed to produce wage slaves and to discipline and punish those that step out of line. *Black Dwarf's* solution was less penetrating than its analysis: 'Mobilise the many thousands of working-class boys and girls in this country who were deeply impressed by the May events in France, for whom the word "revolution" is an exciting word . . . these young people see the skinheads as the nasty, thick little louts they are.'[47] Yet few working-class boys and girls in Britain, skins or otherwise, had been impressed by the unrest in Paris, and 'revolution' was mostly bandied around at demos and dinner parties. Moreover, for the Mods of the early 1960s it was the material culture of France – its fashion and food – which had been central to their aspirational identity; and as they got older, they continued to shop in search of a cosmopolitan 'lifestyle'. For skins, on the other hand, neither education, revolution nor shopping was a way forward.

IT'S A COMMUNITY, A GANG, ISN'T IT?

Class, rather than race, was the obsession of early skins. Indeed, from the late 1960s until the mid-1970s, the cult was more heavily influenced by West Indian culture than any other British youth movement. The shaved head, ankle-length trousers and Crombie overcoat were adopted from the Jamaican 'Rude Boy' style, and the music skins preferred was ska and rocksteady, a precursor of reggae which was at its peak from 1966 to 1968. The *Sunday Times* noted that they borrowed from 'Negroes, whom they call Calebs or Rudies and whom they leave pretty much alone'[48] – a dialogue that was recaptured in Shane Meadows' film *This Is England* (2006).

Many original skinheads came from south-east London where there was a large West Indian population; the journalist Garry Bushell remembers 'going down Lewisham market where you'd pick up the latest Ska as it came in'.[49] They developed their own dance to that music, the Skinhead Stomp. Another remembers: 'You'd go three steps one way and three steps the other and two forward and one back and kick your leg behind you. Everyone seemed to dance the same way. It wouldn't take you two minutes to pull a bird, you know. The birds would all be going like that up and down the floor and you'd just stand in front of them follow them and that's it – you'd clocked it with a bird you know.'[50] (In 1970, the Jamaican artist Symarip cashed in on the craze with the anthemic single 'Skinhead Moonstomp'.) Don Letts, who went on to participate in both the punk and reggae scenes, recalled that when he was 14 in 1970, 'my white mates were skinheads (pre-right-wing version) while we were rude boys (an Anglicised version of the Jamaican real deal) and we met in the local youth clubs, united by these tunes.'[51] And Gary Kingham, an original skin, remembered: 'The whole scene was highly influenced by black culture, the haircut, the length of our trousers, the walk, the dances, some of the talk and of course the music. Much of it was copied from the Rude Boy style. Black and white generally got on well together, inter-mingled and if there was trouble, it would be about women.'[52]

One of the reasons why West Indian culture appealed to skinheads was a shared sense of being marginalised in British society. Skinheads' strong gang culture and tribal identity was an attempt to recover a cohesive working-class community that was being fragmented by the brutal post-war redevelopment of Britain's cities and by the softer changes wrought by affluence, which meant that skilled workers eschewed tower blocks for the suburbs. 'It's a community, a gang, isn't it?' one skin explained. 'It's only another word for community, kids, thugs, whatever.'[53] Hence skin gangs had a sharp sense of terri-tory: they named themselves after the patches they violently defended, using graffiti to mark these out.

In *The Paint House*, a 1972 Penguin collection of interviews with east London skinheads, one of the themes that emerged was their indifference to the consumer society and a detestation of socially mobile members of their own communities as 'traitors'. 'It's not actually middle class, it's people thinking they're middle class', said one of those interviewed. 'Well, they're just a lot of people that think they're better, that's all they are. But they've taken on middle-class attitudes.' This was 'keeping up with the Joneses', 'cause the people next door got a colour television 'n' they 'ave only a black and white one, they go out and get a colour one.' Another gang member agreed: 'The middle class are arse-'ole crawlers . . . they're so insecure, they are neither one thing or another and they never get to be. They're just in a vacuum, a void, a space.'[54]

To some extent their chosen enemies were arbitrary. As one skin-head admitted, 'If the blacks and Pakis weren't 'ere we would fight amongst ourselves . . . when I was younger like, I was a mod and we used to go and fight the grease and 'ippies, wouldn't we? There's always got to be someone who is the scapegoat.'[55] Reviewing *The Paint House* in *The Times*, Stephen Jessel wrote that 'pity is aroused by the emptiness and circumspection of these lives, punctuated and motivated by the welcome and sought after violence of the football terraces and the beating up of Pakistanis, homosexuals, hippies and other apparent undesirables in accordance with their interpretation of the Puritan ethic . . . What terrifies is the mindless ignorance and casual malice of it all.' For Jessel, the interviews revealed 'the colossal difficulties that face teachers and schools in trying to graft agreed social values onto a hardy and resistant stock.'[56]

The skins' anti-authority outlook and their attempt to recover a traditional working-class culture came together in a passion for foot-ball. This was the first British youth cult where sport was as much of a focal point as music. Football had been a cornerstone of British working-class culture since the late nineteenth century, a collective expression of social solidarity and local identity. For skins it represented a link with that world but also an exciting escape from the constraints of parental and police authority. One of Arsenal's 'North Bank' fans recalled his experience in the stadium:

To say it was electrifying would be underestimating it. I mean you can talk about taking speed and smoking pot, but the actual buzz of being there and the noise generating round you and your team comes out and you scream . . . your hair stands up on end. It's like that film *Zulu*. The thin red line and these thousands of black men all steaming down on them. I should imagine that could make you feel something like it, that battle, that chant.[57]

Skinhead never succumbed to commercial or political incorpora-tion to the extent that most youth cultures did. Its association with football hooliganism and Far Right politics in the 1970s made it anathema not only to politicians but also to those in business and the media for whom the conventional teen pop of the Bay City Rollers and even the more challenging world of glam rock offered better investment opportunities. Some parents of skinheads initially liked the style because it was clean-cut, and they often shared their children's views of class and race (having transmitted them in the first place). However, the working-class communities that skins claimed to represent largely rejected them, appalled by the violence and antisocial behaviour. Some skins tried to square the circle by claiming the violence was just a bit of weekend fun and that for the rest of the time they were good boys:

All these things what we was to the older people – hooligans, louts, tearaways – you know, it's not true. I mean I like to think I'm a likeable person as such . . . Even then I was polite and never disrespectful to elderly people. I had neighbours who'd say 'Oh, he's a lovely boy, helped me home with my shopping yesterday' and all that. I mean, just because I done things on a Saturday afternoon on the terraces and Friday night at the club, it doesn't make me a bad person.[58]

However, the culture of football was changing. Annual attendance at Football League matches fell by over 36 per cent between 1971 and 1987, from 28.7 million to 18.2 million, largely as a result of hooliganism. More people chose to watch the game from the comfort and safety of their homes as TV coverage improved. The link between local communities and football clubs was further weakened by the fact that more affluent families chose to drive to large successful clubs rather than support the local team facing relegation. And as money began to flood into the game it became as corporatised as other entertainments, with football players earning money and living lifestyles comparable to those of the pop stars and fashion designers they now socialised with. Like so much of the traditional working-class culture that skins were trying to revive, football had come to reflect what they were rebelling against: a consumerist celebrity world that eschewed the values of the past.

MODERNITY'S MISERY FACTORY

Skinhead shared with other members of the Mod family a sharply urban identity, which set them apart from the substantial body of young Britons who embraced movements such as folk and progressive rock in the 1960s and 70s, both of which expressed a desire to return to a simpler Arcadian past inhabited by artisans, warriors and maidens, or a fantasy world of wizards and dragons, though its fans were forced to make a living in the real world alongside urban Mods. The musical pomposity of prog rock concept albums like Yes's *Tales from Topographic Oceans* (1973) invited the mockery of Mods and later became a foil for punks. To be fair, both the concept album format and the aping of classical music came from the innovations and pretensions of the Beatles and the Who; and the use of synthesisers by Emerson, Lake and Palmer could be as progressive as the electronic experiments of Bowie or Eno at that time. But there remained a difference between groups admired by Mods and those admired by prog rock fans, namely the pre-industrial landscape over which prog's ten-minute solos wafted like the spirit of Merlin.

Folk shared with prog rock a Celtic romanticism, which saw rural Britain as the vestige of a pre-industrial world from which comfort and inspiration could be drawn. Invigorated by Bob Dylan and connected for a time to the hippie movements in Europe and America, the folk revival that had begun in the 1950s peaked in the 70s with the advent of folk rock, epitomised by Fairport Convention and the Cambridge Folk Festival, which had been launched in 1964. Folk rock was at odds with the acoustic puritanism of earlier folk revivals; it had a commensurately wider musical influence and its more politically active fans were at the forefront of the burgeoning Green movement.

Yet the outlook of both folk and progressive rock remained overwhelmingly anti-modern. In his study of the British folk movement, Rob Young refers to Timothy Leary's dictum 'Turn on, tune in, drop out' as a call to resist 'the spectre of modernity': 'Far from being intended to mean "Get stoned and abandon all constructive activity" – the interpretation of thousands of hippy camp followers – Leary's injunction was a Pied Piper's clarion call to the young people of tomorrow to search for a meaningful spiritual path out of modernity's misery factory.'[59] This path was not just the sex, drugs and meditation of journalistic cliché but a different attitude to consumption, which rejected the mass production of new goods in favour of preservation and restoration. These preferences are summarised by the folk musician Vashti Bunyan:

Screening out modernity is exactly what we were doing. Even the food I bought, I would try to buy in plain paper packages rather than the packet – I got quite obsessive about rejecting the modern world in the end. Even bits of old horse harness that you could start to put the pieces together and get a real idea of what it had been like . . . It was before the upsurge of little antique shops – finding something like an old smoothing iron and finding out how things used to be done. Even quite late on, doing stupid things like putting an old kitchen range in the farmhouse we eventually ended up getting . . . most people would be pulling things out and putting in something modern. We took out the modern and put in an old, smoky black range. So yes, we got completely fixated on old versus new.[60]

Like every folk revival since Cecil Sharp, that of the 1970s was a predominantly middle-class affair: most working-class Britons continued to be drawn into the consumer society through both desire and neccessity. Gary Kemp, who was a suedehead child before finding a home for his Mod yearnings in the glam scene of the 1970s, recounted in his memoirs why folk made little sense to his family:

The early-seventies folk revival seemed to come from a general desire to return to the loyalties of a simple past, a reaction to the sixties op-art future and Wilson's white heat utopia that never came. And by early 1975 it definitely hadn't arrived in our street. The Kemps were still with no bathroom and one outside loo shared between three families. My parents, far from interested in middle class folk nostalgia, were desperate to get the luxury that their friends in high-rise places had, and they quite rightly craved an avocado bathroom suite, a warm, dry loo seat, and maybe even a small area outside for greenfly to gather.[61]

One of the paradoxical reasons for Mod's longevity – and its trans-mutation into other subcultures – was that the 1960s had not trans-formed working-class life as much as millions had hoped. Yet as Kemp suggested, frustration with the slow pace of change did not usually foster the kind of cynicism with which some historians have revisited the period more recently: the disappointment of not having acquired a nice bathroom did not lead either parents or children to stop wanting one – nor did they blame the media hype about Swinging London for the plumber's absence.

In short, the 1960s continued to be seen as the bearer of a promise that could still be paid on demand. Consequently Mod, as the youth culture most associated with that decade, continued to fascinate and appeal to subsequent generations. Furthermore, disillusionment with the 1960s did not cause most teenagers to follow music and fashion that rejected modernity in the way that much of folk, progressive rock and, later, Goth did. Most continued to choose youth cultures that proclaimed modernity in some way, at the very least by locating their hopes and dreams in the city.

However, modernity that amounted to no more than urbanity was a pallid form of progress. What appealed to Mods was not just residing or working in the city; it was a particular kind of urban lifestyle: they cherished cities as the servers of technology and social diversity – fast, fun, playgrounds of pluralism. Like all the relatives of Mod, skinhead rejected the rural good life offered by hippies; but they also came to viscerally reject Mod's vision of the cosmopolitan metropolis. It was ironic, because by contesting ownership of the inner city with ethnic minorities and middle-class gentrifiers, skinhead inhabited an idealised landscape with an urban folklore just as retrograde in its own way as the rural visions that shaped the folk movement.

AS QUEER AS A CLOCKWORK ORANGE

Like all youth movements with antisocial elements, from rock 'n' roll through to hip hop, skinhead attracted not only working-class youth but also middle-class teenagers in search of excitement and the kudos of being associated with society's rejects. One of the founders of the movement was the illustrator James Ferguson:

George Melly had a go saying we were all C-stream dumbos. No. Wrong. We were everything. I went to grammar school and I was fine. Lots of others were as well. He was judging it on pure prejudice and that happened a lot. It happens because nine times out of ten it's written about by middle class people who have never been through this kind of thing. For me it felt great. You're amongst your own kind with the music and the clothes. I loved it.

Nor did he embrace the ideas of the Far Right when the cult became more toxic. 'When I read these things about fascism,' wrote Ferguson, 'they've stolen something that meant so much to me.'[62] A number of working-class followers had social aspirations and realised them professionally. Stuart Cosgrove, a Northern Soul-loving Scottish suedehead, went to Reading University, wrote for *Black Echoes* magazine and then became an editor at the *New Musical Express*, where he joined a cadre of working-class writers that included committed Mods like Nick Logan and Paolo Hewitt as well as skin-turned-punk Tony Parsons.

Although skinhead did not find its way into mainstream British culture through design and consumption, it did reach a wider audience through cinema and pulp fiction. Stanley Kubrick's 1971 film adaptation of Anthony Burgess's 1962 dystopian novel *A Clockwork Orange* in particular referenced the cult and had a direct impact on it. Burgess explained that the title was taken from the cockney expression 'as queer as a clockwork orange'. The book tells the story of a teenage gang, the Droogs, who speak a surreal Cockney-Slavic patois and who rape and kill for pleasure. The origins of the plot lie in the trauma of Burgess's pregnant wife Lynne, after she had been beaten up in London by four American soldiers, and in a trip to Leningrad in 1961, where the writer encountered the 'Stilyagi' or 'Style Boys', a violent Russian youth cult which showed him that the phenomenon was not confined to capitalist societies.

The Droogs' savagery is accompanied in the film by the music of Beethoven, Elgar and a soundtrack by the American composer Walter (now Wendy) Carlos, pioneer of the Moog synthesiser and a major influence on Roxy Music's Brian Eno.[63] The gang are dressed in skinhead style, but with added bowler hats. As Tony Parsons remembered: 'It was all there . . . you could see the ghost of the Skins in the uniform of the Droogs – the thin braces, the white strides, the rakish use of hats, the combat boots as combined fashion accessory and blunt instrument. Someone had been paying attention and we were flattered beyond belief.'[64]

Some skinhead gangs even adopted the bowler hat for a time. However, the murder of a pensioner by one such gang in the north of England, similar to a murder depicted in the film, together with other 'copycat' killings, led to a ferocious debate about the influence of the media on juvenile delinquency. Unimpressed by the fact that it had been nominated for four Oscars, the British Home Secretary, Reginald Maudling, demanded to know why the censors had not made cuts. Burgess, who had co-written the screenplay with Kubrick, was hounded by the press and allowed himself to be 'paraded on one dismal talk show after another' to justify his novel. 'If a couple of nuns were raped in Berwick-on-Tweed,' he recalled, 'I would always get a telephone call . . . it was clear that I would never be awarded the OBE.'[65] As a result, the film was withdrawn in 1973 and not available again until 2000.

Almost as influential in spreading word of skinhead were the best-selling 'youthsploitation' novels by Richard Allen. Allen's books overtly celebrated the cult, offering their young readers vindication if they were hardcore skins and vicarious thrills if they were not. Here the hero of the novels explains his 'natural' urges:

Basically, Joe Hawkins had a feeling for violence. Regardless of what the do gooders and the sociologists and psychiatrists claimed some people had an instinctive bent for creating havoc and resorting to jungle savagery. Joe was one of these. Being part of a club which tried to foster a live-and-let-live fellowship did not weaken his desire to unleash brutal assaults on innocent folk. The club was a front to cover his deep, dark nature. A requirement for his suedehead cultism.[66]

As Stewart Home observes in his study of the books, 'Allen is obsessed with reinforcing both sexual and racial stereotypes. While his male characters are simply sadistic, his female characters often have a maso-chistic aspect in their personal make-up.'[67]

Condemning skins in 1969, *Black Dwarf* had commented that there was 'one compensation: only the masculine variety has been spotted, so at least they won't breed'.[68] In fact there were many female skins, known as 'crombies', who attached themselves to male gangs and adopted the boys' highly masculine look, the girls' main distinguishing feature being the fringe they wore at the front of their cropped heads. As one female skin remembered, 'you'd be wearing staprest trousers, Levi jeans, Ben Sherman shirts, braces – very much like the boys really, and at times it was difficult to say whether you were male or female'.[69] This access to masculine style appealed to some middle-class women too, as the following testimony from 1986 confirms:

My first thing was a very half-hearted, ill-informed attempt to try and become a skinhead. I didn't know there was anything else to be. You wore a checked shirt and sort of broguey shoes, and there were also Crombie coats . . . In middle class, suburban Merseyside we were all trying to be skinheads, which was really pathetic. We just weren't that hard, you know. And we used to go around in little Harrington jackets and boy's brogue shoes and have our hair cut really short except for those wisps at the side and the back. But I was very ill during the winter because I would insist on going round with this stupid jacket on.[70]

The style was more ambiguous than critics often supposed. The unisex nature of female skins' style was part of a wider trend towards androgyny in British youth culture during the 1970s and 80s. In fact, female skinhead attire was in counterpoint to the male experiments of glam rock and New Romanticism,[71] which is why feminist punks adopted aspects of their look, especially the DM boot. Moreover, in the 1970s proto-feminist sentiments were latent among female skins, for whom the style was a liberation from the physically restricting and time-consuming 'dolly bird' look – a sense of liberation similar to that which had drawn young women to the crisply cut attire of Mod clothing in the 1960s. As one female skin at the time said: 'I like the clothes 'cause you don't have to dress up, you don't have to put on stilettos and hobble round, you're casual and do what you wanna do.'[72]

Skinhead offered liberating ambiguities for men too. In *A Clockwork Orange*, the gang leader Alex wears mascara and a false eyelash below one eye, a look created for the film by make-up artist Barbara Daly, who not only went on to work with punk and New Romantic fashion designers but did the make-up for Lady Diana at her wedding in 1981. More importantly, there is a striking element of homoeroticism in skinhead culture of the 1970s and 80s with the gangs' focus on male bonding, not to mention the plethora of muscles and crotches on show in many of the pictures taken at the time.

Not surprisingly perhaps, there is little personal testimony about the full depth of skins' relationships. Yet there is no doubt that their macho style and attitude appealed to a homosexual constituency among all classes during the 1980s and 90s. Indeed, as it faded from the football terraces the skinhead style was perpetuated by gay culture, where it provided an escape from perceived effeminacy and reflected a romantic adoration of the muscular, athletic male body that goes back to the Ancient Greeks. Such anxieties and fantasies of homosexual masculinity led to the style being exported from Britain around the world. The adoption of the look could sometimes cause confusion on the streets. Following a British National Party election victory in London's East End in 1993, Michael Dover and his boyfriend recalled that 'quite often in the Bethnal Green area we'd have young schoolboy skin-heads coming up to us and saying, "Allright mate?", cause they actually assumed that if you have short hair you're a BNP supporter. Which is why I wear my pink triangle and rainbow flag.'[73]

Yet despite these important ambiguities, skinhead's global reach was largely effected through neo-Nazi politics. Both in Britain and abroad, it remained a predominantly working-class, heterosexual cult, associated with a violent rejection of the creative fusions that had sired British youth culture in the 1960s.

WHAT'S WRONG WITH BEING PATRIOTIC?

According to Roddy Moreno, founder of Skinheads Against Racial Prejudice (SHARP), 'No true skinheads were racist. Without the Jamaican culture skinheads would not exist. It is their culture mixed with British working class culture that made skinhead what it is.'[74] Yet it really is a myth that the subculture had a benign early phase that was later sullied by right-wing ideas. From the start, the cult contained strong racist elements that reinforced its assertion of white working-class identity and its rejection of the rest of British youth culture. *Black Dwarf*'s 1969 headline, 'SKINHEADS – A YOUTH GROUP FOR THE NATIONAL FRONT?', was not just leftist paranoia.

The Millwall skins in Grosvenor Square in 1968 who shouted 'Students, students, ha, ha ha!' had also taunted protesters with chants of 'Enoch! Enoch!' In his notorious 'Rivers of Blood' speech earlier that year, Enoch Powell had predicted that Britain's civil rights legislation, passed in 1965 and 1968, would be the means by which 'in a few years' time the black man will have the whip hand over the white man'. To avert race war he called for the compulsory repatriation of all non-white Britons, including those who had been born in the country and who, Powell claimed, could never be British.

Powell touched a national nerve and spoke to disaffected youths who believed that young British-born blacks were part of the reason that white working-class culture was decaying. Interviewed in the mid-1970s, a 17-year-old pipe fitter sporting a White Power badge complained that 'A Rasta can wear a Black is Beautiful badge and they all sit up and start clapping. I wear a White is Beautiful badge and get run in for being a racist.'[75] The National Front, Britain's main neo-Nazi party, formed in 1967, played on those anxieties and found tens of thousands of willing supporters among the skinhead fraternity, recruiting successfully at football grounds, a tactic that helped the NF to become Britain's fourth biggest political party by 1977. As Murray Healy has concluded, skins' conservatism 'and their status in the British social memory as the most violent subculture did seem to render skinheads predisposed to right-wing affiliation'.[76]

In the mid-70s there was still a black presence in football gangs, for whom the battles were territorial; the most famous was Cas Pennant, leader of the notorious 'Inter City Firm' who followed West Ham, the premier club of London's East End. As one white skin remembered: 'Yes we did have trouble with the blacks. I mean, there was a club that started up at Mile End that was called "The A Train" and yeah, sure, whenever we chose to go up there, we'd have a battle with the blacks. But we had black guys on our side as well, a few coloured guys who'd stand behind you and fight for you as a brother, no problem.'[77]

The main victims of skinhead gangs were not Afro-Caribbean but Asian. This was partly because people from the former colonies in the Indian subcontinent were seen as physically weaker and more servile than blacks and therefore easier to bully. Des, a garage mechanic from Birmingham, told a reporter in 1972:

I'll tell you why I hate the bloody Pakis. I'll tell you a story. A week or so ago I was walking down the streets with a couple of mates, I wanted a light for my fag, so I walk up to this Paki git and ask him, 'You got a light, mate?' And what do you think the fucker did? I'll tell you. He walks – no, runs – into this shop and buys me a box of matches! Now I ask you! What the fuck could I do with a bleeder like that but hit him? And another thing, have you ever been in their restaurants? Have you seen the way they *grovel* around you, the way they're always trying to please you? I hate them, that's all.[78]

Greater antipathy towards Asian Britons also stemmed from the fact that even among racist skins there was a residual respect for black style. As one London gang explained in a TV interview:

'Sometimes we hit 'em, sometimes we just leave 'em. Pakis ain't so much your enemy; they're just like a pastime.'
'We jump 'em; it's not their colour, you know, 'cos the Jamaicans are alright.'
'Yeah, we got a lotta Jamaican mates; I mean, they don't like Pakistanis either.'[79]

These views highlighted uncomfortable facts about youth culture. Even if music and fashion had fostered some cultural dialogue – though not necessarily unity – between white and black youth, Asians and other minorities were largely regarded as irrelevant. As Rupa Huq has written: 'Asians have simply never assumed a principal place in *Top of the Pops* / MTV youth culture mythology, instead they have been considered perennially unhip.'[80]

The reason for this lies in stereotypes that became embedded in British society after large numbers of Asians arrived in the United Kingdom in the 1960s and 70s. Although teenagers of all ethnicities continued to value family life, Asian teens (especially those of Muslim origin) had their private and public lives more strictly policed by the extended family. The greater premium placed on education by Asian Britons, and their commensurately better performance in school, added to a view of Asians as unwilling, or at best unable, to have fun and rebel. As Rehan Hyder has concluded:

Young Asians have . . . been perceived as essentially conservative figures, bound by the strict conventions of community and more likely to be doing schoolwork or toiling in the local corner shop than playing or enjoying pop music. This is in marked contrast to the fetishization of black, Afro-Caribbean youth, who have been considered perennially cool and hip by white mainstream society – although this is often accompanied by attendant stereotypes of physicality and criminality.[81]

There had been an Asian presence in British music, fashion and design in the 1960s but it was the mystical, erotic India of the sitar, the Kama Sutra and the Bhagavadgita that attracted the likes of George Harrison and Jimi Hendrix. This perception – what Hyder calls 'retro-Orientalism' – was rejected by some artists, notably Steve Marriott who described it as 'little more than a tawdry fad'.[82] But Marriott's opinion didn't alter the prevailing view of young British Asians as coming empty-handed to a party thrown by whites and blacks.

Even the partial, tentative alliance that white working-class Mods had formed with West Indians ruptured in the mid-1970s when skinhead became more overtly racist. As dance-happy ska and rocksteady morphed into the politically radical (and religious) reggae, it formed the basis of a more pronounced black British consciousness which challenged the contradictions of a society that could simultaneously consume black music and fashion while continuing to demonise black people. Both Jamaican musicians, such as Bob Marley, and homegrown bands like Birmingham's Steel Pulse confronted the forces of oppression in black people's lives, promising deliverance from Babylonian captivity and a return to a black Zion in Africa.

The music and message of reggae seemed a long way from the skinheads' favourite song, Desmond Dekker's 'Israelites', which had topped the charts in 1969. Sociologist Dick Hebdige described the consequences:

When he found himself unable to follow the thick dialect and densely packed Biblical allusions, which mark Reggae, [the skinhead] must have felt himself even more hopelessly alienated. Excluded even from the ranks of the excluded, he was left out in the cold, condemned to spend his life in Babylon because the concept of Zion just didn't make sense . . . For the rude boys had come of age and the skins were sentenced to perpetual adolescence.[83]

The message of peace and love to all people that reggae propagated alongside its call for black militancy further alienated skins from the culture they had once admired. As Hebdige concluded, 'The wheel had come full circle and the skinhead, who had sought some refuge from the posturing beatitudes of the pot-smoking hippie in the coterie of the black delinquent young, was confronted with what appeared to be the very attitudes which had originally dictated his withdrawal.'[84]

Whereas Mod's other progeny, Northern Soul and glam, offered escape from a troubled world, skinhead had aggressively confronted it, only to find that fewer and fewer people loved 'Johnny' as a result. Feeling more marginalised than ever, a new generation of skinheads developed a form of thrash punk called Oi! in the late 1970s and early 80s, which rejected both black music and the arty introspection that characterised some of the post-punk New Wave. According to Steve Kent, guitarist of the Business, they were against 'trendy university people using long words, trying to be artistic, losing touch'.[85] Writing in the magazine *Sounds* in 1980, music journalist Garry Bushell named the genre after a cockney expression meaning 'hey', the trademark of the band Cockney Rejects, whose singer Stinky Turner introduced their sets with it. 'Oi! was real punk,' said Bushell. 'Punk had always made a big thing about being from the tower blocks and the working classes having a say. In reality it was all art school kids, posh kids from Bromley like Billy Idol. The real punk . . . the Oi! bands, were just working class kids.'[86]

Some Oi! bands like the 4 Skins publicly rejected Far Right politics but the racist ghost at the feast of skinhead soon showed its face. In the summer of 1981, a compilation album put together by Bushell was released under the title *Strength Through Oi!*. Denials that the title was derived from the Nazi slogan 'Strength through Joy' were met with scepticism when it was revealed that the aggressively posturing skinhead who graced the cover was Nicky Crane, a Far Right activist serving a four-year prison sentence for racist violence.[87] The movement's new heroes were the group Skrewdriver, formed in 1976 by Ian Donaldson after he saw the Sex Pistols play. Donaldson joined the National Front and by 1982 the band were openly espousing Far Right politics, with their leader stating, 'I don't go to church or anything. I think my religion is my race.'[88] With album titles such as *Hail the New Dawn* (1984) and *Blood and Honour* (1985), they influenced neo-Nazi groups in America and Germany, but by the time *White Rider* was released in 1987, skinhead had ceased to be a movement with any mass appeal to British youth.

Some have mourned the passing of skinhead. The anthropologist Ted Polhemus had arrived in Britain from America in 1969 in 'the belief that Britain was a perfect place for a Hippy – a Yellow Submarine sort of place from which the Blue Meanies had been driven away long ago.'[89] He had an unnerving encounter with skins on his arrival, but later came round to a different view:

This fragmented, atomised, individualised culture we now inhabit will never again in the foreseeable future generate such collectivism of the spirit . . . I've come to appreciate the essential honesty of the skin's approach to life

... There wasn't any pretence. Whatever faults they may have had it must be said that they were not con artists pretending to be hip ... A little group of working-class kids tried to make sense of a crazy world and for a moment – perhaps – succeeded in rekindling a little pride in themselves and their working-class heritage.[90]

Skins as guardians of a 'collectivism of the spirit'? It's an interesting idea but a misleading one. Skinhead only seemed authentic if you believed that it accurately resembled the traditional lifestyle it was trying to save. But white working-class culture could not be stripped down to an essential steel frame, like a stolen Ford Cortina in a dodgy garage, resprayed and rolled out as if the world hadn't changed. Even in its core constituency among the poorest and most alienated youths in Britain, by the mid-1980s few wanted to return to what was always a parody of paradise lost.

Aside from the musical interface with Oi!, many punks admired the confrontational, nihilistic aspects of skinhead, its hippie-baiting class-consciousness and violent anti-authoritarianism. The group Sham 69, from Hersham in Surrey, controversially incorporated the movement's fashion style and its crude, male working-class spirit into songs like 'Hurry up Harry', which celebrated a lads' night out at the pub. This gained them a large skinhead following and they were forced to abandon live performances in 1978 after the National Front broke up one of their concerts (although this did not stop Tony Blair using their biggest hit 'If the Kids Are United' to mark his entrance at the 2005 Labour Party conference).

The Sex Pistols' John Lydon claimed Droog leader Alex as one of his role models. 'During the course of managing the Sex Pistols, I did ask Stanley Kubrick to direct a movie about the band,' reported Malcolm McLaren, 'but he told me he had already made that movie and it was called *A Clockwork Orange.*'[91] However, as punk emerged in the clubs of New York and London in the mid-1970s, its links with left-wing politics, reggae and an extrovert fashion aesthetic taken from glam set it against what skinhead had come to stand for. Punk reaffirmed some of the key principles on which British youth culture had been founded by Mod in the 1960s. In doing so it gave birth to new members of the Mod family in the 1980s and 90s who in style and outlook more closely resembled their parent culture.

7

TEARS OF RAGE ROLL DOWN YOUR FACE
Mod in the Punk Era

This is a bloke, with a brain on his shoulders, who is actually saying something he *sincerely* believes is happening in the world, saying it with real venom and real passion. It touches you, and it scares you – it makes you feel uncomfortable. It's like somebody saying, 'The Germans are coming! And there's no way we're gonna stop 'em!'
    Pete Townshend on Johnny Rotten, 1977[1]

No more Queen Elizabeth. And no more Rolling Stones or Beatles. But John Lennon rules, ok?
    Joe Strummer, Leeds University, 1977

IT'S MODERNISM MADE FLESH AND CLOTH

'There was this terrible trough in the mid-70s', remembers Billy Bragg. 'England didn't qualify for the 1974 World Cup, Miss Hall our English teacher left school, and the Faces split.' A teenage, suedehead office junior from Barking, Essex, Bragg found some solace in the remnants of Mod – in his view, 'that most enduring of all British youth cults' – by going to see a Small Faces reunion tour in March 1977.[2] A month later, he launched himself into life as a singer-songwriter after seeing the Jam play in London. 'I was suspicious of Punk', Bragg recalled in his memoir *The Progressive Patriot*, thinking it was 'just another art school prank',[3] but that night in the metropolis he was struck by 'English electric lightning'.[4]

Led by fellow satellite town teenager Paul Weller, the Jam epitomised Mod's influence on punk even as the latter was proclaiming
a revolution. Weller was the first musical figurehead with mass appeal
since Pete Townshend to overtly proclaim his allegiance to Mod. The
Jam sang fast, angry and mournful songs in English accents about
growing up, getting laid and falling in love in class-divided Britain,
while wearing sharp suits, sporting Steve Marriott haircuts and bearing
Union Jacks on their clothes and kit. Mod thereby helped to anglicise
punk rock, which had arrived from America, making it more recognisable, more palatable and ultimately more meaningful to young Britons
with little knowledge of, or interest in, the intellectual radicals who
fostered it from 1972 to 1976.

Yet the cosmopolitanism of Mod helped to ensure that the angli-
cisation of punk didn't make it parochial. Indeed, the long-term global
influence of punk is partly due to the fact that the British version is
more internationally recognisable than its American parent. Even
stripped of its political meanings, punk music and fashion owed its
global reach to London's reputation as a style capital, a status it first
commanded in the 1960s and which was based around the idea of
'street style', created and sold by entrepreneurial youth rather than
by celebrity haute couture.

Punk rock had begun in the bohemian milieu of New York in the
early 1970s as a reaction to the corporate exploitation of youth, the
artistic pretensions of prog rock, the utopianism of the hippie movement and the latent misogyny pervading all youth cultures. American
punks like the Ramones and Richard Hell stripped rock 'n' roll back
to musical and sartorial basics by replacing ten-minute solos with short
howls against authority and alienation, and by simplifying the uniform
of rebellion with a return to the T-shirt, jeans and leather jackets that
had shocked Middle America in the 1950s.

Punk acquired a more European style and sensibility as it crossed
the Atlantic. As a populist form of modernism, 1960s British pop
culture had visibly displayed the subversive influence of Europe on
the taste of post-war British youth; as Billy Bragg puts it, 'It's
modernism, made flesh and cloth.'⁵ Streams of Continental modernism
now washed punk's upper reaches, and they in turn shaped British
art and design over the next decades. Dada, Surrealism and, most of
all, the spectacle of French Situationism, all influenced punk to some

degree, as Jon Savage and Greil Marcus have shown in their respective studies of the movement, *England's Dreaming* and *Lipstick Traces*. 'The Sex Pistols were a commercial proposition and a cultural conspiracy launched to change the music business and make money off the change,' wrote Marcus, 'but Johnny Rotten sang to change the world.'[6]

Just as important as its artistic influences and the urge for change was the fact that British punk shared Mod's obsession with class; and it was that which appealed to young people who knew nothing of Marcel Janco or Guy Debord. Greil Marcus believes that it was 'awareness and acknowledgment of class on both personal and official levels' that distinguished post-war British youth culture from its US counterpart. Mod meant little to Marcus and other Americans after its 1960s heyday: 'I was a huge Who fan from the moment I heard "My Generation"', he said. 'I located the UK version of their first album – and found truth, but I wasn't really interested in what they might be saying to or about Mod life, and never saw *Quadrophenia*.'[7]

Mod gave punk a ready-made link between two of its key ingredients – class politics and Continental sensibility – and helped to popularise punk by giving it a more British message, look and sound. Punk repaid the favour by helping to energise Mod after a decade during which it had fragmented into different subcultures. Over the next five years, Mod took several forms: it was an acknowledged influence on punk music and fashion during the cult's early, most controversial, phase from 1976 to 1979; from 1979 to 1982 it inspired a copycat Mod revival by working-class youths nostalgic for the optimism of the 1960s and disappointed with what they saw as the middle-class posturing of punk's shock troops. At the same time, a new subculture, Two Tone, emerged which fused the politics and style of punk and Mod to create the first truly multiracial youth culture on either side of the Atlantic.

'We declared war on England without meaning to,' announces John Lydon in Julien Temple's film, *The Filth and the Fury*, snorting with laughter. While the Sex Pistols were stating the obvious about the lack of opportunity in class-bound Britain, Lydon recalled, they were unprepared for the violent reaction that engulfed them.[8] Whereas Mods had used the insolence of affluence to dress and dance their way out of class constraints, punk launched an angry assault on those restrictions at a time when they seemed to be tightening their grip on people's lives. Author and music journalist Charles Shaar Murray has pointed up the differences:

Punk was Mod resurgent at a time of economic contraction, social pessimism, and a low budget. Mods were defined in their clothing and presentation as dramatizing their aspirations and the notion of expansion of horizons . . . Punk was almost a retreat from that. They were dramatizing their alienation and their poverty. Mod was a working-class movement which speedily attracted the middle class. Punk was a middle-class movement which presented itself as working class and nevertheless attracted a large middle-class following.[9]

One survey claimed that fewer punk musicians came from middle-class homes (43 per cent) than beat musicians of the 1960s (48 per cent).[10] But other evidence suggests that punk (like Mod before it) did attract a large middle-class following. At one level adolescents loved its shock value, an exemplar of that being their use of the swastika. Whereas Mods had subtly taunted the wartime generation by turning the RAF roundel into a Pop Art emblem, punks provoked with Third Reich references, yet with none of the sincere neo-Nazism that gave political meaning to the skinheads' adoption of it. At another level, middle-class youths were drawn by punk's intellectual origins in European radicalism. And somewhere in between those points of subscription was what the Members, a band from Camberley in Surrey, called 'The Sound of the Suburbs'. Their 1979 song captured a whiff of the original fuel that had ignited Anglo-American youth culture in the 1950s: boredom with suburban conformity, set against the prospect of excitement and fulfilment in the city.

'Led Zeppelin is for middle-aged students to sit and listen to in their bedrooms', Paul Weller announced in 1977. 'What relevance have the old groups today? I think the whole scene now is just a progression that goes Mods . . . Skinheads . . . Punks.'[11] The letters pages of the New Musical Express in the late 1970s were full of complaints that jet-setting rock stars with mansions and champagne parties to match had lost touch with their audience and become part of what one of its journalists, Mick Farren, called 'the turgid mainstream of traditional show business'.[12] It was largely through the NME that the Mod–Punk relationship was transmitted to a wider national audience. The human bridge between the two cultures was formed by its editor, Nick Logan, a 60s Mod who was at the magazine's helm from 1973 to 1978. At the end of 1976 Logan had fixed the *NME*'s annual readers' poll, replacing their choice of the year's most promising act (a side project of Genesis drummer Phil Collins) with the Sex Pistols, in a brazen move that showed that chart fixing was not the prerogative of the Establishment. But as well as hiring the young guns Julie Burchill and Tony Parsons, Logan also brought in a friend of Weller's, Paolo Hewitt, who would become Mod's leading chronicler over the next thirty years, alongside Stuart Cosgrove, a Northern Soul-loving, working-class Scottish suedehead.

Launched in 1952, the *NME* was at the peak of its influence in the 1970s with a readership of over 300,000, who were informed by the magazine's new breed of music journalists setting out to contextualise popular music. Inspired by America's Lester Bangs, these essayists knew their Barthes as well as their Beatles and were committed to promoting British youth culture as a commercial art form at a time when newspapers were still more interested in rock stars' sex and drugs excesses. There were tensions between Logan's Mod- and punk-aligned journalists that reflected those at large among Britain's youth, but they worked together well enough to prevent a rupture at a crucial moment in British popular culture.

In recent years, conventional historians have tended to dismiss punk, as much as radical sociologists once took it far too seriously. Brian Harrison, for example, called the Sex Pistols' anti-royalist message a 'childish publicity stunt'.[13] In another study of the period, Dominic Sandbrook framed punk as one of the ways for a minority of teenagers to annoy Middle England. Only a few 'youngsters', he claimed, were 'skinheads, football hooligans and punks' in the 1970s.[14] Aside from the numerical implausibility of this, the adolescent desire to shock was not empty of meaning. Like adults' commercial or social choices in life, teenagers picked a subculture because it expressed their feelings, however inadequately; and for many those feelings included genuine anger at the shoddy and often nasty limitations of British society. Three of the Pistols were raised in Shepherd's Bush, the same neighbourhood as the Who, and as guitarist Steve Jones said of his childhood there, 'If you weren't born into money then you might as well kiss your fucking life goodbye; you weren't gonna amount to anything.'[15]

What helped punk to become more popular in Britain than in the United States was that the worldwide recession of the 1970s hit the British economy harder and led to higher rates of inflation and youth unemployment. Punk's class commentary therefore resonated with young Britons, living as they did in a society where snobbery was more acute and social mobility less marked than in America. A *Daily Mirror* leader entitled 'Punk Future' made that link quite explicit: 'It's not much fun being young today. 104,000 school leavers have gone straight from their classrooms to an idle and purposeless life on the dole. Is it any wonder youngsters feel disillusioned and betrayed? . . . Punk rock is tailor-made for youngsters who think they only have a punk future.'[16]

WE WERE ALWAYS KIND OF MODDY

The Sex Pistols' 'declaration of war on England' occluded punk's Mod antecedents for a time. Yet the Union Jack was just as prevalent on clothes and musical instruments as it had been in the 1960s, as Jamie Reid and other artists and designers followed the Pop Artists of the Mod era in reclaiming official symbols of British nationhood. Let It Rock, the boutique that Vivienne Westwood ran close to where Quant had begun in 1955, was a laboratory for a renewed assault on national imagery. 'I am English, and I parody the English with the hope that my clothing will have international significance', Westwood declared.[17]

Parody came at a price, with T-shirts retailing at over £15 in her boutique and others like it, when they cost around £1.50 in Oxford Street at the time. Help was at hand, as the *NME* advised its readers that, unlike Mod style, punk 'gear is made from objects that cost nil or nothing', like 'safety pins, antique gym shoes, tattered Levis and all manner of refuse and castoffs'.[18] Yet Robert Elms remembers that the early punk scene echoed its Mod antecedent:

Acme Attractions was consciously a Mod shop in the King's Road in 1975–76, it had a scooter in the shop and sold born-again sixties clothes. You could go in there and buy a pair of straight-legged red trousers when everyone else was wearing flares. If you look at what happened in early punk, it got hijacked by the middle classes very quickly, but for the first nine months '76 into '77 it is Mod. It's a combination of hairdressers and art school students and a couple of unemployed kids, that's exactly the same sort of thing you would have got with Mod . . . I bought my first bondage suit in Citizen Image and it cost something like £80 in 1976, it was incredibly elitist Modernist clothing. What I think in many respects punk was, it was Carnaby Street end of Mod, it was that very dandy dressed up end of Mod . . . it's got lots of the echoes.[19]

For those without the money to spend at Vivienne Westwood's boutique or Citizen Image, the outlets that became associated with punk and post-punk styles were the second-hand clothes store and the market stall. In this respect, the equivalent of Carnaby Street in the period 1975–c.1995 was Camden Market. Formerly an industrial part of north London based around canal and railway traffic, Camden had declined since the 1960s. Later famed for producing the Two Tone group Madness and as the setting for the film *Withnail and I*, its warehouses and cobbled courtyards were first redeveloped by art students in 1973. A decade later what Jonathan Raban called the 'bedsitter-entrepreneurism' of its small traders had created a total youth experience for all comers to the city, from clothes and food stalls, to pub rock venues and Dingwalls, with a weekend crowd estimated in 1990 to be around 200,000.[20]

Musically, punks' parody was described by one critic as 'an extremely brutal bastardisation of Mod'.[21] In *England's Dreaming*, Jon Savage observed that 'The Clash began as a classic Mod group . . . angry, smart, mediated pop. They speeded up the heavily chorded stuttering sound of The Who and The Kinks.'[22] Punks also shared a love of amphetamines with 60s Mods, and speed once more became the drug of choice for young Britons who regularly used drugs as part of their lifestyle.

According to the Sex Pistols' songwriter, Glen Matlock:

We were always kind of moddy. We may not always have worn the clothes but we had the London mod attitude, that laddishness which the other groups didn't have.[23]

Everything seemed to revolve round the Small Faces . . . To me the mods were the real thing. When I met Steve [Jones] and Paul [Cook] they seemed to be from a very similar kind of background. They were into bands like the Faces and the Who.[24]

In his autobiography, John Lydon described the many influences on punk:

We had a very strong soul tradition in the UK since the mods. Before the Pistols' era, I came from the soul circuit. The Soul Boys, an offshoot of the Mods, were essentially working-class kids from rural areas and suburban parts of London. Now these Soul Boy clubs, although very much under-ground, carried on right through 1976 and beyond . . . They were the fashion icon to the early punks . . . Soon the Soul Boys actually changed their fashion and mixed in a lot of Bowie influenes and effeminacy . . . You started to get a crossover with the arty kids . . . Everybody liked Bowie, and it was through him that punk became acceptable to the Soul Boys element. Mod, rockabilly, Glam – everything – had all been absorbed by Punk.[25]

Punk claimed to be a more feminist youth culture than Mod, with some justification. On both sides of the Atlantic the genre produced female-led groups who articulated a more strident femininity and claimed the right to more independence from men, and the right to party along-side them without attracting the traditional stigma of the loose or hysterical woman. Angela McRobbie observed that while 60s Mod 'offered girls a more visible, active and collective role (particularly on the dance floor) than had previous groups' and allowed boys 'the vanity, the soft sharpness that are usually regarded as cissy', the musical genre that Mod established in the 1960s was what she called 'Cock Rock'. In this essentially 'male form of expression' women were either subordinate as in the Rolling Stones' 'Under My Thumb' or else wicked heartbreakers as in the Who's 'I Can See for Miles'. In contrast, McRobbie wrote, 'Punk was the first form of rock not to rest on love songs . . . and one of its effects was to allow female voices to be heard.'[26]

Female-led groups like the Slits and Siouxsie & the Banshees were certainly more obtuse than Mod icons from the 1960s like Martha Reeves or Julie Driscoll. Formed in 1976 by women from two groups, the Flowers of Romance and the Castrators, the Slits declared: 'We're just not interested in questions about women's liberation. You either think chauvinism is shit or you don't. We think it's shit.'[27] Male punks, like male Mods before them, did not always agree. The Nipple Erectors, which had a female bassist, had to suffer sound men cutting their guitar strings and skinheads spitting at them. 'There weren't that many female musicians around', said their founder Shanne Bradley, 'it was tough, I felt I had to be able to play harder and faster than a bloke to be accepted, taken seriously.'[28]

Although John Lydon famously dismissed sex as 'just thirty seconds of squelching noises', a number of songs by his male peers still displayed erotic obsession and unchanged attitudes to women.[29] The Stranglers' 'Bring on the Nubiles' and 'Peaches' (a hit released in the same month as 'God Save the Queen') invoked a parade of sexual objects which echoed singer Hugh Cornwell's opinion that 'a lot of women like to be dominated'.[30] In their study of the gender politics of rock 'n' roll, Simon Reynolds and Joy Press argued that misogyny was one of the lasting influences of the Sixties:

Punk had learned the art of defiance from 60s mod bands whose songs aggressively targeted women; it redirected the riffs and accusatory machismo at society . . . but, inevitably, punk's roots in the masculinism of 60s rock were bound to resurface. At times the misogyny was even more virulent than in the 60s, because punk's general nihilism encouraged a no-holds barred assault on liberal values (including feminism).[31]

Despite this, the playfully challenging ambiguities of glam rock found their way into punk, along with its clothing, hair and make-up styles. 'Ziggy Stardust had a mutant bastard offspring and his name was Johnny Rotten', as David Bowie drily remarked in 1980.[32]

The Sex Pistols' first live performance, on 6 November 1975, was at a former crucible of Mod subculture, Central St Martin's College of Art and Design in Soho, where their manager Malcolm McLaren had been a student. The set included cover versions of the Who's 'Substitute' and the Small Faces' 'Whatcha Gonna Do About It?'. Yet when the album *Never Mind the Bollocks* was released in October 1977, Rotten complained about the 'regressive mod vibe' of the production, which he felt had tempered the anarchic spirit of the band's live performances – although he accepted that if all his influences had been audible, the record would have been 'unlistenable for most people because they wouldn't have had a point of reference'.[33]

It was those points of reference that made British punk musically and stylistically distinct from its American parent – and that transatlantic difference was part of punk's appeal at a time when the Americanisation of British life was continuing apace. The music journalist Nick Kent noted that in 1975, 'Rock was still hopelessly Yank-fixated, which meant that the vast majority of English acts were still singing with pronounced American accents, name-checking American towns and cities in their songs instead of being true to their real roots and writing about their own experiences and regions. Punk would change that.'[34] 'I'm so bored with the USA', sang the Clash, but as Nick Hornby perceptively wrote, 'though we all sang along with them, it wasn't true, not really. We were only bored with our obsession, and that's a different thing entirely.'[35]

As punk flew back and forth across the Atlantic in the mid- to late 70s these differences left some Americans bewildered. 'The levels of violence around here are weird and random', Rob Tyner of the MC5 told the *NME* when he visited London in 1977 from a country where you were around fifty times more likely to be shot.[36] A year later, the Pistols embarked on a disastrous tour of the US – they insisted on going to the south and avoiding Punk's birthplace on the east coast. While in California in January 1978, they met the Ramones and the two groups took an immediate dislike to each other. Legs McNeil, the music critic who had coined the term punk – and who admitted, 'I have an instinctive hate for English people' – was at the meeting and recalled: 'You felt like asking them if they wanted to split for a beer, but the Sex Pistols never dropped the pose . . . They were so obnoxious, so British. It seemed like they were into class, and Punk wasn't about the class system, they were being totally arrogant without humour.'[37] For most British critics, on the other hand, it was the politics of punk that actually validated the movement; as Charles Shaar Murray wrote sarcastically when assessing its legacy in 1986: 'the Brits got hold of it and fucked it up with *politics*, man'.[38]

Despite looking and sounding more like Mods than any of their peers, the Jam also couldn't break America, but Weller made a virtue of the group's failure. This puzzled his hero Pete Townshend when the two men met for the first time in 1980. Townshend found that 'Weller seems willing to deal only with Britain at this stage: he leaves

America to the Americans and is apparently so disdainful of the States that it causes him pain even to talk about the place.'[39]

Yet Anglo-American dialogue did continue in the punk era, ironically with a little help from the Who. Neither as defiantly British as the Jam nor as anarchic as the Sex Pistols, the Clash were the most popular of the British punk bands, a reputation confirmed when they supported the Who on their tour of the United States in 1982. Their biggest success in both countries was their third album, *London Calling*,[40] the title for which came from the opening to the trusted wartime broadcasts of the BBC's World Service. The album's lyrics addressed unemployment, crime and racial tension in contemporary Britain and in his title song, Joe Strummer, the son of a diplomat, assumed a similar degree of moral authority in his call to address the conflicts of the 1970s. The song was an attack on the hollow optimism generated by 1960s pop culture, especially claims that divisions of class and race had been superseded by the sense of belonging to 'my generation'. In a sly reference to Swinging London, Strummer sang of the painful 'swing' of the truncheon, as baton-wielding police used their powers discriminately against black Britons who, in the late 1970s and early 80s, were at least three times more likely to be confronted by the police than their white counterparts.

One of the young blacks for whom police harassment was part of daily life was Strummer's friend Don Letts, who directed the video for 'London Calling'. A black clothier, DJ and filmmaker who also counted Bob Marley and John Lydon among his friends, it was Letts who parked a Mod scooter in the middle of Acme Attractions (he also owned one of the biggest collections of Beatles memorabilia in England). Letts filmed the Clash performing on the rickety, rain-swept Festival Pier on the South Bank of the Thames. The location was rich in symbolism: the pier was one of the few physical remnants of the Festival of Britain, the exhibition staged in 1951 to celebrate Britain's recovery from the war and to showcase modernist art and design.

Further down the Thames was Butler's Wharf, another decaying symbol of Britain's former confidence and power. In the 1980s, it would be redeveloped by Terence Conran and contain his restaurant Le Pont de la Tour, which in the next decade became one of Tony Blair's favourite hang-outs; the prime minister and his wife took Bill and Hillary Clinton for dinner here during a presidential visit to the UK. On 14 February 1976, however, Butler's Wharf had hosted a very different Anglo-American summit: Vivienne Westwood's Valentine's Ball, at which punk announced its arrival from the United States.

Built in the early 1870s when the docks of London's East End were the rough, bustling, cosmopolitan heart of Britain's global trade, Butler's Wharf had contained one of the biggest tea warehouses in the world. When the docks closed in the early 1970s, it became derelict, a visible reminder of Britain's economic decline. By 1975 the wharf's rats and vagrants were joined by a small group of young artists, among them the filmmaker Derek Jarman, who used the wharf as a backdrop to his film about punk, *Jubilee* (1978); another arrival was the painter and sculptor Andrew Logan, who hosted the Valentine's Ball in his studios there. Appropriately, the stage on which the Sex Pistols played that night was constructed of materials taken from the children's section of BIBA, the glam department store which had closed just three months earlier.

A BIGGER THREAT THAN RUSSIAN COMMUNISM

From Steve Jones swearing on Bill Grundy's TV chat show on 1 December 1976 to the sordid death of Sid Vicious on 1 February 1979, punk provoked one of the biggest moral panics about teenagers since mid-century fears that the young were Americanising Britain. However, it was not the American origins of punk that unsettled so many people but the fact that the very British obsession with class was expressed in a louder, more direct, American way. The presenter of one current affairs news programme in 1977 introduced a discussion with community leaders by announcing: 'For the last twelve months punk rock has become almost a battle cry in British society. For many people it's a bigger threat to our way of life than Russian Communism or hyper-inflation and it certainly generates more popular excitement than either of those.'[41]

The Sex Pistols were dropped by EMI, banned from performing on TV and in most concert venues, violently assaulted by royalists, and their single 'God Save the Queen' reputedly kept off the No. 1 spot by a music industry colluding with the government to fix the charts. The venomous reaction to the group showed that the young remained the focal point of anxiety about the state of the nation. It also demonstrated how easily that anxiety could be inflamed by the media; and above all, it revealed how dangerous it was to attack the monarchy in a country in which royalism was still a mainstay of national identity.

In the same way that politicians of the time scared voters into thinking they were on the brink of revolution when in fact most striking workers continued to fight old battles, it suited the Pistols' manager Malcolm McLaren and his cohorts to declare that punk was Year One of a revolution in sound and style. The claim maximised punk's shock value and commercial potential by attracting millions of aspirant rebels from all social classes beyond the small art school constituency from which the movement, like Mod before it, had emerged in Britain. Like the trade union leaders who were fighting for higher wages in order to give their members a larger piece of the consumer pie, punk expressed a widespread desire for a more equal society. It was also marbled with an alternative form of patriotism similar to that which Mod had first articulated. 'You don't write a song like "God Save the Queen"', John Lydon said, 'because you hate the English race. You write a song like "God Save the Queen" because you love them and you're fed up with them being mistreated.'[42]

Released in May 1977, the song was as much an anthem of thwarted aspiration as a nihilistic rant against authority. With its declaration that there is 'no future' it scorned the populist fantasy that the monarchy could unite the country when in fact it sat at the apex of a social hierarchy still dominated by a privately educated, landed minority. The song could also be read as a comment on the fact that the British had no equivalent of the American Dream – that mobilising, aspirational legend by which Americans define class economically, according to how much they earn and own, rather than culturally like the British, according to how one speaks or dresses.

Earlier post-war critiques of the monarchy had come from the intelligentsia, notably playwright John Osborne's 1961 verdict that the British monarchy was 'the gold filling in a mouthful of decay'. Osborne's 'Letter to My Fellow Countrymen' had begun: 'This is a letter of hate. It is for you my countrymen. I mean those of you who have defiled it. The men with manic fingers leading the sightless, feeble, betrayed body of my country to its death.'[43] Punk contained a similarly pained message to Britain from millions of young people who felt rejected or undervalued by a nation that they believed belonged to them too.[44] The outrage that 'God Save the Queen' caused was so great partly because it came from the snarling lips of an articulate working-class man with a larger audience than Britain's original 'Angry Young Man'.

Yet punk was as much an attack on the failures of mid-twentieth-century British liberalism as on conservative institutions. 'The Labour Party had failed the working class', John Lydon later said about Harold Wilson's years in office.[45] Punk's attack on liberalism reflected public discontent with the post-war consensus: that uneasy compact between Left and Right about the value of a welfare state and a regulated economy, which came apart as the Labour governments of 1974–79 failed to get to grips with economic stagnation and civil unrest. Julie Burchill, one of the working-class journalists who made their name at the NME at this time, later argued that punk had much in common with Thatcherism:

Punk was a break with consensus. And we media brats, like our more sussed soulmates who would come up a few years later in the City, were McLaren *and* Thatcher's children . . . We were still non-U upstarts with names like Steve and Paul and Julie and Debbie. What we all shared was Attitude; short-haired, impatient, get-rich-filthy-quick, liberal baiting and hippy-baiting.[46]

On eighteen occasions between 1961 and 1996, Gallup asked whether there was a 'class struggle' in Britain: the number of people who answered 'Yes' rose from 60 per cent in the 1960s to 80 per cent in the 90s.[47] But if the 1970s was a period of civil unrest, it was more because the evolution of modern Britain was moving too slowly for many people rather than because revolution was in the air. The promises of individual freedom, social mobility and political justice made during the 1960s ran into the buffers of economic stagnation, the institutional resilience of the British class system, and visceral right-wing opposition to civil rights in Britain and Northern Ireland. It was this frustration of moderate aspirations – skilfully manipulated by militant trade unions – which caused the mass discontent that allowed this period to be caricatured as one of unrelenting chaos and gloom.

Mrs Thatcher's populist Conservatism cleverly exploited some of the working- and lower middle-class aspirations that had been disappointed in the 1970s. She blamed an unholy alliance of socialism and snobbery for thwarting ambition; and she exaggerated the extent of national decline in order to justify her messianic salvation of Britain through unregulated American-style free market capitalism, while leaving intact institutional barriers to equal opportunity, such as public schools. One of her early supporters was a musician whose work combined the aspirational optimism of Mod with the angry pessimism of punk, a man whose following, according to the critic Simon Reynolds, 'constituted a mini-subculture in its own right'.[48]

THE REAL SPIRIT OF PUNK

In 'Tales from the Riverbank' (1982) Paul Weller sang of a dream that was mixed with nostalgia. Written in his London flat, the song recalled the rivers and canals around his childhood home in Woking, and was inspired by his reading of Kenneth Grahame's *Wind in the Willows*. The song's admission that he'll always hang on to that dream of a fantasy home captures something of Weller's pied piper ability to take British youth forward into the past. Paul Weller was the undisputed figurehead of Mod during the punk era, and while other musicians, from Pete Townshend to Joe Strummer and John Lydon, were a spent force by the mid-1980s, he, like Mod itself, survived and thrived. 'It's like a code, in a way', he told chat show host Jonathan Ross. 'It gives something to my life . . . I'm still a Mod. I'll always be a Mod. You can bury me a Mod.'[49] Yet Weller did not spread Britain's first youth culture by a blind dedication to codes established in the early 1960s: his cross-generational appeal sprang from his ability to maintain a Mod aesthetic in music and dress over thirty years while avoiding pastiche, regularly adapting his sound and style to contemporary taste, from 70s punk to 80s House music.

The Jam established their punk credentials by supporting the Clash on their White Riot tour in 1977. Like most artists of the punk era, Weller was strongly influenced by the Who but he also cited the Beatles, the Kinks and the Small Faces as heroes when it was unfashionable to do so. When Glen Matlock was ejected from the Sex Pistols in 1977, reputedly on the grounds that he liked the Beatles too much, Weller smartly invited him to join the Jam. (Matlock was interested but wouldn't agree to wear a Carnaby Street suit.⁵⁰) And whereas most punks doffed their caps to black music by citing reggae as an influence, Weller's loves were soul, funk and the original Mod passion, jazz.

Weller's popularity was augmented by his upwardly mobile, suburban working-class background. He was born in 1958 to a taxi driver and cleaner in Woking, Surrey, a moderately affluent but unfashionable satellite town south of London. The frustrations of suburbia had inspired the work of artists throughout the twentieth century and Weller too was aching for the excitement and freedom that urban England seemed to promise. As a teenager he got on a train from Woking to Waterloo with a tape recorder just to record the sounds of the city, returning home clutching his captured urban noise like a Victorian butterfly collector. Some of Weller's songs, like 'Mr Clean', were lacerating attacks on suburban middle-class life in the manner of the Kinks' 'David Watts' (which the Jam also covered); the song 'All Around the World' can be heard playing in *Abigail's Party* (1977), Mike Leigh's sneering satire on aspiration in suburban Britain.⁵¹ Generally, however, his songs, from 'A Town Called Malice' (1982) to 'Stanley Road' (1995), eschewed trite generational revolt and celebrated family life and the Woking roots to which he remained attached.

Weller admired John Lydon, who shared his attachment to family roots, but he disliked the destructive politics of punk, epitomised in the Pistols' song 'Anarchy in the UK'. In the 1990s he told an interviewer:

I liked the attitude of Punk but I also thought a lot of it was fake . . . Most of them were bullshitters. I knew what it should have been about: a real street movement, the first working-class musical movement that our generation had had. We'd read all about the Sixties, but it was the first time for us that something similar had happened. That's what I wanted it to be, that's how I perceived it. And I think that's why The Jam clicked. We made our own scene. What we and some of our audiences were about was more the real spirit of Punk.⁵²

Whereas punks who sought to give their rebellion some intellectual weight cited the Dadaists, Weller referenced Pop Art; and when they lauded Debord, Weller cited Colin MacInnes and George Orwell, whose patriotic evocations of English life appealed to him. 'I like his

[Orwell's] version of socialism', Weller told the teenage readers of *Smash Hits* in 1979. 'He had a lot of just basic common sense [and] he realised that the working class had that common sense.'[53] His contrary outlook shocked many when, criticising the Pistols' 'God Save the Queen', he praised the monarchy and told fans of the Jam's voting intentions in the forthcoming general election that would sweep Margaret Thatcher to power: 'The Queen's the best diplomat we've got. She works harder than any of you or I do, or the rest of the country . . . this change-the-world thing is becoming a bit too trendy, we'll be voting Conservative at the next election.'[54]

'Anarchy in the UK holds no sway with the Jam',[55] announced their delighted record label; Polydor even tried to book them to appear at Silver Jubilee street parties. When the Jam left the White Riot tour, the Clash sent a sarcastic telegram: 'Maggie wants you all round for target practice tonight.'[56] Taken aback by the hostile reaction to his comments, Weller recanted his Conservative sympathies but reiterated his patriotism in a manner that kept him apart from many punks. 'We don't love parliament', he said later in 1977, 'but I don't see any point in going up against your own country. If there is such a thing as democracy, then we've got it.'[57]

For the writer D. J. Taylor, growing up in a middle-class Norwich family, Weller's political views and the Jam's preference for suits and ties drew him to the band. Taylor found 'the idea of yobbish teenagers who couldn't sing whining on about anarchy deeply distasteful'; he liked the Jam 'for being English, for singing about council houses and watching the news and not eating your tea. It was always a comfort to know that they were never going to conquer America.'[58] That parochial view, common to fans of many British groups over the years, was not just an expression of defiance towards America; it revealed a confidence in native talent that was beginning to draw the generations closer together at a time when they seemed further apart than ever. Perhaps the most ironic aspect of punk's nihilism was that the Britons growing up in the 1970s were the first to have parents who had themselves experienced, and continued to value, youth culture. 'My parents', recalled Taylor, 'were the kind of cautious middle-class people who faintly disapproved of pop music while remaining routinely aware of it . . . Though my father maintained that The Beatles, along with jeans and fish fingers, were responsible for the decline of Western civilisation, I think he sometimes found that pose rather difficult.'[59] As he later discovered, Taylor's father 'affected to loathe the Fab Four but . . . still inexplicably bought their records. A copy of "She Loves You" consequently rubbed shoulders on the rack next to the *Messiah* and *The Dream of Gerontius*.'[60]

Although the Jam were initially derided for their retro aesthetic and reactionary opinions, the quality of their third album, *All Mod Cons* (1978) turned the group from also-rans into the most critically and commercially successful post-punk artists, superseding the Sex Pistols and the Clash as the figureheads of British popular music until they split up in 1982. While the album sleeve was covered in old Mod symbols, from Italian scooters to ska badges, many felt that Weller had tapped into a British musical past in order to take punk forward. Reviewing *All Mod Cons* in the *NME*, Charles Shaar Murray wrote:

We've heard a lot of stupid, destructive songs about the alleged joys of violence lately and they all stink . . . If these songs mean that one less meaningless street fight gets started then we'll all owe Paul Weller a favour. The Jam brought us the sound of '65 in 1976, and now in 1978 they bring us the sound of '66. Again, they've done it in such a way that even though you can still hear The Who here and there and a few distinct Beatleisms in these ornate descending 12-string chord sequences, it all sounds fresher and newer than anything else this year.[61]

In *Sounds*, skinhead's champion Garry Bushell wrote, 'They just blast away 12 years of blind alley "progression" and take up the mantle of Townshend/Lennon-McCartney for the modern world'; while the *Record Mirror* concluded: 'The Jam have come of age . . . they are not imitators but upholders of a great British tradition.'[62]

Weller's most famous song was composed in his parents' holiday caravan at Selsey Bill on the south coast of England. 'The Eton Rifles', about a fight between state school teenagers and cadets of Britain's top private school, avoided the bluster that often blighted punk songs about class war. The conclusion 'We came out of it naturally the worst' had a poignant ring of acceptance that hair dye, ripped clothes, frenetic chords and trite sloganeering would not destroy the institutions responsible for Britain's toxic level of class-consciousness. Weller even gave an interview to the *Eton College Chronicle* in which he expressed the hope that he hadn't upset any of the pupils. On the contrary, the interviewer replied, many of them loved the song and had helped it to reach No. 3 in the charts; one of them was the future Conservative prime minister, David Cameron, then a 14-year old cadet in the Eton Rifles.

Cameron and his friends may have relished with Schadenfreude the fact that 'a tie and a crest' triumphed in Britain's class war over the ersatz power of mere style that Mods claimed through their own dress code. But what appealed to the Jam's fan base in the affluent white working classes was the anguished realism of their songs which depicted everyday life in modern Britain. Weller's lyrics sprang from the 'kitchen sink' social realism of mid-twentieth-century film and literature but what made his songs resonate was his ability to pipe this into a commentary on the universal limitations of youth culture. That ability was displayed in the song 'When You're Young', which preceded 'Eton Rifles' and charted in the summer of 1979:

> Life is timeless, days are long when you're young
> You used to fall in love with everyone
> Any guitar and any bass drum
> Life is a drink and you get drunk
> when you're young
>
> Life is new and there's things to be done
> You can't wait to be grown up
> Acceptance into the capital world
> You pull on some weed, then you pull on someone
> when you're young

After optimism comes angry defiance and then the realization that aspiration won't change the world on its own:

> But you find out life isn't like that, it's so hard to comprehend
> Why you set up your dreams to have them smashed in the end
> But you don't mind, you've got time on your side
> And they're never gonna make you stand in line
> You're just waiting for the right time

You're fearless and brave, you can't be stopped when you're young
You swear you're never ever gonna work for someone
No corporations for the new age sons
Tears of rage roll down your face but
Still you say, it's fun

And you find out life isn't like that, it's so hard to understand
Why the world is your oyster but your future's a clam

For some teenagers, the answer to an unattractive present and no future was to retreat into the past. One of the oddest episodes in the history of British youth culture was the Mod revival of 1979–82, in which artists far less talented than Weller tried to recreate mid-60s pop Modernism for a cadre of working-class teenagers who rejected the eclecticism that had made both Mod and punk such creative forces. Dressed as carbon copies of the original Mods, they demonstrated how thin the wall was between a subculture being imaginatively reconfigured for a contemporary audience, and one that was merely being copied as an escape from the present.

Zadie Smith's portrait of Ryan Topps in her novel *White Teeth* depicts the perils of such tribal devotion in the 1970s. Ryan, a Mod, is the first lover of the novel's heroine, Clara, a teenage West Indian immigrant for whom British youth culture is a passport with which she enters the new society she finds herself in:

Ryan fancied himself as a bit of a Mod. He wore ill-fitting grey suits with black polo-necks. He wore Chelsea boots after everyone else had stopped wearing them. While the rest of the world discovered the joys of the synthesizer, Ryan swore allegiance to the little men with big guitars: to the Kinks, the Small Faces, the Who. Ryan Topps rode a green Vespa GS scooter which he polished twice a day with a baby's nappy and kept encased in a custom-built corrugated-iron shield. To Ryan's way of thinking, a Vespa was not merely a mode of transport but an ideology, family, friend and lover all rolled into one paragon of late forties engineering. Ryan, as one might expect, had few friends.[63]

I DIDN'T WANT TO DESTROY ANYTHING

When the music journalist Caroline Coon accused Weller of being a revivalist, he famously stepped out with a cardboard sign around his neck bearing the words 'How can I be a revivalist when I'm only fucking eighteen?'[64] An answer to Weller's rhetorical question came in 1979 when the mass media reported the strange sight of young people dressed exactly like some of their parents in the mid-1960s.

The Chords, formed in south-east London in 1978 and like the Jam signed to Polydor, were one of a clutch of Mod revival groups that briefly rose to prominence. Singer and guitarist Billy Hassett explained why they felt it necessary to excavate Mod in such a fastidious way:

I got into it much the same way that all the New Mods did, loving the music of the Beatles and the Stones . . . The whole Sixties thing wasn't acknowledged positively . . . The Beatles had only been broken up five years when punk happened and it became so unfashionable to like the Beatles . . . I loved it when punk came along, I wanted to draw on that energy but I didn't identify with the image . . . Mod wasn't the pinpoint for us, it was the whole era and all we did was wrap it up in one big coat, the parka. That was our statement. I mean, I couldn't be a punk, I didn't want to destroy anything.[65]

Interviewed in *Sounds*, Ian Page of Secret Affair defined Mod as dressing up in order to redress the wealthy's assumed 'right to feel superior, or treat [working-class people] like a soiled pound note'. 'Take their clothes, retain your identity', he implored readers. Page also affirmed Mod's perennial elitism: 'I do not believe everyone is equal. I believe everyone should have equal opportunity to be top dog.' He added that he named his band Secret Affair to suggest a secret society that was 'special, separate and elite'.[66]

Although the Chords were championed by John Peel, they and other revival bands produced little of artistic merit and met with little commercial success. Secret Affair's 'Time for Action', which made it to No. 13 in the charts, was the exception; more typical was the Merton Parkas' 'You Need Wheels', which sputtered briefly into the charts at No. 40 in 1979 and sounded like the cockney music-hall duo Chas and

Dave on a little speed. Interviewed for an *NME* feature on the movement in 1979, the Chords' guitarist Chris Pope declared: 'We want to
do something better than mod achieved in the '60s. It died a death
before it reached a natural conclusion.'[67] Yet although they toured in
support of the Jam, the Chords' songs like 'The British Way of Life'
weren't successful and by 1981, along with other Mod revival bands,
they were dropped by their record company and split up. Creating a
rather lame version of 60s R&B, the bands had followed Northern
Soul fans back to a musical past that betrayed the progressive essence
of Mod. But even Northern Soul fans had developed their own distinctive clothing style, something that this revival markedly failed to do.

Scooter clubs, which had never disappeared, grew in size and
number from 1979 to 1984, their members even mimicking the battles
of the original Mods like an historic re-enactment society. In 1966
several hundred Mods had gathered in Trafalgar Square on Guy Fawkes
Night. They then rode down the Mall in a charge culminating with
one man deliberately crashing his scooter into the gates of Buckingham
Palace. Whether or not this was intended as an attack on royalty is
unclear, but the re-enactment of the event by Mod revivalists in 1984
had even less impact: police broke up the scooter rally outside the
palace before a commemorative charge on the gates could take place.

The Mod revivalists of the late 1970s were nostalgists, clinging to
what they thought was a better past when England had more to offer
the young, from full employment to World Cup victory. The revival
demonstrated that old and young alike could construct a golden age
– an idealised, simplified image of what could be – even when they
were styling themselves as 'Modernists'. The revival mirrored a wider
trend in Britain at the time. In what became known as the heritage
industry, the 1970s and 80s witnessed a rise in the number of people
visiting country houses and other sites of historic interest that for
some were reassuring relics of an age when everything and everyone
had their place.

Music critics panned the groups involved, but the media reported
the Mod revival approvingly as a relief from the filth and fury of
punk. 'They're pushing out punk,' declared the *Daily Mirror*, 'being
smart is all the rage. The boys have short, neat hair and lovely manners,
and the girls spend half their day putting on their make-up. They are
the kind of youngsters most mums can understand. Because most

mums were like that themselves back in the Sixties.' Pearl, a 19-year-old make-up artist from Putney, told reporters, 'I went off punk because the people started to look scruffy and unoriginal.'[68] Not only were cleanliness and smartness set against the scruffiness of punk style; so too was the better relationship these young people seemed to have with parents who had been Mods in the 1960s.

As we saw earlier, one of the less-noticed features of British youth culture in this period is the extent to which it formed intergenerational connections. Family ties endured even in homes that contained the most truculent punk, as some parents accepted that their children's rebellion, however annoying, might be based on a sincerely held set of tastes and attitudes. In a few cases they went even further. When the hippie-turned-punk champion John Peel helped to promote the Damned on his long-running Radio 1 show, the mother of the band's drummer, Rat Scabies (real name, Chris Millar), wrote to the DJ thanking him for 'helping Christopher with his career'.[69]

However, it wasn't just tolerance that bound families together; youth culture, and Mod in particular, also provided a shared experience of style. Whether it was creatively morphing into distinctive subcultures like glam or merely replicating itself, the connections it established across time began to bridge the generation gap. Taking clothes from the wardrobe of the past was nothing new, of course; take, for example, the 1960s fashion for Victorian military jackets. But the Mods of the 1970s didn't just shop in second-hand markets and retro boutiques; they also borrowed their parents' clothes. Two Welsh sisters from Gwent told reporters that most of their clothes 'come out of Mum's wardrobe, where they have been since 1969'.[70] Some parents chided their offspring for not being more imaginative, as Paul Lyons recalls: 'My Dad used to tell me that we had to understand that Mod was just fashionable in the 60s, and that the way we were all carrying on was far too anal.'[71]

Parents did take the cult seriously, though, sometimes giving their children advice about Mod style to ensure they maintained its codes, much as adults once taught children how to cook or fish. Christine Feldman has observed of this period that 'a kind of storytelling culture evolved, from which imitation ensued'.[72] When Paul Lyons started to wear white socks made fashionable by Two Tone bands, his father sat down with him, 'attempting the matey father to son chat about the dreaded foot attire that I wore and even went as far as going into detail about the 60s mod scene that he was a part of. "We never looked like that", he said.'[73] A curious form of rebellion ensued in which children would reassert generational difference by upholding their contemporary twists on Mod style, thereby demonstrating that even when Mod was at its most imitative, the young of each era made it their own.

At the general election of 1979, 42 per cent of new voters supported the Conservative Party, with only 28 per cent opting for each of the other main parties – an almost exact reversal of 1974. For some, therefore, the Mod revival was a troubling sign of a reactionary trend in national politics. In a 1980 *Observer* article called 'Beware the Mods', one fan of the Merton Parkas echoed the views once held by Marc Bolan in 1962 and, more recently, by Paul Weller: 'Being a Mod means being Conservative', he told the newspaper. 'A real Mod wouldn't vote Labour. It means having a job and working to make this country great again.'[74] How typical he was is hard to say; but in any case, what the media noted most about Mods of this period was not their political affiliations but the fact that they seemed to have depoliticised youth culture, taking the sting out of generational revolt and rejecting the radical politics of punk. After interviewing some Mods the *Daily Mirror* concluded: 'The sixties were fun, that was the big thing about them say today's Mods. The Mods' philosophy is simple, Mark says, "We're clean, we like girls, drink and having fun."' Christine from Gwent added, '[Mod boys] have such lovely manners and they look so smart; the ones we know always kiss your hand when you meet them and hold doors open for you. I love it.'[75]

However, those seeking creativity in their otherwise mundane lives soon became disillusioned when they realised that the revival was going nowhere. The DJ and club promoter Paul Hallam was at the heart of the cult and told his young followers that they were on the cusp of a creative revolution. One of them was Mick Ferrante: 'I remember Paul Hallam saying, "Yeah, it's gonna be a whole revolution. There's gonna be Mod poetry, Mod films, Mod art, we're gonna change the world." I actually believed in this shit, we all believed in it.'[76] Paul Lyons realised that he had little in common with his fellow revivalists: 'We'd talk clothes, talk music and I was getting tired of it, it was just: "Hang on, how much further can we go with this? Do I really know you, do I really know what you're like?" It just was getting very, very boring for me.'[77] Mick Ferrante too joined the ranks of the disillusioned: 'That's the problem with the whole Mod thing, you can't really have *Modernism* as it is, because you're always looking back, it's always retro, so it can't work.'[78]

The critic Peter York, in a *Harpers & Queen* article entitled 'Mod: The Second Coming', summarised the Mod revival in September 1979. He too pointed to the apparent paradox:

All over the country, long after the whole hippie progressive thing was supposed to have buried Mod entirely, the Mod aesthetic just kept going, sometimes explicitly as in the scooter clubs and sometimes just in a line of indirect descent. Northern Soul – which was a dance-based life – and skin-head, which has never really gone away, both came from Mod . . . To revive Mod was to revive what was barely history at all. Hence a little attendant *weirdness* . . . One of the central ideas of the Modern Movement is the avoidance of historical reference, which means, in youth-culture terms, that *revivals are wrong* . . . The answer comes from a very articulate group of people who run this New Mod fanzine *Maximum Speed*, which shows both how things can never be the same *and* how the Mod thing has some real continuity in it. This kid said that Mod today is a totally different thing yet it all comes down to a tradition – dressing smartly, Soul music – but the difference is that kids know a lot of things now and will never unknow them, since the recent past is so accessible. The sensibility is Post-Modern.[79]

In his study *Retromania*, Simon Reynolds summed up the appeal of such revivalist cults: 'If Time has become annexed by capitalism's cynical cycles of product shifting, one way to resist that is to reject temporality altogether. The revivalist does this by fixating on one era and saying: "Here I make my stand." By fixing identity to the absolute and abiding supremacy of one sound and style, the revivalist says, "*This* is me."'[80] Yet this unfashionable period of Mod seemed not to have dimmed by the turn of the century. A survey carried out in 2003 by ModCulture, the movement's leading website, found that most people using the site had entered the scene during the 1970s revival. It found that 8.3 per cent of its users had become Mods in the 1960s, 53.5 per cent during the punk era, 21.3 per cent in the Britpop years, while a substantial number, 16.9 per cent, were young people who had become Mods in the last ten years.[81]

It may be that the enduring appeal of the 1960s is the optimism associated with that period, which was especially appealing for working-class teenagers in the punk era who felt that they had no future. As Billy Bragg explained:

There is something authentic about Mod . . . Against a backdrop of the 1960s it seems to sum up that optimism for working-class people to be seen as individuals, not to be seen as a lumpen group like hoodies are; to shine, to get respect for how they dress, never mind what else they do, never mind where they went to school, never mind what their accent sounds like – the aesthetic is all. I don't think any other British youth cultures have that same aesthetic which is Mod: the person as a work of art.[82]

But in the case of the 1970s Mod revival the work of art was a pastiche and the pride it expressed was second-hand optimism borrowed from a previous era, like an elder brother's frayed shirt found in a wardrobe after he's left home to enjoy a more independent life.

YOU MIGHT AS WELL GO TO SLEEP

Young Mods of all kinds clung to the Jam in the hope that the group would succeed where others had failed to imaginatively reconfigure the movement for a new wave of followers. Yet even Weller could not do it alone, and expressed pity for some fans in the economic context of the times: 'It just seemed so desperate,' he said, 'these young working class kids trying their best to dress up and look the part while all around their environment was crumbling.'[83]

The event which did almost as much as Weller to reconfigure and perpetuate Mod over the next twenty years was, ironically, a film which itself sponsored the Mod revival. Executively produced in 1979 by the Who and based on their concept album of 1973, *Quadrophenia* was instrumental in attracting more teenage recruits to that revival, and by the group's own admission, it was designed to cash in on the phenomenon.[84]

Quadrophenia was a film about Mods for the punk generation, based on the true story of Barry Prior, a teenager who committed suicide by riding his Lambretta over a cliff in 1964, after a Mod gathering in Brighton. It told the story of Jimmy, a young Mod who works in the mail room of an advertising agency, lives for the weekends but becomes so obsessed with the cult that he loses his lover, his friends, his job and very nearly his life. Jimmy was played by Phil Daniels, but it was the Sex Pistols' John Lydon who originally got the part before insurance companies refused to underwrite the film if the *enfant terrible* of British rock starred in it. Lesser New Wave figures did make it into *Quadrophenia*: Toyah Willcox, who had also appeared in Jarman's *Jubilee*, got a small part, while Sting of the Police played Ace Face. Sting recreated the infamous courtroom scene of 1964 when, to the cheers of those arraigned, a young Mod had produced a chequebook in the dock to pay his fine for public disorder – a moment that symbolised the freedom that affluence seemed to give the young. In the film, however, one of the triggers for Jimmy's self-destruction is his discovery that Ace is in fact merely a bell-boy at a Brighton hotel, his freedom from servility revealed to be no more than a promissory note in a sea breeze.

The film also addressed the tribal aspect of youth culture, in which teenagers sought individuality through immersion in a movement that demanded a high degree of uniformity. Jimmy's childhood friend, Kev (played by Ray Winstone), is a rocker and when the two meet again, Kev tries to re-establish their friendship:

KEV: I don't give a monkey's arsehole about the Mods and rockers. Underneath we're all the same, aren't we?

JIMMY: No, Kev, that's it. Look, I don't wanna be the same as everybody else. That's why I'm a Mod, see? I mean you gotta be somebody, ain't ya, or you might as well jump in the sea and drown.[85]

This exchange points to Mod's key attraction, as Robert Elms sees it:

As a boy you've got two different things pulling you. One is the desire to be different, to stand out, to want to be the cock of the south. But at the same time to be part of a gang and to fit in. So you want to do two things, which appear to be contradictory: you want to be an individualist and you want to be part of a gang. Well, Mod solved that riddle – it's a gang of individualists.[86]

The DJ, promoter and 70s Mod Eddie Piller agrees that the cult

allows elements of individualism within a group. You're following the strict fascistic codes that apply to dress and ideas and you're applying them so that it gives you enough leeway to be an individual within that movement. And that is what all adolescent boys are searching for. Group membership that allows them some freedom of expression away from their parents. Actually that is a much better reason why Mod is still becoming.[87]

   Many young Britons continued to be put off Mod in the 1970s and 80s by those 'strict fascistic codes', believing that in trying to create an alternative elite Mods had just fostered another kind of conformity. The artist Humphrey Ocean played bass for Ian Dury's first group, Kilburn & the High Roads, who opened for the Who on their British tour of the album *Quadrophenia* in 1973. Born in Sussex in 1951 and privately educated, Ocean explained:

I was never a Mod. They were too clean, you know, they were foppish, took too much care of their clothes . . . and I wanted bohemia. I'd been in school where I'd been told what to do for eight years . . . and that's why I slightly mistrusted Mods because it seemed to be a rather organized movement, and it was a code, and I was intrinsically rebelling against that.[88]

Another man who brushed past Mod is the renowned milliner Stephen Jones who, like Robert Elms, was closely connected to the New Romantics of the early 1980s through his involvement with the Blitz club. As he saw it, Mods 'had a manifesto, which was why I was never a part of it. I understand it and really respect them, but I always thought . . . it's a bit fascist. The fashion I've been interested in is much more inclusive; the Mod thing was about being true to a certain set of ideals that were about constraint.'[89]

   Some of *Quadrophenia*'s extras epitomised that constraining tendency, chastising the film's director, Franc Roddam, for its historical inaccuracies; the film's lack of 'a Mod-like attitude to detail' included the appearance of a 1970s Ford Cortina and rockers wearing Motörhead T-shirts. But the reference to Motörhead was no accident. Heavy metal, which peaked in Britain during the 1970s and 80s, played with occult imagery as much as progressive rock, especially in its graphic objectification of women as vampish sirens. Yet groups like Black Sabbath came from the industrial Midlands of England and their predominantly male blue-collar followers located themselves in the urban industrial world, however crudely they sometimes expressed that identity. In a sense, heavy metal was the stylistic counterpoint to the Mod revival of the New Wave era, in the same way that rockers had been the counterpoint to 1960s Mod. Simple leather- and denim-based fashion and a taste for tattoos and Harleys were all riffs on the American rock 'n' roll culture that Mods abhorred and which many punks (for all their use of Teddy Boy style) also rejected for being too stridently masculine.[90]

The use of Motörhead T-shirts in *Quadrophenia* that purists disliked was exactly the conflation of past and present that made the film so successful. In his study of popular music and British cinema, K. J. Donnelly wrote:

Punk influenced *Quadrophenia* in that it chose to eschew the artifice of the rock opera of a few years previously, like the other film based on a Who album, *Tommy* (1975). It shied away from being a musical and was essentially a drama with songs, representing the mods as an earlier form of youth rebellion along lines that could be understood by a late 1970s punk-influenced audience.[91]

Roddam responded to criticism of the film's inaccuracies by stating that 'The Mod movement not only represented an expression of violence and energy but also one of political mobility, "We've got a voice, mate, you'd better fucking listen to us."' And the film – like Mod – had a global appeal. 'I have come across people who've seen it two hundred times', Roddam later said. 'There was even a Mod club in San Diego with Mexican Mods. They called *Quadrophenia* the Bible.' A sequel was mooted and the director discussed the possibility of Jimmy rising from the mail room to be an advertising executive. 'He would probably have ended up supporting Margaret Thatcher', Roddam ruefully concluded.[92]

The film inspired copycat riots in the summer of 1981, this time with skinheads attacking Mods on the Brighton seafront. One skinhead told the *Brighton Evening Argus* why he despised revivalists: 'The only reason they come here is because of that film *Quadrophenia*. All these young kids just copied it to follow the trend. We hate everyone of course, but we hate the Mods and the Soul Boys the most, 'cos they're flash. I reckon there's going to be a lot of trouble down here in the summer 'cos that's what Skins are all about.'[93]

When it came, the trouble on the seafront was easily contained. On the August Bank Holiday weekend of 1981, 300 Mods were rounded up by police on a grassy promenade in Brighton, told to take off their shoes and crash helmets then made to lie face down for six hours. 'No one is to move or talk', barked a senior officer through a megaphone. 'You might as well go to sleep.'[94] Yet in the spring and summer of 1981 Britain's police were busy combating the most serious inner city riots since those of 1958. Across the country, tens of thousands of young, mostly working-class, black and white men took to the streets to vent their anger at unemployment and racist policing. A Brighton Conservative MP rebuked the sociologist Stanley Cohen for suggesting that there was a connection between the fracas at the seafront and the urban deprivation that lay behind riots in places like Toxteth in Liverpool.

Julie Burchill and Daniel Raven summed up the revivalists, both peaceful and violent, in their study of modern Brighton:

They were a kind of youth culture Amish, stolidly refusing to acknowledge anything that happened to the rest of the world after a certain point in history – 1966 in their case (with a special dispensation for Weller). This seemed a shame . . . because it was precisely the sort of attitude the original mods they so admired would have scorned . . . they derided the rockers on the basis that their musical taste and dress code were locked in a 1950s time warp. It could then be argued that whenever they ogled the Italian tailoring in *Quadrophenia* or sneered to see a schoolmate buy a Duran Duran record, the nu-mods were actually behaving a lot like . . . old rockers.[95]

The police officer's suggestion that they might as well 'go to sleep' may therefore be an appropriate verdict on the Mod revival. Yet another legacy of *Quadrophenia* was the growing ability of youth culture to memorialise itself as part of Britain's national heritage.

THINGS ARE SO DIVERSE

The film's enduring popularity produced one of the world's strangest shrines to the God of Youth. In the middle of the riots, Jimmy escapes from the police and runs down an alleyway where he has quick sex with the girl he is infatuated with. The site of this fictional romantic scene soon became the destination for Mods who come on pilgrimage from all over the world, leave graffiti on the walls and sometimes recreate the couple's frenzied tryst, much to the annoyance of local people.

Although on its release the film was blamed for bringing disrepute to Brighton, it soon came to be seen as encouraging tourism. In 1997, a new generation of city officials helped organise civic receptions to mark the film's re-release. A 'Quadrophenia Express' left London's Victoria station with original cast members and journalists, and was met at the other end by Mods of different generations and the mayor of Brighton, who introduced a screening of the film at the Grand Hotel overlooking the beaches where the battles, real and recreated, had taken place.

The welcome the mayor gave to the 'Quadrophenia Express' stems from the fact that the Mod cult invited patriotism as well as local pride. Yet at the heart of this was the fact that in the 1980s youth culture began to be incorporated into the heritage industry – including those cults once associated with national crisis and decline. Punks with brightly dyed, spiky hair were now gathering on the steps of Eros in London's Piccadilly, and the more enterprising were charging tourists to take pictures of them.

The use of Piccadilly Circus as a hang-out by the young had attracted controversy in 1969 after residents in the area complained to Westminster Council that unkempt, drug-taking hippies were repelling tourists. One woman wrote: 'I have had to apologise to visiting Americans at the filthy appearance of the Circus, and express shame that the centre of London looks so disgusting.' Despite making arrests the police could not disperse what the Met's Assistant Commissioner called 'these beatnik types', and by 1978 a new problem had emerged. What angered Westminster residents most about the punks hanging out at Eros was the fact that they were attracting rather than repelling visitors to the capital. In her letter to the council, a Mrs Bliss noted with horror that 'the behaviour of these Punks has become a tourist attraction and crowds of tourists collect to watch them'.[96] By the early 1980s visitors from around the world could buy picture postcards of these exotic beasts to send home. As a snapshot of quintessentially British life, they were available from souvenir shops alongside traditional pictures of the Royal Family. And in 1992 punk became part of the pantheon of British national achievement when Vivienne Westwood went to Buckingham Palace to receive her first honour from a queen she had once mocked.

In the midst of the moral panic swirling around punk there were already signs that youth culture was no longer seen as an ephemeral trifle to be ridiculed or endured. The formation of an artistic canon in music and fashion that had begun in the late 1960s and was recognised by different generations meant that youth culture was acquiring respectability even as it continued to critique the world it grew up in. And that respectability enabled the government and the tourist industry to enshrine youth culture as a way of selling Britain to the world.

Just as some original Mods decried the commercialisation of their cult in Carnaby Street, punks complained about the same thing happening to theirs. That led some of them into the Oi! movement, but most followed a shining path of musical innovation that became the New Wave of the 1980s.[97] Mark E. Smith, a former factory worker and leader of Manchester band the Fall (who believed punk was mostly 'rich kids pretending to be trash'), observed that

as with many scenes, it became very conservative – with everybody dressing the same and avoiding those that didn't. Small wonder that they soon ran out of things to say . . . To me Punk was and is a quick statement. That's why most of the main players couldn't handle the fall-out of it all, they were like a bunch of shell-shocked army majors stuck in time, endlessly repeating their once-successful war-cries. Nothing wrong with that, I suppose, but I wanted something with a bit more longevity.[98]

But longevity was achieved because punks, like Mods before them, settled down and had kids, a natural process that provided domestic runways for new forms of youth culture to take off. Even when a particular style was not passed on, parents with recent memories of illicit sex and drugs arguably had a better understanding of their children, however awkward a disciplinary conversation with a teenager could be as a result. Yet the parental transmission of youth culture was little understood at the time. In 1984, the sociologist Laurie Taylor mournfully told readers of *The Times* that 'Britain's youth, once thought unconventional and rebellious, is no longer revolting.' The article was illustrated by a picture of a twenty-something punk couple walking down a street holding their small child's hands, and was captioned 'Punk parents: a conservative new generation'. The implication was clear: parental responsibility meant creeping conservatism and the end, not only of youth, but of a person's engagement with youth culture (although the couple in the picture were still wearing their leather jackets and spiky hair with some dignity).[99]

The other thing that fertilized post-punk music and fashion was the creative talent of punk's original *enfant terrible*, John Lydon. The former Sex Pistol launched the New Wave era of 1978–88 with the release of Public Image Ltd's first, eponymous single, a sonic melange for which his new band dressed in tailored suits. For the critic Greil Marcus this was apostasy: 'New Wave', he wrote, 'was a code word not for punk without shock but for punk without meaning. Punk was not a musical genre but a moment in time that took shape as a language anticipating its own destruction . . . [Punk] was not history. It was a chance to create ephemeral events that would serve as judgements on whatever came next – that, too, was the meaning of no future.'[100] However, as Simon Reynolds has shown in his study of the New Wave, *Rip It Up and Start Again*, punk had both a history and a future. For all the Teddy Boy style references, its past lay in the 1960s, in a contrary but symbiotic relationship with Mod. As we have seen, on the one hand Mod helped to anglicise punk, lending it a very British class-consciousness that was absent in its American mentor. On the other, Mod drew from the energy of punk to renew its own assault on class stereotypes, while tempering the more anarchic, antisocial aspects of its sister movement.

Perhaps no other period demonstrates Mod's reproductive fertility more than the era when the past was so aggressively derided. Mod was codified sufficiently to be replicated while being eclectic enough to embrace new forms of expression, which reinvigorated it artistically

and made it appear relevant to successive generations of British youth.
Early in his career, Paul Weller had expressed his belief in musical
eclecticism:

I ain't rock 'n' roll. It's boring . . . leather jackets and greasy black hair, James
Dean and motorbikes, all that rock 'n' roll imagery is a crock of shit . . .
Rock 'n' roll's been dead for years. It died when Elvis went into the army.
The Who never played rock 'n' roll. They were an R&B band. They were
soul, Tamla Motown. I don't think anyone's played real rock 'n' roll for years
. . . You can't put tags on people. Things are so diverse.[101]

The New Wave embraced that diversity by drawing on American
funk, Jamaican reggae and the electronic music that had arrived from
Germany in the 1970s. Jon Savage has argued that a different kind of
'pop culture time' emerged in the punk era when 'a sixties mod jacket
might be worn with zoot-suit trousers and teddy boy brothel creepers'.
'Punk's historical collage', he concludes,

marked the moment when the linear forward motion of the sixties was
replaced by the loop. Suddenly all pop culture time was accessible, on the
same plane, available at once. In retrospect this process had begun during
1966 – at the very height of pop modernism – but it had taken ten years to
become a living, working part of youth culture.[102]

Yet punk's appeal had been limited by the fact that you could not
easily dance to it, and Mod brought to the New Wave a love of dance
music. Millions of British teenagers, like their parents and grandparents
before them, danced because it helped them to forget the anxiety and
disappointments of growing up in Britain; it offered an escape from
the boredom and fatigue of the working week; and it remained one
of the best ways to meet people for sex, friendship and marriage.
From the early Mod discotheques in 1960s London to the Northern
Soul dance floors around Manchester in the early 1970s, Mods had
combined a love of pop and rock with a love of dance.

The most popular form of dance music during the punk era was
disco, a fusion of American soul and funk with the electronic beats
developed in European studios using early synthesisers. Originating
in the gay clubs of New York, disco crossed boundaries of class, race

and sexuality to an extent that punk had hoped to do but never quite managed. American punks regarded disco with contempt as the ultimate form of synthetic, commercial music that encouraged bovine escapism.[103] But while British punks also wore 'Disco Sucks' badges, they happily danced to Anglo-Jamaican ska and reggae. Don Letts argues that this engagement with black music was a legacy of Mod:

There was a quantifiable effect of Jamaican culture on my white mates. In the 60s the skinheads were grooving to the Trojan sound, the Mods were into a bit of ska in the early days, and that went through all the way to punk. There was a quantifiable effect in shaping the identity of what it meant to be British, almost. People always talk about that, but what's also interesting is that all that white culture was having a very big impact on people like myself, or Norman Jay, or Jazzie B, or Goldie, or whoever. It was very much a two-way thing. There were just less of us.[104]

The pattern of musical and social engagement with black culture culminated in Two Tone, a post-punk movement that had little impact in America and showed the extent to which Mod and punk had become entwined in a new kind of 'pop culture time'. In Jon Savage's phrase, 'the twinned totems of white British pop', Mod and punk, had become 'the twinned totems' of British youth, an embrace that would shape the nation's youth culture for the next two decades.[105] Set within that context, in 1979 Two Tone was the first movement successfully to merge rock and dance music. 'Fuck art, let's dance', said a Madness T-shirt at the time. And millions did.

8

SUBSTANCE WRAPPED IN CHEQUERBOARD
Post-Punk Mod and the Making of Multiracial Britain

This is England, this is a white country, we don't want any black wogs and coons living here. We need to make clear to them they are not welcome. England is for white people, man . . . I want all of you here to vote for Enoch, support him, he's on our side. Enoch for Prime Minister! Throw the wogs out! Keep Britain white!

    Eric Clapton addressing fans in concert, Birmingham, 1976[1]

Dance and think at the same time.

    Horace Panter, the Specials' bassist, 2007[2]

WOULD YOU LIKE SOMETHING HARDER?

'Dreadlock Holiday', 10cc's perennially popular reggae song – referencing cricket and roadside rastafarians, pina colada and the offer of 'something harder' – reached No. 1 in the British charts in August 1978. That same year black, white and Asian youth fought running battles with skinheads on the streets of Lewisham, a multiracial district of south London. And the following year, Jerry Dammers, the son of a Church of England clergyman, founded an independent record label which would become the engine room of an alliance that the 'twinned totems', punk and Mod, formed with each other and which created the first multiracial youth culture in the Western world: Two Tone.

Dammers' own band the Specials, and others on the label like the Selecter, the Beat and Madness, combined white Anglo-American punk rock with reggae's faster ancestor ska (itself a fusion of American rhythm and blues and Caribbean calypso). Two Tone's style was an adaptation of the Jamaican Rude Boy look which, as we have seen, had influenced both Mods and skinheads in the 1960s and early 70s, with its sharp 'tonic' suits, porkpie hats, Ben Sherman shirts and loafers. And as well as giving ska a harder rock edge, punk's other legacy was to infuse it with populist left-wing politics. Two Tone became a social movement as well as a commercial success during its brief heyday from 1979 to 1981. It is one of the few times in the history of British youth culture when young people not only anticipated and reflected social change but could claim to have played a part in effecting it. The Specials' lead singer, Terry Hall, remembered: 'It felt really good, and really powerful. It felt like you were part of something important, like we could take on the world. You can be cynical, and I've been through it loads of times thinking, yeah, but what does music actually change? But the Specials were a case of where music really did change things.'[3]

A peculiarly British phenomenon that barely scratched the consciousness of American youth, Two Tone demonstrated that Britain was becoming a more racially integrated society than the United States. In both countries the 1970s was a dangerous time to be black. In Britain the far right of the Conservative Party, effectively led by Enoch Powell, together with violent neo-Nazi groups like the National Front, had mobilised a largely working-class white constituency – in the Front's case through young football hooligan gangs. Mrs Thatcher successfully courted that constituency prior to her election in 1979 by stating that 'some people are really rather afraid of being swamped by people of another culture'.[4] Against that background, Two Tone was an attempt to recover the multiracial spirit of Mod and early skinhead but in the context of contemporary music and politics rather than through an ersatz revival. It had its origins in an awkward alliance between punk and reggae that briefly flourished in the late 1970s.

At the same time that punk was peaking, Bob Marley's two-year residence in London from 1976 to 1978 stimulated the development of home-grown British reggae with groups like south London's Aswad and Birmingham's Steel Pulse, who sang about what it was like to grow up as a black youth in Britain and who would often perform at the same events as punk groups. Always keen to amplify their revolt, punks downplayed the fact that groups like the Rolling Stones had engaged with reggae – in their case thanks to Keith Richards' drug-addled sojourns in Jamaica with West Indian musicians, an exchange that influenced the underrated blues and reggae album *Black and Blue* (1976). An interest in reggae was a natural extension of that genera-tion's embrace of American rhythm and blues, and Eric Clapton's popular 1974 cover of Bob Marley's 'I Shot the Sheriff' had helped the genre to reach a white audience. But two years later when Clapton told his fans that England 'is a white country, we don't want any black wogs and coons living here', he revealed how partial and malformed that interest could be. Yet ironically, in the process he helped race relations in Britain evolve from the cultural day-trippers of his gener-ation to the young people of all races living alongside each other in the punk era.

MORE RIVER THAMES THAN MISSISSIPPI DELTA

The location of the meeting between punk and reggae was not a tropical recording studio but the schools, streets and parks of Britain's cities where young black and white Britons grew up together. Previously, white youths had connected with black culture largely through musical imports from America and the Caribbean, whether it was Motown soul or Trojan ska, but this changed in the late 1970s. As Don Lett explains: 'Popular music of the previous twenty years had been informed by black music – the difference was that the punks weren't being inspired by an alien culture thousands of miles away. They were being turned on by the man next door – more River Thames than Mississippi Delta.'[5]

British reggae, from heavy dub to lovers rock, was the first home-grown music of British-born black youth. For Brinsley Forde of Aswad, 'Our attitude has always been that the band and the music was about our experiences in inner-city London and a lot of the bands at that time were just copying music from Jamaica; they weren't telling their own story . . . Later on we were not only identified with by the black youth but also white kids. Indian kids were identifying because we were talking about what was happening to us.'[6] The original link between punk and reggae musicians was Don Letts, who recalled of his friendship with leading punks, 'We turned each other on through our different cultures. They liked me because I gave them access to Jamaican culture, and they turned me on to a white culture that didn't fucking exist before they came along.'[7] This coming together was celebrated by Bob Marley in his song 'Punky Reggae Party', whose lyrics referenced the Damned, the Clash and the Jam.[8] Marley's American biographer reports that when reggae's creator heard the Clash in London 'he admired their spunky courage and anger in the face of England's social stratification and class-based economic oppression', as well as acknowledging the practical help punks gave to British reggae artists.[9] Yet when questioned by Charles Shaar Murray about 'Punky Reggae Party', Marley admitted that he had had little to do with the writing of the song – he revealed that his producer Lee 'Scratch' Perry had written the lyrics – and didn't seem to know much about groups like the Jam that were mentioned in it.

The initial artistic results of this well-meaning alliance were negligible. Awkward attempts to fuse the bass-heavy, marijuana-influenced sound of reggae and the trebly, amphetamine-fuelled noise of punk resulted in songs like 'Guns of Brixton' and 'White Man in Hammersmith Palais' by the Clash and, less famously but more effectively, 'S.U.S.' and 'Jah War' by the Ruts. Yet the genre was popularised by UB40 and the Police. The latter's drummer, Stewart Copeland, admitted that 'We completely bastardized reggae; we plundered it without remorse; we took from it what was useful to us but we made no attempt to repackage it and deliver it back to the people, which would have been false.'[10] Moreover, punks often romanticised black life in Britain. 'White Man in Hammersmith Palais' was written by Joe Strummer after he had been taken to a reggae gig at the Palais by Letts, who later observed that 'the ghetto is something that you get out of, not into, and Joe had a romanticized idea of what ghetto life was about'.[11]

Most British blacks, on the other hand, had little time for the mystical pan-Africanism of Rastafarianism that permeated reggae, even when it was refracted through the experiences of fellow Britons like Aswad. As Compton Amanor of Two Tone group the Selecter explained: 'We're born here, we're British. The Rasta things always had to encircle itself with the myth of Roots which, in the end, takes your identity away even more, gives you more hang-ups. You talk to kids, say "Where are you from?" and they say "Africa" – but they were born here. It doesn't really mean anything.'[12] In addition, black identity in Britain has always revolved more around African American culture; hence American artists, from James Brown through to Beyoncé, have had more long-term influence on black British youth culture than Bob Marley. The posthumous deification of the dread-locked Marley (similar to that of John Lennon, who died a year before him) has obscured the fact that creatively important though his stay in London was – after all, it produced the album *Exodus* – he was not capable of speaking for British youth, except in the generically mystical 'one love' patois that he employed in much the same way as the hippies had done in the 1960s, and with much the same effect.

In fact, punks and hippies had more in common than either cared to admit. In the early 1970s, after dropping out of boarding school and then art college, Joe Strummer had spent time in the hippie squats of west London, but cut all ties with his past when he joined the Clash. 'Punks were hippies with zips', the sharp-suited punk poet John Cooper Clarke once remarked.[13] It is also worth noting that hippies were instrumental in bringing punk and reggae to a wider audience: the long-haired radio show host John Peel became the greatest promoter of post-punk music in Britain. And it was Peel who was the first to play the Specials' debut single, 'Gangsters', on Radio 1 in May 1979.

IT'S LIKE A ZEBRA CROSSING AS FAR AS YOU CAN SEE

The first big Rock Against Racism (RAR) concert in London's Victoria Park in 1978, headlined by the Clash, was witnessed by a largely white audience. The last RAR event took place in 1981 in Leeds and was headlined by the Specials. Looking out at the crowd, singer Neville Staples remarked: 'It's like a zebra crossing, black and white, black and white as far as you can see.'[14] It was Two Tone which had created this new audience pattern.

RAR was triggered by David Bowie's brief flirtation with fascism during his 'Thin White Duke' phase, when he claimed that 'Adolf Hitler was one of the first rock stars', and by Eric Clapton's racist comments at a concert in Birmingham in the summer of 1976. Whereas Bowie made a full apology for his claim that 'Britain is ready for a Fascist leader', blaming his comments on a combination of drug addiction and an excessive reading of Nietzsche, Clapton never fully retracted his. After initially trying to make light of the rant, claiming he was apolitical and likening the incident to a scene from *Monty Python*, he later reiterated his support for Enoch Powell in several interviews; as late as 2007 he denied that Powell was a racist in an interview with Melvyn Bragg. Given that Clapton was so indebted to the Delta blues, his call to 'Keep Britain white' showed once again that artists and fans could absorb and consume the music of other cultures without respecting the men and women who created them, still less engaging in interracial relations that might form the basis of a more equal society.[15]

RAR was the first political movement to emerge directly from British youth culture. It was launched in 1976 by left-wing activists with support from the Clash, and by 1978 it had organised 300 concerts around Britain that brought together punk and reggae performers. According to Gene October, one of the movement's founders:

Before the Rock Against Racism thing really got going, if you were white, there were parts of town you simply didn't go into, because the blacks would kick the shit out of you, not because they were racist, but because you might be. The black kids wanted to mix and later, after Punk happened and Rock Against Racism got going, they could. You'd walk past a bunch of Rastas and they'd be fine, 'How you going, mate?' You'd get black kids at Punk shows, Punk kids at Reggae shows. That simply couldn't have happened a year earlier. That's how much Rock Against Racism changed things.[16]

It certainly made an impact on Gurinder Chadha, the director of *Bhaji on the Beach* (1993) and *Bend It Like Beckham* (2002). As a teenager, she travelled to the Victoria Park concert from her home in Southall, where racist abuse had been part of her family's daily life since their arrival from Kenya in the early 1960s. 'Before Rock Against Racism there was a sense that it was OK to be racist but with RAR we got to see that there were others willing to speak out about racism and talk about a different kind of Britain', Chadha remembered. 'The whole of the park was jumping up and down to The Clash. It was an incredibly emotional moment because for the first time I felt that I was surrounded by people on my side. That was the first time I thought that something had changed Britain for ever.'[17]

Jerry Dammers was there too but he saw that almost all of the 60,000 concert-goers were white. As he recalled: 'We started out at the same time as RAR so it was part of the same thing and for me it was no good being anti-racist if you didn't involve black people, so what the Specials tried to do was create something more integrated.'[18] In that the Two Tone movement would succeed – and it did so by returning to the source of British youth culture.

WE HAVE TO GET TO THESE PEOPLE

From the 1950s to the 1990s Britain was the portal of black American, Caribbean and African music for the rest of Europe (and sometimes for the whole world). During that period Mods were the most consistent champions of black music: they had been the first white Britons to fall in love with modern jazz, before turning to rhythm and blues, soul, ska and reggae. Little wonder then that both in style and substance, the Two Tone movement was a child of Mod.

Jerry Dammers had been a teenage Mod in the late 1960s, before becoming a skinhead after an unhappy two-week stay on a hippie commune. The son of a radical clergyman in the Church of England, Dammers entered the world as Gerald Dankey in southern India in 1955. The family returned to England the following year and settled in Coventry, an English Detroit, which had became prosperous through its car industry (Dammers would see Two Tone as a multiracial English version of Motown). Shy yet single-minded, his politics were shaped as much by his reverend father as by the irreverence of punk. Like the original Mods, Dammers was into ska and had been writing his own songs since his early teens, setting out to create 'a weird new music that was a Jamaican-British cross-over'.[19] At art school when punk happened, Dammers formed a band, the Coventry Automatics, with bassist Horace Panter; admired by the Clash, they supported them on tour. The idea for the Specials came out of a concert that Dammers played in the south of England in 1978, when the show was disrupted by violent skinheads mounting the stage and assaulting the lead singer of the support act. 'That was the night the Specials concept was born', remembered Dammers:

I idealistically thought, we have to get to these people. It was obvious that a mod and skinhead revival was coming, and I was trying to make sure it didn't go the way of the National Front and the British Movement. I saw punk as a piss-take of rock music, as rock music committing suicide, and it was great and it was really funny, but I couldn't believe people took it as a serious musical genre which they then had to copy. It seemed to be a bit more healthy to have an integrated kind of British music, rather than white people playing rock and black people playing their music. Ska was an integration of the two.[20]

Coventry was an appropriate crucible for Two Tone. By the 1970s, like Detroit, it was a declining industrial city with unemployment reaching 20 per cent, one of the highest rates in Britain. The promise made by politicians in 1973 that the United Kingdom would acquire West German standards of living by joining the EEC had not materialised; in fact West Germany was partly responsible for Coventry's decline. The superiority of German car design and engineering, coupled with industrial relations that were less poisoned by class conflict, had helped to destroy the British car industry. There was a feeling in many towns and cities like Coventry that Britain had won the war but lost the peace.

The city had also acquired a significant black and Asian population, drawn there by the promise of work, whose experience of racial hostility was now exacerbated by the city's economic problems. Nationally, between 1972 and 1981 black unemployment increased 325 per cent in comparison to 138 per cent for all workers.[21] However, during the 1970s and 80s young people of different races grew up alongside each other in large numbers for the first time and therefore became more familiar with each other's culture. They represented a new social geography and an emerging post-colonial culture that the comments of Enoch Powell and Eric Clapton failed to address: how do you, in Clapton's words, 'send back wogs and coons' who are not immigrants but the first numerically substantial generation of British-born black and Asian youth, and who want to be accepted as Britons? Discussing their relations with the police in 1973 the Home Secretary told the Cabinet:

Difficulties arise with young coloured people in particular and many of these were born here or came here as small children and have spent their forma-tive years here. These, the second generation, who are not immigrants at all, have their own difficulties, growing up in two cultures, that of their parents and that of the larger society around them. But as British born and bred they rightly expect to be accepted on the same terms as others regard-less of colour.[22]

Youth clubs, seen by some politicians as a solution to teenage disaffection since they became state funded in 1960, were not helping at all, according to Baron Hunt. Hunt, who had led the expedition to conquer Everest in 1953 that launched the Queen's reign with imperial optimism, concluded in his 1976 report on youth clubs, *Seen But Not Served*: 'The youth services failure to meet the immediate and crucial need of young blacks has been partly responsible for the growth in separate black and white youth clubs. Many authorities have given up artificial attempts to keep youth clubs multi-racial.'[23]

Faced with police harassment, racist teachers and employers, and retreating en masse into self-segregation, many black teenagers rejected the country that seemed to have rejected them, a spirit captured by the Jamaican poet Linton Kwesi Johnson in works like *Inglan Is a Bitch* (1980). But many others began to engage with the 'Bitch' in the late 1970s as a new youth culture emerged. Gurinder Chadha socialised with young whites for the first time through Two Tone. In 2004 she recalled: 'That really for me was the first time that I felt really comfort-able about being black, and Asian and British at the same time in one space.'[24] Chadha and others like her were joined by a generation of white Britons who had grown up alongside other races. For a few, the experience confirmed their prejudices. But many more became less willing to accept the xenophobia and racism of parents, teachers and the rock stars of an earlier age. Two Tone sprang from and spoke to the first generation of young Britons who vocally rejected racism in such large numbers that doing so began to be the norm rather than the drilled preoccupation of leftist groups. Its followers opposed racism not just because they felt it was morally wrong but because doing so was the natural outcome of their lived experience of multicultural Britain – of growing up alongside people of different ethnic backgrounds as neighbours, schoolmates, colleagues, friends and lovers.

The Two Tone label was run from Dammers' modest home in Coventry. Dammers designed the record covers and the company logo himself, referencing the Op Art designs of the 1960s in his use of geometric black and white shapes and using clear, bold typography from the same period. The Two Tone logo, known as 'Walt Jabsco', was a drawing of the archetypal Rude Boy, while that produced by rival label Go!Feet for fellow ska band the Beat depicted a Rude Girl. Dammers admitted that 'When I designed the 2-Tone logo, race was not really on my mind, the black and white check was based on the sticky tape I used to decorate my bike with when I was a "mini mod" aged 10.'[25] Yet Two Tone design soon found its way on to the clothing and accessories of millions of young black, white and Asian Britons and came to visually symbolise the racial unity espoused by the movement.

The 1979 Two Tone tour of Britain, documented in the feature film *Dance Craze*, included Madness, the Specials and the Selecter. It started in Brighton, with publicity shots of the groups taken on the beach in a deliberate attempt to connect Two Tone with its Mod heritage. Indeed, as Horace Panter recalls, 'Our tour was put together rather like a sixties package tour: three bands, low ticket prices, lots of dancing.'[26] On its way around the country the tour's multi-race audience took many by surprise. Suggs of Madness remembers police sometimes being called to venues because concerned members of the public assumed that the large numbers of black and white youth gathered outside spelled trouble.[27] Inside, the concerts were anarchic events, with hundreds of black and white youths clambering on the stage to sing and dance alongside the band as they reached the evening's finale.

For Billy Bragg, whose wife Juliet managed the Selecter, this multiracial Mod/punk hybrid was the high point of the post-punk era: 'It was an incredible moment. I can remember [the Specials' veteran Jamaican trombone player] Rico saying [to Dammers] "Jerry, if your army combine with my army, it's a revolution!" It floated on a tide of what was going on in society.'[28] The Specials' bass player Horace Panter agreed:

I don't like pontificating about 'cultural identity in Thatcher's Britain', but The Specials took the spirit of the time and turned it from negative, apathetic and nihilistic to positive. They made people dance and think at the same time. Just like the blues, where it all came from in the first place: sing about your worries and your feelings and turn them into a celebration. The Specials and the 2-Tone 'movement' became more than just pop music. We were actually out to change things: seven very different people guided by one person's vision.[29]

Madness, from Camden in north London, were the only all-white group on the Two Tone roster and although they regularly attracted a crowd of skinheads, group member Chas Smyth remembers feeling part of a change: 'The multicultural thing was a big deal for us, we felt we were part of a wave, you know. It was dance, it was good time, its ideals were honourable and progressive, pretty cool. Its camaraderie was strong, too.'[30]

Two Tone was a commercial success, dominating the charts from 1979 to 1981. The Specials had seven Top 10 hits in two years and two best-selling albums, while Madness, who left the label and survived the demise of the cult, had 16 Top 10 hits and two best-selling albums. On 7 November 1980 three Two Tone bands made an appearance on *Top of the Pops*. Like all youth cults, Two Tone offered its young adherents pleasure and excitement. Yet it was one of the shortest-lived subcultures in Britain, and it dissipated rapidly once the Specials fell apart, which showed how much the movement had relied on the musical and political direction of a founder who became emotionally fragile under pressure. The group was destroyed by the short-sighted egotism of its members and the burden of expectation placed on Jerry Dammers' shoulders as one of the spokesmen for that generation. 'It was astonishing', wrote the Specials' Horace Panter. 'A band formed by a militant socialist who was sometimes referred to as a benevolent dictator. A band that stood for unity and racial harmony but split up because they couldn't stand each other. A head-on collision between wide-eyed idealism and the coldest, most cynical of businesses.'[31]

A NORMAL PART OF EVERYDAY LIFE

It would be naïve to suggest that Two Tone had an immediate impact on race relations beyond its core following, however large that was for a time. After all, this youth culture lasted only two years and when the Specials split up, record companies soon abandoned the movement, as executives moved on to promote another strange child of the post-punk era, New Romanticism.

For some platoons of this multicultural army Two Tone was just another teenage uniform, issued by retailers eager to cash in on a subculture they neither understood nor particularly cared for. As Horace Panter recalled: 'Whether we liked it or not we were still "pop music", and our fashion stance was as interchangeable as any other commodity. It was difficult to move without seeing black and white check. Pauline Black said that even Evans Outsize were doing it.'[32] The half Anglo-Jewish, half Nigerian lead singer of the Selecter, raised in Essex by white foster parents, Black was the female figurehead of Two Tone, and remembers 'seeing clones of myself in the audience'.[33]

For teenagers growing up in less multiracial neighbourhoods outside the big towns and cities it was predominantly a style, not a lived experience. In Coventry itself, the National Front continued openly to recruit on the city's streets and there was a rise in the number of racially motivated attacks in Coventry and elsewhere in Britain during the 1980s. In the nation's multicultural capital, Two Tone could not prevent the New Cross massacre of 1981, in which thirteen black teenagers were burned to death during a house party after a probable arson attack by white racists. Nor did it dislodge the institutional racism of the police, who failed sufficiently to investigate New Cross and other incidents of racially motivated crime.

Frustration that alliances with white liberals did little to protect black people, still less progress their claims for equality and justice, was the political basis of hip hop's creation and helps to explain its popularity among black youth in England and America. Crucial though reggae and Two Tone were in establishing an identity for the first substantial generation of British-born blacks, hip hop had an attraction for later generations that these earlier musical styles couldn't match.

Public Enemy's 'Fight the Power' appealed to those searching for music that expressed their anger at the continuing ferocity of racial discrimination. In this context, the poetics of the best rap lyrics displayed a literacy and political awareness that Mod, in its image-based obsession with clothing over music, rarely matched, save in the lyrics of Paul Weller and Damon Albarn. Meanwhile, hip hop's celebration of criminality, hypersexuality, its attendant misogyny and homophobia, and the gaudy, conspicuous consumption of 'bling' that characterised so-called Gangsta rap, captivated black youths for whom politics of any kind were either a dead end or just a bore.

Yet Two Tone had a long-term legacy: it set a precedent in Britain for public, multiracial socialising among people from a variety of class backgrounds. Crucially, these interactions were connected more to youthful hedonism than to political discourses or workplace encounters; and they rose above the subterranean, nocturnal world of sex and drugs that had characterised similar interactions in previous generations.

Artistically, its legacy extends beyond the fact that groups as musically diverse as the Prodigy and the Libertines sampled the Specials' work, or that other multiracial groups, like Bloc Party or Plan B, became more common afterwards, significant though these trends were. Although in music and fashion Two Tone was essentially a dialogue between white and West Indian youth, with Asians like Gurinder Chadha involved largely as fans, it was one of the inspirations for Britain's first distinctively Asian subculture. Bhangra, which was brought into the mainstream by artists such as Asian Dub Foundation in 1993, took Two Tone's musical formula and combined traditional Punjabi music and hip hop, while appealing to a diverse fanbase. The artists also employed Bhangra deliberately to challenge the romanticisation of Indian spirituality, which from the Beatles onwards had permeated the image of Asia in British youth culture.

However, Two Tone's most important achievement was that it drew battle lines that would never be entirely erased. Describing the movement as 'substance wrapped in chequerboard', for Mark Lamarr 'these songs may not have ended a war, but at least they made you decide which side you were on'.[34] Forming part of a broad post-punk popular culture, Two Tone marked out generational attitudes to race in the same way that punk had sharpened attitudes to class. The Sex Pistols had made it easier to criticise and ridicule the monarchy. Although around 80 per cent of Britons did not want to abolish the institution, it became acceptable for people to have at most an occasional interest in the monarchy, without ascribing to its essentially conservative ideology of class. As the historian Antony Taylor comments, 'the 1970s showed that the monarchy was no longer above criticism, especially by the young', and this contributed to the process by which the media gradually broke down 'the taboo on reporting royal misdeeds', while also making them a routine object of satire.[35] Similarly Two Tone established that a multiracial society was here to stay. For the first time, a sizeable generation of British-born blacks and Asians came of age in the 1970s and their involvement in Two Tone rebuked Enoch Powell's supporters by demonstrating not only that they had a cultural influence on British life but also that they were a social presence and that large numbers of their white peers wanted to engage with them.

Of course, it was not a straightforward generational divide, just as attitudes to class were not clearly demarcated in that way during the 1960s. Many young Britons, and not just reactionary skinheads, remained anxious or just downright hostile to the idea of a multiracial society, and transmitted that attitude to children born in the 1980s and 90s. But Two Tone did set a social precedent that showed what was possible, in the same way that civil rights legislation set a moral and legal precedent that showed what was not permissible. By setting this precedent the Two Tone movement contributed to a slow but steady reduction in racism in both the private and public spheres. As Paul Gilroy observed in 2004, Two Tone 'made the encounter between black and white a normal part of everyday life; it relieved such friend-ships of the weight they had been made to bear.'[36]

There was a marked rise in mixed-race relationships in the thirty years following the demise of Two Tone. A survey in 1989 showed that 24 per cent of black British men and 18 per cent of black British women had white partners; among young people in their twenties the historic gender gap in such relationships was closing, with 27 per cent of black males in mixed marriages and 28 per cent of black women. (These were conservative figures, since they did not include the generally higher level of non-marital relationships.) Between 1987 and 1997, the overall numbers of mixed marriages almost doubled, giving Britain one of the 'highest levels of rates of interracial marriage anywhere in the western world', according to Yasmin Alibhai-Brown. The result was a rapidly growing mixed-race population, estimated at 350,000, over half of whom were under 18 years of age – in other words, born after 1979.[37] There are caveats to be made: Asians remained less likely to contract mixed marriages and statistical evidence does not make a direct connection between this youth culture and racial integration. However, there can be little doubt that Two Tone represented a step change in the way that young Britons of different races interacted.

This fulcrum of familiarity became apparent at the time of the swansong of Two Tone in 1981, when the Specials' song 'Ghost Town' reached No. 1 just as multiracial rioting in protest against poverty, unemployment and racist policing swept England. As the mournful trombone of Rico kicked in, accompanied by the despairing deadpan vocals of Terry Hall and backed by the angry passion of Neville Staples, the song's video showed the Specials driving around empty London streets hunched in a car. Commenting on a lack of fun and opportunity, 'Ghost Town' provided the soundtrack for a generation of young black and white people. In the words of Angela McRobbie, the song was 'a classic single, envisaging and documenting the new intersections of black and white youth in Britain's cities'.[38] By reaching No. 1 in the charts, it rebuked those who claimed that Mod and its descendants were just consumerism dressed up as rebellion.

Jerry Dammers wrote the song on tour when he felt that his dream was being torn away from him. 'Everyone was getting under pressure and the band was getting tired', he recalled.

It wasn't just that, the country was falling apart. You travelled from town to town and what was happening was terrible. In Liverpool, all the shops were shuttered up, everything was closing down. Margaret Thatcher had apparently gone mad, she was closing down all the industries, throwing millions of people on the dole. We could actually see it by touring around. You could see that frustration and anger in the audience. In Glasgow, there were these little old ladies on the streets selling all their household goods, their cups and saucers. It was unbelievable. It was clear that something was very, very wrong.[39]

IF THOSE NIGGERS DON'T GET OFF THAT FENCE

'We had always considered ourselves as a strictly British phenomenon', wrote Horace Panter of Two Tone, 'and had talked about how difficult it would be to expect French, Germans or Americans to understand what we were about. Most of those countries had only just accepted reggae, and now here was a gang of upstarts from England (not Jamaica) who were playing it differently.'[40] But despite some bemusement, Two Tone groups generally found a welcome on the Continent. 'The audiences were no less enthusiastic than those in England', observed Panter. 'Europe seemed to take to us immediately.'[41] Neville Staples found it more difficult: 'Going to Europe could be a disconcerting experience for the black guys in the band,' he wrote. 'A pattern developed on the continent, where the fans loved us but our reception outside the TV studio or concert hall would verge on the hostile.' That experience became more acute when they travelled through Communist East Germany where black faces were a rarity, but in West Germany in 1980 he found a different audience that included, in his view, 'the most progressive people around'.[42]

America was a different story. However much was wrong with Britain at the time, Two Tone exposed the sharper racial divisions in the United States. As a black teenager born in Britain and growing up in Brixton and Camberwell, Don Letts had been influenced by black American music, style and politics. But, as he observed, 'The social development of black America did not really apply to the UK, the difference being their forefathers had been dragged there kicking and screaming, whilst my parents had willingly bought a ticket to this country from Jamaica.'[43] Moreover, after a century of segregation it was not until the 1960s that a modicum of equality before the law was established in the United States. In addition, Britain had (and continues to have) a lower level of self-segregation than the United States: British youth are statistically more likely than American teenagers to grow up alongside each other in the same neighbourhoods, to go to the same schools, and to be entertained and socialise in the same space.

Two Tone had virtually no impact in the United States – despite the huge efforts that Two Tone groups made during their brief existence to bring their message to a country where mixed marriages were illegal in most states of the Union until 1967. A cover of the *NME* in 1980 heralded the Specials' tour of the US with black and white checks imposed on the Stars and Stripes, and a headline that read 'The 2-Toning of America',[44] but the group returned with mixed feelings about a country whose music had influenced them yet seemed alien on closer inspection. As Horace Panter remembered:

America had always held a fascination for me. Musically it was where it all came from. If there hadn't been blues and country music, there wouldn't have been ska, reggae and rock 'n' roll, with all its subdivisions and cul-de-sacs. There wouldn't have been Searchers, Beatles, Rolling Stones, Kinks or Small Faces to fire the imagination in my pirate radio days. America was where it still lived . . . It was almost like a pilgrimage.[45]

Like previous pilgrims, the Specials discovered that the country of their imagination was more complex than that which they had consumed second-hand through music and film. The group had gained a following on the more open-minded west and east coasts, but in between ska was seen as a curious British hybrid. 'Now you're in the States, are you going to continue playing Jamaican music?' one journalist asked. Dammers laughed and replied: 'We don't *play* Jamaican music.'[46] Bemusement was replaced by hostility in many places, as in Chicago where the band were asked to leave their hotel because the staff objected to having a multiracial group staying there.

The poster girl of Two Tone also discovered two Americas. In her memoirs, Pauline Black wrote: 'The cognoscenti on the east and west coasts who had possibly explored a broader horizon than the World Series (the only world event happening in one country that I know of!) may have been open to new fashions in music, but the vast expanse of "good ole boy and girl" ten-gallon hat wearers and wet T-shirt bosom jigglers inhabiting the Midwest and beyond thought we were a bunch of aliens that had just landed in their backyards.' African Americans were just as puzzled as whites. The small number of blacks who went to see the band 'left bemused', recalled Black, 'or if they were reggae enthusiasts, congratulated us on a job well done, but seemed somewhat baffled as to why we played everything at such breakneck speed'.[47]

However, like every British band that had toured America since the

Beatles, the Selecter didn't just find an ignorance of British pop culture; they experienced a higher level of racism and self-segregation that extended from daily life right into America's cultural matrix. What seemed to disturb Americans was not the existence of black entertainers with an entourage but 'the sight of six black people and three white people laughing, joking and chatting with each other'.[48] Driving through America's vast interior from one liberal coastline to the other, the band often sat in silent restaurants waiting in vain to be served before leaving hungry, hearing the buzz of conversation resume inside once the door swung shut.

American attitudes to racial mixing continued to have a limiting effect on US youth culture. Conventional histories of rock 'n' roll reiterate the idea that Elvis Presley broke America's radio and chart segregation by getting black music played on stations with mainly white audiences. Yet Pauline Black noted that a quarter of a century later, Two Tone stalled in the United States because with a few exceptions broadcasters didn't know what to do with a music that was so visibly, aurally and determinedly multiracial. 'As far as American radio was concerned,' she wrote, 'there was black music and there was white music and although crossover hits regularly happened, these categories still prevailed. 2Tone music didn't lend itself to either side of this racial barrier . . . and fell into the yawning crack between black and white America, then largely disappeared once the bands returned home.'[49] This only exacerbated the perennial problem faced by any artist trying 'to break America', namely that the continent was so vast and its radio stations so localised that it was much harder than in Britain to reach a national audience.

Black noticed that white Americans felt less threatened by the mixed-race group when they realised that these 'aliens' in their midst were from a foreign land. 'I lost count', she remembers, 'of the times that I went into shops and was treated like dog dirt until they heard my accent and discovered I was British and then everything changed and it was "please" and "thank you" and "hope you have a good day y'all." That was how it was in the cities, but it was just plain hostile if you strayed off the interstate roads.'[50] Maltreatment in the southern states culminated in a narrow escape from violent rednecks during an interview with Garry Bushell of *Sounds* at the Southfork Ranch – incidentally the place where the popular TV drama *Dallas* was filmed.

The Selecter were being photographed sitting on a fence in their crisp Mod/Rude Boy attire when a flatbed truck drew up alongside the Two Tone tour bus, with a gang of Texan men on board wielding baseball bats and wearing angry scowls. The tour manager was summoned over to the truck and told, 'If those niggers don't get off that fence and back on that bus right away then there is gonna be trouble.'[51]

Back home, Bushell's article, entitled 'RUDIES UBER DALLAS', and its accompanying photo captured the tension of that moment at Southfork and the oceanic difference in racial attitudes between Britain and America that Two Tone exposed. And it was the racial fence-sitting of young Britons, their refusal to come down on one side or the other, both musically and socially, that had forged one of its most extra-ordinary youth cultures.

SCARY CONCRETE JUNGLES

'By the mid-Eighties, the whole Mod movement was a sad, dwindling affair . . .' observed Terry Rawlings, one of the chronicler-participants in the cult. 'In London at least, [it] was as underground as it was possible to get without being buried. It was more like a little close-knit community that revolved around one or two club nights dotted around the capital and a handful of almost guerrilla-type Mod outfits that fought gamely on, regardless of any or no interest.'[52]

One sign of Mod's temporary waning in the mid-1980s was the fact that a long-awaited screen adaptation of Colin MacInnes's *Absolute Beginners* flopped when it was released in 1986, helping to send Britain's biggest film company, Goldcrest, into liquidation. This was the first attempt to film a novel that since its publication in 1959 had been regarded as *the* literary expression of mid-twentieth-century British youth culture, comparable to the cult status that J. D. Salinger's *Catcher in the Rye* enjoyed in the United States. Paul Weller described *Absolute Beginners* as 'the ultimate Mod book; a book of inspiration'; and in a foreword to the reissue of MacInnes's essays, *England Half English*, in 1986 Weller wrote, 'Mobility, optimism, affluence and a sense of the new. Sounds like a fairy-tale or was it only a film?'[53]

The film was released at the peak of both Margaret Thatcher's popularity and that of Weller's jazz-soul group the Style Council, many of whose songs pointed out that mobility, optimism and affluence was just a fairy tale in the 1980s for those caught on the wrong side of Thatcher's monetarist economic policies. In 1985 Weller had joined Billy Bragg, Gary Kemp, Jerry Dammers, Elvis Costello and the Smiths (among others) on the Red Wedge tour of Britain. With posters designed by the self-proclaimed modernist Neville Brody, Red Wedge aimed to galvanise Left-inclined British youth against the Conservative government. Its failure to impact on the 1987 general election in any way left Weller and others disillusioned with the Labour Party, a feeling that would be revisited when Tony Blair attempted a new alliance with youth in the Britpop era.

Founded after Weller broke up the Jam at the height of their fame, the Style Council (1983–89) was a controversial affair. Joining forces with the Merton Parkas' keyboardist Mick Talbot, Weller left behind the guitar-driven R&B of the Jam, and gave full rein to his passion for soul and jazz, while emphasising Continental European style. On the release of the Style Council's EP *À Paris* in 1983 Weller declared: 'I don't see myself as British anymore. We regard ourselves as European.'[54] The album that followed, *Café Bleu* (1984), with cover shots of a crisply casual duo in Paris, instrumental soul-jazz tunes and sleeve notes from Weller's alter ego 'The Cappuccino Kid' – written in the beat style of Colin MacInnes by Paolo Hewitt – alienated many fans in the post-punk era. But what critics missed was that his use of jazz was a conscious return to some of Mod's roots and by the end of the 1980s he would also be exploring new sounds, engaging with contemporary dance music; his final Style Council album, *Modernism: A New Decade* (1989), was inspired by House music but was rejected by his record label, leaving Weller to face the 1990s as a solo artist.

The box office failure of *Absolute Beginners* had more to do with the fact that by the 1980s, relatively few British teenagers were aware of the novel's significance or had heard of Colin MacInnes. Its setting in the jazz world of 1950s Soho perhaps also puzzled those who were in thrall to the folk memory of the 1960s and believed that British youth culture had begun in that decade. The critics who panned it agreed that the film's failure was largely due to the fact that its director, Julien Temple, decided to eschew the realism of *Quadrophenia* for an episodic musical format that was designed to appeal to the first generation of teenagers raised on the pop video – a move that alienated older Mods who were aware of the novel's significance and resented the fact that many of its themes were lost in translation. This despite Temple's punk credentials and his marshalling of talents spanning three eras of Mod-related British music: Ray Davies, David Bowie, Paul Weller and Jerry Dammers all acted in, and/or scored some of the music for the film.

Modernism in its broader sense had a bad press by the 1980s. Modernist architecture in particular appeared to have failed aesthetically and socially, in its professed aim of making Britain a better place to live. As the architectural critic Owen Hatherley wrote, 'England loves the 1960s: its indie rock obsesses over a retread of the last time it seemed internationally significant, its populace yearns for the 1966 of *Revolver* and being good at football . . . the exception to this is in architecture.'[55] While music and fashion were incorporated by commercial and political elites into a canon of British culture that defined the nation – and the National Trust took charge of Paul McCartney's and John Lennon's childhood terraced houses, both of which were listed as Grade II buildings – architecture did not become part of the heritage industry. According to Hatherley: 'The sixties [heritage] industry was always based on pop culture rather than the wider modernisation of housing because it had less dispute within it.'[56]

For teenagers living in tower blocks made unsavoury by poverty and anger, modernism – if it was understood at all – seemed disconnected from a youth culture that promised style as a substitute for wealth and power. Yet the extent of tower block living was exaggerated. Construction peaked in 1966, when they accounted for 26 per cent of local authority housing construction; in the 1970s, when high rises began to come under attack, construction fell back to 10 per cent, the same level as it had been during the housebuilding boom of 1953–59.[57] That was of course little consolation for those already trapped in them.

With its pounding punk-ska beat, the 1979 Specials' song 'Concrete Jungle' depicted the life of a young man living in fear of crime and racist gangs in Coventry's high-rise flats. The Jam song 'The Planner's Dream Goes Wrong' (1982) was another attack on Brutalist social housing, in which Paul Weller suggested a class divide between architects and those forced to live in the places they created; as he later commented, 'the people who design the scary concrete jungles can all go back to their mock-Tudor country homes at the weekend'.[58] In a 1981 article for *The Face* entitled 'The Other Side of Futurism' Weller tried to square his faith in Mod style with some of the environmental consequences of the modern movement. 'We are now living *A Clockwork Orange*,' he wrote, 'the crumbling tenements, the piss-stench lifts, the hungry roaming groups of teenagers, muggings, rape, murder, the whole savagery of *A Clockwork Orange*. That whole barren landscape is here and has been collecting for the last ten years.'[59]

Whereas early Mods had absorbed and celebrated the influence of French culture, in everything from hairstyle and clothing to food and interior design, architectural modernism was now blamed on the inhumane ideology of one man – its Swiss-French godfather, Le Corbusier. Although he had not designed a single building in Britain, he and his British followers were attacked for doing more damage than the Luftwaffe bombs. Nazi destruction of the nation's cities had enabled the likes of Basil Spence to apply their ideas on a blank, rubble-strewn canvas, notably designing a new cathedral in Coventry which became a symbol of Anglo-German reconciliation. 'Has he done any harm?' Spence had asked in the *Sunday Telegraph* on Le Corbusier's death in 1965. 'His arrogance was typically Gallic, and he sometimes ignored the requirements of ordinary people', he wrote, concluding, 'I think if you're a slave to any idea in architecture it would do harm . . . You have to accept the challenge of quality, and then apply it to what already exists, trying to make it part of the environment.'[60] Spence sometimes failed to apply that wisdom. In the same year, his design for the concrete tower blocks of 'Hutchesontown' arose in Glasgow's Gorbals, their crude balconies jutting like an arrogant chin over the rotting landscape of what had once been Britain's largest shipbuilding community (and from which John Stephen had escaped to London in 1952).

The stabbing of architectural modernism intensified in the 1980s as Margaret Thatcher implemented her vision of post-industrial Britain. Christopher Booker, who had attacked the aspirant modernity of mid-twentieth-century British youth in his widely read 1969 book *The Neophiliacs*, took his critique to new heights when he blamed Le-Corbusier-inspired architecture for the riots of black youth in

Tottenham's Broadwater Farm Estate in 1985, during which a policeman was killed. Coincidentally, an exhibition of Le Corbusier was showing at the Hayward Gallery on London's South Bank when some of his attackers went on trial. This, together with the riots, prompted a splenetic article for the *Daily Mail* called 'Concrete Jungle', in which Booker wrote: 'The huge windswept housing estates into which millions had been kennelled were not just soul-destroying to look at. They were literally the most inhuman form of architecture ever conceived by the mind of man, creating frustration and loneliness, as well as their by-products, vandalism and crime, on an almost unimaginable scale.' He concluded that 'the real tribute to the power of Le Corbusier's ideas in London is not that being staged in the Hayward Gallery. It is the one unfolding in that courtroom at the Old Bailey.'[61]

Blaming the concrete walkways and 'kennels' of Broadwater Farm for rioting not only ignored the fact that poverty, unemployment and racist policing were at the root of young blacks' anger. Booker and other peddlers of 'neophiliac' clichés ignored the fact that modernist architecture remained quite popular in the affluent parts of Britain's inner cities and suburbs. The owners of Wells Coates' famous Isokon flats in Hampstead, for example, were not provoked into violent disorder at the sight of the harmonious lines and curves of its white-washed concrete walls and balconies; nor was there an epidemic of mugging and rape in the lifts of Ernö Goldfinger's Trellick Tower. Built in 1972, Trellick Tower was home to a mixture of working- and middle-class families, most of them content to live in a well-managed tower block, given a Grade II listing by English Heritage, as preservation bodies began, tentatively, to protect the best examples of architectural modernism.[62] Millions also worked happily enough in buildings that exemplified it, from the journalists of the *NME* at Seifert's King's Reach Tower to the brokers at Rogers's Lloyds of London. In the City and other commercial districts across Britain and in the wider world, modernism continued to rise in myriad forms as banks, insurance companies and governments commissioned architects to design offices which, tall or not, tried to assert that wealth and power in the late twentieth century were inseparable from modernity and progress.

A SENSE OF SPACE MADE FOR AN EASIER LIFE

When people arrived home from work to Barratt or period homes that weren't built in a modernist fashion, many got to work on their interiors to create a parallel universe of style. Despite a significant revival of traditional country chintz, led by Laura Ashley in the 1980s, in countless other working and middle-class homes around Britain the impact of modernist design continued to be felt from the 1970s to the 1990s. Thus in 1972, true to both his business acumen and his modernist beliefs, Terence Conran launched one of his most successful lines, the 'Bauhaus' chair. It was an affordable replica of the 1925 chrome-plated tubular steel creation by Marcel Breuer, the Jewish-Hungarian designer who had been one of the Bauhaus founders and who had designed furniture for the Isokon flats. Dismissing Breuer's chair at the time, Evelyn Waugh had written that 'iron furniture bent out of shape would be more offensive than worm-eaten wood'.[63] Half a century later it did not offend the thousands of Habitat customers who placed it in their homes as a practical and pleasing sign of their taste.

In 1974 Conran published *The House Book*, following it with *The Kitchen Book* (1977), *The Bed and Bath Book* (1978) and *The Cook Book* (1980), which sold millions of copies in their various editions. *The House Book* combined quotes from Le Corbusier with those of rock stars in order to make explicit the link between modernism and youth culture that Conran had articulated since the 1960s (a later edition of *The House Book* even included a line from Liam Gallagher).[64] In the 1970s and 80s Conran's chain of Habitat stores became ever more successful by continuing to associate eclectic modern design with youthful aspiration; by the time the company went public in 1981, there were almost fifty stores in the UK and France.[65] Contemporary furniture at the time, said Conran reflecting on his career, 'wasn't associated with comfort; it was too austere for that. But what Modernism did was it helped to show people that a sense of space made for an easier life.'[66] For those who were unconcerned with modernism as a movement, the practical appeal of a style devoted to maximising space by decluttering the home was huge.

The success of retailers like Conran – and later IKEA – was assisted by wider social trends that literally gave the young more space. Home ownership rose significantly between 1970 and 1990 and as non-marital co-habitation lost its stigma the number of couples living together or with friends of either sex increased dramatically. In 1967 Cressida Lindsay's novel *No Wonderland* was advertised as 'a startling novel of London's Mod set, where boys and girls live together without shame and without apology'.[67] In the next decade, the popular sitcom *Man About the House* (1973–76), for example, traded on the fact that two single women shared a flat with a single male, Robin Tripp. Orgies didn't usually ensue but young lives were policed less as a result. At the same time, communes began to decline, along with the hippie counter-culture that had spawned them.[68] Yet the real barometer of youth lifestyles was not perhaps how many people lived together but how many lived alone.

One of the biggest changes in British life in the last quarter of the twentieth century was the rising number of people choosing to live on their own. From 1971 to 1991, the number of one-person households in Britain rose from 18 to 27 per cent and in the subsequent twenty years it rose again, to 34 per cent. The fastest growing group were young adults aged between 18 and 34; by the mid-1990s, for example, men in their thirties formed the largest group of men living alone.[69] This was part of a global trend produced by rising incomes and divorce rates, and to a lesser extent by an increase in social security provided by the state. The trend was pronounced in the secular and wealthy northern European countries where people had more money to rent or buy their own home and where the social stigma of living alone declined more rapidly. By the start of the twenty-first century Britain had the fifth-highest rate of one-person households in the world after the Netherlands, Germany, Norway and Sweden.[70] Among the core 18–24 age group, more young Britons (46 per cent) lived independently than their counterparts in any other EU countries except Germany and Sweden.[71]

Another key trend was that the generations began to live apart more than ever before. As the elderly population increased, and the state made more provision for them, senior citizens chose to maintain their independence for as long as possible before being shunted into care homes by children who no longer felt obliged to house them (only Asian Britons maintained the tradition of caring for the elderly within the family home).[72] This physical separation was ironic because it took place in exactly the same period that the generations were beginning to share a common 'youth' culture in which styles in music, fashion and design were transmitted more frequently across different age groups.

The historian Brian Harrison has described as a 'family revolution' the vast changes to British habitats and households in the last quarter of the twentieth century:

Unplanned and rapid, it had been predicted by few, yet it was a revolution in British social arrangements fully comparable with and perhaps more lasting than the growth of class consciousness during the industrial revolution. It was all the more startling in Britain for the reticence and even Puritanism that had moulded British public life . . . After the 1960s British institutions – the law, the taxation system, building societies, schools, churches, political parties – stumbled awkwardly in its wake.[73]

When assessing the impact of youth culture on British life in the twentieth century, commentators have too often focused on sex and drugs, neither of which people entirely renounced as they moved into adulthood and marriage. But Mod – always more a dream of opportunity than a promise or expectation of it – had a bigger impact in other, more material areas of interior life. As modernist designers in the early twentieth century had hoped, the British home became a screen on which young consumers could project their personality. As one edition of *The House Book* put it: 'The house is the repository of our unmet needs, our unfulfilled dreams, or our nostalgic longings. It cannot really satisfy any of them but perhaps that is why we have so much satisfaction in making the attempt.'[74]

Despite the perennially low budgets of most first-time buyers, the recessions of the 1970s and 80s, and the steady inflation of property prices, the appetite for interior decor didn't abate. In the early 1970s the average weekly wage was £32, yet in 1974 the weekly household spend on furniture and furnishings was £1.33, rising to £2.74 per week by 1979. These figures continued to rise throughout the 1980s, from £3.36 per week in 1982 to £5.28 by the end of the decade.[75] Many young people combined money-saving DIY with the acquisition of decorative objects and affordable gadgets, just as early Mod teenagers had made do with customising cheap suits and dresses while buying a scooter, or as punks and others bought second-hand clothes or market stall copies. Although it is difficult to quantify the part that youth culture played in these trends, what can be said with some certainty is that as young people gained more space to live independently, youth culture began to flourish beyond adolescence, a development that complemented the fact that the generations had more in common with each other.

As people found new ways to prolong the social life and patterns of consumption once associated with teenagers, the parameters of the youth market continued to expand. Advertisers were complicit in that trend, redefining youth and encouraging people to believe that gaining a partner, a home, and even children did not prevent them from engaging with popular music, fashion and design. While in the 1950s 'youth' had been commercially defined as the 14–24 age group, by the end of the century it came to include those in their late thirties, while some market research companies thought that men and women up to the age of 44 could be regarded as being in their 'late youth'. Furthermore, the concept of youth, with all its attendant characteristics of beauty, vitality, sexiness and dynamism, was increasingly used to sell products to anyone who had ever been young, creating a more multigenerational 'youth' market. Thus during the 1980s and 90s pop, rock and dance music were commonly used in TV and cinema advertising, replacing the tailor-made jingles once satirised by the Who in *Sell Out*. As Billy Bragg observes of the punk generation,

me and Weller and Rotten and all that lot, we were the last generation to grow up in an atmosphere where pop music belonged to us alone. Our parents had absolutely no idea of pop music at all and weren't interested in it. Unlike my son now: the bands he's into are basically bands he hears in my car . . . I think the generation gap has all but disappeared in cultural terms because pop music has become a universal medium. If you have a number one hit now, the chances of your song advertising a car are pretty high.[76]

That did not end public concerns about youth and subcultures, however. What emerged in the wake of the 1960s was a multi-tiered youth culture in which different generations articulated what it was to be young at different stages of the life cycle, ranging from pubescence to middle age. Teenagers remained at the creative and commercial fulcrum of it all – and at the nexus of moral panics about it, as the rave movement of the 1990s would dramatically show. But as the so-called permissive society of the 1960s bedded down into a broadly accepted way of life, generational identity was expressed less than ever through transgressive sexual and social behaviour and more through a superior knowledge of contemporary style and the latest trends.

From the 1970s to the 1990s there was a rise in the number of magazines aimed at aspirational young men and women whose adulthood was loaded with style and outlook gained from their teenage involvement in youth culture. Direct heirs of the unisex Mod magazine *Rave*, these taste-forming publications combined features on music and fashion with items about homes, accessories, food, sex and holidays. The most influential was *The Face*, launched in 1980 by 1960s Mod Nick Logan: its first cover story was a profile of the Two Tone movement. Logan, who had been an editor at the *New Musical Express* before launching the teen pop magazine *Smash Hits*, conceived *The Face* as a unisex title that would combine the intellectual standards and irreverent humour of post-1960s music journalism with the ear-to-the-ground awareness of a cutting-edge fanzine and the design sensibility of the best lifestyle magazines; it spawned a number of imitators such as *i-D*, as well as Logan's other title, *Arena*. At its peak in 1987, *The Face* had a circulation of 350,000 per issue, not far short of the half a million that *Smash Hits* managed at the height of its popularity among teens around the same time.

Logan named his magazine after the original Mod word for a style leader but as with the Small Faces there was more to it than a name. Crucially the magazine set out to popularise modernist design, employing Neville Brody as its art director. Brody and other designers were heavily influenced by the visual language of modernism and worked not only at the hubs of youth culture in music and fashion but also in product design, thereby helping modernism to enter the homes of independent young adults as well as the bedrooms of disgruntled teenagers, not just through wardrobes and record collections but through furniture and crockery.

Indeed, the economic recessions that had begun in the 1970s may have been an added incentive for designers to work in the agencies of youth. 'The general malaise', concluded the critic Hugh Aldersey-Williams, found expression in album cover art, one of the few areas of design to flourish, where the escapist fantasies of . . . Roger Dean for bands like Pink Floyd and Yes gave way to the urgent typographic cries of Malcolm Garrett, Peter Saville and Neville Brody, which spoke more directly of industrial design and unrest. This graphic specialism continued to thrive until the demise of the twelve-inch record with the introduction of compact discs in the 1990s.[77]

One examplar of that trend was Barney Bubbles. Born Colin Fulcher in 1942, after grammar school he was captivated by the Pop Art he encountered amid the Mod scene of Twickenham Art School, later combining this with a love of pre-war Russian Constructivism. Bubbles was spotted by Terence Conran and appointed senior graphic designer for the Conran Group in 1965 for which he produced a variety of Habitat homeware designs. He also became involved with the counter-culture, working as art director for an issue of *Oz* magazine, doing light shows at the UFO club and gaining a reputation for prodigious LSD consumption before his appointment in 1977 as the art director of Stiff Records, one of Britain's leading independent record labels in the New Wave era. Among the album covers he designed were Elvis Costello's *Armed Forces* and Ian Dury & the Blockheads' *Do It Yourself*. The latter was one of Dury's typical celebrations of British life, which Bubbles embellished with a pattern taken from the catalogue of Crown, Britain's largest wallpaper manufacturer. A total of thirty-one different covers of *Do It Yourself* were released, each with a different Crown pattern: it was a Pop Art cover for the post-punk age, the New Wave equivalent of the *Sgt. Pepper* sleeve, and it captured both the DIY aesthetic of punk and the growing popularity of home improvement. Perhaps Bubbles was also ridiculing the taste of more conservative home-owners, because one sign of changing tastes was the decline in wallpaper sales, down by 40 per cent between 1971 and 1976, as younger people swapped pattern for swathes of complementary colours.[78]

Barney Bubbles was a manic depressive, and one of his last projects before his suicide in 1983 was to direct the promo for the Specials' 'Ghost Town'. Among the millions of British teenagers who saw that video and were excited by the song's commentary on urban decay were a 16-year-old working-class boy from Salford and an 11-year-old middle-class boy from Chelmsford. Many years later, Shaun Ryder and

Damon Albarn would collaborate on the Gorillaz song 'Dare'; in the meantime those two boys from very different backgrounds shared a love of Two Tone.[79] That, along with other Mod-related influences, shaped their outlook when they emerged into public life – one from drug-dealing at the Hacienda club in Manchester, the other from painting at Goldsmith College in London – to become figureheads of two key youth cultures of the 1990s. Dubbed 'Baggy' and 'Britpop' by the media, both movements would continue Two Tone's marriage of the 'twin totems' of British youth culture.

TAKE ME BACK TO DEAR OLD BLIGHTY

Although many black British youths took to hip hop music and fashion in the aftermath of Two Tone, white British youth did not generally do so – in stark contrast to white Americans, for many of whom rap became the new rock. One reason for that transatlantic divergence is that in the 1980s British rock music remained more innovative than its American counterpart. That was partly because it displayed a more ambiguous masculine sensibility inherited from Mod, but mainly because in Britain rock music formed close connections with the dance cultures of Europe and America – another Mod legacy that Two Tone had exemplified.

Most Britpop and Baggy groups were formed during the so-called Indie explosion that took its name in the independent labels like Two Tone and Stiff which flourished in the 1970s. The two most influential Indie groups came from Manchester and purveyed a uniquely British sensibility, combining a love of 60s British pop with 70s punk. The Smiths sang about unrequited love, loneliness, inadequacy and youthful sensitivities, personified by Morrissey, whose camp, maudlin style exemplified the ongoing reformation of British masculinity that Mods had pioneered in the early 1960s. Morrissey's attachment to the style of that period was also apparent in his taste for crisply designed record sleeves which referenced the post-war 'New Wave' in film and drama – by using photographs of northern working-class heroines like the playwright Shelagh Delaney, or homo-erotic images of Continental film stars, such as Jean Marais, displayed on the cover of 'This Charming Man' (1983).

Like John Lydon before him (and Noel Gallagher after) Stephen Morrissey came from a working-class Irish immigrant family. Raised on the margins of society, he shared with both men a patriotism taut with anger. (His identity he defensively expressed in 2004's 'Irish Blood, English Heart'.) Morrissey also shared with John Lydon a fierce anti-monarchism which, combined with his enigmatic sexual ambiguity, influenced the penultimate Smiths studio album and title song, *The Queen Is Dead* (1986). With a cover graced with a still of the French film actor Alain Delon (an original Mod icon) from the 1964 film *L'Insoumis*, the song mocked the emasculation of Prince Charles during the long wait for his mother to die so that he could be king. Opening with a snatch of the First World War music hall song 'Take Me Back to Dear Old Blighty', it climaxed with a surreal taunt at the ageing heir to the throne, supposedly longing to wear his mother's bridal veil. Derek Jarman's film promo for the song included a twirling guitar painted with a Union Jack, together with a young crop-haired and topless woman fluttering the British flag into the air on industrial waste ground. This was 'God Save the Queen' for the post-punk, Indie generation.

'I think we need more brains in popular music', said Morrissey in 1984.[80] His political literacy was apparent in 'Panic', a song released in July 1986, which attacked the superficiality of BBC pop radio with less irony and more righteous anger than the Who's mocking of commercial radio on *Sell Out* nineteen years earlier. Borrowing chords from T. Rex's 'Metal Guru', the song was written when news of the 1986 Chernobyl nuclear disaster was announced on BBC Radio 1, breezily followed by DJ Steve Wright playing Wham's 'I'm Your Man'. Visually realised by another Jarman promo, the song was a call to arms to youth from Dublin to Birmingham and the chorus's incite-ment to execute the DJ whose music failed to speak to them captured youths' periodic disillusionment with the commercialisation of their culture. The vain refusal of some BBC DJs to play the record added to its rebellious allure so that 'Panic' became a chart hit – and the sort of commercial success its fans claimed to despise.

Although the group eventually had an influence on US Alt rock artists like the Killers and Interpol, the Smiths barely touched America at the time. Their arcane European cultural references and ambiguous masculinity seemed to say nothing to young Americans about *their*

lives. The Bostonian poet and songwriter Joe Pernice records the taunts
the band's American followers endured in this extract from his novel-
ised account of Smiths fandom, *Meat Is Murder*:

For me the Smiths were the great pasty white hope. R.E.M. ran a close second
. . . but the Brits had an emotional edge . . . Did the small group of us who
liked 'faggot' British music feel like we were better than them? Of course
we did. Amen to that, Brother. The following exchange illustrates the nearly
religious and potentially violent musical loyalty of some of my peers:

'I think the Smiths are a much better band than Kansas.'

'You better not say that up the park on a Friday night, or you'll get your
fuckin' ass kicked. What are you, a fag?'

No, I was not a fag, and thankfully 'the park' was not one of my usual
haunts.[81]

In Britain, the daytime DJs of Radio 1 rarely played The Smiths'
music but John Peel's nocturnal exposure of the group – along with
so many other Indie artists – helped their four studio albums to reach
either No. 1 or No. 2 in the British charts. (In America their chart
position averaged only 96.) The Smiths' following in Britain was
largely middle class and white, and their name became an easily
mocked byword for the self-indulgent angst of cosseted teenagers.
But the band's influence was felt in all corners of Britpop and beyond.
As much a fan of David Bowie as he was of the Stooges, Morrissey
publicly approved of Suede's own homoerotic, Bowie-influenced
songs; and Blur's employment of former Smiths producer Stephen
Street is another example of Morrissey's legacy to the young men
and women who forged Britpop.[82] Even Noel Gallagher acknowledged
the influence of his fellow Irish-Mancunian during the 1980s: 'None
of my mates liked [the Smiths] – they were more hooligan types.
They came into work and said, "Fuckin' hell, did you see that poof
on *Top of the Pops* with the bush [flowers] in his back pocket?" But I
thought it was life-changing.'[83] Gallagher's life, and that of millions
more young Britons, was also changed by another band.

Formed a year after the Smiths in 1983, the Stone Roses fused British
Indie rock with House, the new American dance music that emerged
from the black gay nightclubs of Chicago and became more popular
in Europe than in the United States, where it was eclipsed by hip hop.

The Roses' fusion – captured best on 'Fool's Gold' (1989) – was as significant in the history of British popular music as the incorporation of American rhythm and blues by the Beatles had been in the 1960s. The Roses' founders, Ian Brown and John Squire, both set out as Mod-punks, with Brown running Northern Soul nights in a Salford club and both being involved in the northern Mod scooter scene.[84]

The Stone Roses and the Smiths imploded under the usual burdens that destroy pop groups: the weight of fans' expectation, bad record deals, personal animus and drug addiction. But Morrissey's solo career was also soured by accusations of racism when he flirted with skinhead culture, both in the imagery he used and in songs like 'Suedehead', 'National Front Disco' and 'Bengali in Platforms', the last of which appeared to mock the dated fashion sense of Asian immigrants. Many were alarmed by his 1992 performance at Madstock, a music festival headlined by former Two Tone band Madness in north London. Hip-swaying in a gold lamé shirt, Morrissey waved the Union Jack while performing in front of a picture of two female skinheads, prompting the usually adulatory NME to ask 'FLYING THE FLAG OR FLIRTING WITH DISASTER?' Interviews over the next decade confirmed suspicions. 'I don't really think black people and white people will ever really get on or like each other', he said on one occasion, adding: 'England is not England in any real sense of the word, it has been internationalised and that's screechingly evident wherever you look around the country. The English people are not strong enough to defend their sense of history. Patriotism doesn't really matter any more. So I think England has died.'[85] Morrissey not only seemed to attack multiculturalism but also dance music, suggesting that rock and dance were respective paradigms of white and black culture. He described reggae as 'vile', rap as 'the degree zero of music' and House as just 'a doorway for the drug culture'.[86] Although Morrissey's comments didn't resemble Clapton's rant which had provoked Two Tone into being, the furore over Madstock showed that Dammers had helped define a British youth culture that celebrated racial integration to an extent that Morrissey's views were no longer welcome.

The Stone Roses, on the other hand, were hailed as saviours because they engaged with contemporary Anglo-American dance culture and therefore represented a cosmopolitan idea of what British youth should look like in the late twentieth century that accorded with the modernist tradition. The Union Jack that adorned their debut album was painted by Squire with huge drips of paint that echoed the style of Jackson Pollock, and attracted none of the criticism that Morrissey's flag had done.

Most accounts of the mid to late 1980s portray Britain as a place where a property- and service-driven economic boom, coupled with nationalist Euroscepticism, made inner-city rioting a thing of the past and Mrs Thatcher's Conservatism triumphant, at least in England. Closer inspection shows a country that was grateful for rising living standards but unwilling to embrace the Thatcherite narrative about the 'permissive society' of the 1960s as a period when Britain lost its competitive edge and moral bearings. More people owned their own homes but the way they lived in them, and raised children, was changing fast. By 1991 two-thirds of unmarried British women – most of them between the ages of 18 and 28 – were 'living in sin' with their partners (or future husbands), compared to only one in twenty in 1961. The number of single mothers in the UK rose from 160,000 in 1981 to 430,000 in 1991, by which time the nuclear family of mum, dad and two kids had been relegated to third in the table of most common British households, after co-habiting unmarried couples and people living alone.[87]

While Conservatives condemned the single mother as the epitome of an amoral welfare-dependent society that had originated in the 1960s, most Britons continued to see the decade as a post-war golden age. According to a national survey carried out in 1986, 70 per cent of people across all age groups believed the 1960s to have been the best decade of the century in Britain.[88] That consensus was based on the real freedoms that liberal social legislation had secured between c.1965 and c.1975, and on a hazier folk memory of the period's youth culture and its global successes. Little wonder then that the music and fashion of the 1960s should have influenced that of the 1980s, gestating other Mod-related movements a decade later.

Reviewing the Stone Roses' influential debut album in 1989, the *NME* noted 'a hugely successful attempt to hurdle the boundaries of time. Undeniably reminiscent of the arse-end of the '60s, the brighter, psychedelic side of The Beatles, but sharpened by an exuberant '80s edge.'[89] The magazine recorded the virulent anti-Thatcherism and anti-monarchism of Ian, John, Mani and Reni that was de rigueur for post-punk bands. But it also noted that on their European tour later that year, Parisians 'stared in wonder' at coach parties of Roses fans from Lancashire who 'have the brass to go skitting across the Continent in search of high times' with the Channel Tunnel still five years from completion. 'I've hitched all the way down from Blackburn', beamed one teenage girl, 'because I can't live without them.' These mostly working-class teenagers were, concluded the NME, the 'latest mani-festation of Mrs Thatcher's economic miracle'.[90]

The ascendancy of Thatcher and Reagan and their deregulation of capitalism in the final years of the Cold War coincided with the rise of postmodernism as a philosophical movement and cultural practice. Not surprisingly, it emerged in the United States as an attack on modernist architecture and then swept across Europe in the 1970s and 80s, seducing both Left and Right. 'Let us then romp', invited the critic Charles Jencks, 'through the desolation of modern architecture, like some Martian tourist out on an earthbound excursion . . . bemused by the sad but instructive mistakes of a former architectural civilisa-tion.'[91]

Postmodernism questioned the apparent certainties and strictures of the modernist movement, claiming to offer choice instead of canons: a supermarket of style that mirrored the fantastic consumer choice being offered by the entrepreneurial society bulldozed into being by the New Right. In response to Mies van der Rohe's dictum that 'less is more' the American architect Robert Venturi famously retorted 'less is a bore'.[92] An early British example of that outlook was the TV-am Building at Camden Lock (1981–3) by Terry Farrell – a mix of different styles finessed with decorative eggcups on the roofline, all of which housed a de-unionised TV company that Mrs Thatcher approvingly visited in 1985.

By then, postmodernism claimed dominion over youth culture – not just through Mod revivals of the sort noted by Peter York, but also in the 'sampling' of virtually any music by DJs, in the parallel craze for home-produced 'mix tapes', and in the plunder of historic images by the video promos industry that burgeoned after the launch of MTV in 1981. No one reached into the fancy dress box of history quite like New Romantic pop groups, whether it was Bowie-loving Soul Boys like Spandau Ballet or the punk-turned-dandy highwayman,

Adam Ant. In cinema too, change was visible: if the lunar dresses and brutalist architecture of Antonioni's *Blow Up* had seemed to epitomize the pop modernism of the 1960s, then the dystopian Asiatic-Euro-American visual mélange of Ridley Scott's *Blade Runner* (1982) was, for some critics, the sign of a fractured culture. However, like the Tyrell Corporation's replicants, something was clearly wrong.

To its critics, postmodernism was not only a wilful misreading of modernism as a monolithic movement; it also provided a handy justification of anything-goes, free-market economics. Analysing the design of New Wave record covers in 1983 in an article for *The Face* entitled 'The Age of Plunder', Jon Savage linked the politics and style of the period:

In refashioning the past in our image, in tailoring the past to our own preconceptions, the past is recuperated: instead of being a door out of our time, it merely leads to another airless room. The past is then turned into the most disposable of consumer commodities, and is thus dismissible: the lessons which it can teach us are thought trivial, are ignored amongst a pile of garbage. A proper study of the past can reveal, however, desires and spirits not all in accordance with Mrs Thatcher's mealy-mouthed ideology as it spreads like scum to fill every available surface, and it is up to us to address ourselves to them. What pop does or doesn't do, ceases to be important.[93]

Perhaps the fishiest aspect of postmodernism was that the style it most liked to plunder was the very thing it set itself against. Post-modern design may have come up with some fresh and witty juxta-position, but in everything from architecture and furniture to music and fashion its practitioners visibly relied on the aesthetic treasure trove of modernism and perpetuated its tropes by doing so. Perhaps the two movements were, as one critic suggested, 'not fundamentally opposed, but aspects of each other . . . both have an ambivalent sensibility that can be located in Britain's twentieth century.'[94] The contemporary record cover art which illustrated Savage's article – produced for bands like New Order and Bauhaus – were all a testament to the power of the modernist aesthetic. As Savage knew, what pop did or didn't do *did* matter. Young Britons may have liked a bit of fancy dress and a lot of tongue-in-cheek irony, but they still required a future and demanded a say in the present. That's one reason why modernism in its most popular form survived the ideological onslaught of the 1980s.

The Stone Roses' 1990 outdoor concert at Spike Island, a desolate brownfield site near Manchester, marked the symbolic start both of the dance-rock fusion known as Baggy, or 'Madchester', and of Britpop, both of which exhibited the enduring appeal of Mod. When frontman Ian Brown sang 'I Am the Resurrection' across the windswept post-industrial landscape, fans heard more than the messianic self-regard common to rock stars; they also caught a reassuring proclamation that the Stone Roses were, in the words of John Robb, 'the resurrection of British pop'.[95] But Spike Island also marked the beginning of the end of youth culture as it had been experienced in America and Europe since the 1950s. For Britpop and Baggy would turn out to be the last hurrahs of the music and fashion movements of the pre-digital age – capable of reaching, defining and conferring some meaning on the life of a whole generation.

9

THERE'S A GREAT BIG CRACK IN THE UNION JACK
Britpop, Mod and the Rebranding of Britain

[The Union Jack] is the greatest flag in the world and it's going down the shitter. We're here to do something about it.
   Liam Gallagher to Alan McGee on the day Oasis signed to Creation Records, 1993[1]

When we hear Liam's voice, it's our voice. It's everyone's voice.
   Pete Townshend, 1996[2]

HOPE, OPTIMISM AND FUN

As night fell on Saturday 10 August 1996, Noel Gallagher surveyed an audience of over 100,000 people in the grounds of Knebworth, a nineteenth-century country house in Hertfordshire remodelled by Sir Edwin Lutyens, one of the godfathers of modern British architecture. Its most famous owner had been the Victorian novelist, dandy and Conservative politician Edward Bulwer-Lytton, to whom the description of the working class as 'the great unwashed' is attributed. Since 1974, large numbers of the great unwashed had attended concerts at Knebworth by the likes of Pink Floyd and Led Zeppelin, as the Lytton family (like many British country estate owners) reluctantly opened their grounds to public entertainment in order to maintain their property. Lord Montagu's Jazz Festival at Beaulieu in 1960, attended by many of the early Mods, had been one of the first of such events. In contrast, Oasis's audience at Knebworth was the largest gathering for a single concert in British history. Supported by the Prodigy and Ocean Colour Scene, over two nights they played in front of 250,000 fans from all over Britain after 2.6 million people had applied for tickets.

As the concert reached its climax Noel Gallagher shouted, 'This is history! Right here, right now, this is history!' Indeed, it can be argued that Knebworth was Woodstock for the Britpop generation: the concert illustrated music's occasional ability to bring together young people from all backgrounds on a grand scale and foster a sense of leaving one's mark on the nation as a whole, if only for a brief moment. Noting that one in twenty-four Britons had tried to be there, the critic John Harris remarked that 'if Britpop was built on the hope that rock music could tie the UK into a moment of blissful musical unity', Knebworth 'represented its high watermark . . . For that brief moment [Oasis] may just have been bigger than the Beatles.'[3] But what kind of history was really being made at Knebworth? At its peak from 1993 to 1999, Britpop music, fashion, art and design were all laden with Mod styles and symbols. Yet that cultural renaissance referenced the 1960s to such an extent that the artists of the period were accused of creative atrophy.

Britpop was the most patriotic youth culture to emerge in Britain since the 1960s and was one of the few popular expressions of Britishness at a time when Scotland and England were becoming more politically divided than at any time since the eighteenth century. 'There's a great big crack in the Union Jack', sang Suede's Brett Anderson mournfully in one of the group's last songs. Since the 1960s, the end of Empire and the decline of industry, together with increasing secularisation and the diminishing role of the monarchy, had eroded the economic and cultural framework of British national identity that had existed since Victorian times. North of the border, discontent with the Union had turned Scottish nationalism from an intellectual protest vote against English dominance into a broad political movement that threatened to take Scotland out of the Union. In an attempt to contain the threat, Tony Blair's government set in motion one of the biggest constitutional changes in the Union's 300-year history: the devolution of political power to Scotland and Wales that culminated in the opening of Scottish and Welsh parliaments in 1999.

Academic surveys confirmed the decline in British identity. In 1974 65 per cent of respondents in Scotland said their identity was Scottish while 31 per cent defined themselves as British; in 1999 77 per cent said Scottish and 17 per cent British. But British identity was also eroding in England. While in 1992 31 per cent of people living in England said they had a specifically English identity and 63 per cent described themselves as British, in 1999 the respective figures were 44 per cent English and 44 per cent British.[4] This shift was more pronounced among the young. A *Sunday Times* poll of English teen-agers in 1997 showed that traditional sources of patriotism like the monarchy and the military meant less to the young than music, fashion and football; it also showed that around two-thirds now considered themselves to be English rather than British.[5] How ironic therefore that a youth culture which had set out to define post-imperial secular modernity, at the end of the twentieth century should briefly fill the cracks in a national identity that had been constructed largely to maintain Protestantism and build a global Empire.

Furthermore, although Britpop was one of the most anti-American youth cultures ever produced in the UK, it was sponsored by one of the most slavishly pro-American British governments of the twentieth century. At the same time the country's lifestyle was visibly becoming more American, as was evident in the spread of shopping malls, fast-food chains and obesity – the last of these making it harder for men and women to squeeze into close-fitting Mod-style clothes. And while Blur's album *Parklife* – with images of dog racing at Walthamstow stadium on its cover, the finishing post deliberately resembling a Mod roundel – celebrated traditional working-class culture, the pre-war traditions of that culture continued to be eroded, both by consumerism and by the 'intrusion' of women into national life during the post-Thatcher era.

In common with its Mod mentor, Britpop became associated with populist liberalism – although it too first emerged under a Conservative government. During the premiership of Mrs Thatcher's successor, John Major, in 1996 the government announced that 'London is universally recognised as a centre of style and innovation. Our fashion, music and culture are the envy of our European neighbours.'[6] Yet Conservatives failed to manipulate fashion and music because youth culture was still largely seen as a progressive impulse associated with the liberal social climate of the 1960s. It was the Labour Party which co-opted Britpop to promote itself as a dynamic political force, also using it as part of a wider 'rebranding' of Britain that was intended to revive the concept of Britishness. But Labour too discovered that youth culture was a slippery creature that defied conventional alliances. Critics accused Blair and Blur alike of fostering a retrograde youth culture based on a cocktail of nostalgia, xenophobia and even racism. In his study of the 1990s, *When Surface Was Depth*, Michael Bracewell wrote:

What was being proclaimed was a kind of heritage pop, in which the styling and values of an earlier England – the England of the Beatles and brand-new Wimpy Bars – was evoked by Thatcher's grown-up children to offer a cultural database of received ideas of Britishness, from which a response to the realities of Major's classless Britain could be impishly composed. For the kids, it was rather like running riot in an interactive museum of English popular culture. Britpop, importantly, seemed to lack the anxiety and self-referring irony of the pop that had come before it. It seemed, somehow, deeply materialistic.[7]

Like the movers of Swinging London, the shakers of Britpop were themselves attacked for being a vain metropolitan elite, representative of little except the tightening grip of celebrity-driven consumer culture – a charge they sometimes invited as tabloids captured debauched nights in Soho (still considered a vortex of misadventure) by some of its leading players. As usual, critics came from within the Mod fraternity as well as from those who were perennially sceptical about the merits of popular culture. Self-appointed working-class guardians of Mod objected to it being popularised for a wider middle-class audience and thereby losing the cult's proletarian essence; ironically, it was that essence that Mod had originally sought to escape. As in the 1960s, some elders of this style council resented their loss of control over a movement that had outgrown its circle of original followers, its mass appeal overrunning the stockade of authenticity they had built to protect their elitist subculture. As Ashley Heath noted at the time, 'Mod has become the most sacred and the most silly of all British style cults. Mod is, above all, the cult that is too cool to ever really acknowledge itself and, whenever it does try, diehard prime movers will always be there to point out the pale, retrograde pastiche.'[8]

Yet despite all those paradoxes, Britpop demonstrated again the extent to which Mod, more than any other youth culture, was creatively regenerated over time, in a way that simultaneously provided each generation with an identity of its own while also fostering creative and social relationships between the generations. When *Melody Maker* announced the arrival of 'The New Mod Generation' in 1994, it described contemporary bands like Blur as 'New Mod icons' and presented a 'teenage modette' who said '[I've] always liked my Dad's music.'[9]

Britpop was an eclectic movement that spanned the varied music of Pulp, Suede and Oasis, and in fashion the work of Paul Smith and Ozwald Boateng. In different ways they all created a contemporary version of Mod style that sought to maintain a British aesthetic in a globalised world yet without becoming parochial by disconnecting themselves from foreign influences. As in the 1960s, the quality of British popular culture and the pleasure it gave to millions coincided with a period of relative affluence and optimism. Youth (and overall) unemployment remained higher than it had been in the 1960s; but it fell to pre-Thatcher levels as a fragile economic boom based on consumer credit and property speculation led to consistent growth rates of between 1 and 3 per cent in the fifteen years from 1992 to 2007.

In 1996 *Newsweek* declared that London was 'the coolest city on the planet'.[10] The following year, over three decades after *Time* told the world that London was swinging, another American magazine, *Vanity Fair*, proclaimed 'LONDON SWINGS AGAIN!' 'As it was in the mid-60s,' wrote David Kamp in a special feature, 'the British capital is a cultural trailblazer, teeming with new and youthful icons of art, pop music, fashion, food and film. Even its politicians are cool.'[11] What chimed with British readers was that the capital's new vibrancy echoed the 1960s:

Any mental images we have of a 'swinging' London, of a city in glorious thrall to a thriving youth culture, are indelibly 60s ones . . . There's more than a little self-conscious similarity between London's 60s and 90s because Britons in their 20s and 30s – the current tastemaking generation – have studied their forebears well. You pick up hints of this everywhere – in the smart, slim cut of the mod suits . . . in the renewed vogue for Vespa scooters . . . and most conspicuously in the music that has come to be known as 'Britpop'.[12]

Like the original *Time* article, *Vanity Fair* claimed that London had replaced Paris as the fashion and food capital of Europe, with Terence Conran appearing as a conductor of currents between the pop world and modern lifestyle. The hollowness of the feature was not that it spun a London scene into a national fantasy: the trends it observed were manifest across Britain, in cities from Bristol and Manchester to Leeds and Edinburgh. What made the article largely irrelevant this time was that America wasn't actually taking much notice of Britain. Indeed, the article never appeared in the United States: it was cooked up for the magazine's UK edition to pander to British vanity.[13]

'Cool Britannia', the phrase used by the media to laud the British renaissance, also had an American provenance without being noticed by Americans. The phrase originally came from a song by the Bonzo Dog Doo Dah Band, an eccentric British group whose combination of music hall, jazz and rock had attracted admirers including the Beatles in the 60s. The song artfully played on the title of 'Rule, Britannia!' Written by the Scottish poet James Thomson in 1740 and set to music by the English composer Thomas Arne, 'Rule, Britannia!' had originally been used as pro-Union propaganda to help unite the Scots and the English. In 1996 the title of the Bonzos' long-forgotten song was chosen by the American ice cream company Ben & Jerry's to launch a new flavour, and by 1997 it was used, wrote author Andy Beckett, first as 'shorthand for the Government's entire arts policy', and then to mock New Labour as a whole.[14]

The heart of Cool Britannia was what Stuart Maconie dubbed 'Britpop' in a 1993 article for *Select* magazine. This, as he pointed out, was really the belated commercial triumph of post-punk culture, refracted and popularised through Mod music, fashion and design and utilising sounds and symbols embedded in British culture since the 1960s.[15] As Paul Tunkin, a former Essex art student and founding DJ of legendary neo-Mod London nightclub Blow Up, recalled:

My first introduction to Mod was through investigating the original bands that Bowie covered on *Pin Ups*. For Blow Up I wanted to juxtapose original 60s music with a strong blast of energy from the 80s new wave and the

emerging British bands later to be filed under Britpop . . . It was a regeneration of Mod . . . a new agenda, new music, new style, to make a raid
on the mainstream rather than being in the sidelines as with the 80s Indie
scene.[16]

Indie had only partially entered the British mainstream in the 1980s
and had registered in America only among a few cognoscenti who
laid the foundations of American Alternative rock.[17] 'From being this
weird outsider thing we were suddenly in the thick of the mainstream',
remembers Blur's bassist Alex James.[18] This was the world of John
Peel played on primetime radio, wrapped in a Union Jack and booming
out of speakers not just in locked bedrooms and student bars but
from white vans, town centre bars and nightclubs.

The emerging Britpop canon omitted recalcitrant artists like
Radiohead, whose *OK Computer* (1997) was a *Dark Side of the Moon* for
its time. Expressing antipathy to the social and environmental effects
of the consumer society, *OK Computer* spoke to the first generation of
Western youth whose lives were simultaneously augmented and
invaded by the personal computer and mobile phone. (Although ill
at ease with the temper of their time Radiohead were among the first
to use the internet to sell direct to fans.) The prevailing mood in
Britain was captured by a gushing *Guardian* editorial of 1994 that
echoed Harold Macmillan's celebration of mass affluence in 1957: 'We
have never had it so good. We are in the middle of a Britpop renaissance', while another feature announced: 'Where doom, gloom and
despair have been the watchwords of rock credibility in the past few
years, these groups speak of hope, optimism and fun.'[19]

That optimism was contrasted with the aggressive cynicism of
grunge and hip hop, in a way that suggested the American Dream
was alive and well – in Britain. Grunge was a white American counterpoint to hip hop that had its origins in so-called 'slacker' culture, given
a literate voice by Douglas Coupland in his 1991 novel *Generation X*.
Jon Savage read the music 'as telling unattractive home truths about
a country losing its empire and hit by recession; as representing the
final, delayed impact of British punk on America.' (The title of
Nirvana's 1991 album *Nevermind* was a statement of apathy deliberately
echoing the Sex Pistols' *Never Mind the Bollocks*.[20]) Slackers howled
against the American Dream but in studied awe of daytime TV rather

than with the political activism that had driven the baby boomer revolt against Middle America. Grunge was popular among white middle-class teenagers everywhere, who found a reluctance to tidy their rooms expressed in the jaded abuse that Cobain screamed into his micro-phone.

Whether trading on the indolence of the Seattle slacker or the insolence of the Bronx gangsta, the apathy and anger of white and black America had less appeal to British youth than the huge popularity of Britpop and techno-based dance music. Conversely, aside from the Spice Girls, the British only had sporadic success in America, for example Oasis's 'Wonderwall' (1995), Supergrass's Kinks-inspired hymn to youth, 'Alright' (1995) and Blur's 'Song 2' (1997), the latter inspired by 'low-fi' Alt rock and as such a readmission of American influence. 'The gap between British and American tastes has never been wider', wrote Neil Spencer.[21]

YANKS GO HOME!

'I'm sick of your smug limey attitude', the Red Hot Chili Peppers' Michael Balzary told a journalist in 1994. 'You British think you're so fucking great. OK, name me one British band that means shit any more. Name one! You can't. You're so fucking la-de-dah and you don't mean shit.'[22] Liam Gallagher later told the BBC, 'To make it in America you've got to be shit or live there. And I'm not fucking living there.'[23]

In Britain, Oasis hyped a rivalry with Blur based on a Mason–Dixon line of class between the north and south of England that periodically arose in British youth culture. 'Blur are a bunch of middle-class wankers trying to play hardball with a bunch of working-class heroes', said Noel Gallagher in 1995, in the same period as Prime Minister John Major professed his desire to create 'a classless society'.[24] Their rivalry culminated in a battle for chart supremacy that year, which was reported on primetime BBC news. Oasis portrayed themselves as gritty northerners, the authentic voice of rock 'n' roll from Britain's old industrial heartlands – all 'Cigarettes and Alcohol' and what Liam Gallagher called 'ordinary day lads', next to Blur's effete southerners, affecting cockney vowels to attain a putative authenticity.[25]

Their rivalry was of little interest outside Britain and what united the two groups was a shared desire to reinvigorate a canon of British music and style in order to counter American influence.[26] At times with wit and intelligence, and at times with self-pity and vanity, Britpop defined itself against American music, style and sensibility. Both what it had to say and what it failed to do tell us much about how young Britons saw themselves in the late twentieth century.

On their 1994 tour of the United States Blur were thrown out of radio stations when they gave interviews in which they mocked their hosts; and playing to small, indifferent crowds, their gigs descended into drunken bouts of fist-fighting and bus-trashing that shocked even their roadies. This was partly the self-pity of young Englishmen disdaining success in America only after it had eluded them. But the anger went deeper than disappointment with their reception. Rarely in post-war British culture had anti-American sentiment been so prevalent outside left-wing political movements. Journalist Toby Young, who once worked for *Vanity Fair*, believed that 'a new generation had come of age':

They had grown up loathing and despising American mass culture; and when it came to music, movies, TV, computer games, it was all America, and I think a generation of Brits who came of age in the mid-90s really resented this, you know, they felt a nationalistic resentment of the fact that America enjoyed this unchallenged cultural hegemony, and consequently there emerged this kind of protest movement, if you like, this new music, these new fashions, which were more anti-American, and they were British in a slightly caricatured way. And that was enough for the world to go nuts for a while about London's second coming.[27]

Britpop artists encouraged that feeling, some messianically presenting themselves as saviours of a corrupted national aesthetic. Like most artists at any time they exaggerated the extent to which an inadequate culture required an injection of their genius; Oasis performed their first single on *Top of the Pops* in front of an image of the Union Jack disappearing down a plughole, which illustrated their view that they had arrived to rescue it. Britpop artists literally wrapped youth in the flag as Mods and punks had done before. Whether the Union Jack adorned Noel Gallagher's guitar or hugged Spice Girl Geri

Halliwell's body at the 1997 Brit Awards, it once more became a fashionable cliché rather than a flirtation with Fascism, and was displayed on countless products bought by their fans. Britpoppers retrieved the Union Jack from the Far Right and from football hooligans, returning it to the mast of cosmopolitan post-imperial Britain where it had been raised, with the pulley of Pop Art irony, by the art school modernists of the late 1950s.[28]

However, it was on Blur's unsuccessful first tour of the United States that two albums gestated which came to define Britpop's relationship both to its Mod ancestry and to contemporary America more effectively than the hubristic statements and flags on guitars. *Modern Life Is Rubbish* (1993) and *Parklife* (1994) were partly inspired by homesickness. 'I started to really miss simple things', said Damon Albarn. 'I missed people queuing up in shops, I missed people saying "goodnight" on the BBC. I missed having fifteen minutes between commercial breaks. I missed people having some respect for my geographical roots, because Americans don't care if you're from Land's End or Inverness. I missed everything about England.'[29] Homesickness was compounded by a distaste for aspects of American life: 'I just became very disillusioned with what I was seeing and I started to make a lot of connections between America and home; all these American things we embraced – plastic mouldings and obesity and money for nothing . . . I saw it coming over and I started to write songs about it.'[30] Albarn therefore spoke not merely of cultural differences but of similarities, primarily the shopping mall America that Britain had embraced in the satellite towns and suburbs from where many Britpop artists came.

Blur's frontman was expressing a concern about the Americanisation of Britain which, as we have seen, had been a creative pulsar within British youth culture since Mods first articulated it. When Suede's frontman, Brett Anderson, appeared on the cover of *Select* magazine in 1993 to announce the arrival of Britpop, he was set against a British flag under the headline 'YANKS GO HOME!' Anderson disliked the jingoism but he summed up what had united all British musical artists since the Beatles: a desire to express their originality. As he later recalled: 'You're hit on the head with this rush of Americana. The whole world is culturally devoured by America. We actually reflected and celebrated our own culture. That was really exciting.'[31]

The king of the 'Cavaliers' in the 1970s: former Mod David Bowie takes the cult's reformation of masculinity a stage further – his space-age guises, accompanied by an artful fusion of soul, funk and electronica, shaped the look and sound of the Mod family into the 1980s and 90s.

'The music was vibrant, pulsating, irrepressible': Northern Soul dancers at an 'all-nighter' in 1975 show off the fashions and dance moves that kept aspects of Mod alive and formed the basis of modern club culture.

Above left: Selling a lifestyle: four shop assistants (the Hellier and Young twins) in BIBA's Kensington boutique, 1966. Women came to shop from all over England, and by the time BIBA was linked to glam it sold everything from dresses to paint and wallpaper.

Above right: Julie Driscoll, a blues and soul singer whose style influenced the look of female Mods in the 1960s as well as women who became skinheads and suedeheads in the 1970s.

Left: A suedehead couple embrace while striking a defiant pose in 1970.

Opposite page, top: 'Scary concrete jungles': the Jam stand in the shadow of modernist architecture for the cover of their second album, *This Is The Modern World* (1977).

Opposite page, bottom left: Paul Weller strides past adoring Mod revivalists in the courtyard of an Oxford pub in 1984.

Opposite page, bottom right: Mod rides again in the punk era: Jimmy (Phil Daniels) and Steph (Leslie Ash) in *Quadrophenia* (1979), before Jimmy's Mod world goes over a cliff.

Opposite, top: 'The Punk and the Godfather': Paul Weller and Pete Townshend, with author Paolo Hewitt on the left.

Opposite, below: Neil Primett (*centre*), founder of the retailer 80s Casual Classics, with staff members, modelling some of the European sports clothing associated with the Casuals youth cult.

Top: Pauline Black, in her trademark 'pork pie' hat, performs with the Selecter at the Apollo Theatre in Hammersmith in 1979.

Bottom: Two Tone Britain: black and white youth defy stereotypes to enjoy a Specials concert together in Coventry, 1981.

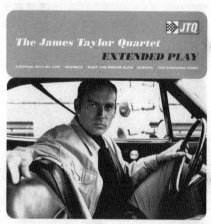

Top: Blur display their Mod influences in Clacton in 1993.

Above: Cover of the James Taylor Quartet's *Extended Play*, released in 1994 on Eddie Piller's Acid Jazz label, adapting the music and style of Mod's jazz origins for a new generation.

Left: Noel Gallagher playing his trademark guitar at an Oasis concert, Maine Road, Manchester, 1996.

Top: The 'post-punk Bauhaus' and home of British club culture: ravers in 1988 at Tony Wilson's Hacienda Club in Manchester, located in the same street that housed the original Twisted Wheel club.

Above left: Britpop goes to Japan: a flyer for Paul Tunkin's neo-Mod club, Blow Up.

Right: Mod and modernism: a 2008 pocket tube map, displaying the 'target'. This was an appropriate marriage as Harry Beck's schematic 1931 map of the London Underground is considered a masterpiece of modernist design.

Top left: 'A Heritage of Modernism': Ben Sherman, the British clothing brand founded in 1963, showing contemporary Mod style in 2013.

Top right: The Times celebrates Bradley Wiggins' gold medal at the 2012 London Olympics.

Below: Jonathan Le Roy, co-founder with brother Adam of the renowned Brighton boutique Jump The Gun, meets friends on the seafront in 2011.

Yet far from being a decade-long Last Night of the Proms for teen-agers, Britpop artists were often critical of Britain. 'It annoys me when we're accused of having this nostalgic romance with a mythical lost Britain', said Albarn. 'Where are these songs about how great the country is? Nearly every one is tempered by cynicism and aggression.'[32] The social scientist Rupa Huq agreed that 'the integral element of irony and playfulness in Britpop's theory and practice places it above simply being a vehicle for straight white boys with guitars committed to the idea of Englishness. The celebration of Britain in Blur's work is a love/hate relationship with Blighty: a more complex conjecture of textual layers than simply a one-way celebration.'[33] Talking about *Modern Life Is Rubbish*, Albarn explained:

This album doesn't celebrate England. A lot of it is triggered by things which are quite sinister such as the Americanisation of England . . . I'm talking about bubble culture; people feeling content in these huge domes that have one temperature and are filled with this lobotomized music. That's all happening here and a lot of feelings about it are on the album. Ours is the sort of Englishness a war wouldn't change. It's to do with a latitude and a history.[34]

The album cover essayed the strength and weaknesses of Mod culture. The front image was of a British steam train, the *Mallard*, which held the world speed record for a steam-driven locomotive when in active service from 1938 until 1963, and whose blue streamlined body, designed by Sir Nigel Gresley, had once been an exemplar of modernist design in form and function. Blur had the *Mallard* painted in the style of a Hornby train set that would have adorned middle-class homes in mid-century Britain. Here was nostalgia for a muscular British form of modernism, one that was less tainted by America, but rooted in the nation's past.

Yet while tapping into that nostalgia made fortunes for a few, Britpop was not the media invention it was later made out to be. Record companies were at first wary of it, so in thrall were they to the dictates of the American market. Food Records executive David Balfe rejected *Modern Life Is Rubbish* because he thought it would only sell to a few Indie fans and to even fewer in the United States. Furious arguments erupted. As Blur's drummer Dave Rowntree remembers: 'Damon said, quite rightly, we are going to focus on Englishness and say very clearly we can make English music a force to be reckoned with . . . Balfe ridiculed him: "Well, Damon, you can look in your crystal ball and predict the future but I have to look at the market as it stands at the moment." Fucking cunt. He had no faith.'[35] *Parklife*'s eponymous song was 'A Day in the Life' for its time, with the cockney rap about an English slacker's routine spoken by a middle-aged Phil Daniels, still recognised as the star of *Quadrophenia*.

Of course, Damon Albarn's view of American modernity – all plastic mouldings and obesity – was as much of a cliché as the American stereotypes of Britain satirised by Mike Myers in his creation of the sex- and fashion-obsessed, groovy, world-saving Austin Powers. The success of *Austin Powers: International Man of Mystery* (1997) in the US (where it grossed $53 million) owed much to the fact that, like James Bond and Harry Potter, it was that rarity: a British commercial cinema brand. The favourable review given of the film by the *New York Times* was headlined 'IT'S A MOD, MOD, MOD, MOD WORLD';[36] but there was no repetition of the British Invasion of the 1960s. 'The Union Jack is flying more limply than it has for years', the BPI, representing the British music industry, had announced gloomily in 1991; 'our share of world sales is in steep decline.'[37] Little had changed a decade later. In 1984, 28 per cent of the best-selling albums in the US were British; by 1999 the number had fallen to 0.2 per cent and in 2002 the US press reported that 'for the first time since 1963, there is not one British artist in the American Top 100 singles chart'.[38]

Whereas in Britain, Mod had creatively regenerated itself since the 1960s, forming a connected series of subcultures recognisable to Britons of all ages, in America it had remained stuck in the clichés of Swinging London and the British Invasion of 1964–75. In a strange way, this marked a return to how America had seen the British before that era – as an unmodern country stuck in the past.

AN UNRULY NINETIES MONGREL

The essential look of the Britpopper, from teenagers to thirty-some-things, rebuked the fashion styles of grunge and hip hop. Britpop clothing was a fusion of different aspects of Mod style from the 1960s to the 1980s, including items like the suede desert boot, the Ben Sherman shirt and the Harrington jacket, which had been staples of both the skinhead and Two Tone movements. This was combined with Sergio Tachini tops, Adidas trainers and other European brands of sportswear favoured by the football Casuals of the 1980s, of which more in the next chapter. Damon Albarn accurately dubbed the style 'mod-ual', although the term never caught on.[39] There was also a return to suit- and hat-wearing among young British men; suits became tailored along Mod lines more in this period than at any time since the early 1980s. At a conference on Britishness during the time of anxiety about it, Billy Bragg was asked by a schoolteacher what the English national costume was, if it was kilts for the Scots. He replied: 'Oh, I saw some kids in our national dress the other day: they had parkas on and Italian suits and their pork pie hats. Their parka from the American army, their suits from Italy, their pork pie hat from Jamaica, I mean they were wearing our national costume – they were Mods. Arguably the most marketable aesthetic that we have ever come up with, more than punk.'[40]

It was certainly marketable in the 1990s. A number of independent British clothing labels began to flourish amid the demand for a contem- porary Mod style; and their designs were then copied and sold in high street chains like Next. The Duffer of St. George was one of the most successful; a 1994 long-sleeved top proclaimed the origins of the move- ment, with 'modernist' in black felt lettering glued across a tight-fitting white cotton chest. Young designers at the time were eager to refute any suggestion of nostalgia in their work. Burro, set up by Olaf Parker, with his wife Sue and brother Tim, dressed Jarvis Cocker, Paul Weller and many of their fans. 'It was contemporary mod, late mod, not The Jam', explained the Parkers. 'We didn't go about it saying "Let's look at a picture of the Small Faces and copy the clothes."'[41] Critics agreed. Announcing that 'Mod . . . the coolest of British style cults comes round again', the *Guardian* observed that 'A quintessentially British feel is emerging in male street fashion following a period dominated by American skatewear [and] hip-hop clothing.' But like the music of the time, it was a contemporary hybrid. 'British cults, from the seventies suedeheads to the eighties casuals, are being blatantly plundered and thrown together', concluded the *Guardian*, and 'since all these styles stemmed from the original modernist blue- print, the result is an unruly nineties mongrel.'[42]

One of those unruly mongrels was the designer Ozwald Boateng who riffed on the Mod suit, employing primary colours with tweeds and wool. 'It was an exciting time, like a reinvention of the sixties and punk, maybe it was reminiscent a bit of the past, but with a forward vision', Boateng later said. 'You have these times when Britain was exciting . . . I was doing my bit on the Row, McQueen was doing his bit in Paris and the Gallaghers were doing what they were doing all round the world. It was a great time.'[43] Born in Muswell Hill in 1967 to middle-class Ghanaian parents, Boateng was first inspired by the sharp suits his schoolteacher father wore; he was later mentored by Tommy Nutter, a leading Mod-inspired tailor of the late 1960s. Headquartered in Savile Row, Boateng's emphasis on formal menswear also drew on the uniform of blazer, shirt, tie and trousers/skirt of British schoolchildren. Like the nineteenth-century class culture from which the tradition of school uniforms came, the collegiate uniformity it imposes on British children was often adapted to suit prevailing youth fashions. Just as Etonian prefects wore flamboyant waistcoats to denote their authority, so in state schools children wore badges on their blazers to display allegiance to certain pop groups; or else they would knot their ties in a certain way. Boateng's comment that 'style is belonging' expressed a widely held belief that there is a quintessential British style – formal yet flamboyant – that offers its wearers membership of a club.[44]

The work of Paul Smith is another example of the aesthetic links between 1960s Mod style and later British fashion. Born in 1946 in Nottingham, Smith had left school at 15 with ambitions to be a racing cyclist before an accident pushed him into clothing design and an apprenticeship in Savile Row. For Paul Smith, Mod was not a puritanical code but a feature used in conjunction with other styles, especially the dandyism of the late 1960s. As he recalled in an interview:

I had no money to get from Nottingham to London, so the only way I could get to London was by selling something. I used to make ties out of quarter yards of fabric on my mum's sewing machine and silk screen T-shirts, then come to London and sell them. I used to have them in a bag and people would say, 'What do you do?' and I would say, 'I'm a designer – want to buy a T-shirt?!' . . . I'm often linked with Mod, but personally I never dressed in that way. I used to buy Ben Sherman shirts, with the button-down collar,

Oxford shirts . . . I used to visit Carnaby Street a lot, which was a melange of Mod and hippie, because the low-rise trouser that a Mod would wear was also what a hippie would wear, but the Mod would wear a button-down-collar shirt and the hippie would wear a flowery shirt. There was just a lot of 'dandyness' everywhere. You had a lot of guys who liked girls but who looked like girls.[45]

Working with Pauline Denyer, a former RCA graduate and his future wife, Smith opened his first store in Nottingham in 1970, where his headquarters remain. But it wasn't until the 1990s that his regeneration of Mod styles achieved a mass audience. What he called 'classics with a twist' were symbolised by his trademark multicoloured bar code, printed on to a Mini Cooper and then used to adorn a range of products. 'It seems to have this really wide appeal', he said of the Mod influence on his work. 'We still get the old musicians coming in, but we also get the new ones like Kasabian, Franz Ferdinand, Razorlight . . . and then I get letters and all sorts of things sent in by 11-year-olds, 14-year-olds.'[46]

Smith's style, coupled with the way he reached an international audience, made him the true heir of John Stephen, who had been among the first to understand that the manner in which style was retailed mattered to young people. The interiors of Smith's stores variously referenced the late nineteenth-century English gentleman's tailor, early twentieth-century artistic modernism and the Dandy Mod look of the 1960s. His shops around the world mirrored that in London's Covent Garden where interiors of mahogany shelves, glass cabinets, oak floors and woven rugs displayed his clothes alongside contemporary *objets d'art* by British designers and Dinky cars that recalled Smith's 1950s childhood. 'Smith relies heavily on historical signposts in order to forge nostalgic connections to the older Britain that dominates the imaginative geographies of fashion exports', the fashion theorist Alison Goodrum has written. '[But] rather than the simple appropriation of references to British heritage, gentlemanly values and age-old tailoring . . . the design aesthetic of Smith's stores mix[es] the signs of Britain's past with modern and indeed avant-garde Britishness.'[47]

The ambiguity of that British 'retro-futurism' helped to make designers like Smith popular around the world.[48] Like music produced under the Britpop banner, Mod-inspired fashion of the 1990s not only captivated much of the nation's youth but it was also a commercial success in Continental Europe and Asia. Far from being the concern of a few parochially minded teenagers affected by a peculiar form of nostalgia, the international reach of contemporary Mod fashion showed that a certain idea of British style had become globally established since the 1960s. As the DJ Gilles Peterson remarked in 2011, 'Going to places like Barcelona or Milan or anywhere round the world you will still find Mod tribes and you can still see how influential this quintessentially British look and style has been and continues to be.'[49] The milliner Stephen Jones agrees: 'I think that internationally if people want to know what's happening in youth culture, they look to Britain . . . because this country is where so much youth culture is started. If you look at Japanese street style so much of it is based on Britain, and Japanese street style is about the esoteric, the unusual . . . but very, very obsessive.'[50]

The appeal of Western youth culture in Asia had already been apparent during the Beatles' ascendancy, but 'big in Japan' remained a condescending cliché of the music industry, used to denote failure in America. Even when taken seriously, Japanese popular culture was often seen as a postmodern melange of styles assembled from East and West. Yet Mod's appeal to Japanese youth had been constant from the 1960s onwards, spreading from fashion and scooters to a particular taste in furniture and other domestic products. This appeal was refreshed by the success of *Quadrophenia* in the 1980s and then by Britpop in the 1990s, periods during which Paul Weller became one of the most successful musical artists in Japanese history. The Japanese Mod movement was more popular with women than it was in Britain, a tendency that observers like the singer Ronnie Fujiyama attributed to the fact that 'Mod is a good look for skinny Japanese girls': the angular haircuts and dresses suited the dominant female aesthetic of *kawaii* where the svelte, gamine figure is privileged over the voluptuous.[51] Hence the female Mod look popularised by Mary Quant was still revered there in the 1990s, seen not just as impishly androgynous but reaching 'a level of near virtuousness' among Japanese women, according to one critic.[52]

For Japanese men and women, Mod's appeal seemed to rest on its association with commercial and technological progress. Research also suggests that, as in Europe, Mod's popularity was based on the fact that it was cosmopolitan and yet recognisably British. 'It's Western but non-American', explained Fumio Nawa, a member of the Tokyo band, the Marquee, 'because Japan is usually deeply influenced by American culture, I felt this British culture thing was so fresh and attractive.'[53] Musically, 'this British thing' was also a way of consuming black music through a white filter, which made it more amenable to Asian youth in a society where blackness was often regarded with suspicion. 'We admire white R&B groups who admire black R&B', explained one female Mod musician. 'We love the primitive rhythm unique to whites who cannot express blackness completely.' She added that her group was 'putting a yellow spin' on the white British inter-pretation of black music – a comment that her interviewer Christine Feldman described as 'a truly transnational statement about Mod's peculiar relationship to race and style'.[54]

Although firmly rooted in the 1960s, Mod style in Asia and Europe was not attached to a particular period or genre of music, a fact that enabled it to surf changing musical trends. One female Mod from Tokyo told interviewers: 'I am a Modernist so I like modern music . . . So I am interested in Techno', to which she added her belief that 60s Mod was in any case 'a forerunner to the Techno-oriented Rave culture'. Christine Feldman concluded from her international research that 'Mod is past and it is present. It is British and it is global. [Its] 60s view of modernity has become somehow endearingly antiquated in its retro-futurism and yet has been deemed more progressive and interesting than contemporary realities by its current adherents.'[55]

INFLUENCE IS NOT PASTICHE

The international appeal of British popular culture in the 1990s was enhanced by the extent to which contemporary art was overtly linked to music and fashion, both in the alliances forged between practitioners and by the fostering of the idea that youth culture in Britain was synonymous with a broader modernity.

Art and design had never ceased to influence pop and, as we have seen, a specifically modernist aesthetic continued to have a wide influ-ence through the designers involved in the post-punk music culture of the 1970s and 80s. What was different about the 1990s was that the Young British Artists, or YBAs, explicitly employed Pop Art in their work as much as musicians referenced the Kinks or the Who. Predominantly born in the 1960s, the YBAs had been developing their ideas throughout the 1980s before they came to public notice. Sponsored by the Lisson Gallery before Charles Saatchi and Jay Jopling took them up, their work had initially been known as New Object Sculpture.

The YBAs launched themselves in the summer of 1988 at the 'Freeze' show organised by Damien Hirst, then a second-year student at Goldsmiths College in south-east London. 'Freeze' was held in the disused Port of London Authority building by the Thames. Unlike the squatted warehouse in which punk's launch party had taken place in 1976, this space had been loaned to Hirst by the Docklands Development Corporation. The LDCC, which also funded the show, was busy transforming the derelict commercial heart of imperial London into the deregulated banking capital of Europe.

What united a generation of artists as disparate as Gavin Turk and Sarah Lucas was that they eschewed the austere, conceptual Minimalism that had dominated Western art in the 1970s, and they skipped over the theoretical concerns of critical postmodernism which by the 1980s had become the dominant intellectual language of art. The YBA's jokey installations displayed the influence of Pop Art and Surrealism – a combination that mirrored the marriage of Mod and punk which had given birth to Britpop. This was an art that sought to be part of a common, non-partitioned culture, and did so by deliberately referencing British youth culture.

Jeremy Deller's and Mark Leckey's works are some of the best illustrations of how artists of the 1990s pioneered this fresh engagement with the pleasures of pop. This can be seen in Deller's *Acid Brass* (1998) where the artist asked the Williams Fairey Brass Band (based at the Aviation Works in Stockport) to perform a series of Acid House anthems. In the project *We Are the Mods* (1998), Deller set up a digital recording studio at the De La Warr Pavilion in Bexhill-on-Sea inviting local retired people to make a record. In both cases, Deller linked traditional and contemporary pop cultures, while making a tacit link between different strands of modernism. Designed by the architects Mendelsohn and Chermayeff in 1935, the De La Warr Pavilion was an appropriate setting for We Are the Mods, as it was recognised (and preserved) as one of the first modernist public buildings in Britain. Mark Leckey's work, meanwhile, included Fiorucci Made Me Hardcore (1999) a video depicting dancing teenagers at various Northern Soul nightclubs, which uses archival footage donated to the artist by Northern Soulers themselves.

The 1997 'Sensation' exhibition of YBA work at the Royal Academy was one of the most influential showcases of contemporary art since the ICA had launched British Pop Art with 'This Is Tomorrow' in 1956. (The RA was a fitting venue because by then several leading Academicians were elderly Pop Artists, such as Peter Blake who in the 1990s also designed the cover for Stanley Road, Paul Weller's best-selling homage to his parents and his childhood roots in Woking.) The American art critic Brooks Adams discerned in the work of several of the artists 'a Pop, Mod or Techno influence and an attitude of imperturbable Kool (i.e. cool with a touch of toxic perversity)';[56] Gavin Turk's Pop (1993), a life-size wax rendition of himself as the cartoon punk Sid Vicious holding a pistol, placed in a glass case, was an example of that.

Like Britpop bands, the YBAs were all accused of plundering the past without displaying any originality. Yet critics defended them on the grounds that 'influence is not pastiche' and pointed favourably to the links between art and youth culture.[57] Richard Shone, an editor of the august Burlington Magazine, compared the way that YBAs exhibited their works in improvised galleries in abandoned offices, factories and warehouses (where DJs played at launches) to the underground dance clubs that were springing up, as rave gripped large sections of British youth at the same time.[58]

In his memoirs, Alex James, who like fellow Blur members Damon Albarn and Graham Coxon had been at Goldsmiths College with Damien Hirst, compared the worlds of music and art. 'Britpop was never a scene,' he wrote, 'the good bands never really saw eye to eye. The burgeoning art explosion was exactly the opposite. The artists were unified as a group and . . . they didn't plagiarise each other.'[59] The transaction between art and pop was a mutually beneficial one, in which musicians gleaned some intellectual cachet from the association while in return artists felt part of mass culture. A notable collaboration was Hirst's direction of the promo for 'Country House', the song with which Blur won the so-called 'Battle of the Bands' with Oasis in 1995.

Defenders of the YBAs argued that the alliances between art and pop forged since the 1960s marked 'a democratisation of the art world' rather than a corruption of it (Warhol's sponsorship of the Velvet Underground being a chief example).[60] Asking, 'What does it mean to be "new" in Britain?' Richard Shone wrote:

For 'new' we must nearly always substitute 'current' or 'fashionable' or 'present day' when applied to episodes in British culture. It has rarely implied 'Modernist', as it has in Continental European countries or in the United States. Looking back over the undulating foothills of 20th century art in Britain, there have been moments of unexpected newness but they did not take their place in the historic narrative of international Modernism.[61]

Critics of the YBAs dismissed their work as sensationalist gimmickry; Damien Hirst's musings on mortality using preserved animal carcasses bore the brunt of that criticism. That critique was essentially a debate about which art forms merited inclusion in the modern movement. The cultural historian Peter Gay expressed admiration for Hirst but argued that Pop Art had corrupted rather than democratised modernism, writing 'the makers of these entertainments claim to have seriously contributed to modernist culture, but they have only scrambled and distorted the frontiers of what used to be clear distinctions'.[62] This echoed Christopher Booker's criticism of pop in the 1960s. Beyond the world of art criticism, the creative links between art, pop and democracy became more established in the public domain by the 1990s, as British music and fashion were incorporated by political elites into accepted ideas of what constituted national culture. At the same time, the idea that youth was synonymous with modernity did become more awkward and debatable as Mod culture aged, however gracefully, effectively entering its fortieth year in 1998.

MOD LIFE CRISIS

'Rock 'n' roll is not just an important part of our culture, it's an important part of our way of life', said Tony Blair at the Q Awards on 9 November 1994, at which stars ranging from Ray Davies to Dave Gilmour and Noel Gallagher were present. Speaking without notes at the start of the ceremony, the Labour leader continued:

In Parliament you can have debates about all sorts of industries . . . if you had a debate about the music industry, they'd think it rather strange, but that actually just shows how far Parliament is behind the times . . . The great bands that I used to listen to – The Stones and The Beatles and The Kinks – their records are going to live forever, and the records of today's bands . . . will also live on because they are part of a vibrant culture. I think we should be proud in Britain of our record industry and proud that people still think that this is the place to make it.[63]

Blair's comments were extraordinary, not because he acknowledged that the best of popular culture stood comparison with established art forms – which by then was a liberal cliché – but because he asserted that rock music and fashion had marked the life of the nation so indelibly that it was something Britons of all ages should be proud of. This was not simply a way of getting down with the kids in order to secure their votes; in the late twentieth century an engagement with youth culture emerged as a way for politicians to promote themselves as avatars of modernity, a concept that potentially attracted voters of all ages.

If the commercial triumph of 1980s Indie rock was analogous to the Labour Party returning to power after eighteen years of Conservative rule then Blair's manipulation of youth culture was the political equivalent of advertisers expanding the parameters of the youth market in order to sell vitality to the middle-aged. One result of that expansion was the growing profitability of the so-called 'creative industries' that Blair celebrated. An umbrella term for thirteen sectors ranging from architecture to video games, between 1998 and 2003 the creative industries did form a larger proportion of the British economy and its exports than in any country in the world after the United States. Although its 'gross value added' (used to measure the output of an economic sector) halved from 14.9 to 7.3 per cent in that period (largely as a result of digital piracy), the creative industries still were worth twice as much as the British tourist industry and were comparable in size to the financial services industry, employing

2.7 per cent of the nation's workforce.[64] Alan McGee, the man who discovered Oasis and owned Creation Records (named after 1960s Mod band the Creation), was appointed by Blair to the Creative Industries Task Force, a government quango designed to create an alternative 'cabinet' of commercial artists and with it the impression that youth culture and political liberalism were symbiotic (members also included Paul Smith and Richard Branson).

Noel Gallagher joined McGee and other captains of the creative industries at Blair's Downing Street inauguration party in November 1997. Damon Albarn was so disillusioned with New Labour's manipulation of music that he did not attend – yet Albarn provided the clearest intellectual validation of Blair's concept of pop music as a socially unifying national heritage: 'There was a time when pop music wouldn't have been able to define what being English was all about, but that's changed now. If you draw a line from the Kinks in the Sixties, through The Jam [in the 70s] and the Smiths [in the 80s], to Blur in the Nineties, it would define this thing called Englishness as well as anything.'[65] This pop canon, as sharply defined as any of the traditional arts, was open to criticism for precisely that reason, but it helped to establish connections across generations. Perhaps the long-term significance of Britpop was not so much that it enhanced national identity or demonstrated British insecurity about American influence but that it highlighted the decline of generational revolt as one of the forces that drove Anglo-American youth culture forwards.

The canon demonstrated that all pop led back to Abbey Road and it excluded those who took roads less travelled. But limiting though this canon was, it did signify a narrowing generation gap in Britain. Paul Weller was one of the few songwriters successfully to relaunch their career based not on a revival of former glories but on critically and commercially successful contemporary work that won him a new generation of fans. The media dubbed him the 'Modfather', a mantle he accepted and a phrase which suggested that generational revolts were being replaced by the subtle intergenerational relationships that characterise other art forms and social movements; critics less content with this trend dubbed Weller's music 'Dadrock'.

Glastonbury was a testament to the blurring of generational boundaries. When Michael Eavis founded it as the English Woodstock in 1970, it was part of the haphazard free festival movement of hippie

counter-culture; later, in the punk era and during the early rave movement of 1988–94, it became the playground for drug-fuelled hedonism,
radical politics and occasional police confrontation. Yet from the mid-
1990s the people attending ranged from teenagers to those in their
sixties; some parents even brought children to what became a sort of
Butlins for the white middle classes. Once the preserve of those in
their teens and twenties, pop and rock concerts became a common
pursuit. In 2000, a survey of 'young' people's leisure activities by the
British Market Research Bureau found that 33.4 per cent of 15- to
24-year-olds regularly attended such concerts; but the figure for the
25 to 34 age group was 36.3 per cent, while older age groups still
appeared to be rocking in significant numbers, with 31.1 per cent of
35- to 44-year-olds regularly going to concerts and 22 per cent of 45-
to 54-year-olds.[66] Another report, in 2010, showed that while most
people went to their first music festival at 18, the average age of the
festival-goer had risen to 31.[67]

The size and number of British festivals grew to accommodate this
larger audience. Complaints about ticket prices and the introduction
of security fences had dogged festivals since the early 1970s when
hippies had objected to paying for their entertainment. When Britain's
most successful former hippie, Richard Branson, launched the V
Festival in 1996, clichés about the 'sell-out' were reiterated – yet the
more interesting trend was that festivals had come to represent a youth
culture that was multigenerational. The first V Festival was headlined
by Pulp and Paul Weller – the sort of combination that had made
Modernists riot at the Beaulieu Jazz Festival in 1960.

The development of a common youth culture didn't just unite
families when a parent's own music and fashion was being replayed
by their children. Even when Mum and Dad's brush with youth culture
had been fleeting or superficial, an osmotic familiarity with it made
youth culture less threatening to elders than it had once been. The
spark of rebellion still flew from the flinty moral and spatial restrictions placed on behaviour by parents and teachers, but young people
never ceased to require the support of their elders, and they usually
got it. In other words, the family didn't just accommodate youth
culture; family life often provided the platform for it.

The memoirs of British musical artists from the 1960s to the 90s
reveal how much they yearned for parental approval. Born in 1966,

Louise Wener grew up in a middle-class Jewish family in suburban Essex. Her father, a fan of 1940s jazz, had no time for his daughter's heroes David Bowie and Paul Weller and he had little more for her attempts to emulate them. After forming the band Sleeper with boyfriend Jon Stewart at Manchester University, only the dole and Stewart's occasional drug-dealing kept a roof over their heads.[68] But when Sleeper appeared on *Top of the Pops* with their hit song 'Inbetweener', she recalled a change in her family's attitude:

When my Mum goes shopping in Ilford the following weekend, 'Inbetweener' is playing on the stereo in Clark's. Mum is overcome with pride and tells the shop assistant that it's her daughter singing on the radio. The assistant has seen us on the television. She's so impressed, she offers my Mum a free pack of innersoles. The innersole moment feels significant and in light of our debut appearance on *Top of the Pops*, our relationships with our families are subtly changing. My Mum has stopped reminding me that I have useful retail experience from my days working at Mothercare and Jon's Dad is no longer asking him if he's thought about getting a job on a cruise ship.[69]

After Sleeper split up, a teaching career saved Stewart from the world of cruise ships – at the Brighton Institute of Modern Music, a real life 'school of rock' that was yet another sign of how artistically reputable pop had become.[70]

Brighton was also the base for British Sea Power (BSP), a post-Britpop Indie rock group formed in 2000 whose first album *The Decline of British Sea Power* (2003) exhibited the ironic wit and post-imperial themes common in British popular music since the mid-1960s. Although acclaimed by David Bowie and Jarvis Cocker, the group's biggest fan was the elderly father of its founding members, Scott and Neil Wilkinson. A shipping clerk from Sunderland who had been an anti-aircraft gunner in the Second World War, Mr Wilkinson's knowledge of pop had not sailed far beyond Flanagan and Allen before he immersed himself in his sons' world, suggesting ideas for albums and requesting regular morning briefings to keep himself and Mrs Wilkinson informed of their progress.

In *Do It For Your Mum*, Roy Wilkinson, BSP's manager and elder brother of the two band members, told how their father was 'brought all kinds of new proxy glories' through his children's career: 'Dad has often seemed to be in the band as well', observed the author:[71]

As Dad approached his eightieth birthday, we looked on with surprise and amazement as he transformed himself into a connoisseur of indie-rock. He immersed himself in the records of anyone he saw as a potential rival of British Sea Power . . . Apropos of nothing I would find myself closely inter-rogated on the opening track of Nirvana's *In Utero* album . . . [One day] he made a pot of tea and then carried it into the dining room, his voice full of passion and disbelief . . . His pitch and volume suggested someone warning pedestrians about a runaway car. 'This lot!' he shrilled, directing his ire towards various musical peers of BSP, 'British Sea Power make all those other shites look like they aren't even trying! The other lot, they're not even at the races!'[72]

The objects of his worst invective were BSP's American counterparts; the Strokes, for example, were dismissed as 'Kentucky fucking Fried Chicken'. Never satisfied with the group's modest commercial success compared to those 'charlatans' U2, Mr Wilkinson finally exhaled a sigh of relief after a new £35 million wing of Britain's National Maritime Museum was opened in Greenwich. Carved outside the building next to words by Shakespeare was a British Sea Power lyric. 'That's more like it,' said their father. 'Shakespeare. That's the kind of company this band should be keeping.'[73]

Though such devotion could be embarrassing it was usually repaid, artistically as well as financially. Songs that celebrated familial love remained less common than ones about romantic and sexual relation-ships, but they appeared more frequently from the 1970s onwards, and were just as artful as the paintings with which Whistler and Hockney had paid tribute to their mothers. Public Image's 'Death Disco' (1979) and the Verve's 'The Drugs Don't Work' (1997), for example, both mourned the loss of parents who had died of cancer. (The extent to which commentators ignored this aspect of British youth culture was apparent when the conservative philosopher, Roger Scruton, cited 'The Drugs Don't Work' – which reached No. 1 in the UK charts – as evidence that the young had seen the futility of taking recreational drugs. In fact, the drugs in Richard Ashcroft's song referred to the painful chemotherapy that his father had endured.)[74]

Of course, Mod was not solely responsible for these intergenerational connections. Pushy parents, proud of their children's success in forms of art and entertainment they didn't understand, were nothing new. But the family of interrelated subcultures that Mod spawned after the 1960s did make those connections between parents and children more possible.

An important sinew of that relationship was the use of technology, which modernists of all kinds had celebrated throughout the twentieth century. Gadgets made pop music a common part of daily life in Britain between the 1960s and the 1990s, contributing to its multigenerational appeal while simultaneously providing each generation with its mark of technological progress and expertise.

The portable transistor radio that had so annoyed the bowler-hatted commuter when Ringo used it in *A Hard Day's Night* remained a controversial symbol of youth's influence on culture and the environment. First marketed in America in the 50s, it became ubiquitous in Britain by the time the Beatles split up, with close to four million bought annually by 1970. The introduction of the more powerful 'boom box' (or 'ghetto blaster') by the Dutch company Philips in the mid-1970s enabled bass-heavy radio and cassette playing, and took the home hi-fi into the street, as did the car stereo.

The launch of MTV in 1981 brought pop simultaneously into the homes, bars and other public spaces around the clock, as well as expanding the visual culture of youth by fostering the video promo – an art form in which British artists led the world for a decade. Sony's 1980 introduction of the Walkman re-privatized music a generation before the iPod; but by the time it was pumping pop quietly into millions of ears, music was more ubiquitous than ever, deepening the sense of a shared pop heritage and narrowing the generation gap.

Digital technology began to make Mod soundtracks readily available; gone were the days when Northern Soul DJs hunted down rare singles, of which only a handful of pressings had survived. One such collection of '60s Mod Anthems for the In Crowd' was entitled *Mod Life Crisis*. The cover's red, white and blue Pop Art arrow pointed to a nest of scooter headlights illuminating that cliché of the menopausal Western male: the urge to buy a motorbike and take to the road like Peter Fonda or Phil Daniels. Of course, this was a cynical cash-in on middle-aged nostalgia and the perennial desire for eternal youth; moreover, the 'Dadrock' trend was not free of generational tensions.

I WANT A REFUND ON MY ADOLESCENCE

Monarchs and politicians had associated with the stars of British popular culture since the turn of the twentieth century in order to appear more in touch with the 'common people', as a Pulp song satirically put it. The strategy had met with some success, but overt public alliances between pop stars and political parties never last.

As a strategy to mobilise the young to vote, the concept of Cool Britannia failed. Turnout for the under-25 age group had averaged 74.4 per cent of eligible voters throughout the 1970s and 80s after the franchise was extended to 18-year-olds. But despite Noel Gallagher exhorting the young to vote for Blair, it fell significantly in the first two general elections that Blair won, down to 59.7 per cent in 1997, and down again to 49.4 per cent in 2001.[75] This was partly due to an awareness that policy differences between Left and Right were less marked than before. Political apathy among the young was compounded by their realisation that having a prime minister who was into the Kinks did not mean having a government that would improve their lives.

Disillusionment with New Labour came to a head when Tony Blair limited welfare benefits for teenagers and announced the introduction of tuition fees for university students, which came into effect in September 1998. The *NME*'s response was to lambast what it called 'Britain's first rock 'n' roll government', restating the belief that youth culture should be by and for the young: 'Our music, our culture, our collective sweat from our groovy brows, has been bundled up and neatly repackaged and given a cute little brand name and is being used by New Labour spin doctors to give this hideously reactionary New Labour government a cachet of radical credibility. New Labour is taking us for granted and taking the piss.'[76] Indeed, a number of musicians – including Jarvis Cocker and Noel Gallagher – pointed out that their music had been developed while they were on the dole in the 1980s.

Anxious to show that the intergenerational alliances in art and politics were still mutually beneficial, the prime minister responded with a 'New Deal for Musicians', which enabled aspiring bands to access unemployment benefit for thirteen months if they could demonstrate evidence of 'talent and commitment'. Predictable images of feckless, Left-leaning teenagers with guitars, drums and decks auditioning before a committee of junior civil servants from the Department of Work and Pensions led to the conservative media denouncing it as 'a charter for scroungers'.[77]

As well as disillusionment with the political incorporation of youth culture, Britpop highlighted how rebellion against one's parents, if it took place at all, was not always a rejection of conservatism but could also be a desire to translate parents' tastes or liberal values into a contemporary context. Ray Davies's use of music hall motifs in the 1960s had been influenced by his father, a professional musician who, said Davies, took him as a boy to a theatre in Finsbury Park to hear 'the dying gasp of English music hall'.[78] Damon Albarn's father, Keith, was an art lecturer who had managed the psychedelic rock group Soft Machine in the late 1960s, and who provided his son with a family environment in which he could develop his own musical experiments. Yet Albarn's generation laboured, as Davies's had not, under expectations created by the pop culture of the 1960s.

The idea of the 1960s as a golden age hung over liberal America too. In *Generation X*, his 1991 novel about disaffected American youth, Douglas Coupland coined the phrase 'legislated nostalgia', which he defined as 'to force a body of people to have memories they do not actually possess: *How can I be part of the 1960s generation when I don't even remember any of it?*'[79] A simultaneous yearning to have sampled the exciting modernity of the 1960s and a desire to escape this 'legislated nostalgia' was one of the creative tensions within Britpop. 'I resent the eighties', Jarvis Cocker once remarked. 'I'd been born in the sixties, and you'd see stuff on telly about how great it was, and by the time it came to your formative years where you're thinking "Come on then, let's have a bit of that" it's all going in the opposite direction. I often said I wanted a refund on my adolescence.'[80] That feeling of having missed out on Sixties wealth – what Douglas Coupland called 'boomer envy' – was experienced by young people on both sides of the Atlantic, especially when the cheap education, virtually full employment and affordable housing that the 60s generation had enjoyed was contrasted with the far tougher circumstances of the Thatcher and Reagan years. In Britain 'boomer envy' was compounded by jealous longing for an era when global cultural power seemed to have rested with Britain.[81]

It is in this context that Britain's obsession with the 1960s should be seen: it is a yearning for a time when British popular culture had been the most innovative and influential in the Western world. In 1965, 52 per cent of the number one singles in the US were by British musicians but from the late 1970s onwards there was a steady decline, with the number falling to 18 per cent in 1986 and then down to single figures in the following decade; and despite a brief recovery in 1997, by the end of the century there were no British number ones in the American charts.

America continued to have a relatively greater influence on the British charts. Number one records by native artists reached a peak in 1967 of 88.5 per cent then fell to between 60 and 70 per cent in subsequent decades. To some extent that illustrates the robustness of British popular music across different genres.[82] Britpop improved the balance of power for a time. Between 1991 and 2000, the total number of domestic records in the British charts rose from 58.3 per cent of the total to 68.2, while those of foreign (mostly American) origin fell from 35.6 to 27.5 per cent. This was part of a global trend. As Simon Frith observed, 'in almost every national music market, the sales percentage of domestic repertoire steadily increased in the 1990s', probably due to a wider resistance to American cultural domination when the United States became the unchallenged superpower as the Cold War came to an end.[83]

However, as a strategy to halt Americanisation beyond the music charts, Cool Britannia was no more effective than its Swinging London precursor; Britpop's artistic figureheads were pitifully ill equipped to reverse the tide of transatlantic material culture. As in Mod's heyday, the way things were retailed as well as the products sold continued to become more American. In the decade to 2001, as Union Jacks were once more stretched over guitars, busts, bottoms and bags, more than 600 new shopping malls were erected in the United Kingdom, representing 42 per cent of the total opened since 1968, with most of the increase due to out-of-town developments. With almost 1,500 shopping malls by the end of the twentieth century, Britain had the largest number of any country outside the United

States.[84] Alan McGee had grown up in East Kilbride, a new town built in Scotland's industrial central belt during the 1950s. A modernist architectural panorama that like most new towns proclaimed post-war optimism, its centre was not a church or a town hall but a shopping mall.

The retailing equivalent of the grey squirrel, this glossy, air-conditioned, car-reliant American phenomenon accelerated the decline of the traditional British high street before internet shopping moved in for the kill. Shopping malls helped to destroy the independent shops, run by young entrepreneurs, which had transformed the music and fashion industries of Britain since the late 1950s. Most young people didn't care much. Street markets and boutiques could still attract a discerning clientele, but most teenagers flocked to malls to shop, steal or just to hang out with their friends.

Like their older relatives, most young Britons wanted the material benefits of American lifestyle; but they also wanted to retain their distinctiveness in an American-dominated global culture. The repackaging of Indie music with Mod styles that produced Britpop was a response to anxiety about that American influence; and as *the* signifier of a distinctive British youth culture, Mod – not for the first or last time – was the style that lent itself most practically to that emotional need.

ARE PEOPLE REALLY SO SELECTIVE IN WHAT THEY LISTEN TO?

More than most manifestations of Mod culture, the music associated with Britpop was dominated by white guitar bands, old and new. This led some academics to accuse Britpop of peddling a reactionary nationalism that was not only uncritical of British society but also excluded black and Asian youth from the party. Some journalists agreed by contrasting Britpop with the contemporaneous rave scene as a positive exemplar of eclectic, multiracial youth culture. Jon Savage remarked that 'Britpop is a synthesis of white styles with any black influence bled out',[85] while Simon Reynolds wrote in 1995:

Britpop is an evasion of the multi-racial, technology-mediated nature of UK pop culture in the 1990s. If it started a few years ago as a revolt against

American grunge . . . it has now extended itself into the symbolic erasure of black Britain, as manifested in jungle and trip hop. For Britpopsters, the 60s have a mythic status as a lost golden age which is alarmingly analogous to the Empire for football hooligans and the BNP. Even more than the insularity of Britpop's quintessentially English canon, it's the sheer whiteness of its sound that is staggering . . . take Blur, whose homage to the music-hall pop tradition manages to sever The Kinks from R&B, Madness from ska, and Ian Dury from the Blockheads' fluency in funk and disco.[86]

Some of this concern was based on the elements of skinhead and Casual style still in fashion at the time. When Blur appeared in a publicity shot dressed in Fred Perry polo shirts with a Great Dane on a lead and the words 'British image 1' graffitied above them, the *NME* accused them of joining Morrissey in 'flirting with Fascist imagery'.[87]

Britpop fans may have found solace in a sense of ethnic solidarity and in the familial bonds that a heritage of Mod-related music and fashion offered them, but most criticism supposed that Britpop and rave were two distinct and paradigmatic youth cultures. In fact, the two had strong commercial, artistic and social links, through the friendship between Tony Wilson and Alan McGee, and in the crossover music of the bands they managed, notably Manchester's Happy Mondays and Glasgow's Primal Scream. A testament to that musical cross-fertilisation was the latter's *Screamadelica* (1991) which won the first Mercury Prize in 1992. Produced by the DJ Andy Weatherall, it employed a range of genres from gospel and soul to House, techno and Indie rock, and became an aural template for the less tribal youth cultures of the next century. Such music refuted the charge that the architects of Britpop were just peddling Mod-affected nostalgia for the 1960s. 'This is the most important time in British music since punk', said McGee of the creative alliances forged in the 1990s.[88]

Although Britpop's following was largely white, there is no proof that young people at the time made an existential choice between 'white' Britpop and 'multicultural' rave. 'Are people really so selective in what they listen to?' asked the Stone Roses' John Squire when interviewed by Stuart Maconie. 'Everyone I know has a cross section of music in their collection.' Lead singer Ian Brown added, 'I would hate it to get like America where music is really compartmentalised.'[89] Extensive anecdotal evidence suggests that most youths happily went to both rock concerts and nightclubs and, like the Japanese fans of Britpop quoted above, their definition of 'modern' was based on a simultaneous enjoyment of retro-style and the latest electronic music. Indeed, what emerged in this period was a greater dialogue between the subcultures of rock and dance music that laid the foundations for a less tribal youth culture – although one in which Mod retained its emotional potency as a connecting narrative between different periods and styles.

The Face reiterated the claim that Britpop had 'defined a new Englishness' that was modern in outlook because 'it's an attitude based not on a nostalgic Carry On Mr. Kipling Britain, but a Britain that you will recognise as the one you live in.'[90] In response, Andy Bennett offered a more subtle picture of British youth than the dichotomy that dominated the debate: 'Britpop is symptomatic of the pluralism which is increasingly becoming a feature of the identity politics of British youth', he wrote, concluding:

It could be argued that like reggae, South Asian dance music and rap, Britpop is simply another resource through which young people in Britain can choose culturally to situate themselves . . . The cultural fragmentation which has led some to seek ways in which to revive traditional notions of Britishness has, at the same time, given rise to new ways of looking at Britain as a nation and considering what it means to be British . . . Thus Britpop is not necessarily about a Britain you will recognise as the one you live in – it is rather about a particular 'version' of Britain in which you may choose to live if you wish.[91]

Whichever version of Britain they chose, one of the things that Britpoppers and ravers shared was a sense of being British and of inhabiting youth cultures that continued to look, sound and feel different to those of America. As we shall see, rave was often celebrated in the youth media in just as nationalistic a way as Britpop, using the specific language, style and symbols of Mod to distinguish it from American dance culture. Yet politicians were wary of rave not because it was too black but because it was more closely connected to drug use. Dance culture therefore escaped the clammy hands of political incorporation that compromised the public image of Britpop, while also acquiring a counter-cultural reputation that eluded Britpop, despite the latter's origins in the independent milieu of post-punk music and fashion.

There had always been purists within the Mod movement who objected to what they saw as a corruption of it by new artistic developments. The Style Council had kept Mod's roots alive in the 1980s, in the jazz and soul music they played and in the group's Continental aesthetic. Yet they had been booed off stage at the Albert Hall in 1989 when Weller brought on guest vocalists to perform soul and hip hop numbers. As the Style Council's drummer, Steve White, remarked, 'That's the same kind of nonsense the folkies did when Dylan played at the Albert Hall with the Band, it's absolutely ridiculous.'[92] However, by the 1990s purist voices within the Mod movement were less prominent than before, a fact evidenced by the Acid Jazz movement.

Acid Jazz emerged out of a multiracial southern English 'rare groove' dance scene in the 1980s, which revolved around the retrieval of 'soul jazz' records by artists like Jimmy Smith and Donald Byrd who had been at their peak in the 1960s and 70s. Contemporaneous with Acid House, this small but significant branch of the Mod family was given a name and a sharper focus by DJs associated with Acid Jazz Records, the magazine *Straight No Chaser* (named after a Thelonious Monk album) and 'Talkin' Loud and Saying Something', a club afternoon at the Camden venue, Dingwalls, started in 1987 by Gilles Peterson. An eclectic DJ who played global jazz-related music from Brazil to Nigeria, Peterson formed a creative alliance with 1970s Mod Eddie Piller, the manager of a contemporary jazz group, the James Taylor Quartet, whose mother had run the Small Faces fan club in the 1960s. As Piller remembered:

I knew that my mum had some famous friends, but I didn't really know who the Small Faces were, or what they had achieved, until she bought me a Small Faces album and said, 'Here's my band, here are the fan club letters' . . . In '79 my father was taking me to school and I put on a tape that I'd made and I was quite pleased with it, and it had the Chords, The Jam, the Small Faces, the Kinks . . . and he goes 'What's this?' and I said, 'This is Mod. This is what I'm into, Dad.' He goes, 'This ain't Mod. This is pop. Mod is Tubby Hayes. Mod is Willie Dixon.' He was a Mod though he wouldn't have called himself that. He would have said he was a Modernist Jazz fan . . . from '58 onwards.[93]

'The Mod movement had ground to a halt and needed some direction', Peterson recalled of the late 1980s, 'and Eddie found it by tapping into the scene I was coming from, which was more about progressive movement, mixing the styles.'[94] At its peak in the first half of the 1990s, what made Acid Jazz different to Northern Soul was that it spawned original groups, such as the Brand New Heavies, Incognito, Corduroy and the Young Disciples, who mixed styles including hip hop into their jazz-fusion. 'For me, Acid Jazz was Acid House for the weirdos in the back room,' remembered Peterson, 'and experimenting with drugs was a big part of it.'[95]

Acid Jazz was recognised by the more astute media before Britpop got under way, though it reached a peak of popularity in the mid-1990s on the coat-tails of Britpop. The cult's apparel was 'slightly Sixties with a Nineties edge', one member told the *Observer* in a 1991 article called 'it's a Mod, Mod, Mod world'. As well as close-cropped hair and the hats once worn by jazz stars like Thelonious Monk, followers sported the so-called 'Yardie-cardi', a suede-trimmed cardigan favoured by West Indian Casuals, and they mixed all this with contemporary Mod-inflected designs by retailers like the Duffer of St George.[96]

According to Gilles Peterson, the movement's demise was partly due to a tendency within later Mod culture towards nostalgia. 'It was a great time', he concluded, 'but after two years I was beginning to feel the sound, the music and name was ghettoizing itself, it was becoming a Mod thing, a retro thing.'[97] Nonetheless, this was the first time since the early 1960s that jazz of any kind had been a commercial force in British youth culture, and it formed part of the burgeoning link between dance and rock music that was a feature of the Britpop era.

The two cultures were drawn closer by Blur at a critical moment in Britpop's genesis. In March 1994, just weeks before swathes of American youth mourned the death of Kurt Cobain, Blur's 'Girls and Boys' reached No. 5 in the British charts and quickly stormed those of Continental Europe and Asia, expressing a very different kind of teen spirit. Written while Albarn was on holiday in Mallorca with his partner and fellow musician Justine Frischmann, it was a vivid portrait of young Brits enjoying sun, sex and sangria on cheap package holidays to Mediterranean resorts. Sung in English accents and set to a jaunty electronic Euro-disco beat, 'Girls and Boys' was one of the first British songs to celebrate the hedonistic holiday dance culture that exploded in the 1990s; and perhaps the last irony of Britpop was that, for all its posturing about America, in the long run it was dance culture that drew British youth closer to Europe and put some warm blue Mediterranean water between them and young Americans. It was not usually the suave urban Continental culture admired by the early Mods; indeed at times it looked and felt more like Blackpool or Brighton in a heatwave. Fuelled by alcohol and drugs, entranced by a music created in West Germany and black America, and clothed in an abiding sense of British style, millions of young people plunged into the Continental Europe that Mods had dreamed about ever since the 1950s.

IO

AS ENGLISH AS FISH AND CHIPS
Mod and the Explosion of British Dance Culture

Raving, in all its forms, is now as English as fish and chips or football.
  Tony Marcus, *Mixmag*, 1995[1]

Young British people make a lot of noise and this can be a bad thing.
  José Maria Ribas, Spanish minister for tourism, 2001[2]

HERE COME THE MIRROR MEN

'To tell you the truth, I feel a bit sorry for men these days', Geri Halliwell told *NME* readers before wearing her Union Jack minidress at the 1997 Brit Awards. 'There's less work, the male suicide rate is going up, there's no real defined role for them anywhere . . . They don't know what to do and maybe some of them want to stick together and act like lads to make them feel better.' Reassuringly for male readers, when asked what sort of man she was attracted to, Geri said that although the film *Malcolm X* had made her cry, 'someone I wanted to shag might just be any bloke with a six pack who had a bit of sexuality about him'.[3] Ironically, one of her fellow Spice Girls would marry a footballer who became the poster boy for a competing strand of masculinity.

Metrosexual was a term coined in 1994 by Mark Simpson, the British author and biographer of Britpop's campest founding father, Morrissey.

In an article called 'Here Come the Mirror Men',[4] Simpson defined this archetype as an affluent, narcissistic male of indeterminate sexuality between the ages of 18 and 45, given to a dandyish love of clothes, grooming and physical fitness who inhabits post-industrial urban society and who enjoys shopping as a leisure activity just as much as women. He identified David Beckham as an exemplar of this British male.

Simpson was describing not just a footballer in a sarong but a Mod, straight out of the pages of *Rave* magazine thirty years earlier. The term metrosexual did not arrive in America for almost a decade, and it never became as accepted there as it did in Europe. Mod had attached to British youth culture a prototype of metrosexual masculinity in the 1960s, which became embedded in Britain through a combination of broad social trends and the legitimacy that some Mod-related youth cultures gave them. One of those cultures barely registered in the mass media despite its connection to the nation's favourite sport.

The cult of Casuals, at its peak in the 1980s when it probably numbered tens of thousands, took its name from a love of smart casual clothing. They were a close relation of the most troublesome member of the Mod family – that cousin with learning difficulties who never entirely left the neighbourhood when property prices rose and the delicatessen appeared: the skinhead. Some Casuals shared with skinheads a macho tribalism that revolved around football. Yet they were generally more affluent and used clothes as a signifier of aspiration, rather than as a suit of armour against the arrows of feminism and effeminacy, as skinheads had tended to do.

'These so-called Casuals were nothing more than an Eighties version of Mod', wrote Terry Rawlings in his survey of Mod culture.[5] Although they were by no means all Conservative voters, the cult appealed to aspirational working-class men and women who bought into Margaret Thatcher's property-owning, consumer democracy. This is the context in which Robert Elms places them:

It was a striking return to the fanatical elitism of mod, played out largely against the backdrop of the football terraces in a moribund phase. Casual was a return to classic working-class sartorial values, a cycle reasserting itself, but also a dramatic sign of changing times, a logo-crazed celebration of consumerism in Thatcher's new England. In the same way as the middle classes were starting to be hungry for the trappings of continental civility – extra virgin olive oil, espresso coffee and bottled mineral water – and the big bang braggarts were hooked on Porsches, Dom Perignon and tables at swish new Conran restaurants, so working-class boys identified their own chic objects of desire. Of course they went for clothes . . . soon every market stall was full of snide Lacoste, fakes manufactured for Essex in Thailand. Kids were carrying razorblades to slice off the croc from the real thing and attach it to their dodgy Tesco top.[6]

Casuals' taste for European sportswear descended from the original Mods, who had asserted their European sensibility by wearing cycling shirts as well as sharp suits from France and Italy. Precise origins, like those of most youth cultures, are unclear and disputed; but the first Casuals seem to have emerged in Liverpool in 1978 where they were known as 'Scallies' (from 'scallywag'). Their favourite brand was Adidas, as one fan, Gary Aspden, remembered: 'I just used to love it when you got these shoes and you got these little pieces [the tags] written in German . . . it just seemed so exotic.'[7] Adidas was founded seventy years earlier than Nike, in 1924, by Adolf 'Adi' Dassler, whose shoes had been worn by Jesse Owens in the gold medal wins that so angered Hitler at the 1936 Berlin Olympics (an early example of a sports star endorsing a brand).

Like earlier Mods, Casuals' taste for European apparel was a deliberate parody of middle-class style, because the brands of clothing and footwear they chose were associated with sports like tennis, skiing, rugby, sailing and golf. Few went near Wimbledon, Cowes week or the Open but instead wore the relevant clothing to watch football. Italy gave the Casuals Fila (founded in 1911), Diadora and Ellesse (skiwear companies founded in 1948 and 1959 respectively), and Sergio Tacchini (founded by a tennis player of that name in 1966). As well as Adidas, Germany provided Puma founded by Dassler's brother Rudi in 1947. Sweden gave the Casuals Marc O'Polo (Stockholm, 1967), France Daniel Hechter (ski and tennis wear, 1962) and Lacoste, founded by a former French tennis player in 1933 (its crocodile the first example of a brand logo displayed on outer clothing). There were a few British brands on the approved style list too: Gola, founded in Leicester in 1905, became known for its 1972 kitbag; and Reebok, whose training shoes sported a valued Union Jack tag, was launched in Bolton in

1960.[8] And as we have seen, it was an Englishman who had given Mods the brand replete with meaning since the 1950s: the earliest Casuals to emerge from Manchester were known as 'Perry Boys' because of their love of the shirt created by Fred Perry.

Casuals relied on back-street shops like that of Wade Smith in Manchester, who in the 1980s made a quarter of a million pounds a year importing rare Adidas trainers from Germany that were unavailable in the high street. But this was not the boutique world of the 1960s and 70s. A growing obsession with 'designer' brands reflected the perennial working-class desire to 'Fix Up, Look Sharp', as Dizzee Rascal, a fan of the polo shirt, later put it; but it was also a matter of commercial supply. Affordable, independent boutiques like Quant and Stephen declined in number during the 1970s, usually because high-street retailers bought them out in order to acquire street credibility. Those designers who survived, like Vivienne Westwood, did so by going haute couture, with their artistic credibility intact but even more out of the financial reach of teenagers. Increasingly too, the contemporary heirs to Quant and Westwood were not setting up boutiques at all; instead, the likes of John Galliano and Alexander McQueen were headhunted by the big fashion houses.

Mods' original need to establish themselves as an elite within (and above) the rest of the working classes – capable of better taste if not always greater wealth – was now replayed in a consumerist obsession with labels that more than any other strand of Modernism simply created an alternative uniform that rendered them a herd. One London Casual, Bob Morris, explained:

It's called an 'upping' . . . an 'upping' is really being one step ahead of everyone else, having that item of clothing that no one else can get. In the working classes, even though we're poor, we always want to look like we ain't poor. We wanna drive a big car and we wanna wear good gear and I think that's the essence of Mod. That's what we've got in working-class culture; we've got aspirations to be better than we actually are.

I saw one of my mates, when the sportswear thing came in '81–'82, on the tube and he had a Sergio on him and he was covered in plaster and I said, 'Stu what are you doing wearing that to work, that's seventy quid!' Seventy quid was about a week's wages and he went, 'Yeah well everyone's got 'em now' . . . And that was a very very Mod thing to say.[9]

Casual spread rapidly without the conventional help of magazines, television or cinema; instead it travelled through the nation's nightclubs and football stadia, some of which became venues for mass, informal fashion parades. An early noticeboard of the cult was a Liverpool FC fanzine called *The End*, produced by Peter Hooton. A man of left-wing leanings, he became a key figure in the rave movement of the 1990s as lead singer in the 'Madchester' group the Farm. Hooton remembers the moment in 1978 when he felt part of something new: 'We were in the paddock at Old Trafford getting taunted by the Mancs: "Everton, show us yer scarves!" By that time the Casual revolution had taken off, we were pretty distinctive and laughed: "We don't have scarves, we've got our Fred Perry and Adidas Sambas on."'[10] Paul Webster, an Arsenal fan, recalls how 'London went casual crazy with every team in the capital having their own well-turned-out crew. It quickly became more important to be seen to be the best-dressed mob than to be the hardest.'[11] Tribal loyalties were maintained with each 'crew' or 'firm' choosing certain labels over others in a sort of alternative team strip.

As well as linking the north and south of England the cult extended into Scotland and Wales. In Edinburgh, Hibernian FC (followed by Irvine Welsh, author of *Trainspotting*,) produced the notorious Hibs Casuals.[12] Gareth, a telecoms project manager from the Cardiff City 'Soul Crew', saw it as enabling his friends to challenge the dominance of Britain's capital city. 'This is a big culture,' he said in 2004, 'in London the world's your oyster. You can be anything you want. But when it comes to football, suddenly we're on a level playing field. It's our chance to show how confident we are, how well we dress, how loud we sing. It's a civic pride thing.'[13] His friend Craig agreed: 'The thing about Cardiff is that there's a limit to what most young people can achieve. Casual is an acceptable way for us to aspire to something. The old Marc Bolan quote [*sic*] about mod culture sums it up: "Clean living under difficult circumstances."'[14]

OU EST LE CENTRE ADIDAS?

Amid the creeping Americanisation of national life, football had been one of the few ways that the British had maintained a distance from the United States in the twentieth century; simultaneously football had connected them to the rest of the world. The Casuals cult coincided with the availability of cheaper Continental air and rail travel and the dominance of English football teams in European tournaments between 1978 and 1984.

Whereas earlier tribes had to rely on savvy retailers like Wade Smith to import favoured European brands, later Casuals could afford to travel to the Continent to obtain them at source. 'Shopping trips to Europe became such a big part of the scene in Manchester', said one, adding, 'There were no McDonald's in the north of England in those days. Germany had hundreds of 'em and I learned to order a Big Mac meal in German way before I had to do it in English. "Ein grosse Big Mac meal, mit coke, danke."'[15] Peter Hooton remembers a trip to Paris to watch Liverpool in the European Cup Final in 1981: 'We got to Paris on the Saturday and the game wasn't until the Wednesday . . . we spent the Saturday to the Wednesday looking for this place called the Adidas Centre that didn't exist. We were asking everyone in our broken French "Ou est le Centre Adidas?" and getting this blank look. It was this Holy Grail for Liverpool fans.' Those who couldn't afford their favourite brands resorted to stealing them: 'Even in the late 70s and early 80s, Liverpool shops were security-conscious whereas these places abroad didn't expect people to come into their shops and steal . . . There were Scousers scattered across Germany in various prisons.'[16] Such was the embarrassment in Continental boardrooms about a brand's association with hooligans that some tried to limit supplies to British outlets. This only led to more European 'shopping', whereby enterprising Casuals travelled across the Continent using InterRail – a discount rail ticket commonly used by students on their gap years – in another strange echo of middle-class life.

This was the first British youth culture that wasn't originally attached to a genre of music, which was one reason why the mass media took little notice of it. In the early 1980s, the media was distracted by the colourful, Bowie-influenced New Romantics, and few observers made any links between the two. Yet it was David Bowie who, more than any musical artist, had unwittingly shaped Casual style, in particular with the experimental album *Low* (1977), on the cover of which he sported a wedge haircut and a duffel coat in mimicry of 1930s Oxbridge student style. 'Berlin-phase Bowie might not have seemed important at the time,' wrote Kevin Sampson and Dave

Rimmer in *The Face*, 'but in the Scotland Road area of Liverpool it was breaking down doors for the world of youth culture . . . The resulting image was at once aggressive, effeminate and extremely attractive . . . it was the distinctive hairstyle that stamped SCALLY all over them, the unique and wonderful lopsided wedge – a haircut popular in the last great Depression – ridiculously "claimed" by the hair stylist Trevor Sorbie at Vidal Sassoon.'[17] *The Face* article, called 'The Ins and Outs of High Street Fashion' and published in 1983, was the first coverage of this subculture in the national media. 'This is young, urban, male Britain – modern as hell, and how', the authors concluded, 'though drinking, stealing, claiming and clubbing were all important, obsession with clothes gripped young Merseyside something murderous . . . the age of Football Chic was upon us.'[18]

For some, it was a genuine style movement. Steve White, a Bermondsey boy, who went on to a successful career as drummer for the Style Council and for Paul Weller's solo projects, remembers his time as a Casual with fondness:

In London there was much more an influence of style and actually going to clubs. I used to go to places like the Lyceum, the Hammersmith Palace as a youngster. We would all be wearing a form of Casual . . . wearing our polo tops, our pegs and loafers – a little bit of Northern Soul and a little bit of football culture, and it was a really nice mix. There wasn't any kind of racism. Again there was a lot of black kids that were into it, a lot of white kids that were into it, and as I say, it might be seen as a soft southern take on the whole thing but for me it was a really good scene. I really enjoyed it . . . [but] I do think it got a bad name . . . the couple of crap films that have come out, depicting it as all Fila tops and Stanley knives, and that's done nothing to the image.[19]

There were many female Casuals too, just as there had once been female skinheads. 'A. J.' from Manchester explained that

girls of the period were bang into the whole thing too. The same haircuts, the same excessive jewellery, and the same fashions – like we wore loafers, they wore court shoes, we wore golf jumpers, they wore the cardigans . . . in fact for a good while you couldn't move in Manchester for girls peeking out from beneath long fringes in sheepskin coats and tartan skirts.[20]

Unlike skins, a significant minority of Casuals were Afro-Caribbean; indeed reggae singers like Gregory Isaacs had helped to shape the look in the late 1970s. Bev Thompson regarded membership of the Leicester City 'Baby Squad' as a symbol of belonging to Britain:

I wanted equal rights. . . Part of being a Casual for me was showing that we weren't scared. Leicester was a big place for the National Front and we were told to keep out of the way or run if we see skinheads and I think the Casual movement gave us a sense of identity where we could stand and be strong. And that was probably the first time where first, second generation [blacks] in Britain, we felt like this was home. We identified with them. Wearing British labels kind of stamped that. Wearing [an] Aquascutum outfit . . . I couldn't get more British than that.[21]

Thompson believes that Casuals anticipated metrosexuality: 'back then [in the 80s] guys were really vain about their hair, about their clothing, about their trainers, the whole shebang, you didn't want to get roughed up and you certainly didn't want to get your garms mashed up'.[22] Yet the fact remains that vanity and violence sometimes went hand in hand. The national media belatedly picked up on the cult through its connection with hooliganism. 'SPOT THE REAL THUG' said one tabloid newspaper in 1985. Displaying a photo of a 'traditional' skinhead football hooligan next to a coiffured Casual, it asked readers: 'Can you tell the violent thug from the true soccer fan? The bovver booted model looks ready for a punch up but the casually dressed model is wearing the new disguise. And he is the real villain. His £300 outfit may look smart but tucked in the pocket of his Italian bomber jacket could well be a lethal Stanley knife.'[23] The media made much of the odd bank manager and fireman in hooligan gangs, and ten of West Ham's notorious 140-strong Inter City Firm cited their occupation as 'rock musicians'. But studies showed that the majority (around 90 per cent) were lower working class, from skilled manual workers to the unemployed, like most men involved in football gangs since the First World War.[24]

The first issue of the men's magazine Loaded in 1994 displayed the actor Gary Oldman on its cover. Five years earlier Oldman had starred in Alan Clarke's The Firm (1989), one of a genre of British films like Nick Love's Football Factory (2004) that portrayed the lives of a gang of style-conscious hooligans. In the film, the Firm are led by their 'top boy', 'Bex' Bissell. 'I would like you to meet a very old friend of mine and yours, put your hands together for . . . Stanley', says Bissell as he brandishes a Stanley knife with intent to carve a tattoo in a teenager's arm to signal his induction into the gang. A staple of the British toolbox and a symbol of DIY home improvements, the Stanley knife was an appropriate choice of weapon given their aspirations. But it was a corrupted aesthetic, for while these aspirational youths outwardly rejected 'cloth-capped bullshit', they remained trapped in a violent, proletarian male cosmos largely of their own making. Hooliganism was a prime example of the less savoury forms of British youth culture that were exported to the Continent alongside the music and fashions that enjoyed government support and public approval; its ready adoption across Europe was also a reminder that the Continent was not just home to coffee machines, scooters and ski wear.

The swaying, charging tribes of well-dressed hooligans were defeated in the 1990s by CCTV policing and the introduction of all-seat stadia – which had long been a feature of American sport – following a series of human disasters such as Heysel. But they also fell victim to the changing nature of football. By the time the Premier League was launched in the 1992–93 season, the game's annual turnover was £46 million, a figure that rose to £570 million in 2001–2. Some fans complained about the sport being taken over by men with real wealth and not just its trappings, but women and senior citizens driven away by hooliganism began to return; and as the century-long white working-class tradition of racist chanting finally began to decline, even a few young blacks and Asians appeared as spectators to augment the older black presence on the pitch.[25]

When football became fashionable again in the 1990s, Casual style was incorporated into the Britpop look by the lads Geri Halliwell had pitied. Blur's Damon Albarn told readers of the *Modern Review*:

In these seemingly dark ages of cultural recapitulation, the archetypal yob has become the prodigal son. He is no longer just a menace to society, the local lager hooligan: he has bettered himself, refined his vulgarity. He has become a social climber, a renaissance man . . . old yobs of the Eighties, resplendent in their Sergio Tacchini and Kappa tops, have been absorbed into Nineties Britain. In many ways they are its success story.[26]

Casuals and their imitators rarely acknowledged that by the end of the century multinational corporations based in Asia or America had taken over most European sportswear brands (with the notable exception of Germany's Adidas). So-called 'Lacoste Lefties' knew the irony of fetishising brands associated with the economic globalisation that led to the decline of British manufacturing, especially when it hurt close to home. As Jonny Owen recalled: 'When the Burberry factory moved from South Wales to China they only moved 'cause they could make shirts cheaper . . . so the Cardiff Soul Crew were like "That's it . . . if you move our factories, we won't wear your shirts anymore. Go on, fuck off!"'[27] Of course, for Lacoste Lefties and Thatcherites alike, labels stitched in China could still provide a sense of distinction and a connection to the extended Mod family, but the real engagement with Europe took place not on the football terraces of Britain but on its dance floors.

FAHREN AUF DER AUTOBAHN

The last British youth culture of the twentieth century to be shaped by Mod's European outlook originated in the country that had been a crucible of modernism. Techno emerged from the industrial and commercial centres of West Germany around the time that Britain belatedly entered the European Community in 1973 and became the distinguishing feature of British dance culture over the following decades. The influence of techno on everything from House and drum and bass in the 1980s and 90s to grime and dubstep in the 2000s, connected the youth of Britain to the rest of Europe as never before, and distinguished their culture from that of America without destroying transatlantic ties.

In the autumn of 1975, four young men in sharp suits, with short hair neatly combed, arrived in Liverpool from Germany. But they were not returning home from a creative sojourn in Hamburg. Kraftwerk arrived from their home town of Düsseldorf, and like the Beatles they changed the course of Western popular music. Led by Ralf Hütter and Florian Schneider, they had been raised in occupied West Germany's industrial powerhouse just a few years after the Beatles were born during the Luftwaffe's blitz of Liverpool. Already nearing 30 when their first successful album, *Autobahn*, was released in 1975 – its title track describing the experience of driving on Germany's motorways – Kraftwerk had emerged from the West German avant-garde music scene of the 1960s, which included the classical composer Karl Heinz Stockhausen and the psychedelic rock group Can. Düsseldorf was also the capital of the German fashion industry.

Kraftwerk were among the first to experiment with synthesisers, while also developing the art of VJ-ing by incorporating back-projected film into their performances. With catchy hooks, serenely robotic expressions, fine tailoring and graphics taken directly from Bauhaus designs, Kraftwerk (meaning power station) celebrated the modern world of cars and robots, speed and computing.[28] Their stage personas expressed a camp, chilling detachment from it all that completely eschewed the conventional phallic posturing of the Anglo-American rock god. Style Council drummer Steve White cites Kraftwerk as a member of the Mod family when asked to define popular Modernism: 'What we are really looking for is pioneers in music or in art, or in literature and fashion; that's the aesthetic and idea of Mod. Miles Davis was a modernist, Bowie was a modernist . . . I think Kraftwerk were a Mod band.'[29]

Coincidentally, a few days after Kraftwerk's concert in Liverpool, one of the Beatles was back in town: at another venue in the city, and in front of a much larger audience, Paul McCartney performed with Wings on his latest world tour. Yet as Wolfgang Flür, the group's drummer, later reflected, 'Kraftwerk were bringing a new kind of pop music to Liverpool. We were the most modern act in the city.'[30] And with *Autobahn* reaching No. 11 in the 1975 album charts, it seemed that running underneath the post-war Germanophobia of the British people was a steady current of receptivity to Continental music and style, even though Kraftwerk's performances played to stereotypes of humourless Teutonic automata. In some respects, these godfathers of electronic music were a pop version of the sneaking British fondness for German cars and engineering.

'From the beginning', recalled Wolfgang Flür, Britain 'was the country in which we had the most and the most enthusiastic fans.'[31] The feeling was mutual because for Kraftwerk the source of post-war youth culture was not America but Britain. Flür recalled the excitement he felt in 1975 as the group arrived in the country: '"England" had always been a magical word to me. I thought of all the radio and television programmes about The Beatles, The Hollies, The Pretty Things and The Who and so many other famous bands that I'd seen ten years ago. Now that I was travelling there with my own band, one of my greatest dreams was about to be fulfilled.'[32]

Not only had they made it into the Top 20 in 1975, they had also appeared on BBC's *Tomorrow's World*, a popular science and technology programme that showed what the modern world would look like in viewers' lifetime. The sharp-suited Modernists from Düsseldorf also influenced David Bowie on *Low* two years later, as well as a string of 80s electro-pop acts, from the Human League to Gary Numan and the Pet Shop Boys. However, it was through dance culture that their influence was most keenly felt. When, in 2002, there were no British acts in the US Top 100 – for the first time since 1963 – American commentators noted that this was not just the result of Britpop hubris, but also of the British taste for electronic music:

The musical split between the United States and the UK sunders one of pop culture's most venerable alliances . . . To some extent, the breach represents a disparity in musical taste. The many styles of arty post-disco grouped under the heading 'electronica,' for example, are more popular in Britain than in the United States. The Brit drought also reveals limited UK expertise in some of today's best-selling genres, notably hip-hop, country, and nu-metal.[33]

This was ironic, for it was in the United States that the split began, when a group of DJs began to mix the sounds of African American soul music and European techno to create the sonic basis of modern dance culture.

HOUSE IS GAY MUSIC

Whereas British popular music recovered its distinctiveness in the early 1960s dance music remained in thrall to America until the late 1980s. During the 1960s, Mods had moved to jazz, ska and Motown soul in the first nightclubs designed solely for dancing. The term 'rave' seems to have first been used in the 1950s to describe bohemian parties in the Soho area. It became ubiquitous in the early 1960s when Mods used it to describe any all-night, drug-fuelled dance party, and it became firmly attached to Mod culture when it became the title of the most influential youth magazine of the period, *Rave*, published from 1965 to 1971. But it was not until the 1970s that a separate subculture developed around dance music.

The roots of what came to be known as rave lay in the Northern Soul scene of the 1970s.[34] However, there was a crucial difference between Northern Soul and the dance cultures set in train by disco: the latter's impulse to change, their desire for perpetual motion and sense of modernity that Mod seemed to have left behind at the entrance to the Wigan Casino. Whereas Northern Soulers relied on an ever-diminishing store of 1960s American soul, techno was a contemporary genre that lent itself to musical experimentation. In the mid-1980s, African American DJs in Chicago, led by Frankie Knuckles, experimented with a harder, more aggressive form of techno. They used it to give soul-based disco a faster more infectious beat, while retaining its melodic, harmonic qualities.

Like many Mods, Paul Weller endorsed the new genre. 'At the time I really believed that garage house was the new mod music', he later said.[35] The reason lay in its origins in soul. Speaking to *The Face* in 1983 about 'the State of the Nation's dress' at the height of the Style Council's fame, Weller said, 'I still think of myself as a modernist . . . but people have missed the point. The true mod legacy is all those soul boys and girls walking down the high streets.' Weller added that while pop should be 'taken as seriously as the other arts', the best thing about the Tate Gallery was its polished floor: 'if it belonged to me I'd turn it into a disco.'[36]

House was a cocktail of American and European musical styles that was distilled in the multiracial gay clubs of Chicago like the Warehouse and then transmitted to Europe by touring American DJs and pirate radio stations, at the same time as hip hop became America's biggest global export since the arrival of McDonald's and Nike in the 1970s. But just as punk had been more successful in the UK because of the nation's more acute class-consciousness so House became more popular here because of Britain's less acute racial divisions and more liberal attitude to sexuality. Public Enemy's Chuck D bluntly articulated American opinion in an interview with the British critic Simon

Reynolds: 'it's sophisticated, anti-black, the most ARTIFICIAL shit I ever heard. It represents the gay scene, it's separating blacks from their past and their culture, *it's upwardly mobile.*'[37] These comments are revealing, as by 'keeping it real' hip hop artists perpetuated a stereotype of blacks as working class and angry.

Hence the fact that Frankie Knuckles remained virtually unknown in his own country. House never had disco's *Saturday Night Fever* to make it acceptable to a straight American audience and it had to compete with the macho minstrelsy of hip hop; in contrast disco never had to compete with the soul or funk genres from which it borrowed so heavily. In 1990 a despairing letter by a reader from Oregon to *The Face* declared: 'Americans may have MTV, but all you can see on it is bad metal, their music in general is a pale imitation of the stuff from England. Fashion? Not even a glimmer of acid house style. America may have their own rivalry, LA vs NY, but neither compares with the originality of Manny or Londinium.'[38]

In Europe, House music soon broke out of its gay ghetto and captivated a far larger and socially more diverse audience, numbering several million in Britain alone during its peak years between 1988 and 1998. For young Europeans in search of a good time and a degree of racial harmony less dependent than hip hop on the peddling of stereotypes, House music was the Holy Grail. And when it was combined with the illegal consumption of Ecstasy, it acquired a subversive, hedonistic appeal that Northern Soul and disco had both, for different reasons, lost.

In his study *Hip-Hop America*, Nelson George, the pre-eminent chronicler of the genre, wrote, 'The Brits once boasted that the sun never set on the British Empire, but now they live under a perpetual cloud cover.'[39] For George, the only rays of light were provided by America's most ubiquitous cultural product of the late twentieth century. Hip hop, he claimed, 'has outlived all its detractors and even surprised most ardent early supporters by always changing, and with each change, expanding its audience. It has outgunned punk, post-punk, New Wave, Rave, House, techno, and every other much-hyped musical form of the age.'[40] Except that in Britain and the rest of Europe it simply didn't.

Partly this resistance was a question of style, argues the DJ Mike Pickering: 'When it [hip hop] went mainstream, it became gangsta rap, which most people found tasteless and it focused on having loads of money and jewellery and bling as they call it. We're far too aloof for that, it's not Mod to walk around dripping in jewellery.'[41] It also jarred because, far from living under perpetual cloud cover, the British had actually evolved a post-imperial youth culture that reflected a progressive society. Sheryl Garratt, who edited *The Face* and was personally involved in rave, described the difference between Britain and America: 'What's great about Britain is it's not exclusively an English-American dialogue. We've got lots of stuff from the Caribbean, lots of stuff from Europe, we're very open to influences from all over the world . . . [America] is a very diverse country but schools are more or less segregated, neighbourhoods are more or less segregated. Here, everybody's on top of each other.'[42]

As Mike Pickering observed when he played in America in the 1980s and 90s:

The only clubs that I would play in New York and Chicago were almost all 99% gay and predominantly black. . . . White middle-class America, they would never go near homosexual, black music in warehouses. Whereas a British kid, even if he was slightly middle class, would go, 'I'm going to check out that scene', that's the main difference. We're a nation of discoverers as far as culture is concerned and as a nation we're less hung up on race or sexuality. They're not like us, they don't move on very quickly, it's an old-fashioned place compared to Britain.[43]

This wasn't just British conceit. Derrick May, America's leading techno DJ, who had been instrumental in the music's global development, remarked on the difference between the two continents after his first tour of Europe:

You gotta remember, we were brought up with this racial conflict thing, instilled in us since babies. If you're a kid in Detroit, [you might] never even have to *see* a white person, unless they're on TV. The closest association I had with people outside my race was when I started travelling to Europe. The first time I went to the UK, man, I played for five thousand white kids. It really expanded my horizons.[44]

Horizons were also expanded by the unprecedented fusion of rock and dance music that accompanied the rave movement in Britain.

The crucible for all these developments was a nightclub, described by one critic as a 'post-punk Bauhaus' for British youth – the Hacienda.[45]

IT WAS THE POLITICS OF JOY

Glasgow, Manchester, Liverpool, Coventry and other post-industrial cities and towns in Britain were the geographical bedrock of post-punk in the 1980s and 90s, on which several strands of Mod-related youth culture were built, from Two Tone to rave. DJ Dave Haslam's study of Manchester concluded:

Where once the Manchester mill owners and merchants, mill hands and factory operatives created the wealth that financed the Empire, now the city dominates English pop culture, trading in music, the sounds from the city's streets resonating around the globe. Away from the centres of political power – and you can't get much further away than a bedroom in Burnage or dance floor in Ancoats – Manchester's mavericks and misfits have created a magnificent, unofficial underground culture.[46]

Connecting it all was the impresario Tony Wilson, who once said that his only failing was 'an excess of civic pride'. Wilson finished the job that Jerry Dammers had begun: making people dance and think at the same time.

Born in Salford in 1950, Tony Wilson was a grammar school and Cambridge-educated local TV presenter. He was also a radical entrepreneur. 'The musicians own everything. The company owns nothing. All our bands have the freedom to fuck off', he famously wrote in his own blood on a piece of paper framed in the offices of his record label, Factory Records.[47] Inspired by seeing the Sex Pistols' first performance in Manchester, along with his Glaswegian friend Alan McGee, Wilson made his name in the post-punk era. Sensing the growing importance of electronic music, he and McGee pioneered the fusion of rock and dance genres that became Baggy with bands like New Order, Primal Scream, the Stone Roses and the Happy Mondays.

Several of their members emerged out of the Casuals, their knowledge of soul, funk and House music as well as Indie rock informed by the sense of belonging to an interconnected family of Mod. As Gary 'Mani' Mounfield of the Stone Roses, and later Primal Scream, explained: 'We were mad for Tamla and Northern Soul . . . I've still got my scooter, a Lambretta SX200 white standard, it's a fucking knicker-dropping machine. Mod influenced us all, even now for sure – Temps, Four Tops, the fucking Who, awesome! Entwistle, brilliant apart from the beard!'[48]

Wilson's belief in modernism was more intellectual but just as passionate as Mani's. The design of Factory's record covers and merchandising contributed to the movement's aesthetic impact on British popular culture in the 1980s and 90s. Peter Saville, Factory's art director, looked back on his work in an interview in 2009:

You're involved in this thing called the new wave, and [it's] your first intro-duction to modernism. Post-punk. They fit together, they make sense, there's a kind of discipline. There's an ideology evident in the aesthetic. When you look at this stuff, the modernists, it's about a changing time – a new order, a new way of life, a new system . . . Pop art was the only thing I knew anything about but . . . my content was coming from the canon. I was seeing all these things that middle class Britain had been denied. I was asking – 'why don't we have this?' If Mart Stam made that great tubular chair, why don't we have one? If the Bauhaus proposed all these ways of living, why don't we live like that? Why isn't anything in 1970s Britain like it could be? So – with this carte blanche of a record cover almost every month or so, a single or an album or whatever, I kind of curated a proposition. Of – how I would like modern life to be. What do I want in my life. And if I can't have it I'll have a picture of it.[49]

With money from the commercial success of New Order songs (versions of which were played by radio and nightclub DJs alike) Wilson set up the Hacienda club in 1982 in a red-brick former yacht-builder's workshop and warehouse next to Rochdale Canal. It was an audacious bid to fuse the two strands of British youth culture. The Hacienda didn't just contain a stage for live performances as well as a huge dance floor; it was designed to foster an overtly modernistic environment.

Ben Kelly, the designer brought in by Saville, had studied at the RCA in the 70s and had previously designed the interior of Vivienne

Westwood's boutique, Seditionaries. The bars at the Hacienda were named after the English Soviet spies, Philby and Burgess, and here ravers could sit on a hundred Alvar Aalto bar stools before re-entering the club.[50] With the clean lines of its steel beams painted yellow and black, it was, said one critic, 'an industrial fantasy'[51] that, like the Factory name and logo, restated the modernist aesthetic in what had become a post-industrial city. Kelly said he was 'trying to poke fun at post-modernism, which had reared its ugly head at the time, and which I felt very uncomfortable with.'[52]

A former factory worker and Factory co-founder, DJ Mike Pickering, who had been involved in Northern Soul as a youth, was clear about their intent. 'It stemmed from Saville,' he said. 'The whole thing had to do with Italian anarchists and modernists and it came from the "Situationist Review" – that's where the name the Hacienda came from, "The Hacienda must be built" . . . We were all into Italian anarchists and the simplicity and the sleekness of it all.'[53] If the references to Situationism linked the project to the punk background of Wilson and Kelly, then the overall aesthetic connected it to the broader modernist movement:

It was totally modernism and the Hacienda was like walking into a space-ship. It was so modernistic and that followed on from everything we did at Factory. I mean we were all ex-Mods and . . . Mod is short for Modern, that's what we were doing. The colours, the simplicity, it was all modernism . . . Most of the clubs at that time were kind of like old pubs – you stuck to the carpet if you stood in one place for too long. We got rid of all that, we built a place that reflected our lifestyle . . . we had no carpets, it was all beautiful bare surfaces. Sleek lines. No swirly patterns – there were stripes, though![54]

The club also had a corresponding admission policy, as Pickering recalls:

One of the reasons the Hacienda was different to other clubs at that time was because I reversed the door policy. In those days what I call 'thugs in ties' could get in by wearing the shittiest of clothes, as long as they weren't trainers . . . with a tie, and be a real meathead, you'd get in all the other clubs, but if you turned up in a beautiful Armani top, or even Fred Perry with great gazelles on, they'd go 'You're not coming in.' We reversed that completely, so immediately for the 'Perrys', as they were called – like Casuals, which was another continuation of Mod – it was the first place they had to go to, instead of hanging round the Arndale, and that created a really fertile ground for young music makers or DJs or film makers.[55]

From the Hacienda, rave spread as quickly through Britain as Merseybeat had done from the Cavern Club, soon embracing all social classes. 'It was here's the drugs, here's the dance, let's fucking go', remembers Wilson. 'There were no moral questions. It was the politics of joy.'[56] Alan McGee recalls his first trip to the Hacienda: 'We walked in and there were 2,000 people going absolutely mental. Wilson was in the corner in the cocktail bar holding court. He gave me a hug, I gave him a hug. I looked on stage: there were 600 kids on stage – I'll never forget it – and there was Shaun Ryder sweating profusely, out of his mind, leading the charge of 600 people punching the air.'[57]

By the time Britpop was in full swing in the mid-1990s the bouncy, melodic beats of House had swept the nation's bars and clubs. Estimates by the leisure industry in 1993 put the annual value of the rave market at £1.8 billion, with over 50 million attendances at clubs, most by people aged between 16 and 24, each spending on average £35 on admission charges, soft drinks and recreational drugs.[58] As with jazz and rhythm and blues in the 1960s, Britain was the prism and the portal through which a version of America was transmitted to the rest of Europe. Within a few years of House arriving in the UK, it was crossing the English Channel fast on its way to becoming Europe's most popular dance music since the Second World War.

Although Britpop and rave shared millions of fans, what made clubbing different in the 1990s was that most participants were in their teens and twenties, whereas rock openly celebrated its multi-generational constituency. In that respect rave also differed from disco, which since the 1970s had managed to cross the generational divide by becoming a staple of birthday and wedding parties from Easterhouse to Esher. What made rave a younger pursuit? Aside from its association with a strange and misunderstood drug, it was a more recent phenomenon than rock and for a time electronic dance music seemed capable of greater innovation with its dizzying production of new sub-genres. As James Barton, the Liverpudlian founder of the 'super-club' Cream, recalled: 'It was a really exciting time. I was nineteen and my brothers had come through punk. I caught the back end of that, seeing The Clash before they split, then The Jam. But acid house felt like a music which my brothers hadn't loaned me. It wasn't handed down, it felt like *ours*. We were in the middle of what felt like a revolution.'[59]

Rave was not confined to clubs. From 1988 until 1994, an illegal party scene was developed by young DJs and promoters in fields near Britain's cities. Some critics saw this aspect of the rave movement as the antithesis of Mod culture because clothes were less of a focal point than music and drugs (and when dancing at night in a field it was hard to tell what shoes people were wearing). For Eddie Piller the arrival of rave marked an important shift in the history of youth culture:

The sea change is quite easy to spot, because up to the late '80s you had a series of either new youth cultures or revivals, and then Acid House came along. And that was like Year Zero in the cultural revolution. Everything that had come before was over . . . If people are tripping they're not necessarily interested in how they look and they're not interested in the music because all they want is bang-bang-bang so they can reach a personal nirvana through the heartbeat manipulation of House music – and that happened for about a year. And it killed all youth culture. You were either a Head – an Acid Head – or not. And that had never happened before.[60]

For Robert Elms Acid House was a conscious 'rejection of the Mod ethic':

Now Mod is overtly elitist, always was, and all of the Mod offshoots as I understand them: New Romantic, early punk, the Casuals, are all elitist. They're all about saying I'm in with the in crowd, I'm the only one with these trainers, I'm the only one who's got that record. Acid House was exactly the opposite of that, it was about getting as many people in a field as you can or putting your arms round each other while taking this silly drug. In many respects that was a hippie thing . . . which I always hated: it was anti-urban, that's why it took place in fields . . . I think that although it was dancing it was hippie dancing, it was dancing that was all over the place, it wasn't dancing in a Mod sense, it wasn't about looking cool, none of that. It wasn't meant to be cool: Acid House, it was the opposite of cool.[61]

There were acknowledged links to hippie culture in the rave movement, not least the fact that 1988 was dubbed by promoters the 'Second Summer of Love'. Among the many tribes that gathered in rave's metaphorical tent were the New Age travellers, or 'Crusties', whose anti-consumerist, environmental and spiritual concerns echoed those of the original hippies, as did their rejection of mass-produced style in favour of crafted clothing. However, they differed from their 1960s counterparts in that they were partying with other tribes rather than setting themselves apart as 'Tomorrow's People'.

Yet fashion remained important for many ravers, especially the so-called neo Mods who orbited Andy Weatherall's club Boy's Own in London Bridge. As Simon Reynolds recalls, 'The Boy's Own aesthetic was an update of sixties mod: the same homosocial obsessions with the sharpest clothes, the obscurest import dance singles from Black America, and the pills that allowed you to skip sleep and spend the weekend dancing.'[62] There was also a subtle class divide between ravers who dressed like beach bums (known briefly as Acid Teds) and the men who sharpened up to dance in a field or a club, echoing the divisions that had led to fighting on beaches in the 1960s. The 'mod versus rockers, Balearic Beat versus Acid Ted antagonism', Reynolds observed, 'was grounded in an enduring divide that runs through British pop history: an upper working-class superiority complex vis-a-vis the undiscriminating unskilled proles'.[63] One thing that united them all was a yellow face with a facile smile.

Just as Mods had used the RAF target and the British flag to make their points about class prejudice and military service, so the 'Smiley' was used by ravers to make a point about the corporate regulation of time and the state's policing of leisure. The logo had been designed in 1963 by an American advertiser, Harvey Ball, for an insurance company to cheer up workers whose morale had sunk following a corporate merger at the firm. The stick-on Smiley was appropriated by the psychedelic movement, first appearing at free festivals in Britain in the early 1970s, but it was not until the logo's adoption by ravers that it came to stand for a specific youth culture. Smiley's first appearance in this context was on the cover of 'Beat Dis', a 1988 hit by Brixton-born Tim Simenon (known as 'Bomb the Bass'); a year later both appeared on the cover of the *NME* when it endorsed the movement (its headline 'HAIL THE DJ!' rebuked Morrissey's chant of 'Hang the DJ' in the song 'Panic').

In 1993, the *Sunday Times* observed that rave was bringing together 'The Lost Tribes' of British youth culture. A reporter noticed that 'Young men with shaved heads and pigtails, stripped to the waist, are executing vaguely oriental hand movements. Freeze-framed by strobes in clouds of dry ice, revivalist hippies and mods are swaying in the maelstrom. Rastas, ragga girls, ravers, there is no stylistic cohesion to the assembly, as there would have been in the (g)olden days of youth culture.'[64] What initially fostered this 'tribal gathering' was a drug that provoked the biggest moral panic about young people since the Sex Pistols insulted the Queen.

LET'S GO MENTAL, LET'S GO FATAL

More even than recreational sex, drug use had become the focus of anxiety about the young when it became more widespread in the 1960s. 'Taking drugs has become part of a culture of defiance and rejection' for hundreds of thousands of youngsters, declared the *Observer* in 1967.[65] However, until the 1990s drugs were not as big a part of youth culture as governments, the media or parents often feared. For example, after Mick Jagger's prosecution for marijuana possession in 1967, which famously attracted sympathy from the editor of *The Times*, a Gallup poll found that 73 per cent of 18- to 20-year-olds were against the legalisation of cannabis, and when asked 'what is the most serious threat to the well-being of young people today?', a majority of men (55 per cent) and women (63 per cent) placed soft drugs well above alcohol or smoking.[66] The Dangerous Drugs Act of 1964, brought in to deal with Mods' love of speed, was extended by the 1971 Misuse of Drugs Act, which over the years proscribed an array of substances from magic mushrooms to ketamine. However, campaigns that appeared in teen magazines of the 1960s and 70s to dissuade young people focused on wealth, rather than health risks, warning teenagers that 'drugs are expensive and would mean sacrificing records, clothes, holidays'.[67]

Drug use, like every other form of teenage consumption, did not take place in a generational vacuum but depended on individual circumstances. A survey by the Metropolitan Police in Britain's capital city conducted between 1970 and 1974 shone light on the extent to which the social background of the 17–21 age group shaped their choice of drugs as much as it did their choice of clothes or music. Hallucinogenic drugs were found to be most prevalent among middle-class students, while marijuana use was also highest in that group and among West Indian youths.[68]

But there were signs that marijuana was spreading to the 'skilled working class', especially in inner London 'bedsit land', where, said one report from Lambeth, 'a sense of boredom and frustration pervades and where there is an awareness that the potential for development and enjoyment in work or in leisure is small.'[69] Narcotics therefore remained part of a culture of consolation as much as a tool of liberation, providing a temporary escape from boring or painful circumstances (not least disillusionment with youth culture itself). What concerned the Home Office most were police reports that drugs of all kinds were being used more frequently in association with the new disco dance culture that emerged in the 1970s in both city and suburbs. The probation service in Bexley, a suburb of south-east London, reported that while drug-dealing still went on in pubs, 'local discotheques are becoming suspect as centres where drugs are being used, mainly by the older adolescents who are either seeking some increased perception of the music or need drugs to overcome difficulties in mixing with their peers.'[70]

It was precisely this form of recreational use, combined with electronic music, that made taking Ecstasy a mass pursuit in Britain from the late 1980s until the end of the century, creating a symbiotic link between dance music and drugs that embraced people of all social backgrounds and circumstances to an unprecedented degree in British youth culture. First synthesised in 1912 by a German pharmaceutical company, Ecstasy had enough stimulant in its chemical compound to provide the energy needed to dance all night ('a trembly effervescence that makes you feel like you've got champagne for blood', according to Simon Reynolds); but it also had psychotropic properties that enabled ravers to feel 'loved up', to be more tactile and empathetic with friends and strangers alike ('a penicillin for the psyche' according to Reynolds again).[71] Mocking psychedelia in 1968, Ray Davies had said, 'You still can't beat going to the pictures, a couple of pints and a fag. The Kinks all agree that Sunday dinner is the greatest realisation of heaven.'[72] The idea that Sunday dinner was the stairway to heaven seemed hopelessly out of date twenty years later.

Given that Casuals compared the adrenalin rush of street and stadium combat to the rush they got from drugs, it is not surprising that they tried Ecstasy. But in one of the most unusual transformations in the history of British youth culture, Casuals' discovery of 'E' led some to embrace members of rival gangs. Mark Moore recalled that in London 'You were getting a lot of the football firms down at Spectrum and The Trip. The bouncers were quite close to the street and they kept saying "it's going to kick off in here", 'cos of there being rival firms in the same club. But they were all on E, so they were just hugging each other, they couldn't be bothered to fight.'[73] An emblem of what some called 'the emotional hooligan' or 'love thug' was a T-shirt popular in the summer of 1990. Produced by the neo-Mod boutique brand Burro, its slogan read 'No Alla Violenza'.

Louise Gray noted that while the tabloid media conflated sex and drugs, Ecstasy actually fostered tactile empathy more than it did lust. As a consequence, although millions of young people became lovers by meeting at raves, the drug dissolved much of the sexual frustration and aggression that traditionally marred large gatherings of hormonal young people:

That was one of the reasons why you could have such an extraordinary mix of people – male gays, but also working class boys who hadn't had any contact with the trendy culture, and maybe in another life they might have gone queer-bashing or Paki-bashing. Suddenly they were thrown into this environment where everyone was kissy-kissy, but it didn't matter, they weren't threatened in any way.[74]

A popular song that signalled this partial cessation of hostilities was the Farm's 'All Together Now' (1990), written by former Casual Peter Hooton, about the football match that took place between British and German troops in no-man's-land during the 'truce' of Christmas 1914. A suitable metaphor for the 'kissy-kissy' peace between some British football tribes the song was also a fitting epitaph for this branch of Mod as it merged into the rapidly flowing currents of European dance culture collectively known as rave. Even Britpoppers whose work was relatively uninformed by electronic music got involved. Noel Gallagher recalled the difference that the drug made to his experience of the Hacienda: 'I think it was with Ecstasy really; I think that it was the new posh designer drug . . . it was very exciting when it first happened, going to the Hacienda and listening to this music that was fucking unspeakably rubbish, and then you had an E and it was like listening to fucking classical music.'[75]

The *Sun* newspaper (which had originally welcomed the cult, even offering a free Smiley T-shirt) changed tack when it realised drugs were involved. 'Reporting' from one nightclub, the *Sun* said,

The screaming teenager jerked like a demented doll as the LSD [*sic*] he swallowed an hour earlier took its terrible toll. The boy had become sucked into the hellish nightmare engulfing thousands of youngsters as the Acid House scourge sweeps Britain . . . Callous organisers and drug dealers simply looked on and LAUGHED . . . DJs encouraged the frenzied crowd with chants of 'Are you on? Let's go MENTAL, let's go FATAL.'[76]

And just a page away from the newspaper's daily topless woman was a report about 'OUTRAGEOUS sex romps taking place on the dancefloor'. The *Sun* warned readers that they might wake up in bed with an ugly stranger because their judgement would be impaired by the drug.

As DJs became the objects of desire and fantasy, like rock stars, Manchester author and DJ Dave Haslam remembers one moment of madness at the Hacienda: 'A girl came into the DJ box, lay down and took all her clothes off. She was naked, and started pulling at my trousers. I was wise enough to know it was E taking effect, rather than anything to do with me, but it was just one of those things, there was a lot of craziness in the air.'[77] The evidence suggests that for most women nightclubs actually became safer places in the 1990s, as alcohol-fuelled aggression gave way to a more empathetic environment. 'I would feel totally comfortable going to a rave solo', remembers one Hacienda regular. 'Unlike discos and many pubs [where] people look at you as being there to pick someone up . . . I wouldn't hesitate to go raving on my own. It'd be fine for a woman to go to a rave, pop anything they want to, skin up a huge joint, and no one bats an eyelid.'[78]

As well as predictable concern about drug use, rave attracted criticism from the Left for being escapist, as disco had done in the 1970s; the *New Statesman* dismissed House on the grounds that its 'pleasures come not from resistance but from surrender'.[79] Official concern on the other hand resulted in the Criminal Justice and Public Order Act of 1994, which gave the police authority to shut down any 'gathering on land in the open air of 100 or more persons (whether or not trespassers) at which amplified music is played during the night'. Lest ravers evaded capture by playing Beethoven's 'Ode to Joy', the Act defined the music in question as that which 'includes sounds wholly or predominantly characterised by the emission of a succession of repetitive beats' – in other words House or techno and its variants. At a trial of party organisers in Dundee the arresting officer, an Inspector Brown, described Acid House as 'just a din, a noise which goes on and on. No rhythms, no words.' When asked by the judge if the DJ 'had played country or Beatles music, would it have made a difference?', Brown replied, 'Probably.'[80] Police harassment became a more common experience for ravers than for any previous youth movement. At one raid, on 'Love Decade' near Leeds, ravers barricaded themselves in a warehouse for three hours until hundreds of police in riot gear broke in using a fork lift truck. They took 836 clubbers away to twenty-six police stations across Yorkshire in hired coaches, making it one of the biggest mass arrests in British history.

Paradoxically, the legal assault on dance culture worked in its favour. By being contained within the system of entertainment licences, rave was brought back from orbital fields to the city, where it could be watched on CCTV and where it once more became a predominantly urban experience. The epitome of that trend was the archly named Ministry of Sound, founded in 1991 by James Palumbo, the Eton-educated son of an Arts Council chairman and ardent developer of modernist architecture. Palumbo turned a disused warehouse at the Elephant & Castle in south London into a 'superclub' that twenty years later was the heart of a global franchise with annual sales of around £80 million through merchandising and from 600 events staged across every continent. In the span of British youth culture the Elephant & Castle was a fitting location for Britain's most famous nightclub because it was the neighbourhood where Teddy Boys were first noticed amid the rubble of the early 1950s; it was also where one of the UK's first shopping centres had opened in 1965 – a garish concrete complex which by the time ravers were queuing to hear Carl Cox had become a dilapidated eyesore.

This urban clubbing experience was celebrated in the film *Human Traffic* (1999), a *Quadrophenia* for its time that paid direct homage to the earlier film. Made by a 25-year-old Welshman, Justin Kerrigan, it was an unsentimental portrayal of a group of friends living in Cardiff who use raving to escape from their dead-end jobs in clothes stores and fast-food outlets. As the central character Jip dances around his bedsit – a *Quadrophenia* poster adorning one of the walls – getting ready for a night out, he shouts, 'Come on! The weekend has landed!' Later, Jip leads a crowded bar in an alternative rendition of the national anthem that concludes 'Who is the Queen?' – a moment that captured the post-punk indifference towards the monarchy among many British youths.

An unintended yet important by-product of the 1994 Criminal Justice Act was rising attendance at licensed outdoor British music festivals. Eager to attract the growing number of ravers, pop and rock promoters began routinely to provide dance tents where the best DJs would play; within a year of the Act being passed, Glastonbury sold its 65,000 tickets twice as fast as before.[81] More important still, leading to the rise of urban 'superclubs' like the Ministry of Sound, the Criminal Justice Act inadvertently stimulated the growth of Continental youth tourism, as entrepreneurs set up branches of their clubs in Mediterranean resorts.

BRITANNIA RULES THE RAVES!

The European aspect of British youth culture first expressed by the Mods of the 1960s became a prominent part of the rave scene in the 1990s. Not only were Continental clothing brands a component of clubbers' style; now, Europe itself became a space for youth to party to an extent that wasn't permitted in the UK. Unable to afford a Mediterranean holiday, early Mods had made do with 'a package tour of the soul', using the acquisition of a Lacoste polo shirt as a substitute for feeling Riviera sand between their toes. Their younger incarnations were able to enjoy a package tour of the body.

'In essence these Mod youths were trying to create new youth communities by the sea,' observed historian David Fowler about the Brighton scooter rallies of the 1960s.[82] The same could be said of their counterparts in the 1990s. As well as giving British youth more space in which to party, the package holiday disrupted the experience of time. The weekend, sanctified by Mods as time out from the routine of work and family life, turned into a week or two of abandon for many teenagers enjoying their first extended period away from the constraints of the parental home.

As Mediterranean clubbing became less a subculture with a suntan and more a common rite of passage, the spread of these cantons of hedonism was part of a burgeoning European tourist industry that was increasingly geared to young people. Between 1981 and 1997, the number of holidays abroad taken by British people rose from 13.13 million to 29.14 million, a sevenfold increase on the number taken at the start of the 1970s when foreign travel became affordable to a majority. The tourist industry was assisted by advertising campaigns that unashamedly promoted the sex on offer to the young, around a third of whom were travelling without their parents for the first time.[83] Britart patron Charles Saatchi's agency was responsible for the most infamous billboards, which included BEAVER ESPANA (a riff on the song 'Y Viva España', the 1974 chart hit that signalled the first wave of Euro tourism). But the one that received the most complaints (possibly because it objectified *men* in order to sell sex to *women*) was a picture of a muscular, headless, well-endowed man in tight white briefs with the caption GIRLS: FANCY A PACKAGE HOLIDAY?

The most popular destination was the Spanish island of Ibiza 80 kilometres off the coast of Valencia. Although referenced in a 1969 Pink Floyd song, Ibiza owed its development to British youth tourism in the rave era; by 2001 it was attracting over 600,000 young Britons every year. Clubs there exhibited modern design as bracing as any at home – like Ku, the world's biggest club (now called Privilege), with a swimming pool and capacity for 10,000 people. One awestruck visitor wrote: 'A night out in Ku . . . might have you believing you had blinked and been transported to the city centre of the first European space station. Under a high glass roof, it is a futurist vision of stages, podiums and steel walkways that weave up through monstrous tropical plant life.'[84]

Ibiza also became the home of 'ambient' electronic music, pioneered by former glam rocker Brian Eno under the influence of the minimalist American composer John Cage. (Eno's most influential album in this context was the appropriately named *Ambient 1/Music For Airports*, released on Virgin in 1978.) Sampling an incredible array of genres from soul to classical, by the mid-1990s ambient attracted a wider audience beyond its core following of teenagers mastering their come-downs with soothing music; now known as 'chill-out music', it became background to many dinner parties. 'Chill out' entered the British lexicon in the mid-1990s as a ubiquitous term for any form of relax-ation from everyday stress.

In 1998, Britain's vice-consul in Ibiza resigned in protest at the 'degenerate, out of control' behaviour of the young Britons he was diplomatically responsible for.[85] But his resignation didn't undermine the growing reputation of DJs like Pete Tong and Paul Oakenfold who by then were playing to huge audiences on Radio 1. As Sheryl Garratt observed, 'Remix culture, the notion that the DJs remaking the records could be as important as the original artists, was beginning to take hold. Until then British dance music had rarely been anything more than a pale imitation of American styles, but now it was finding a new confidence, a new irreverence, and a voice of its own.'[86] The result of that artistic confidence and credibility was that in 2002 Norman Jay became the first DJ to be honoured with the MBE, almost forty years after the Beatles became the first pop group to accept that honour from the Queen.

Surveying the 'Best of British' dance music in 2007, *Mixmag* presented a cover that silhouetted the Queen against a Union Jack but instead of her mouth being torn off – as Jamie Reid had done for the cover of 'God Save the Queen' exactly thirty years before – the monarch's head was obscured by the Smiley logo. BRITANNIA RULES THE RAVES! proclaimed *Mixmag*. The country's most popular dance magazine explained 'why it's all going off in jolly old Blighty': 'This time around the good stuff is homegrown – British clubs and artists are taking chances again. And instead of one dominant sound ruling clubland, there are scores of different scenes and sounds . . . One day, future generations will say, "This was their finest hour."'[87]

Churchillian rhetoric didn't impress the United States, which resisted British dance culture until the arrival of dubstep in the following century. This was because of the continuing dominance of hip hop and because drugs of all kinds were more often seen as a self-destructive last resort of poor, amoral losers rather than as an aid to excitement or relaxation; in Britain they were more or less tolerated as a resource for young people. That British youths consumed more drugs than their American counterparts was apparent in surveys. One conducted by *Mixmag* and the *Guardian* in 2012 showed that while similar numbers of American and British youth had used cannabis in the previous twelve months, more Britons used the drugs most associated with rave culture. Only 19.8 per cent of young Americans surveyed had used cocaine in the previous year, compared to 41.8 per cent of Britons, and just 26.5 per cent of the former had used Ecstasy compared to 53.7 per cent of the latter.[88]

This transatlantic difference was vividly demonstrated at a New Music Seminar held in New York in 1990 at which British and American music industry figureheads sat down to discuss transatlantic business. Tony Wilson chaired a seminar called 'WAKE UP AMERICA, YOU'RE DEAD'. After presenting a potted history of the previous three years that took in Acid House, Madchester and Ibiza, Wilson told his American counterparts: 'The music and the rhythms that you lot created have changed British and European pop music, it's changed Australian pop music, it's happening in Japan, it's happening all over the world. Do you find it strange that it isn't strong in America?'[89] He then forecast that British rock and dance acts would 'export back to America the black dance music they'd ignored, just as the Stones and Beatles [did] in the sixties'.[90] But what really annoyed Wilson's American colleagues was his revelation that the Happy Mondays were former drug dealers, a moment enhanced by the appearance of the actor and comedian Keith Allen (a friend of Damien Hirst and Blur's Alex James) who boasted of having thousands of Ecstasy tablets back in his hotel room. As Simon Reynolds noted in his account of the event, 'the joke fell on stony-faced ground, because "drug pusher" had a different connotation in an America beset with gang-related bloodshed'. In Britain the image of the Ecstasy dealer was that of 'a harmless minor villain'.[91] That British outlook was captured in the song 'Ebeneezer Goode' by Aberdeen group the Shamen, which reached No. 1 in 1992, attracting criticism for the refrain 'Eezer Goode, Eezer Goode', which cheekily celebrated a '*very* naughty' character and his wares (played in the promo by the Scottish comedian Jerry Sadowitz).

The American equivalent of Ibiza was the 'spring break' flight to

Mexico, but techno and House were as absent from the DJ's decks in Cancún as they were in Cincinnati, as was the attendant Ecstasy culture. Spring break was rooted in college life, in a country where tuition fees cost up to ten times more than in Britain and higher education was open to fewer people. That, together with the higher cost of foreign travel for most Americans, meant that the Hispanic party spots of the New World were populated by predominantly middle-class youth, whereas those of Spain were affordable to large numbers of working-class people.

No other British youth culture since the 1960s when Mod was at its height had drawn together so many people from different social backgrounds. Looking back on rave in 1998, Sheryl Garratt wrote:

Raves began to gather up all the disparate threads of youth culture and knit them back together. Black and white, male and female, rock and soul fans, crusties and Sloanes. There were no elitist door policies here. Anyone could go on an adventure to wonderland: all they needed was the price of a ticket, some access to transport, and a pill if they wanted . . . In 1987, Mrs Thatcher had declared that 'there is no such thing as society' and that we should all rely on ourselves. In fields and warehouses and aircraft hangars around Britain, for a while it felt as if we were building an alternative society of our own.[92]

It's easy to mock the communality of rave culture as an artificial one that barely survived the chill-out zones of the nightclub or beach bar, still less the shaky journey home by car or plane. There is no statistical evidence to prove how many socially transgressive relationships lasted beyond the fading memories of damaged synapses. However, the real problem with Garratt's conclusion is not that it is too utopian but that it isn't imaginative enough, because the alternative society that she and her friends built left the warehouses and entered the high street, albeit in a diluted form.

In the short term, Wilson's wake-up call to America would return to haunt him, as violent (and mostly white) drug gangs forced the premature closure of his beloved Hacienda. Factory Communications crashed on 24 November 1992, owing more than £2 million. When Wilson died from cancer aged 57 in 2007, the Union Jack on Manchester Town Hall was lowered to half-mast as a mark of respect, the first time this had been done to honour anyone from his milieu. Wilson's coffin was given the Factory catalogue number FAC 501 and Peter Saville designed his black granite headstone.

The popular modernism that Wilson had graphically promoted didn't end with his headstone but lived on in the design of countless bars and nightclubs throughout Britain in the late twentieth century. As Saville explained to one interviewer, the ubiquity of modern design began with youth culture:

The bedroom walls of all young people are covered with pictures of the pop stars and groups they love. Then they hit twenty and the ephemera of this thing they loved is put away under the bed . . . By bringing cultural references other than a picture of the artist to bear, what Malcolm [Garrett] and I did with covers, and Neville [Brody] also with *The Face*, was create a visual influence which the recipient could take with them *into their adult life*.[93]

URBAN MODERNISTS

The 'hearts and minds' revolution in British taste, which had begun in the 1960s, was accompanied by a return to the city. The suburbanisation of Britain, which took place between the 1870s and the 1970s, was reversed in the last quarter of the twentieth century, as millions of extant and aspirant middle-class people, most of them in their twenties and thirties, began to move back to the city. They were not just trying to shorten their journey time into work: refugees from the suburbs went in search of an urban, cosmopolitan lifestyle, which had been celebrated in and mediated through British youth culture since the 1960s.

So-called gentrification of the inner cities was first noticed in the mid-1960s. Areas like Islington in London had been left to decay as people and industry moved out in search of gardens and garages. They offered pioneering, often bohemian, newcomers cheap property and a more multicultural milieu, as immigrants, most from former British colonies, settled in cities alongside the white working-class population that either couldn't afford or didn't want to leave their communities. Forming the seedbed in which the Two Tone movement had germinated, these variegated urban communities laid the foundations for the revival of British urban life and a commensurate celebration of modernity in popular culture.

During the 1970s, when teenage attitudes to suburban life had framed so many lyrics of British popular music, suburban drift continued apace, as the city for many older people symbolised the economic stagnation and social conflicts of the time. The decade therefore witnessed the severe depopulation of Britain's cities: between 1971 and 1981, London lost three-quarters of a million people and the six next-largest cities together lost in excess of half a million. However, in the twenty years that followed there was a clear trend towards reurbanisation, with Britain's major cities recovering from the population losses of the 1970s.[94] Eight of Britain's major cities recorded a consistent increase in repopulation in the 1980s and 1990s; London grew by 6.9 per cent, Glasgow by 3.7 per cent, Leeds by 2.8 per cent, Manchester by 4.2 per cent and Sheffield by 3.7 per cent. The geographer Michael Pacione concluded that 'Where repopulation of the city centres occurred, a large proportion of the new residents were socially mobile young adults seeking proximity to work and leisure facilities and the "stylishness" of city centre living.'[95]

The specific appeal of the city to the aspirant young is again borne out by statistical evidence, which shows that between 1993 and 2003 there was a 10 per cent rise in the population of London's under-45 age group, while during the same time period the proportion of the population of the city aged 45 and over fell by 1.6 per cent.[96] By the end of the 1990s, 62 per cent of the city centre populations of both Manchester and Liverpool comprised people in the 18–34 age group. In Manchester 42 per cent of the working-age population were defined as 'living young, professional lifestyles', and for both cities an astonishing 75 per cent of the overall adult population were recorded as being single and unmarried.[97]

Lifestyle magazines promoted commercial modernism to this urban audience. For example, *Wallpaper* magazine (subtitled 'the stuff that surrounds you') followed a template set in the 1960s with features on what it called 'international design interiors and lifestyle', including everything from furniture to fashion and travel, which won it a regular readership of 120,000. The 1996 launch cover made clear the identity of its target audience with the headline 'URBAN MODERNISTS' over a shot of an attractive young couple, posed like David Hockney's *Mr and Mrs Clark and Percy* (1970–71), with the female partner standing confidently over a seated male, against a minimalist interior. Of course reality on the streets was often different to that displayed in lifestyle magazines, just as the poverty, boredom and loneliness that existed in rural Britain clashed with the cosy images of settled tradition often peddled by magazines like *Country Life*. Despite significantly reduced crime rates in the late 1990s, possession of an Alessi kettle remained no protection against burglary or street crime, and tension between old and new urban populations was sometimes acute.

However, the more important caveat to the story of reurbanisation is that many young people wanted to live in the city but could not afford to because of the rise in house prices during the urban property booms of the 1980s and 90s, which were triggered partly by the rising demand for city life by their richer peers.[98] Most of those who could not afford the move still used the city for after-work leisure – a factor in the huge increase in the number of first wine bars and later gastro pubs. Serving wine as well as beer with restaurant-grade food, often playing pop music (with electronic varieties in the ascendant) and welcoming women as much as men, these places were conduits of popular modernism, not least because the style employed by Saville and Kelly at the Hacienda was reproduced in so many of them.

The good life to be found in the city was defined everywhere in song, film and advertising as fast, sexy and cosmopolitan. Yet the real and the longed-for move into the city was not just a libertarian escape from the sexual and social stultification long associated with suburbs; it also embraced an aspirational form of working-class culture based less on poverty, crime and vulgarity, and more on style, hedonism and wit. The roots of that image lay in the legends of Swinging London and in the broader reimagining of the post-industrial city in later years, of which the Hacienda was a prime example (after closure, the club was turned into luxury flats, developers trading on the building's provenance).

All this was in marked contrast to the pattern of American life in the last quarter of the twentieth century where suburbs remained the locus of aspiration and success. Of course gentrification also took place in US cities but not to the same extent as in Britain, with consequences for youth culture and attendant lifestyles, as Camden resident Robert Elms attested:

This [Mod] is an urban story, it's an inner city story. Now inner city America is black in almost all of their cities . . . Most of white America gave up the cities to black people and Hispanic people a long time ago, so that's where you'll see similarities to British youth culture, you'll see dance crazes, see new clothes coming . . . Black America does that, white working-class England does it . . . Cities provide streets for parading on. Football grounds were places for people to parade in and you travel to another city and you showed off, it's all part of that mentality.[99]

'They don't move on very quickly, it's an old-fashioned place compared to Britain', said Mike Pickering when asked to explain the difference between the two countries, adding, 'I think we're proud of ourselves as a youth culture, but we're not that proud of our country. They're proud of their country but it's all that jingoistic bollocks.'[100]

'You know, Tony, you'll never make money unless you focus', Richard Branson once told the Hacienda's founder.[101] Someone who didn't need that advice was Ingvar Kamprad, and if one enterprise signified the appeal of popular modernism to people of all social backgrounds in the late twentieth century, it was IKEA. Swedish modernism in household design had been popular with the British middle classes since the 1950s, but after IKEA launched in the UK in 1987 it became the favoured style of millions: not just young professionals moving back into the city but millions more in suburbs and rural areas. Its 1996 TV campaign 'Chuck out your chintz' openly attacked conservative British style, and by the end of the century IKEA had a million customers a day, its British sales making up more of the total (12 per cent) of the company's turnover than any country except Germany (20 per cent). In the 1980s, Terence Conran had appeared on the Noel Edmonds show with a Lambretta scooter to illustrate the link between Britain's first youth culture and the broader aesthetic movement to which he belonged; later he sold the Habitat chain to IKEA, reluctantly admitting that the Swedish store's more affordable flatpack modernist revolution had superseded the one he had begun.

To what extent these revolutionary changes to British life were the direct legacy of the nation's first youth culture will always be guesswork. But Modernism certainly had an influence beyond teenage fashion and far beyond the expectations of the young men and women who had once gathered at Ronnie Scott's in Soho to design a new way of being British. Few of those directly involved in Mod culture since the 1960s have described its legacy better than Terry Rawlings:

Nowadays Mod is an everyday term, as solidly a part of our society as Coleman's mustard, bangers and mash and cricket on the green. Its elements are woven into the nation's very fabric and its imagery is everywhere you look – scooters and scooter-riding Mods are used to advertise and push everything from Lucozade to tampons. Mods are always the stock, fail-safe fashion spread in just about every lifestyle magazine available, and the humble target design is a staple of a thousand logos and corporate IDs from popular TV shows such as *Shooting Stars* to commercial operations like Parcel Force.[102]

Just like the original Mods who had grown up, created a home of their own, got married and had children, the Mod movement had acquired a family of interrelated subcultures, most of which had themselves grown up and become part of mainstream popular culture by the beginning of the new millennium. What future could there be for a youth culture that had once proclaimed itself to be the future, but which now contained so much of the recent past?

Conclusion

A Heritage of Modernism

The archetypal Mod was male, sixteen years old, rode a scooter, swallowed pep pills by the hundred, was obsessed by cool and dug it. He was also one hundred per cent hung up on himself, on his clothes, hair and image; he thought of women as a completely inferior race. In every way, he was a miserable narcissistic little runt.

Nick Cohn, 'Yellow Socks Are Out', 1989[1]

I'm not being nationalistic but its great when you can feel proud about English pop music again . . . Anyway, Mod will always be around in some shape or form because it's so classic, it's so ingrained in our culture and history. It'll always be there whether it's in high fashion or just in street fashion . . . I think we won. Mods rule!

Paul Weller, 1995[2]

FAMILY OF STYLE

'A Heritage of Modernism.' Those were the words that greeted shoppers in 2012 at Ben Sherman's thirty-two stores worldwide, from flagship shops in London's Carnaby Street and Savile Row to Osaka, Berlin, New York, Moscow, Johannesburg and Melbourne. It was a strange epithet for an Anglo-American clothing brand that became globally renowned through association with a teenage movement that fetishised the future.

'A heritage of modernism' may have seemed like an epitaph for British youth culture, but it was actually a sign of vitality. It evinced a dual sense of tradition and progress at a time when youth culture was accused on the one hand of fragmenting into an amorphous 'supermarket of style', while on the other hand being condemned for fostering a primitive, tribal gang culture.[3]

As this book has tried to show, Mod was a uniquely British hybrid of American, European and Afro-Caribbean styles in music, fashion and design, forming the DNA of British youth culture from the late 1950s to the late 1990s. Started in London by a highly elitist and self-regarding group of aspirant individuals, Mod was transformed via the mass media into a national youth movement that appealed to people from all social backgrounds and shaped the physical environment of many more who never belonged to it.

Steeped since its creation in the progressive art and design movements of the twentieth century, for a time Mod became a commercial and popular form of modernism. Closely linked to the British cultural renaissance of the 1960s, it helped to effect a democratisation of taste that was previously ascribed only to the most educated in society. Contemporary style was sold through a concept of lifestyle in which young consumers could construct an identity for themselves based around the twin ideas of social mobility and cosmopolitanism. As well as clothing, records and gadgets, young consumers were offered domestic habitats that expressed those same ideas through interior design and furnishing which would influence them well into middle age and beyond.

While remaining forever associated with the optimism of the 1960s, Mod parented several other youth cultures that were raised in more pessimistic times. Some of those trends and tribes exposed the shallows of Mod's claim to represent modernity – from the violent, racist skinheads of the 1970s to the thieving, brand-obsessed Casuals of the 1980s, not to mention the accompanying misogyny that ran through the entire history of the movement. However, the potent, idealised modernity of Britain's first youth culture did create an extended family of style that connected millions of people across time and space in a shared pursuit of freedom. As well as influencing the look and sound of post-millennium groups like Franz Ferdinand and the Last Shadow Puppets it was also embraced by some rappers, like Tinie Tempah, who showed the influence of so-called 'hipster' Mod style in the sharper, more formal appearance with which they challenged the crudity of 'bling' usually associated with hip hop.

One of many attempts to define Mod's enduring appeal comes from author and broadcaster Robert Elms:

It is the core ethic and the core aesthetic of not just a youth culture . . . It's a cultural statement that goes way beyond youth culture: you don't have to be young to be a Mod. So far as I'm concerned Sir Paul McCartney is still a Mod, you know Paul Weller is still a Mod. There are guys I know who are in their seventies: Jay Simon, who used to run the Ivy clothes shop in Richmond, was a Mod in 1958 and is still a Mod to this day. Because it's a set of values and aspirations, it's about always wanting to be clean, always wanting to look good, always wanting to know what's happening. So you don't grow out of it. It's a world view, that's what it is, because it does say everything that I am – I'm urban, I like city life, I like modern life, I embrace the now . . . I like cosmopolitanism I like things from different places . . . I think if you've ever been a Mod you don't un-become one.[4]

If Mod was a family of styles, it was also a style that was transmitted through the family. Like most youth cultures, Mod celebrated sex and drugs but relationships between parents and children rarely broke down because of different tastes, lifestyles or political views. Generational identity was more of a healthy dissonance within families than a toxic rupture, a fact illustrated by the extent to which even the wildest musicans and designers of the Sixties valued family life and referenced the music and fashion of the past in their work. Moreover, a variety of latter-day Mods (Elms among them) found their wardrobe and music plundered by their children, usually without much encouragement, so that Fred Perry tops could be found adorning the fittest young chests at the hippest inner city bars, as well as being stretched over middle-aged beer bellies at suburban carveries.

In the early twenty-first century, even rave – which in the 1980s and 90s had prided itself on being a thoroughly modern subculture pursued solely by young people – acquired its own heritage of taste and lifestyle that spanned generations. Studies in Britain and elsewhere found that sizeable networks of middle-aged professionals (aged between 40 and 55) were attending electronic dance music parties and clubs while maintaining their careers and family life. They concluded that this did not usually reflect a refusal to accept the physical process of ageing or to grow up emotionally; rather, what these men and women expressed was a desire to have 'sustainable fun' within an adult life that balanced work, family, health and leisure.

Other middle-aged people who had left raving behind nevertheless claimed that their experience of it had improved family life and become 'a platform for the development of understanding between parents and their children'. Talking about her 21-year-old son, one of these 'party parents as role models', a women in her mid-40s, explained to an interviewer: 'I think we had quite a big influence on his interest in dance music, and his choice of dance music, and what he's now into. He's got into DJing and doing his own parties . . . And I think it would be true to say that that really came from us, from what we were interested in doing, the music and the clubs that we went to.'[5] Corresponding interviews with youngsters suggested that what they inherited from parents was not just a music collection but 'a cultural identity' – a transfer of taste in which an elder's outlook was regarded like a 'family heirloom', as something to be treasured.[6]

These trends were captured in 2011 by an advert for the services directory Yellow Pages. A previous campaign from 1983 had featured a tweedy old man searching in vain for a book called *Flyfishing* by J. R. Hartley by trudging around second-hand bookshops, until his daughter helps him find a copy through Yellow Pages and he is revealed as the author. The 2011 version instead featured a middle-aged DJ, dressed in a parka, visiting record stores in search of a trance record from 1992. Returning home disappointed, his teenage daughter hands him her phone and thanks to its Internet app for Yellow Pages, dad finds the record before revealing his identity as the tune's creator, Dave V. Lately. 'What we do hasn't changed. Just the way we do it,' announces the voiceover.

That could be said of all youth cultures, but perhaps none more so than Britain's first. Thanks to both the public freedom it signified and the domestic ways in which it was transmitted, Mod remained a defining symbol of the more democratic and secular post-imperial Britain that emerged in the 1960s. 'The mod look is here to stay', wrote Jonathan Aitken in his contemporary survey of the period, 'it has given the wearers, as well as the creators, a certain new kind of patriotism, an international pride in the clothes and in the spirit that the clothes have helped to create.'[7] In terms of sexual morality the 1960s may have marked the end of Victorian Britain, but the cultural renaissance of the period still expressed a rather Victorian idea of British superiority and progress – this time based on pop culture rather than industry, military might or religious certainty.

While Mod restored some national pride after the end of empire, it could not halt the spread of American popular culture; nor, conversely, could it import American social mobility. Rising living standards gave millions of Britons a middle-class income, but unlike most Americans the British continued to define themselves according to the culture into which they were born rather than what they came to earn, own or know. Between 1964 and 2007, the number of people defining themselves as middle class rose from 30 to just 37 per cent, compared to 57 per cent seeing themselves as working class – this despite the fact that the number of people who still endured working-class pay and conditions in 2007 was estimated to be 31 per cent: a large gap between perception and reality.[8] Experts concluded that one reason for this downwardly mobile perception was that being middle class was considered 'boring' compared to 'cooler working-class credibility'.[9]

Ideas of 'cool' had emerged from Afro-American jazz before fanning outward into a global air-stream of style and attitude, but in Britain, more than anywhere, 'cool' became associated with working-class youth. Like the black music and style of America and the Caribbean, a certain idea of British working-class culture no longer belonged exclusively to the working classes.[10] The critic Owen Jones argued that Britain was poisoned by a 'demonisation of the working class'. Snobbery was certainly still rife in Britain as the ubiquitous use of the term 'chav' showed; but the location of cool among the 'lower orders' showed that a romanticisation of working-class culture remained a feature of post-industrial Britain – or at least the more hedonistic, creative aspects of that culture to be found in youth movements. Mod offered working-class followers 'an upward mobility that cherishes where kids come from', while for wealthier followers it provided a smart rebellion that coveted material aspects of middle-class lifestyle without ever troubling the institutional foundations on which that lifestyle was built.[11] In a paradoxical sense, therefore, Mods were complicit in the social stasis they abhorred.

For all those who ascribed to this form of 'cool' – and the many who did not – the harsh reality of many working-class lives was brought home following the shooting of a young man in the impoverished north London neighbourhood of Tottenham on 4 August 2011.

A FRAME OF MIND

The Mod-inflected British rock group Kaiser Chiefs predicted an urban riot in a song of that name in 2004. There was little left of patriotic 90s optimism about British youth culture by the time the Kaiser Chiefs' prediction came true in August 2011. In three days and nights of mayhem that left five people murdered, thousands of young people looted shops, set alight buildings and attacked the police. Newspapers and magazines as different as the *Daily Star* and *The Economist* used the headline 'Anarchy in the UK' to sum up the events, illustrating that punk was still associated with destruction. But with rampant consumerism at the heart of so much looting, perhaps the Mod idea of spending your way out of social class had reached a terrible, logical conclusion.

There were predictable calls for more discipline in homes, schools and on the streets. Water cannon politics was joined by welfare politics, with equally predictable claims that poverty and racist policing were to blame. There was even an attempt to wag a white finger at black youth culture. The historian David Starkey claimed that young 'whites have become black', telling BBC viewers that 'a particular sort of violent, destructive, nihilistic gangster culture has become the fashion and black and white boys operate in this language together.'[12]

As people of all colours and classes scuttled into courthouses around the country, with gang leaders joined by university graduates, few commentators properly addressed the issue of consumerism. 'SUPERMARKET SWEEP!' yelled one laughing teenager as he left a store with a shopping trolley full of stolen goods – referencing the TV game show, first launched in America in 1965, that had contestants running around a fake studio supermarket loading up their trolleys in the time that they 'won' by answering general knowledge questions. Wasn't this 'shopping with violence' the product of an avaricious, celebrity-led youth culture in thrall to consumption for its own sake, in which many young people seemed unable to validate themselves except through acquisition of the latest branded goods? It sounded eerily like Jeff Dexter's description of Mod as 'the original wannabe culture'. So was Britain's first youth culture somehow to blame?

Mods' narcissistic obsession with style had certainly helped to create the consumer society, providing a model of how the aspirations of young Britons could be commercially exploited; hence the *NME* editor's verdict that 'Modernism is just about shopping'. But there was a difference. The hyper-consumerism that drove the riots was shopping stripped of values: acquisition was not a marker of enduring taste but a corrupt and transient badge of success. Mods on the other hand used style to accrue cultural capital and assert a putative social status in a contemptuous world. And possessing a degree of education as well as a refusal to defer to their 'betters', many were well aware of the modernist design incorporated by the products they displayed on their bodies and in their homes.

In 1921, T. S. Eliot wrote parts of the *The Waste Land* in the same shelter on Margate seafront that Mods gathered in during the brawls of 1964. The connection between a classic of literary modernism and the youth culture that mugged the movement's name may seem incidental. Certainly, few teenagers had Eliot in mind while strutting down Carnaby Street and fewer still when they fought rockers on the beaches of Margate. Yet the original Mods and some of their successors evidently saw their lives as an engagement with aspects of American and European modernism that were connected to the artistic giants celebrated in more intellectual circles. As the critic Stephen Hale put it, 'this youthful modernist gang purloined the word from its ivory tower and brought it down to the streets'.[13]

The history of Mod culture shows that many of its followers were conscious of redesigning the British way of life in a way that Walter Gropius at least may have understood. In his history of fashion, Christopher Breward concluded that more than any other youth movement, Mod had shaped British life:

[Mod's] sharp Italianate mohair suits, stiffly lacquered short hair, and unapologetic consumerism (of clothes, scooters, pills and dance music) afforded a superior social weaponry that was far more subtle in its assault on mainstream complacency than the flick-knives, brothel creepers and bike chains of the reactionary Ted. The challenge presented by the Mod was not embodied in physical violence or the status of an outsider, but in his subversive potential as a threat to the older assurances of class and gender-based hierarchies and traditions.

It was the figure of the Mod who formed the focus for the expanding boutique culture of Carnaby Street in the late 1960s. He set a precedent for the tide of countercultural retail outlets which engulfed first the King's Road and later Covent Garden and Camden Town in the 1970s and 1980s; he lent his distinctive look to a spate of successful pop groups; and he put London on the map as an acknowledged global centre for subversive street-level creativity. The rather naïve optimism which had accompanied this assault on conservative mores fuelled a global genealogy of interconnected musical tastes [and] visual imagery.[14]

With a few exceptions, Mods in their many guises did pursue a less nihilistic, more progressive view of class in Britain, one that sought to challenge and subvert stereotypes rather than surrendering to them. Put simply, Mod was not shopping with violence but shopping with taste, as the Pimlico teenager had remarked in 1964: 'Being mod is a frame of mind. You can't just buy it off some geezer in a shop.' Mod as a 'frame of mind' was essential to its cross-generational appeal – an attitude subjective and flexible enough to allow adaptation while maintaining aesthetic standards.

HUMANIST LINES OF ENQUIRY

Aesthetic standards were questioned with increasing frequency in the last quarter of the twentieth century. 'Style is dead' – that was the conclusion of 'Postmodernism: Style and Subversion', an exhibition at London's Victoria & Albert Museum in 2011, which traced the development of art and design from 1970 to 1990. The curators argued that thanks to affluence and technology the swell of post-war opportunity became a tsunami of choice that swept away the belief that any culture was worthy enough to define civilisation at any given time. How fitting that 160 years after Britain proclaimed itself to be the world's most modern country at the Great Exhibition of 1851, curators at the museum of decorative arts founded as a result of that same exhibition should declare that 'we are all postmodern now'.[15] But was it true?

Only if you think that choice began in the same year as the Beatles split up. There never was a rule book of modernism nor a rigid aesthetic canon that stemmed from it, but rather several complementary streams of thought and practice. In youth culture, the practice of 'bricolage' in fashion and of 'mashing' in music were almost as prevalent in Carnaby Street and Abbey Road in 1965 as they were when YouTube launched in 2005. Furthermore, if modernism was dead, then why did the styles associated with it visibly persist in twenty-first-century Britain, and why should they continue to be replayed and redisplayed in British youth culture?

Perhaps it was because practitioners still believed in them. The graphic designer Neville Brody, who did so much to purvey modern style at *The Face* when postmodernism became fashionable in the 1980s, commented: 'For me, Post Modernism felt like a kind of facade built to cover over the cracks of a divided world, a surface of plucked effects and stylistic devices emptied of meaning, an extrusion of hollow traces and flat outlines forcing 2D into apparent depth. I was never a Post Modernist, rather a Modernist exploring humanist lines of enquiry in the collapsing world behind a wall of decoration.'[16]

Perhaps it was also because millions of people still desired smart clothes, stylish interiors and comfortable furniture, arranged within a narrative of progress, and not just picked at random in a supermarket of style detached from function and meaning. In the words of Ted Polhemus, such a 'Supermarket of Style is not . . . a subculture which provides a sense of belonging in return for a lifelong stylistic and ideological commitment.'[17] That was precisely what Mod continued to offer its followers, not least through the internet, which helped to develop a more global and multi-generational Mod community in the twenty-first century.

The Internet's digital attic made the once painstaking search for the heritage of Modernism as easy as ordering a pizza. Young newcomers accessed websites to learn Mod's aesthetic codes, to purchase appropriate merchandise and to link up with each other at the numerous dance clubs, scooter rallies and conventions that took place regularly. Christine Feldman's pioneering fieldwork investigated how these twenty-first-century Mods viewed their world. A typical example was 19-year-old Anthony Doggett from Manchester, born in 1987:

When I was younger, I was into, like, Indie bands – the Strokes and, um, the Libertines . . . and then I liked the Jam and then it just kind of led on from there. I started to go to Mod dos and then got more into music that's to do with the Mod scene . . . From speaking to the original ones, you can see that it's a lot different and it still seems quite fresh and quite lively, so I wouldn't say it's a 'retro-thing', 'cause that makes it sound really dated. I think you have to be a certain type of person to appreciate it, as well. I suppose it is like looking back, but it's looking forward as well.[18]

To young followers like Anthony, the heritage of modernism was not such a paradoxical concept. And far from being a form of cultural necrophilia in a shadowy online world of retro-mania, it was actually experienced as a living, breathing, publicly shared tradition. That was true of any noteworthy youth culture, as Nick Hornby observed:

Kids are listening to Hendrix and Pink Floyd . . . which is partly because it is culture: there is a library of rock 'n' roll. So it's not nostalgia that draws people back to Bob Dylan in the same way that it's not nostalgia that draws young people to Camus or Salinger. These are the greats and this is what you've got to listen to if you're going to be seriously interested in this sort of thing.[19]

But what if 'looking forward', in Anthony's words, was not such an inviting prospect?

WE ARE ALL MODERNISTS NOW

For all its success Mod remained to some extent a culture of consolation. Its idealised vision of modernity had always contained a melancholic acceptance of present realities. That was visible in the cheap suits that were bought off the peg then tailored to look like they had come from Savile Row; it could be detected in the scooters, lovingly polished and ridden by men and women for whom *Roman Holiday* remained just a film. And of course that melancholy was audible in the exquisite anguish of Miles Davis's trumpet on *Kind of Blue* or in the Who's 'Substitute' – that song about the disguises that white working-class Mods used to mask their own anguish.

Yet Mod could still generate anger as well as melancholy, periodically reminding people of its original discontent with social stasis. When the son of a stockbroker courted the British electorate in 2010 a year before the urban riots, he tried to win the votes of what he called 'the Jam generation'. David Cameron told the press how much he had loved the song 'Eton Rifles' when he was a teenager at Britain's top private school: '"Eton Rifles" – inevitably I was one – in the Corps – it meant a lot, some of those early Jam albums we used to listen to', adding: 'I don't see why the Left should be the only ones allowed to listen to protest songs.'[20] The irony under which Cameron's love of the Jam groaned was perhaps no worse than the irony of Pete Townshend not dying before he got old. But the future prime minister touched a nerve and moved Weller to reply, 'It's about class war . . . if you can't take the time or have the intellect to see what the song's about, you haven't got much chance of running the country have you?'[21]

Two years later as prime minister, Cameron joined the Queen at the opening ceremony of the London 2012 Olympics in a celebration of Britain that placed youth culture – including the music of his beloved Jam – at the very heart of national life. The 2012 Olympics were widely regarded as a cultural success and not just an athletic one. With the main site close to where some of the worst rioting had occurred in north and east London just a year earlier, the event took on a redemptive quality as young Britons showed what they could achieve through self-discipline and team spirit rather than dissipation and gang culture (although it should be remembered that the Olympics are as much a mixture of state investment and corporate branding as any youth club or shopping centre, deemed to be the paradigmatic locations of teenage life during the riots).

Perhaps the most notable aspect of the London Olympics and Paralympics as a spectacle of youth was not the achievement seen on medal podiums but that conveyed in the opening and closing cere- monies. For in those four extraordinary spectacles, more than at any other post-war state ceremony in the UK, British youth culture was presented to the world as an essence of national life that was a source of quirky patriotism to the British, and one that was globally recog- nised and valued.

As well as dance routines accompanied by the music of the Jam, David Bowie, the Sex Pistols and the Prodigy, there were live perfor- mances by Paul McCartney, the Arctic Monkeys, Dizzee Rascal and Coldplay. And it was the surviving members of the Who that played out the closing ceremony on 12 August, performing 'My Generation', while another generation represented by the Kaiser Chiefs played a cover of 'Pinball Wizard' (and not 'I Predict a Riot'). From Soho down to Brighton and out into the world, crossing time and space, Mod appeared still to be the DNA of British youth culture. Perhaps Paul Weller's 1995 declaration 'I think we won. Mods rule!' was not as bombastically vain as it had seemed at the height of Britpop.

In that respect, the 32-year-old cyclist Bradley Wiggins provided an almost poetic link between the athletic and cultural success on display in 2012. The only man to have won the Tour de France and Olympic Gold in the same year, Wiggins was a self-confessed Mod, speaking fluent French, owning a collection of 1960s scooters and guitars, and sporting a haircut to match. He was also a symbolic link to the early Modernists who had worn French and Italian cycle jerseys in homage to their Continental cycling heroes.

It was not surprising that soon after Wiggins became a national hero he endorsed Fred Perry, the sports clothing brand associated with Mod longer than any other. But more important than his commercial endorsement was the way that *The Times* celebrated Wiggins' victory. The front cover of the newspaper showed a photograph of the cyclist, head down in pursuit of Gold, with a red, white and blue Mod roundel that he had stuck on his helmet. The headline next to it – MOD RULE – published by a newspaper associated with the British Establishment since the eighteenth century, was a victory of sorts for the millions of young people who at one time or another had adopted this very British style in order partly to affront that Establishment and create their own alternative elite.

On the long journey from cult to culture – via commercial exploitation, moral panic, political incorporation and celebrity excess – Britain's first youth culture failed to disguise the errors of twentieth-century modernism, like the Brutalist civic architecture and the soulless shopping malls that accompanied modernism's development. While swinging to the beat of progress, Mods also failed to disguise the errors bred in their own subcultural bones, like the cloying nostalgia, fatuous nationalism and boorish misogyny that were present in some of the youth movements that claimed Mod as an inspiration.

But from the boutiques of Brighton to the aisles of IKEA, in countless homes and public spaces, modernism strutted its stuff. Any walk around a British village, town or city in the early twenty-first century could demonstrate the enduring popularity of Mod style as it decorated the male and female bodies of different classes, races, and ages. It would be vain to think that all those people ascribed to the manifestos and meanings that Mod transmitted over the decades. But as a result of this peculiar, ubiquitous youth culture, it is true to say that more British people came to see themselves as modern than ever before; and by doing so they helped to change the way that Britain was seen all around the world. Perhaps, in that sense, we are all modernists now.

Notes

Author's Note

1. The broader term 'modernity' has two common usages: first, it describes the journey towards industrialisation, urban living and (usually) some form of democracy, which has dominated Western life for the last 300 years and which became a global force in the twentieth century. But 'modernity' can also be defined as a kind of sensibility, an affinity for that way of life, which has been expressed both by champions of the city like the poet Charles Baudelaire and by critics like the sociologist Max Weber, who warned against the constraints of its 'iron cage'. For an excellent discussion of these terms and their application to recent British history, see Harry Cocks, 'Modernity and Modernism', in Francesca Carnevali and Julie Marie-Strange, *Twentieth-Century Britain: Economic, Cultural and Social Change* (2nd ed., Longman, 2007), p. 28.

Introduction: The Simple Things You See Are All Complicated

1. Paul McCartney, interviewed in *All My Loving: A Film of Pop* Music (dir., Tony Palmer), 23 May 1968; reproduced in Tony Palmer, *All You Need Is Love: The Story of Popular Music*, ed. by Paul Medlicott (Futura, 1977), p. 258.
2. David Fowler, *Youth Culture in Modern Britain, c.1920–1970* (Palgrave, 2008), p. 128.
3. Jon Savage, *Teenage: The Creation of Youth 1875–1945* (Chatto & Windus, 2007), p. 465.
4. Andy Bennett, *Cultures of Popular Music* (Open University Press, 2001), p. 21.
5. 'The Ace Face's Forgotten Story', Steve Turner interview with Pete Meaden, *NME*, 17 November 1979; reprinted in Paolo Hewitt (ed.), *The Sharper Word: A Mod Anthology* (2nd ed., Helter Skelter, 2002), p. 169.
6. Thom Gunn, 'Elvis Presley', in Gunn, *The Sense of Movement* (Faber, 1957).
7. Mary Quant, *Quant by Quant* (Pan, 1967), pp. 80–1.

8. Dick Hebdige, *Subculture: The Meaning of Style* (1979; reprint, Routledge, 1991), p. 52.

9. Patrick Uden, cited in Hewitt (ed.), *The Sharper Word*; Steve Sparks, cited in Jonathon Green, *Days in the Life: Voices from the English Underground, 1961–1971* (Minerva, 1989), pp. 35–6. Sparks recounted that originally 'there were like 120 mods, period'.

10. *NME*, 7 February 1965.

11. Christopher Breward, 'The Dandy Laid Bare', in Stella Bruzzi and Pamela Church-Gibson, *Fashion Cultures: Theories, Explorations and Analysis* (Routledge, 2000), p. 229. See also Alice Cicolini, *The New English Dandy* (Thames & Hudson, 2005), for an excellent survey of dandyism in modern British fashion.

12. Martin Daunton and Bernhard Rieger, Introduction to Daunton and Rieger (eds), *Meanings of Modernity: Britain from the Late Victorian Era to World War II* (Berg, 2001), pp. 14–15. See also Harry Cocks, 'Modernity and Modernism', in Francesca Carnevali and Julie-Marie Strange, *Twentieth Century Britain: Economic, Cultural and Social Change* (2nd ed., Longman, 2007).

13. Ian Christie, 'Mass-Market Modernism', in Christopher Wilk (ed.), *Modernism: Designing a New World, 1914–1939* (V&A Publishing, 2006), p. 391.

14. Charles Harrison, *Modernism* (Tate, 1997), pp. 6–16.

15. K. & K. Baynes, 'Behind the Scene', *Design*, August 1966.

16. Nigel Whiteley, *Pop Design: From Modernism to Mod*, (Design Council, 1987), p. 125. For more on the impact of Pop Art in relation to British culture as a whole, see Anne Massey, *The Independent Group: Modernism and Mass Culture in Britain, 1945–59* (Manchester University Press, 1995).

17. Michael Bracewell, *Pop Life in Albion from Wilde to Goldie* (HarperCollins, 2007), p. 114.

18. Terence Conran, *Q&A: A Sort of Autobiography* (Harper Collins, 2001), pp. 36, 74.

19. David Hicks, *On Living – with Taste* (Macmillan, 1968), pp. 10–11.

20. Richard Barnes, cited in Terry Rawlings, *Mod: A Very British Phenomenon* (Omnibus, 2000), p. 9.

21. Modis Eksteins, 'Spirited', review of Jon Savage's *Teenage*, *Times Literary Supplement*, 31 August 2007.

22. Sarah Thornton, 'The Social Logic of Subcultural Capital' (1995), in Ken Gelder (ed.), *The Subcultures Reader* (2nd ed., Routledge, 2005), pp. 184–92.

23. Christine Feldman, *'We Are The Mods': A Transnational History of a Youth Subculture* (Peter Lang, 2009), p. 5.

24. Savage, *Teenage*, p. xiv.

25. Simon Reynolds, *Retromania: Pop Culture's Addiction to Its Own Past* (Faber, 2011), pp. 184–5.

26. *Daily Telegraph*, 1 June 1966.

27. Bill Osgerby, pre-publication cover quote for Feldman, *'We Are The Mods'*.

28. Reynolds, *Retromania*, pp. xxviii–xxix.

29. Hewitt (ed.), *The Sharper World*, p. 12.

30. Patrick Uden, cited in ibid., p. 57.

31. Lázló Moholy-Nagy, *The New Vision* (1939), p.14; cited in Whiteley, *Pop Design*, p. 229. Moholy-Nagy (1895–1946) was a Jewish Hungarian and a cousin of the conductor Sir Georg Solti.

1 Clean Living under Difficult Circumstances

1. Pete Townshend, interview with Jann Wenner for *Rolling Stone*, August 1968; reprinted in Peter Herbst (ed.), *The Rolling Stone Interviews: Talking with the Legends of Rock & Roll* (St Martin's Press/Rolling Stone Press, 1981), pp. 38–9.

2. Jeff Dexter, cited in Paolo Hewitt (ed.), *The Sharper Word: A Mod Anthology* (2nd ed., Helter Skelter, 2002), p. 47.

3. Colin MacInnes, *Absolute Beginners* (Allison & Busby, 1959; reprinted 1980), p. 66.

4. David Reynolds, *Rich Relations: The American Occupation of Britain 1942–45* (Harper Collins, 1995), pp. 434–5.

5. George Orwell, 'Letter to *Partisan Review*', in Sonia Orwell and Ian Angus (eds), *The Collected Essays, Journalism and Letters of George Orwell, Vol. II: My Country Right or Left, 1940–1943* (Penguin, 1970), pp. 207–8.

6. Bill Osgerby, *Youth Media* (Routledge, 2004), pp. 20, 27.

7. See David Fowler, *The First Teenagers: The Lifestyle of Young Wage-earners in Interwar Britain* (Woburn, 1995), pp. 95, 101. Fowler estimated that youth wages rose between 300 and 500 per cent in the 1920s and 30s, with 50 per cent being retained after living costs, making young people better off than their parents.

8. John Davis, *Youth and the Condition of Britain: Images of Adolescent Conflict* (Athlone, 1990), p. 166.

9. Mark Abrams, *Teenage Consumer Spending in 1959* (London Press Exchange, 1961), p. 10.

10. The first published use of the term 'teenager' was by the American *Popular Science* magazine in 1941; by 1951 the US advertising industry used it to denote a distinct category in society with 'a degree of autonomy and independence unmatched by previous generations',

according to *Advertising Age,* 26 February 1951; cited in Osgerby, *Youth Media*, pp. 20, 22.

11.   Ibid., p. 27.

12.   Richard Hoggart, *The Uses of Literacy: Aspects of Working Class Life* (1957; new edition, Penguin Classics, 2009), p. 221.

13.   Ibid., p. 220.

14.   For a full discussion of commercial television, Americanisation and the responses to it during the 1950s, see Richard Weight, *Patriots: National Identity in Britain 1940–2000* (Macmillan, 2002), Chs 3 and 4.

15.   Francis Williams, *The American Invasion* (Anthony Blond, 1962), p. 11.

16.   For the best discussion of the emergence of the Teddy Boy and media responses to it, see Adrian Horn, *Juke Box Britain: Americanisation and Youth Culture 1945–60* (Manchester University Press, 2009), Ch. 5. Teddy Boy gangs emerged in working-class districts of inner London like the Elephant & Castle, and a *Picture Post* feature in January 1954 was followed by extensive coverage in the national media from 1955 to 1957. As Horn points out, the extent of moral panic about violent Teddy Boy gangs has been exaggerated. He concludes that in the 1950s they were seen as 'not so much a threat but as more of a colourful distraction'; see ibid., p. 130.

17.   Colin MacInnes, 'Sharp Schmutter', in *Twentieth Century,* August 1959, reprinted in MacInnes, *England, Half English* (MacGibbon & Kee, 1961), p. 154.

18.   Johnny Stuart, *Rockers!* (Plexus, 1987), p. 47. Its release was also delayed, this time by the studio. Joseph Losey went on to make some of the best films about Britain's class divide in collaboration with Harold Pinter.

19.   George Melly, *Revolt into Style: The Pop Arts in Britain* (Allen Lane, 1970), p. 36.

20.   *Daily Mail,* 5 September 1956.

21.   Cited in Stanley Cohen, *Folk Devils and Moral Panics* (3rd ed., Routledge, 2002), p. 28.

22.   Colin MacInnes, 'Young England, Half English', in MacInnes, *England, Half English*, pp. 14–15.

23.   Ibid., p. 15.

24.   Lewis MacAdams, *Birth of the Cool: Beat, Bebop and the American Avant-Garde* (Scribner, 2002), p. 20. Some attribute the term to the bebop tenor saxophonist Lester Young, though there is no written evidence of this. In any case, 'cool' does not appear in Cab Calloway's landmark 1938 glossary of street slang, *Cab Calloway's Cat-ologue: A Hepster's Dictionary.*

25. Ibid., p. 45.

26. Ibid., p. 24.

27. Ibid., p. 13.

28. For more on this subject, see Graham Marsh and J. P. Gaul, *The Ivy Look: Classic American Clothing – An Illustrated Pocket Guide* (Francis Lincoln, 2010). Brooks Brothers supplied all the clothes to the *Mad Men* series.

29. Paolo Hewitt and Mark Baxter, *The Fashion of Football: From Best to Beckham, from Mod to Label Slave* (Mainstream, 2004), pp. 33–4.

30. Joshua Sims, *Rock Fashion* (Omnibus, 1999), p. 80.

31. For more on this subject, see Graham Marsh and Glyn Callingham, *Blue Note Album Cover Art* (Chronicle Books, 2002).

32. David Fowler, *The First Teenagers: The Lifestyle of Young Wage-earners in Interwar Britain* (Woburn, 1995), pp. 131–2.

33. Terry Rawlings, *Mod: A Very British Phenomenon* (Omnibus, 2000), p. 11.

34. Ibid., p. 50.

35. Ian 'Mac' McLagan, *All The Rage: My High Life with the Small Faces, the Faces, the Rolling Stones and Many More* (2nd ed., Pan, 2000), pp. 23–4.

36. George McKay, *Glastonbury: A Very English Fair* (Victor Gollancz, 2000), pp. 2–3.

37. Introduction to *All What Jazz*, his 1970 collection of jazz criticism, reprinted in Philip Larkin, *Required Writing: Miscellaneous Pieces 1955–1982* (Faber, 1983), p. 297.

38. Melly, *Revolt into Style*, pp. 27–8.

39. Len Deighton, interview with the author, 13 February 2009.

40. MacInnes, *Absolute Beginners*, p. 64. For MacInnes's description of the clothing style of 'the modernist number' – Dean Swift, the novel's jazz-loving model – and probably the first description of a Mod in print, see p. 66.

41. Interview with Roger Daltrey, in *Seven Ages of Rock*, prod. William Naylor, VH1, 19 May 2007.

42. Jane Wilson, 'Teenagers', in *Len Deighton's London Dossier* (Penguin, 1967), p. 20.

43. Philip Norman, *The Stones* (2nd ed., Penguin, 1993), pp. 56–7. Brian Jones also named his illegitimate son Julian, after one of his bebop heroes, Julian 'Cannonball' Adderley. The Marquee club moved to Wardour Street in 1964.

44. Andrew Loog Oldham, *Stoned* (Secker & Warburg, 2000), pp. 46–7.

45. Quant remembers that the sixteen-year-old Andrew Loog Oldham, 'who had all the confidence in the world', described himself 'as my assistant cum window dresser cum everything else': Mary Quant, *Quant by Quant* (Pan, 1967), p. 104.

46. Oldham, *Stoned*, pp. 76–7.

47. http://www.themarqueeclub.net/harold-pendleton

48. For more on the origins of the discotheque in 1940s France, see Bill Brewster and Frank Broughton, *Last Night a DJ Saved My Life: The History of the Disc Jockey* (2nd ed., Headline, 2006), pp. 59–64.

49. Oldham, *Stoned*, pp. 77–8.

50. Brewster and Broughton, *Last Night a DJ Saved My Life*, pp. 71–2.

51. 'Massive Swing to R&B', *Melody Maker*, 18 April 1965.

52. There are no accurate figures on the size of the movement at any given time. In 1963, the *Hairdressers' Journal* estimated that Mods made up around 35 per cent of the male teenage population, when giving its readers' advice on how best to exploit the market. Mod magazines each claimed to have readerships of between 250,000 and 500,000 per issue: see Julie Burchill, *Damaged Gods: Cults and Heroes Reappraised* (Arrow, 1987), p. 36. The figure of half a million Mods by 1965 was cited by Jonathon Green, *All Dressed Up: The Sixties and the Counterculture* (Jonathan Cape, 1998), p. 45.

53. *The Mod*, No. 9. November 1964.

54. 'Small Faces Get Their Fans Going!', *NME*, 15 October 1965.

55. Ian Hebditch, 'Weekend', an extract from his 1969 PhD thesis, 'I Do Like to Be Beside the Seaside', cited in Paolo Hewitt (ed.), *The Sharper Word: A Mod Anthology* (Helter Skelter, 2002), p. 134.

56. 'Now They're the Big Faces', *Rave*, No. 7, September 1965.

57. Paolo Hewitt and John Hellier, *Steve Marriott: All Too Beautiful* (Helter Skelter, 2004), p. 103.

58. Ibid., p. 91. 'Whatcha Gonna Do About It?' was written, in conjunction with Brian Potter, by Ian Samwell who was also responsible for Cliff Richard's 'Move It'.

59. Tony Fletcher, *Dear Boy: The Life of Keith Moon* (Omnibus, 1998), p. 110.

60. Cited in Dave Marsh, *Before I Get Old: The Story of the Who* (Plexus, 1983) p. 149.

61. Pete Townshend, interview with Jann Wenner for *Rolling Stone*, August 1968, reprinted in Peter Herbst (ed.), *The Rolling Stone Interviews: Talking with the Legends of Rock & Roll* (St Martin's Press/Rolling Stone Press, 1981), p. 38.

62. Ibid.

63. Ringo repeated his comment 'I'm a mocker' in the film *A Hard Day's Night* when a journalist asks him the same question.

64. Jonathan Gould, *Can't Buy Me Love: The Beatles, Britain and America* (Piatkus, 2007), pp. 130–5.

65. Ray Coleman, *John Winston Lennon: Vol. 1, 1940–1966* (Sidgwick & Jackson,

1984), p. 154. Asked at a press conference in Hong Kong in 1964 what the Beatles thought of Mods' colourful clothing, Lennon said, 'They've got to get away from the in-betweens, haven't they? What else can they do, you know. They're fine.' The new look the Beatles returned with from Hamburg in 1962 was famously influenced by their West German friends, the designers Jürgen Vollmer and Astrid Kirchherr, both of whom were linked to the German Mod movement, or 'Exis'. The Beatles were also influenced by the Mods they saw on their first visit to London in January 1962. Tony Bramwell, their friend and later the CEO of Apple Records, said they were fascinated by 'all these kids running round in white hipsters and cycling shirts'. For more on the Beatles' attitude to Mod, see Paolo Hewitt, *Fab Gear: The Beatles and Fashion* (Prestel, 2011), pp. 55–9.

66. Ibid., p. 158.

67. Paul Gorman, *The Look: Adventures in Rock & Pop Fashion* (Adelita, 2006), p. 44. Millings appeared briefly in *A Hard Day's Night* measuring McCartney for a suit, before Lennon cuts his tape. The 'face' Jeff Dexter pointed Millings towards Anello & Davide, a favoured Mod shop, to obtain the Beatles' footwear for the film.

68. 'The Young Take the Wheel', *Town*, September 1962.

69. Cited in *Tynan, Timeshift*, tx: BBC4, 2 March 2005.

70. Jonathon Green, *Days in the Life: Voices from the English Underground 1961–1971* (Minerva, 1989), p. 38.

71. Christine Feldman, *'We Are The Mods': A Transnational History of a Youth Subculture* (Peter Lang, 2009), p. 5.

2 I'm a Mocker

1. Mick Taylor, cited in David Nowell, *Too Darn Soulful: The Story of Northern Soul* (Robson Books, 2001), p. 27.

2. D. G. Blanchflower and A. J. Oswald, 'The Determination of White Collar Pay', Oxford Economic Papers, New Series, Vol. 42, No. 2 (April 1990) pp. 356–78.

3. David Fowler, *The First Teenagers: The Lifestyle of Young Wage-earners in Interwar Britain* (Woburn, 1995), pp. 127–8.

4. Paolo Hewitt, *The Soul Stylists: Six Decades of Modernism – from Mods to Casuals* (Mainstream, 2000), p. 52.

5. In September 1962, Marc Feld's friend Peter Sugar told the interviewer for *Town* magazine that he earned £12 a week in a hairdresser's; he gave his mother 50 shillings a week (£2.50) and spent the rest of his wages mostly on clothes and taxis. Those Mods who were office juniors would

also have earned around £12 a week in the early 1960s. One contemporary study of British youth, Charles Hamblett's and Jane Deverson's *Generation X* (Tandem, 1964), pp. 12–13, estimated that a Mod would pay about £30 for a suit, up to £5 for a shirt, £5 for shoes, and £2 for a hat.

6. *Almost Grown*, Episode 2, Granada TV, 1992.

7. Barry Carter, 'Way-Outspoken: Young Mods Have Their Say on the Scene', *Rave*, May 1964.

8. Richard Barnes, *Mods!* (Plexus, 1979), p. 15.

9. Paul Smith, interview with the author, 24 February 2011.

10. Jonathan Gould, *Can't Buy Me Love: The Beatles, Britain and America* (Piatkus, 2007), pp. 130–5.

11. Dick Hebdige, *Subculture: The Meaning of Style* (1979; reprinted, Routledge, 1991), pp. 52–4.

12. Colin MacInnes, 'Sharp Schmutter', *Twentieth Century*, August 1959, reprinted in MacInnes, *England, Half English* (MacGibbon & Kee, 1961), p. 154.

13. Ibid.

14. Harold Macmillan, *Britain, the Commonwealth and Europe* (Conservative Central Office, 1961), p. 5.

15. Mary Quant, *Quant by Quant* (Pan, 1967), p. 81.

16. Terry Rawlings, *Mod: A Very British Phenomenon* (Omnibus, 2000), p. 50.

17. Ibid., pp. 16–17.

18. Barnes, *Mods!*, p. 9.

19. Christine Feldman, *'We Are the Mods': A Transnational History of a Youth Subculture* (Peter Lang, 2009), p. 29.

20. *Rave*, No. 40, May 1967.

21. Paolo Hewitt (ed.), *The Sharper Word: A Mod Anthology* (2nd ed., Helter Skelter, 2002), p. 9.

22. Julie Burchill, *Damaged Gods: Cults and Heroes Reappraised* (Arrow, 1987), pp. 33–4.

23. *Ipcress File*, soundtrack, Track 12: 'Button mushrooms and birds'. This was written especially for Caine and did not feature in Deighton's novel.

24. Len Deighton, interview with the author, 13 February 2009.

25. Michael Caine, *What's It All About? The Autobiography* (Random House, 1992), p. 175. According to Caine, in order 'to de-gay my role' the director and producer made him use the supermarket trolley 'as a weapon'; and 'the cooking we made fast, expert' and 'macho' by having Caine (actually Deighton) break two eggs with one hand.

26. Len Deighton, *The Action Cookbook* (Penguin, 1967), p. 34.

27. Len Deighton, interview with the author, 13 February 2009.

28. Len Deighton, *The Ipcress File* (3rd ed., Panther, 1966), p. 22. Deighton was influenced both by the crime writer Dashiell Hammett and, like Colin MacInnes, by the beat writers; he also designed the cover of one of the first British editions of Kerouac's *On the Road*.

29. Ibid., pp. 23, 25.

30. Len Deighton, *Funeral In Berlin* (Penguin, 1966), p. 23.

31. Ibid., p. 25.

32. Dick Hebdige, *Hiding in the Light: On Images and Things* (Routledge, 1988), p. 75.

33. Rawlings, *Mod*, pp. 20–1.

34. Barnes, *Mods!*, p. 122.

35. The craze for mirrors and spotlights reached a peak in the summer of 1964. It is seen as the defining mark of the Mod scooter only because most pictures of Mods were taken around this time as a result of press interest in the seaside disturbances.

36. Rawlings, *Mod*, p. 134.

37. Nick Cohn, *Today There Are No Gentlemen: The Changes in Englishmen's Clothes since the War* (Weidenfeld & Nicolson, 1971), p. 78.

38. 'The Ace Face's Forgotten Story', Steve Turner interview with Pete Meaden, *NME*, 17 November 1979; reprinted in Hewitt (ed.), *The Sharper Word*.

39. Angela McRobbie, *Feminism and Youth Culture* (2nd ed., Macmillan, 2000). This feminist critique of Mod originally appeared in the seminal *Resistance through Rituals* essay collection, edited by Tony Hall and Stuart Jefferson in 1976.

40. Val Palmer, interviewed on 'Modcast Episode 2', 5 February 2011, with Martin Freeman, Paolo Hewitt and Val Palmer; retrieved from http://www.themodcast.co.uk, 1 June 2012.

41. Barnes, *Mods!*, p. 16.

42. Feldman, *'We Are the Mods'*, p. 31.

43. McRobbie, *Feminism and Youth Culture*, p. 20. Another, interviewed in the *Sunday Times* colour supplement that year, said, 'My Dad's trying to get me to join the Young Conservatives . . . but I like this set. They're nice and they say what they mean.' See Kathleen Halton, 'Changing Faces', *Sunday Times* colour supplement, 2 August 1964.

44. Hewitt, *Soul Stylists*, pp. 67–9.

45. Deighton, *London Dossier*, 27.

46. McRobbie, *Feminism and Youth Culture*, pp. 20–1.

47. Ian 'Mac' McLagan, *All The Rage: My High Life with the Small Faces, the Faces, the Rolling Stones and Many More* (2nd ed., Pan, 2000), p. 14.

48. Cited in Nigel Whiteley, *Pop Design: Modernism to Mod* (Design Council, 1987), p. 102.

49. Hewitt, *Soul Stylists*, p. 45.

50. Ibid., p. 60.

51. *Daily Mirror*, 31 March 1964, quoted in Johnny Stuart, *Rockers!* (Plexus, 1987), pp. 83–4.

52. Carter, 'Way-Outspoken'.

53. Nik Cohn, *Ball the Wall: Nik Cohn in the Age of Rock* (Picador, 1989), p. 295.

54. *Mod Monthly*, July 1965.

55. Hewitt (ed.), *Soul Stylists*, p. 65.

56. Ibid., pp. 73–4.

57. Ibid., p. 65.

58. Rawlings, *Mod*, p. 50.

59. Peter Burton, excerpt from *Parallel Lives* (Gay Men's Press, 1985), reproduced in Hewitt (ed.), *The Sharper Word*, pp. 100–1.

60. Simon Napier-Bell, *Black Vinyl White Powder* (Ebury Press, 2001), pp. 90–1.

61. Ibid., p. 91.

62. Jon Savage, *The Kinks: The Official Biography* (Faber, 1984), p. 60.

63. 'John Stephen (1934–2004)', obituary, *The Times*, 10 February 2004.

64. Barnes, *Mods!*, p. 10.

65. Jeremy Reed, *orange and sunshine: the party that lasted a decade* (SAF Publishing, 2006), Preface.

66. Shari Benstock and Suzanne Ferris, *On Fashion* (Rutgers University Press, 1994), p. 157.

67. Hewitt (ed.), *The Sharper Word*, pp. 9–13.

68. *Rave*, May 1966.

69. Rawlings, *Mod*, p. 71.

70. See, for example, Fernand Gautier, 'How To Cut the New French Line', *Hairdressers' Journal*, 25 October 1963.

71. Barnes, *Mods!*, p. 11.

72. *Rave*, No. 22, December 1965.

73. Ibid.

74. Nik Cohn, 'Ready, Steady, Gone', *Observer*, 27 August 1967.

75. *Guardian*, 2 December 1964, reprinted from the *Journal of the Institute of Race Relations*.

76. Some rockers were quite explicit in their condemnation of racism. One of those interviewed stated in 1964: 'It's more than just the fun and scare of it what makes you a Rocker . . . feel strongly about racial discrimination. Lots of my mates don't like coloured people . . . I don't

hold with that. I've worked with Jamaicans and I get along with them fine. Most of the people that don't like Negroes are just ignorant.' See Stuart, *Rockers!*, p. 78.

77. Paolo Hewitt, 'Maximum Mod, 1965–68', in *Mod* (NME Publications, 2005), p. 40.

78. Ibid., p. 39.

79. Geno Washington, 'Everyone Got Real Sharp', in ibid., p. 40.

80. *Melody Maker*, 12 June 1965.

81. Ray Coleman, *John Winston Lennon: Vol. 1, 1940–1966* (Sidgwick & Jackson, 1984), p. 244.

82. Ibid.

83. *Melody Maker*, 4 June 1966.

84. Hewitt, *Soul Stylists*, p. 56.

85. Ibid., p. 57.

86. Cited in Andrew Loog Oldham, *Stoned* (Secker & Warburg, 2000), p. 79.

87. Prince Buster, interview with the author, June 2003.

88. *Mod*, p. 10.

89. Rawlings, *Mod*, p. 39.

90. *The Ska Explosion: 25 Years of 2Tone* (Q Publications, 2004), p. 9.

91. *NME*, 10 October 1968.

92. Hewitt, *Soul Stylists*, p. 56.

93. PRO/HO300/08, LCC Children's Department, 'West End Jazz and Dance Clubs', Report for a Meeting with the Home Secretary and Minister of Health, 15 September 1964.

94. Robert Hewison, *Art and Society in the Sixties, 1960–75* (Methuen, 1986), p. 131.

3 I Took the M1

1. 'The Ace Face's Forgotten Story', Steve Turner interview with Pete Meaden, *NME*, 17 November 1979; reprinted in Paolo Hewitt (ed.), *The Sharper Word: A Mod Anthology* (2nd ed., Helter Skelter, 2002), p. 178.

2. *Daily Telegraph*, 30 December 1995.

3. Philip Norman, *Shout! The True Story of The Beatles* (2nd ed., Pan Books, 2004), p. 208.

4. Bill Osgerby, *Youth Media* (Routledge, 2004), p. 154. In popular music, Vera Lynn had been the first Briton to top the American charts, with 'Auf Wiederseh'n Sweetheart' in 1952, followed by Acker Bilk's 'Stranger on the Shore' a decade later. But neither had been associated with a cultural movement nor with specific ideas of modernity.

5. Ibid., p. 29.

6.   Bill Adler (ed.), *Love Letters to the Beatles* (Blond, 1964), p. 81.

7.   Peter Guralnick, *Careless Love: The Unmaking of Elvis Presley* (Abacus, 2000), p. 207.

8.   Ibid., p. 426. An FBI agent reported these comments during a meeting with Elvis in 1970 when he was offering his services to President Nixon in the US government's war on drugs.

9.   Barry Carter, 'Way-Out Spoken: Young Mods Have Their Say on the Scene', *Rave*, May 1964.

10. 'Salute to the MBEatles', *NME*, 18 June 1965.

11. Ibid.

12. *Daily Mirror*, 23 July 1969.

13. NA/INF6/160, *Fashion Fanfare* (1967), final script.

14. NA/FO366/3429, *Sunday Express*, 16 February 1964. The Home Secretary, Rab Butler, was forced to issue a denial in the House of Commons.

15. Andrew Loog Oldham, *2Stoned* (Vintage, 2003), p. 3.

16. Barry Miles, *The British Invasion* (Sterling, 2009), pp. 294–5.

17. Lester Bangs, 'The British Invasion', in Anthony DeCurtis and James Henke (eds), *The Rolling Stone Illustrated History of Rock 'n' Roll* (3rd ed., Random House, 1992), p. 199.

18. John Dougan, *The Who Sell Out* (Continuum, 2010), pp. 8–9.

19. Jeffery A. Miron and Elina Tetelbaum, 'Does the Minimum Legal Drinking Age Save Lives?' *Economic Inquiry* 47:2 (2009), 317–36.

20. I am grateful to Dr Michael Peplar for this reference.

21. *The Times*, 23 December 1964.

22. Pete Townshend, interviewed for *The History of Rock 'n' Roll*, Warner Bros TV, 1995.

23. Jon Savage, *The Kinks: The Official Autobiography* (Faber, 1984), p. 71. *Arthur* was also conceived as a tribute to Davies' brother-in-law of that name, who had emigrated to Australia after becoming disillusioned with post-war Britain; see ibid., p. 109.

24. Charlie Gillett, *The Sound of the City: The Rise of Rock 'n' Roll* (3rd-ed., Souvenir Press, 1996), p. 277.

25. Tony Fletcher, *Dear Boy: The Life of Keith Moon* (Omnibus, 1998), p. 158. Unlike Lennon and McCartney, Moon didn't like the experimentalism of *Pet Sounds*, though he didn't say so at the meeting.

26. Ian MacDonald, *Revolution in the Head: The Beatles' Records and the Sixties* (2nd revised ed., Vintage, 2008), p. 234.

27.   John Lennon was famously attached to his mother and his aunt Mimi, and Keith Richards' memoir reveals that even the bad boy of British rock was raised by a warm, working-class family to which he stayed close. In April 1962, for example, he wrote a letter to his aunt Patty

about his first meeting with Mick Jagger, about the music they loved and the girls they took to their local R&B club: Keith Richards, with James Fox, *Life* (Weidenfeld & Nicolson, 2010), pp. 77–9.

28. Cited in Clark Wilkerson, *Who Are You: The Life of Pete Townshend* (Omnibus, 2008), p. 7.

29. Nick Hornby, *31 Songs* (Penguin, 2003), pp. 130–1.

30. John Crosby, *Weekend Telegraph*, 16 April 1965; reprinted in Ray Connolly (ed.), *In the Sixties: The Writing That Captured a Decade* (Pavilion Books, 1995), pp. 77–82.

31. See Meirion Hughes and Robert Stradling, *The English Musical Renaissance, 1840–1940: Constructing a National Music* (2nd ed., Manchester University Press, 2001).

32. *NME*, 6 January 1968.

33. Robert Hewison, *Too Much: Art and Society in the Sixties* (Methuen, 1986), p. 66.

34. See Mark Jenkins, 'The End of the British Invasion: Why can't Britpop Crack the *Billboard* Hot 100 Anymore?', *Slate*, 3 May 2002.

35. Pat Long, *The History of the NME, 1952–2012* (Portico, 2012), p. 28. *NME* sales declined between 1968 and 1972 under pressure from the 'underground' press, before the magazine revived again thanks to a new wave of music journalists like Nick Kent and Charles Shaar Murray, selling over 200,000 copies a week in 1973. The actual readership was probably much larger, IPC estimating that each copy was passed on and read by three more people; see ibid., p. 68.

36. Joe Boyd, *White Bicycles: Making Music in the 1960s* (Serpent's Tail, 2007), p. 137.

37. Ibid.

38. Cited in Shawn Levy, *Ready, Steady, Go! Swinging London and the Invention of Cool* (Fourth Estate, 2002), p. 9.

39. Paul McCartney, interviewed for *How the Brits Rocked America*, Episode 1, BBC4, tx: 10 February 2012.

40. Jonathan Gould, *Can't Buy Me Love: The Beatles, Britain and America* (Piatkus, 2007), p. 133.

41. Quoted in Christine Feldman, *'We Are the Mods': A Transnational History of a Youth Subculture* (Peter Lang, 2009), p. 127.

42. Mary Quant, *Quant by Quant* (Pan, 1967), p. 113.

43. Ibid., p. 121.

44. Front and rear cover of the US edition of *Quant by Quant* (Ballantine, 1967).

45. Quant, *Quant by Quant*, p. 110.

46. Ibid., p. 111.

47. Feldman, 'We Are the Mods', p. 122.
48. Ibid., p. 130. That youth culture was seen as a limited British version of the American Dream was sometimes made explicit: for example, a 1972 *Time* article on Twiggy and her boyfriend manager (a former labourer) was called 'Show Business: The English Dream'.
49. Ibid., p. 127.
50. *Newsweek*, 25 November 1968, cited in Bill Osgerby, *Playboys in Paradise: Masculinity, Youth and Leisure-style in Modern America* (Berg, 2001), p. 185.
51. Vidal Sassoon, *Vidal: The Autobiography* (Pan, 2010), p. 174.
52. Ibid., p. 173.
53. Hardy Amies, *ABC of Men's Fashion* (Newnes, 1964; reprinted, V&A Publishing, 2007), p. 11.
54. June Harris, 'Decca Music Man Likes British Clothes', *Disc*, 29 February 1964.
55. See Ruth Padel, *I'm a Man: Sex, Gods and Rock 'n' Roll* (Faber, 2000), p. 158.
56. Feldman, 'We Are the Mods', p. 114.
57. Cited in Arthur Marwick, *The Sixties: Cultural Revolution in Britain, France, Italy, and the United States c.1958–c.1974* (Oxford University Press, 1998) p. 468.
58. Craig Werner, *A Change Is Gonna Come: Music, Race and the Soul of America* (Canongate, 2002), pp. 80–1; 83–4.
59. Feldman, 'We Are the Mods', p. 120.
60. Werner, *A Change Is Gonna Come*, p. 85.
61. Cited in Gillett, *The Sound of the City*, p. 272. The story was originally told by Eric Burdon in an interview, 'Englishman Who Sings the Blues', for *Ebony*, August 1966. *Ebony*, modelled closely on *Life* magazine, was founded in 1945 as a glossy monthly magazine for African Americans, aimed at the expanding black middle class of the post-war era. The fact that a white working-class boy from Newcastle was interviewed at all on the subject of the blues is a measure of how much African Americans welcomed the British Invasion and the progressive racial attitudes it contained, compared to those of white America.
62. Andrew Loog Oldham, *2Stoned* (Vintage, 2003), pp. 5–6.
63. Philip Norman, *The Stones* (2nd ed., Penguin), p. 108.
64. Oldham, *2Stoned*, pp. 8–9.
65. Philip Norman, *Shout! The True Story of The Beatles* (2nd ed., Pan Books, 2004), p. 213.
66. Mark Paytress, *The Rolling Stones Off the Record: Outrageous Opinions and Unrehearsed Interviews* (2nd ed., Omnibus, 2005), p. 101.
67. Jeff Stein (dir.), *The Kids Are Alright* (Pioneer Entertainment, 2003), Ch. 1.

68. Ibid., Ch. 8.
69. Dave Davies, *Kink: An Autobiography* (Boxtree, 1996), p. 83.
70. 'Les Mods', dir. Alain de Sedony, tx: 18 March 1965.
71. Callum G. Brown, *Religion and Society in Twentieth-Century Britain* (Longman, 2006), p. 281.
72. Ronald Bruce Flowers, *Religion in Strange Times* (Mercer University Press, 1982), p. 39.
73. Quant, *Quant by Quant*, p. 125.
74. *Evening Standard*, 4 March 1966.
75. Osgerby, *Playboys in Paradise*, pp. 159–60.
76. Herbert Gans, 'Who's O-O-Oh in America', *Vogue*, 15 March 1965.
77. *Time*, 15 April 1966.
78. Feldman, 'We Are the Mods', p. 124.
79. Ibid., p. 130. The letter was one of several hostile reader responses to the Twiggy craze.
80. *Mod* (NME Publications, 2005), p. 41.
81. David Reynolds and David Dimbleby, *An Ocean Apart: The Relationship between Britain and America in the Twentieth Century* (Hodder & Stoughton, 1988), pp. 275–6.
82. James Macmillan and Bernard Harris, *The American Take-Over of Britain* (Leslie Frewin, 1968), p. 6.
83. *The Times*, 29 March 1965.
84. Louis Barfe, *Turned Out Nice Again: The Story of British Light Entertainment* (Atlantic, 2008), p. 177.
85. Colin MacInnes, *Absolute Beginners* (Allison & Busby, 1959; reprinted, 1980), pp. 52–3.

4 Never Let the Music Get in the Way of the Act

1. Harry Matthews, interviewed in Barry Carter, 'Way-Outspoken: Young Mods Have Their Say on the Scene', *Rave*, May 1964.
2. Terence Conran, *Q&A: A Sort of Autobiography* (HarperCollins, 2001), p. 36.
3. 'Les Mods', dir. Alain de Sedony, tx: 18 March 1965.
4. *Daily Mail*, 31 July 1968.
5. Margaret McFadyen, interviewed in Carter, 'Way-Outspoken'.
6. John Dougan, *The Who Sell Out* (Continuum, 2010), pp. 41–2.
7. Nick Cohn, excerpt from 'Today There Are No Gentlemen', 1971, reproduced in Cohn, *Ball the Wall* (Picador, 1989), p. 294.
8. Rainer Metzger, *London in the Sixties* (Thames & Hudson, 2012), p. 67.

9.   Nigel Whiteley, *Pop Design: Modernism to Mod* (Design Council, 1987), p. 91.
10. Len Deighton, interview with the author, 13 February 2009.
11. William Coldstream (1908–87) was co-founder, with Graham Bell, of the realist Euston Road group of painters, professor of fine art at the Slade School, and later chair of the British Film Institute from 1964 to 1971, during an important period when cinema captured the 'youth-quake' (albeit largely funded by American capital).
12. Nick Hasted, *You Really Got Me: The Story of the Kinks* (Omnibus, 2011), p. 60.
13. Ray Davies, interviewed by Alan Yentob, *Imagine*, BBC1, tx: 17 July 2011.
14. Dave Marsh, *Before I Get Old: The Story of the Who* (Plexus, 1983), p. 48.
15. Ibid., p. 49.
16. See Pete Townshend, interview with Jann Wenner for *Rolling Stone*, August 1968, reprinted in Peter Herbst (ed.), *The Rolling Stone Interviews: Talking with the Legends of Rock & Roll* (St Martin's Press / Rolling Stone Press, 1981), p. 34. The cost of replacing their equipment almost bankrupted the group at one point.
17. Marsh, *Before I Get Old*, p. 307.
18. Ibid., p. 168.
19. Andrew Motion, *The Lamberts: George, Constant and Kit* (Hogarth Press, 1987), p. 305.
20. Christopher Booker, *The Neophiliacs: The Revolution in English Life in the Fifties and Sixties* (2nd ed., Pimlico, 1992), pp. 239–40. Booker noted that 'the pop art industry was almost as flourishing in 1964 as pop music itself'.
21. George Melly, 'The Who and the Wherefore', *Observer*, 21 November 1965.
22. Jonathan Aitken, *Young Meteors* (Secker & Warburg, 1967), p. 261.
23. Jonathan Miller's review of the New Generation show at the Whitechapel Gallery appeared in the *New Statesman*, 29 May 1964; cited in Robert Hewison, *Too Much: Art and Society in the Sixties, 1960–75* (Methuen, 1986), p. 71.
24. Melly, 'The Who and the Wherefore'.
25. *Rave*, August 1965.
26. *Melody Maker*, 3 July 1965.
27. See John Hill, 'Television and Pop: The Case of the 1950s', in John Corner (ed.), *Popular Television in Britain: Studies in Cultural History* (British Film Institute, 1991).
28. Chris Roberts, 'Mecca for Mods?', *Melody Maker*, 25 January 1964.
29. David Fowler, *Youth Culture in Modern Britain, c.1920–1970* (Palgrave, 2008), p. 134.
30. George Melly, *Revolt into Style: The Pop Arts in Britain* (Allen Lane, 1970), p. 170.

31. Dave Clark 'We always have a ball on the swingiest of shows', in *Ready, Steady, Go! Associated Rediffusion's Top TV Pop Show* (TV Publications Ltd., 1964), p. 6.

32. Shawn Levy, *Ready, Steady, Go!: Swinging London and the Invention of Cool* (Fourth Estate, 2002), p. 128.

33. Fowler, *Youth Culture in Modern Britain*, pp. 134–5.

34. Ibid., p. 135.

35. Melly, *Revolt into Style*, p. 171.

36. Cathy McGowan, 'Getting the Fab Gear', in *Ready, Steady, Go! Associated Rediffusion's Top TV Pop Show*, p. 10.

37. Paolo Hewitt, *The Soul Stylists: Six Decades of Modernism – from Mods to Casuals* (Edinburgh, Mainstream, 2000), p. 69.

38. Twiggy, *Twiggy: An Autobiography* (Hart-Davis, 1976), pp. 17–18.

39. John Levesley, 'Where the Way-Out Ones Came In', *Rave*, May 1964.

40. Hewitt, *The Soul Stylists*, p. 87.

41. Roberts, 'Mecca for Mods?'

42. Levy, *Invention of Cool*, p. 130

43. Melly, *Revolt into Style*, p. 172.

44. David Mellor, *The Sixties Art Scene in London* (Phaidon, 1993), p. 43.

45. Ibid., p. 126.

46. Ibid., p. 47.

47. Ibid.

48. Martin Harrison, *Young Meteors: British Photojournalism: 1957–1965* (Jonathan Cape, 1998), p. 68.

49. I am grateful to Paolo Hewitt for this reference.

50. See Marco Livingstone, *Pop Art: A Continuing History* (Thames & Hudson, 2000).

51. Mark Wilkerson, *Who Are You: The Life of Pete Townshend* (Omnibus, 2008), p. 45.

52. Dick Hebdige, *Subculture: The Meaning of Style* (1979; reprint, Routledge, 1991), pp. 104–5.

53. Jon Savage, 'The Who Signal the Start of Swinging London', *Observer*, 31 July 2011.

54. Anne Filer, cited in *Almost Grown*, Episode 1, 'That's What I Want', Granada 1992.

55. Daphne Larner, cited in ibid.

56. Richard Lester, *Boutique London – A History: King's Road to Carnaby Street* (ACC Editions, 2010), pp. 68–70.

57. Robert Hewison, *Too Much Too Much: Art and Society in the Sixties, 1960–75* (Methuen, 1986), p. 71

58. Cheryl Buckley, *Designing Modern Britain* (Reaktion Books, 2007), p. 153.

59. Mary Quant, interview with the author for *Tasty!*, BBC Radio 3 Sunday Feature, tx: 20 December 2009.

60. Mary Quant, *Autobiography* (Headline, 2012), p. 147.

61. J. B. Priestley, 'Dandy Days', *New Statesman*, 1 November 1966.

62. One of the more absurd points made in the revisionist critique of youth culture is David Fowler's assertion that few Carnaby Street stores had the word 'Mod' in them, as if culture (commercial or otherwise) has to label itself in such a crude way to be invested with meaning by those involved in it. By the same token, the Carnaby Street boutique owned by Henry Moss called 'Pussy Galore' might have run into trouble. See Fowler, *Youth Culture in Modern Britain*, p. 133. Mod Male was run by two teenage Mods, Ken Slater from Stamford Bridge and Keith Lewis from Haringey.

63. Ibid., p. 134.

64. *Boyfriend*, 8 January 1966.

65. Jeremy Reed, *John Stephen: King of Carnaby Street* (Haus Publishing, 2010), p. 222. For more on this aspect of his achievement, see Alistair O'Neill, 'John Stephen: A Carnaby Street Presentation of Masculinity 1957–1975', *Fashion Theory*, Vol. 4, No. 4, pp. 487–508.

66. Reed, *John Stephen*, p. 260. The figures come from a survey carried out by Westminster Council.

67. The pivotal moment came in 1966, when Selfridges spent £1 million launching Miss Selfridge. Initially an in-store 'boutique' in Oxford Street, it was soon a 'concession' within department stores around Britain and later became a successful high-street chain; it was acquired by Philip Green's Arcadia Group in 1999. Chain stores' vigorous response to the boutique revolution in the late 1960s is why, even before shopping malls got going, the market share of independents fell from 54.2 to 46.5 per cent between 1961 and 1970, while that of multiples grew from 28 to 36.8 per cent. See Sonia Ashmore, 'I Think They're All Mad: Shopping in Swinging London', in Christopher Breward, David Gilbert and Jenny Lister (eds), *Swinging Sixties: Fashion in London and Beyond 1955–1970* (V&A Publishing, 2006), pp. 58–77.

68. Arthur Marwick, *The Sixties: Cultural Revolution in Britain, France, Italy, and the United States, c.1958–c.1974* (Oxford University Press, 1998), p. 456.

69. Ibid., p. 462.

70. See Marianne Amar, 'Pop Music and Protest in France', in David Mellor and Laurent Gervereau (eds), *The Sixties, Britain and France: The Utopian Years, 1962–73* (Philip Wilson, 1997), pp. 220–9.

71. Robert and Isabelle Tombs, *That Sweet Enemy: Britain and France, the History of a Love-Hate Relationship* (Heinemann, 2007), pp. 632–3.

72. *In Gear* (Rank Organisation, 1966); *Look at Life: Swingin' London* (Simply Media, 2010).

73. Quant, *Autobiography*, p. 98.

74. Marwick, *The Sixties*, p. 468

75. Ibid., p. 465.

76. Barbara Hulanicki, *From A to BIBA: The Autobiography of Barbara Hulanicki* (2nd ed., V&A Publishing, 2007), p. 81.

77. *NME*, 25 June 1965.

78. Christine Feldman, *'We Are the Mods': A Transnational History of a Youth Subculture* (Peter Lang, 2009), p. 65.

79. Ibid., p. 69.

80. Ibid., p. 70.

81. Ibid., p. 83.

82. Ibid., p. 73.

83. Ibid., p. 86.

84. Andy Bennett, *Cultures of Popular Music* (Open University Press, 2001), p. 17.

85. *Storyville: How the Beatles Rocked the Kremlin*, BBC4, tx: 6 September 2009.

86. *NME*, 22 October 1965.

87. Colin MacInnes, 'Sharp Schmutter', *Twentieth Century*, August 1959; reprinted in MacInnes, *England, Half English* (MacGibbon & Kee, 1961), p. 153.

88. Christopher Breward, 'Aestheticism in the Marketplace: Fashion, Lifestyle and Popular Taste', in Stephen Calloway and Lynn Federle Orr (eds), *The Cult of Beauty: The Aesthetic Movement 1860–1900* (V&A Publishing, 2011), p. 194.

89. Cited in ibid., p. 199. For a full study of how the concept of lifestyle was marketed through interior design from the late nineteenth century onwards, see Deborah Cohen, *Household Gods: The British and Their Possessions* (Yale University Press, 2006).

90. *Homes for Today and Tomorrow* (HMSO, 1961), p. 3.

91. Hugh Casson, 'Technique for Living', *Sunday Times Colour Magazine*, 2 February 1964. As director of the Festival of Britain, Casson (1910–99) shaped its bracing modernist design, made more palatable with touches of British folk art, which filtered into furniture showrooms over the next forty years. After being knighted for that achievement, he was professor of interior design at the Royal College of Art from 1955 to 1975, where he continued to spread the modernist influence on British designers.

92. Walter Gropius, 'Programme of the Staatliche Bauhaus in Weimar', in Barbican Art Gallery, *Bauhaus: Art as Life* (Koenig Books, 2012), p. 15.

93. Mary Quant, interview with the author for *Tasty!*.

94. *Vidal Sassoon: A Cut Above*, BBC1, Imagine, tx: 30 May 2011.

95. Cited in Levy, *Ready, Steady, Go!*, p. 36. A version was also popularised by Twiggy.

96. Conran, *Q&A*, p. 36.

97. Ibid., p. 74.

98. Ibid., pp. 49–50.

99. Ibid., p. 71.

100. Ibid., p. 75.

101. Ibid., p. 73.

102. *Observer*, 26 June 2011.

103. Hewitt, *The Soul Stylists*, p. 55.

104. Conran, *Q&A*, p. 73. One of Conran's early restaurant ventures was a café designed entirely around the Vespa, but it fell through when his prospective partner, Giovanni Agnelli of Piaggio, died suddenly.

105. Richard Barnes, *Mods!* (Plexus, 1979), p. x.

106. Conran, *Q&A*, p. 74.

107. Sara Maitland (ed.), *Very Heaven: Looking Back at the 1960s* (Virago, 1988), p. 24.

108. See Barry Curtis, 'A New Domestic Landscape: British Interior Design, 1962–73', in Mellor and Gervereau (eds), *The Sixties, Britain and France*, p. 190. Another link between youth and popular Modernism, noted by Curtis, is that during the massive expansion of British universities in the 1960s (most of it at the hands of modernists architects), £160 was allocated for the fixtures and fittings of each study bedroom in halls of residence.

109. Angela McRobbie, *Feminism and Youth Culture* (2nd ed., Macmillan, 2000), pp. 19–20.

110. Paul Barker, 'The Margate Offenders', *New Society*, 30 July 1964; reprinted in Timothy Raison (ed.), *Youth in New Society* (Hart-Davis, 1966), p. 126.

111. Penny Sparke, 'At Home with Modernity: The New Domestic Scene', in Christopher Breward and Ghislaine Wood (eds), *British Design from 1945: Innovation in the Modern Age* (V&A Publishing, 2012), p. 126.

112. Ibid.

113. Ibid., p. 136.

114. Ali Catterall and Simon Wells, *Your Face Here: British Cult Movies since the Sixties* (4th Estate, 2002), p. 41.

115. *Queen* was owned by Jocelyn Stevens, a financial backer of Radio Caroline.

116. Harrison, *Young Meteors*, p. 66.

117. Ken and Kate Baynes, 'Behind the Scene', *Design Magazine*, August 1966.

118. R. D. Anderson, *Universities and Elites in Britain since 1800* (Cambridge University Press, 1995), p. 15; see also Carol Dyhouse, *Students: A Gendered History* (Routledge, 2006), pp. 97–119, and Stéphan Vincent-Lancrin, 'The Reversal of Gender Inequalities in Higher Education: An On-going Trend', in *Higher Education to 2030, Volume 1: Demography* (OECD, 2008), p. 267.

119. *Almost Grown*, Episode 1, 'That's What I Want', Granada 1992.

120. Ruth Inglis, 'Bedsit World,' *Observer*, 20 February 1966.

121. NA/HO303/79, 'Cinema and the Teenagers', Pearl & Dean Group, 1966.

122. See for example, Fowler, *Youth Culture in Modern* Britain, pp. 174–5.

123. Len Deighton, *London Dossier* (Penguin, 1967), p. 26.

124. *Observer*, 1 December 1968.

125. Jonathan Gould, *Can't Buy Me Love: The Beatles, Britain and America* (Piatkus, 2007), p. 130–5.

126. Richard Williams, interview with the author, 24 November 2009.

127. Cited in Geoffrey Aquilina Ross, *The Day of the Peacock: Style for Men 1963–1973* (V&A Publishing, 2012), p. 108.

128. Ibid., pp. 60–1.

129. Ibid., p. 129.

130. Ibid., pp. 60–1.

131. *Rave*, February 1966.

132. *Disc Weekly*, 1 October 1966.

133. Marsh, *Before I Get Old*, p. 277.

134. Cited in Dougan, *The Who Sell Out*, p. 119. Cohn was writing in *Queen* magazine.

135. This description of Pink Floyd was coined by *Town* magazine.

136. Marsh, *Before I Get Old*, p. 240.

137. *Melody Maker*, 22 October 1966.

138. Quote in Natalie Rudd, *Peter Blake* (Tate Publishing, 2003), p. 49.

139. Cited in Reed, *John Stephen*, p. 228.

140. Simon Reynolds and Joy Press, *The Sex Revolts: Gender, Rebellion and Rock 'n' Roll* (Serpent's Tail, 1995), pp. 160–1.

141. Charles Shaar Murray, interview with the author, 21 March 2012.

142. Charles Shaar Murray, 'Flowered Up!' *MOJO Psychedelic!*, February 2005, cited in Dougan, *The Who Sell Out*, p. 50.

143. Bill Osgerby, *Playboys in Paradise: Masculinity, Youth and Leisure-style in Modern America* (Berg, 2001), p. 185.

144. See Terry Rawlings, *Mod: A Very British Phenomenon* (Omnibus, 2000), p. 150.

145. Nick Mason, *Inside Out: A Personal History of Pink Floyd* (Phoenix, 2005), pp. 93–4.

146. Tom Wolfe, *The Pump House Gang* (Bantam, 1968), p. 67.

147. Ibid.

148. Paul Gorman, *The Look: Adventures in Rock and Pop Fashion* (Adelita, 2006), p. 47.

149. Ibid.

150. George Martin, cited in Simon Napier-Bell, *Black Vinyl White Powder* (Ebury Press, 2002), p. 73. Even the *Ready, Steady Go!* Studios were run by a group of ex-naval officers, and Vicki Wickham remembered that 'the five floors of the building were referred to as "decks" and the times of the day as "bells". The notice board read like a ship's bulletin': ibid.

151. Paolo Hewitt and John Hellier, *Steve Marriott: All Too Beautiful* (Helter Skelter, 2004), p. xv.

152. Ray Davies, cited in Napier-Bell, *Black Vinyl White Powder*, p. 72.

153. Ray Coleman, *John Ono Lennon, Vol. 2: 1967–1980* (Sidgwick and Jackson, 1984), pp. 144–5.

154. Ibid., p. 147.

155. Ibid., p. 159.

156. Ibid.

157. Nick Cohn, *Today There Are No Gentlemen: The Changes in Englishmen's Clothes since the War* (Weidenfeld & Nicolson, 1971), p. 78.

158. *The Mod*, No. 7, September 1965.

159. Ibid.

160. Pete Townshend, interview with Jann Wenner for *Rolling Stone*, p. 42.

161. *The Mod*, No. 7, September 1965.

162. Kit Lambert, interviewed in 'Les Mods'.

163. Deighton, *London Dossier*, p. 20.

5 Ecstatic Exaggerations

1. Dave Godin, *Blues & Soul*, Issue No. 50, December 1970, p. 18.

2. John Lennon, cited in Simon Napier-Bell, *Black Vinyl White Powder* (Ebury Press, 2002), p. 168.

3. Simon Frith, *Sound Effects: Youth, Leisure and the Politics of Rock* (Constable, 1983), pp. 219–20.

4. Gary Kemp, *I Know This Much: From Soho to Spandau* (4th Estate, 2009), p. 22.

5. Ibid., pp. 42–3.

6. Angela McRobbie, 'Settling Accounts with Subcultures', in Simon Frith and A. Goodwin (eds), *On Record: Rock, Pop and the Written Word* (Routledge, 1990), pp. 68–9.

7. Terry Rawlings, *Mod: A Very British Phenomenon* (Omnibus, 2000), p. 124.

8. Ibid., p. 125.

9. Ina Zweiniger-Bargielowska, 'Living Standards and Consumption', in Paul Addison and Harriet Jones (eds), *A Companion to Contemporary Britain* (Blackwell, 2005), p. 234.

10. *Daily Mirror*, 20 July 1967. Opinion polls showed a rise in the number approving the change, from 63 per cent opposed in 1954 to 49 per cent in 1965, with 56 per cent of the 18 to 20 age group in favour.

11. See John Davies, *Youth and the Condition of Britain: Images of Adolescent Conflict* (Athlone, 1990), pp. 125–31.

12. *The Times*, 27 June 1974.

13. Edward Phelps, 'Young Adults and Electoral Turnout in Britain: Towards a Generational Model of Political Participation' (Sussex European Institute, 2006) pp. 16–18.

14. BBC1, *Nationwide*, 13 September 1979.

15. David Nowell, *Too Darn Soulful: The Story of Northern Soul* (Robson Books, 2001), p. 53.

16. Mike Pickering, interview with the author, 25 April 2012.

17. William Hunt, interview the author, 14 May 2012.

18. Ibid.

19. Bill Brewster and Frank Broughton, *Last Night a DJ Saved My Life: The History of the Disc Jockey* (2nd ed., Headline, 2006), p. 98.

20. Stuart Maconie, *Cider with Roadies* (Ebury Press, 2005), p. 65.

21. Chris Hunt, 'For Dancers Only: The Story of Wigan Casino', *Mojo Collections*, Spring 2002.

22. Brewster and Broughton, *Last Night a DJ Saved My Life*, p. 94.

23. Paolo Hewitt, *The Sharper Word*, p. 144.

24. Brewster and Broughton, *Last Night A DJ Saved My Life*, p. 94.

25. Jazzie B, interviewed for *Soul Britannia*, Episode 3, 'Keep On Movin', BBC Four, tx: 4 August 2007.

26. Tim Ashibende, cited in Vron Ware and Les Back, *Out of Whiteness: Color, Politics and Culture* (University of Chicago Press, 2002), p. 104.

27. Brewster and Broughton, *Last Night a DJ Saved My Life*, p. 97.

28. Nowell, *Too Darn Soulful*, p. 157.

29. Dominic Sandbrook, *Seasons in the Sun: The Battle for Britain, 1974–1979* (Allen Lane, 2012), p. 24.

30. Brewster and Broughton, *Last Night a DJ Saved My Life*, p. 87.

31. Rawlings, *Mod*, pp. 120–2.

32. Brewster and Broughton, *Last Night a DJ Saved My Life*, p. 98.

33. Nowell, *Too Darn Soulful*, p. 6.

34. Robert Elms, *The Way We Wore: A Life in Threads* (Picador, 2006), pp. 125–6.

35. Ibid., p. 125.

36. Brewster and Broughton, *Last Night a DJ Saved My Life*, p. 103.

37. Ibid., p. 92.

38. Maconie, *Cider with Roadies*, p. 78.

39. Hugo Wilcken, *Low* (Continuum, 2005), p. 3.

40. Mark Fisher, 'K-Punk, or the GlamPunk ArtPop Discontinuum' (2004), http://k-punk.abstractdynamics.org/archives/004115.html, accessed 1 April 2012.

41. Mick Rock, *Glam! An Eyewitness Account* (Omnibus Press, 2005), p. 50.

42. David Bowie, Foreword to Rock, *Glam!*.

43. Cited in Barney Hoskins, *Glam! Bowie, Bolan and the Glitter Rock Revolution* (Faber, 1998), p. 21.

44. The Kinks and the Mannish Boys were supporting Gerry and the Pacemakers through the north of England.

45. Michael Wale, 'David Bowie: Rock and Theatre', *The Times*, 24 January 1973.

46. Ibid.

47. Rock, *Glam!*, p. 57.

48. Cited in Paolo Hewitt and Terry Rawlings, *My Favourite Shirt: A History of Ben Sherman Style* (Ben Sherman Group Ltd., 2004), p. 40.

49. Peter Doggett, *The Man Who Sold the World: David Bowie and the 1970s* (Bodley Head, 2011) pp. 35–6.

50. Kemp, *I Know This Much*, pp. 53–4.

51. David Buckley, *Strange Fascination: David Bowie – The Definitive Story* (2nd ed., Virgin Books, 2005), p. 12.

52. Ibid, p. 40.

53. Rock, *Glam!*, p. 15.

54. Callum G. Brown, *Religion and Society in Twentieth-Century Britain* (Longman, 2006), p. 244.

55. Penny Summerfield, 'Women in Britain since 1945: Companionate Marriage and the Double Burden', in James Obelkevich and Peter Caterall (eds) *Understanding Post-War British Society* (Routledge, 1994), p. 67.

56. Angela McRobbie, *Feminism and Youth Culture* (2nd ed., Macmillan, 2000), pp. 20–1.

57. The number of women in work rose from 31 per cent of the workforce in 1951 to 45 per cent in 1987, mainly due to married women getting jobs – a key factor in the rising divorce rate, as women gained the economic independence to afford a divorce. However, most of those jobs were low grade, especially if you were black or Asian. For

example, in 1980, women made up 70 per cent of office staff – and 99 per cent of typists and secretaries – but only 14 per cent were office managers. See Summerfield, 'Women in Britain since 1945', pp. 62, 65.

58. Michael Watts, 'Oh You Pretty Thing', *Melody Maker*, 22 January 1972; reprinted in Hanif Kureishi and Jon Savage (eds), *The Faber Book of Pop* (Faber, 1995), p. 393.

59. Cited in Alwyn W. Turner, *Crisis? What Crisis? Britain in the 1970s* (Aurum, 2008), p. 91.

60. Cecil King, *The Cecil King Diary, 1970–74* (Jonathan Cape, 1975), p. 332.

61. Wilcken, *Low*, p. 14.

62. Robert J. Wybrow, *Britain Speaks Out, 1937–1987* (Palgrave, 1989), p. 110.

63. NA/FCO13/518, Fanfare for Europe Press Release, 24 July 1972.

64. Anthony Gishford and Victor Caudery (eds), *Fanfare for Europe: Official Programme Book* (1973), p. 143.

65. Stanley Reynolds, 'Orwell Did Better', *The Times*, 24 March 1975. Despite the current dominance of Eastern European countries and Britain's poor showing since the turn of the century, the UK remains top of the Eurovision league table.

66. Peter York, 'The German Connection', *Harpers & Queen*, December 1977; reprinted in York, *Style Wars* (Sidgwick & Jackson, 1980), pp. 172–3.

67. *NME*, 13 January 1973.

68. Cited in Turner, *Crisis? What Crisis?*, p. 3.

69. Napier-Bell, *Black Vinyl White Powder*, p. 168.

70. Ibid., p. 161.

71. Watts, 'Oh You Pretty Thing', p. 394.

72. Eric Hopkins, *The Rise and Decline of the English Working Classes 1918–1990: A Social History* (Weidenfeld & Nicolson, 1991), p. 254.

73. Watts, 'Oh You Pretty Thing', p. 394.

74. Rock, *Glam!*, p. 27.

75. Jon Savage, 'David Bowie: The Gender Bender', *The Face*, November 1980; reprinted in Jon Savage, *Time Travel – From the Sex Pistols to Nirvana: Pop, Media and Sexuality, 1977–96* (Vintage, 1997), pp. 113–14.

76. Tom Robinson, cited in Buckley, *Strange Fascination*, p. 106.

77. Hoskins, *Glam!*, p. 61.

78. Napier-Bell, *Black Vinyl White Powder*, p. 159.

79. Dick Hebdige, *Subculture: The Meaning of Style* (Routledge, 1979), pp. 61–2.

80. Bowie, Foreword to Rock, *Glam!*

81. Cited in Nick Stevenson, *David Bowie: Fame, Sound and Vision* (Polity, 2006), pp. 170–1.

82. Hopkins, *The Rise and Decline of the English Working Classes*, p. 255.

83. Hoskins, *Glam!*, p. 64.
84. Rock, *Glam!*, p. 24.
85. Stevenson, *David Bowie*, pp. 148– 9.
86. Rock, *Glam!*, p. 39.
87. Hoskins, *Glam!*, pp. 12–13.
88. David Bowie, Foreword to Rock, *Glam!*
89. Buckley, *The Thrill of It All: The Story of Bryan Ferry & Roxy Music* (Andre Deutsch, 2004), p. 172.
90. Ibid., p. 174.
91. Ibid., p. 175.
92. Ibid.
93. Ted Polhemus, *Street Style from Sidewalk to Catwalk* (Thames and Hudson, 1994), p. 75.
94. Simon Puxley, liner notes, *Roxy Music* (Virgin EG Records Ltd, 1972).
95. Alwyn W. Turner, *BIBA: The Biba Experience* (Antique Collectors' Club, 2004), pp. 14, 16.
96. Tony Benn, cited in ibid., pp. 8–9.
97. Ibid., p. 8.
98. Barbara Hulanicki, 'Biba', in Christopher Breward and Ghislaine Wood (eds), *British Design from 1948: Innovation in the Modern Age* (V&A Publishing, 2012), p. 222.
99. Barbara Hulanicki, *From A to BIBA* (V&A Publishing, 2012), p. 97.
100. Kate McIntryre, 'The Most "In" Shops for Gear', in Elain Harwood and Alan Powers (eds) *The Sixties: Life, Style, Architecture – Journal of the Twentieth Century Society*, No. 6, 2002, 40.
101. Cited in Turner, *BIBA*, p. 48.
102. Cited in ibid.
103. Cited in ibid. p. 49.
104. Cited in ibid., p. 47.
105. David Bowie, Foreword to Rock, *Glam!*
106. Kemp, *I Know This Much*, p. 26.

6 A Pack of Weasels Squeaking for Blood

1. George Melly, *Revolt into Style: The Pop Arts in Britain* (Allen Lane, 1970), p. 152.
2. Cited in Dick Hebdige, 'This Is England! And They Don't Live Here!', in Nick Knight, *Skinhead* (Omnibus, 1982), p. 31.
3. Cited in Peter Everett, *You'll Never Be 16 Again: An Illustrated History of the British Teenager* (BBC, 1986), p. 104.

4. Susie Daniel and Pete McGuire (eds), *The Paint House: Words from an East End Gang* (Penguin, 1972), p. 72.

5. *The Times*, 3 October 1972.

6. The term was first used by the sociologist Jock Young in 1971 in a collection of essays, *Images of Deviancy*, edited by Stanley Cohen. It was popularised by Cohen's classic study of the Mods and rocker battles, *Folk Devils and Moral Panics* (1972). Both were heavily influenced by Marshall MacLuhan's *Understanding Media* (1964).

7. Cited in Stanley Cohen, *Folk Devils and Moral Panics: The Creation of the Mods and Rockers* (3rd ed., Routledge, 2002), p. 37.

8. Cited in ibid., p. 38.

9. BBC TV, 'Mods & Rockers', *Panorama*, tx: 6 April 1964. These Mods were interviewed a week after the Easter disturbances at Clacton.

10. 'Montagues and Capulets at Margate', leader article, *Guardian*, 19 May 1964.

11. Paul Barker with Dr Alan Little, 'The Bank Holiday Offenders', *Sunday Mirror*, 2 August 1964.

12. Ibid. The survey, commissioned by *New Society* magazine, noted that 'the boys themselves did not remark on any distinction between them in terms of class.'

13. Cohen, *Folk Devils*, p. 89.

14. Cited in ibid., p. 88.

15. Cited in ibid.

16. R. Grayson, 'Mods, Rockers and Juvenile Delinquency in 1964: The Government Response', *Contemporary British History*, Vol. 12, No. 1, Spring 1998, pp. 19–47.

17. Nik Cohn, 'Ready, Steady, Gone', *Observer Magazine*, 27 August 1967.

18. Melly, *Revolt into Style*, p. 152.

19. Cited in Terry Rawlings, *Mod: A Very British Phenomenon* (Omnibus, 2000), p. 74.

20. David Fowler, *Youth Culture in Modern Britain, c.1920–1970* (Palgrave, 2008), p. 139.

21. Nick Jones, 'Who Killed Flower Power?', *Melody Maker*, 28 October 1967.

22. See, for example, Anthony Heath and Clive Payne, *Twentieth-Century Trends in Social Mobility in Britain*, Centre for Research into Elections and Social Trends, Working Paper 70 (Glasgow, 1999), and Peter Saunders, *Social Mobility Myths* (Civitas: Institute for the Study of Civil Society, 2010).

23. Cited in Charles Hambert and Jane Deverson, *Generation X: Today's Generation Talking about Itself* (Tandem, 1964) pp. 9–10.

24. Barker with Little, 'The Bank Holiday Offenders'.

25. *Melody Maker*, April 1964. Paul McCartney was careful to tread a compromising path along the shingle of youth culture. While he disapproved of the Mod/rocker riots he said they were caused more by alcohol than music, concluding, 'Blame the booze not the beat.'

26. Keith Moon, cited in Simon Napier-Bell, *Black Vinyl, White Powder* (Ebury, 2002), p. 102. For a readable, though romanticized, account of a groupie's life in rock's heyday in the 1960s and 70s, see Pamela des Barres, *I'm with the Band: Confessions of a Groupie* (2nd ed., Helter Skelter, 2005).

27. Cited in Paolo Hewitt and John Hellier, *Steve Marriott: All Too Beautiful* (Helter Skelter, 2004), p. 164.

28. Ibid., p. 165.

29. Cited in Rawlings, *Mod*, p. 74.

30. Cited in ibid., p. 77.

31. NA/ED124/257, Memo on juvenile delinquency by the Association of Headmistresses to the Minister for Education, 1 February 1965.

32. Dick Hebdige, *Hiding in the Light: On Images and Things* (Routledge, 1988), p. 19; cited in Bill Osgerby, *Youth Media* (Routledge, 2004), p. 61.

33. Her Majesty Queen Elizabeth II, *The Queen's Christmas Speeches 1952–2010* (Kindle edition) pp. 279–82.

34. Eric Hopkins, *The Rise and Decline of the English Working Classes 1918–1990: A Social History* (Weidenfeld & Nicolson, 1991), p.123. The American share of manufactured exports also fell, from 27.3 to 17.7 per cent between 1950 and 1970, though it retained a healthy comparative share.

35. James Banks, Richard Blundell, Antoine Bozio and Carl Emmerson 'Releasing Jobs for the Young? Early Retirement and Youth Unemployment in the United Kingdom', Institute for Fiscal Studies, Working Paper W10/02 (2008), 11.

36. Chris Difford, cited in Paolo Hewitt and Terry Rawlings, *My Favourite Shirt: A History of Ben Sherman Style* (Ben Sherman Group Ltd., 2004), p. 131.

37. Ibid., p.13. Sugarman died in 1987.

38. 'Cult Violence', leader article, *The Times*, 20 April 1977.

39. Cited in Everett, *You'll Never Be 16 Again*, p. 104.

40. 'No Love From Johnny', *Daily Mirror*, 3rd September 1969.

41. *Oz*, June 1969.

42. Pete Fowler, '1972: The Emergence of the Skinheads', in Hanif Kureishi and Jon Savage (eds),*The Faber Book of Pop* (Faber, 1995), p. 379.

43. *Black Dwarf*, August 1969.

44. Hopkins, *The Rise and Decline of the English Working Classes*, pp. 156–7.

45. Everett, *You'll Never Be 16 Again*, p. 104.

46. Cited in ibid., p. 106.

47. *Black Dwarf*, August 1969.
48. *Sunday Times*, 17 September 1969.
49. *Two-Tone Britain*, Channel 4, tx: 29 November 2004.
50. Everett, *You'll Never Be 16 Again*, p. 107.
51. Don Letts, liner notes to *Young, Gifted and Black: 50 Classic Reggae Hits* (Trojan Records, 2002).
52. Cited in Paolo Hewitt, *The Soul Stylists: Six Decades of Modernism – from Mods to Casuals* (Edinburgh, Mainstream, 2000) pp. 100–1.
53. Cited in John Clarke, 'The Skinheads and the Magical Recovery of Community', in Stuart Hall and Tony Jefferson (eds) *Resistance through Rituals: Youth Subcultures in Postwar Britain* (Hutchinson, 1976) p. 101.
54. Cited in Daniel and McGuire, *The Paint House*, pp. 73-4.
55. Cited in ibid., p. 71.
56. Stephen Jessel, 'London Skinheads' Views, Opinions and Prejudices', *The Times*, 3 October 1972.
57. Cited Everett, *You'll Never Be 16 Again*, p. 109.
58. Cited in ibid., p. 106. This skinhead was a college-educated electrician; out of a sample of 500 convictions, he was one of the 10 per cent of skilled workers who were interviewed for a government report on football hooliganism in 1968.
59. Rob Young, *Electric Eden: Unearthing Britain's Visionary Music* (Faber, 2011), pp. 40–1; 139.
60. Cited in ibid., p. 14.
61. Gary Kemp, *I Know This Much: From Soho to Spandau* (4th Estate, 2009), p. 68.
62. Cited in Hewitt, *Soul Stylists*, p. 114.
63. Kubrick wanted to use music from Pink Floyd's 1970 album *Atom Heart Mother* but Roger Waters refused.
64. Cited in Ali Catterall and Simon Wells, *Your Face Here: British Cult Movies since the Sixties* (4th Estate, 2002), p. 128.
65. Cited in ibid., p. 130.
66. Richard Allen, *Top-Gear Skin* (1974), quoted in Stewart Home, 'Gender, Sexuality and Control: Richard Allen and Other New English Library Youthsploitation Novels of the 1970s', *Smile 11* (London, 1989).
67. Ibid.
68. *Black Dwarf*, June 1969.
69. Interviewed in *Almost Grown*, Episode 4, 'Do What You Like', Granada TV, 1992.
70. Cited in Everett, *You'll Never Be 16 Again*, p. 110.
71. See Angela McRobbie and Jenny Garber, 'Girls and Subcultures', in Hall and Jefferson (eds), *Resistance through Rituals*, p. 215.

72. Interviewed in *Almost Grown*, Episode 4, 'Do What You Like', Granada TV, 1992.

73. Cited in Murray Healy, 'Real Men, Phallicism and Fascism', in Ken Gelder (ed.), *The Subcultures Reader* (2nd ed., Routledge, 2005), p. 380.

74. Cited in Ted Polhemus, Introduction to Gavin Watson, *Skins* (2nd ed., Independent Music Press, 2008), p. 11.

75. Cited in Hebdige, 'This Is England!', p. 32.

76. Healy, 'Real Men, Phallicism and Fascism', p. 368.

77. Cited in Everett, *You'll Never Be 16 Again*, p. 107.

78. Fowler, '1972', p. 379.

79. *Two-Tone Britain*.

80. Rupa Huq, 'Asian Kool? Bhangra and Beyond', in S. Sharma and J. Hutnyk (eds) *Dis-orienting Rythms: The Politics of the New Asian Dance Music* (Zed Books, 1996), p. 63. For an excellent personal insight into how British youth culture still offered a pathway into being British for 'first generation' Asians, see Hanif Kureishi's account of being a Beatles fan, 'Eight Arms to Hold You', in Kureishi, *Dreaming and Scheming: Reflections on Writing and Politics* (Faber, 2002), pp. 105–120.

81. Rehan Hyder, *Brimful of Asia: Negotiating Ethnicity on the UK Music Scene* (Ashgate, 2004), pp. 57–8.

82. Cited in ibid., pp. 59–60.

83. Dick Hebdige, 'Reggae, Rastas and Rudies', in Hall and Jefferson (eds), *Resistance through Rituals*, p. 150.

84. Ibid., p. 152.

85. Cited in John Robb, *Punk Rock: An Oral History* (Ebury Press, 2006), p. 47.

86. Cited in Healy, 'Real Men, Phallicism and Fascism', p. 369.

87. Cited in ibid., p. 376.

88. Cited in Racial Volunteer Force, *Diamond in the Dust: The Ian Stuart Biography* (2004), retrieved at http://www.skrewdriver.net/diamond.html.

89. Polhemus, Introduction to Watson, *Skins*, p. 10.

90. Ibid., pp. 10–12.

91. Cited in Catterall and Wells, *Your Face Here*, p. 130. Drummer Paul Cook boasted of having read just two books in his life: *The Profession of Violence*, a biography of cockney gangsters the Kray twins by John Pearson (a skinhead favourite), and *A Clockwork Orange*.

7 Tears of Rage Roll Down Your Face

1. Pete Townshend, cited in Greil Marcus, *Lipstick Traces: A Secret History of the Twentieth Century* (Harvard University Press, 1990), pp. 1–2.

2.   Billy Bragg, *The Progressive Patriot: A Search for Belonging* (Bantam, 2006), p. 186.

3.   Ibid., p. 185.

4.   Ibid., p. 187.

5.   Billy Bragg, interview with the author, 20 April 2009.

6.   Greil Marcus, *Lipstick Traces: A Secret History of the Twentieth Century* (Harvard University Press, 1990), p. 2.

7.   Greil Marcus, interview with the author, 18 January 2012.

8.   Julien Temple (dir.), *The Filth and the Fury: A Sex Pistols Film* (Film Four, 2000).

9.   Charles Shaar Murray, interview with the author, 21 March 2012.

10. Dave Laing, *One Chord Wonders: Power and Meaning in Punk Rock* (Open University Press, 1985), pp. 121–2.

11. Cited in John Reed, *Paul Weller: My Ever Changing Moods* (Omnibus, 2005), 49.

12. Cited in Dominic Sandbrook, *Seasons in the Sun: The Battle for Britain, 1974–1979* (Allen Lane, 2012), p. 540.

13. Brian Harrison, *Finding a Role: The United Kingdom, 1970–1990* (Oxford, 2010), p. 436.

14. Sandbrook, *Seasons in the Sun*, p. 553.

15. Temple, *The Filth and the Fury*.

16. *Daily Mirror*, 22 June 1977.

17. Cited in Kevin Davey, 'Vivienne Westwood: The Shadow Monarch', in Davey, *English Imaginaries: Six Studies in Anglo-British Modernity* (Lawrence & Wishart, 1999), p. 115.

18. Sandbrook, *Seasons in the Sun*, p. 552.

19. Robert Elms, interview with the author, 30 July 2010.

20. Christopher Breward, *Fashioning London: Clothing and the Modern Metropolis* (Berg, 2004), pp. 177, 184.

21. Reed, *Paul Weller*, p. 47.

22. Jon Savage, *England's Dreaming: Anarchy, Sex Pistols, Punk Rock and Beyond* (Faber, 1992).

23. Cited in Paul Gorman, *The Look: Adventures in Rock and Pop Fashion* (Adelita 2006), p. 162.

24. Cited in John Robb, *Punk: An Oral History* (Ebury, 2006) p. 9. The interviews in Robb's collection testify to the influence of both Mod and glam rock on many other punks.

25. John Lydon, *No Irish, No Blacks, No Dogs* (Hodder, 1993), pp. 217–18.

26. Angela McRobbie, *Feminism and Youth Culture* (2nd ed., Macmillan, 2000), pp. 151–2.

27. Viv Albertine, *NME*, June 1977.

28. The Shanne Bradley Interview, *Punk 77* (August 2001), http://www.punk77.co.uk/groups/nippleerectorsshanneinterview.htm, accessed 19 June 2012.

29. McRobbie, *Feminism and Youth Culture*, p. 152.

30. Cited in Simon Reynolds and Joy Press, *The Sex Revolts: Gender, Rebellion and Rock 'n' Roll* (Serpent's Tail, 1995), p. 34.

31. Ibid., p. 33.

32. Mick Rock, *Glam! An Eyewitness Account* (Omnibus Press, 2005), p. 124.

33. Simon Reynolds, *Rip It Up and Start Again: Postpunk 1978–84* (Faber, 2006), p. 5.

34. Nick Kent, *Apathy for the Devil: A 1970s Memoir* (Faber, 2010), p. 227.

35. Nick Hornby, *31 Songs* (Penguin, 2003), p. 84.

36. Sandbrook, *Seasons in the Sun*, p. 553.

37. Legs McNeil, cited in Savage, *England's Dreaming*, p. 460.

38. Charles Shaar Murray, 'I Fought the Biz and the Biz Won: Punk Ten Years On', in Murray, *Shots from the Hip* (Penguin, 1991), p. 399.

39. Cited in Paolo Hewitt, *Paul Weller – The Changing Man: The Music, Life and Times of a British Songwriting Legend* (Bantam Press, 2007), p. 11.

40. The cover of *London Calling* – one of ten classic album covers reproduced on postage stamps by the Royal Mail in 2010 – features a grainy photograph of Paul Simenon smashing his bass guitar on stage in New York in 1979, in a borrowing of the Who's destructive stage act, which the Pistols had also emulated. Ray Lowry's simple green and pink design that frames the photo also mimicked the 1956 cover of Elvis Presley's eponymous album. Lowry was one of several graphic designers whose work spanned the hippie and post-punk eras, contributing to both *Oz* magazine and *The Face*.

41. Temple, *The Filth and the Fury*.

42. Ibid.

43. John Osborne, 'A Letter to My Fellow Countrymen', *Tribune*, 18 August 1961; reprinted in Osborne, *Damn You England: Collected Prose* (Faber, 1994), p. 193.

44. Ibid.

45. Temple, *The Filth and the Fury*. Rotten re-assumed his birth name after leaving the Pistols.

46. Julie Burchill, 'McLaren's Children', *20/20 Magazine*, 1990; reprinted in Burchill, *Sex and Sensibility* (Grafton, 1992), pp. 95–6.

47. Andrew Adonis and Stephen Pollard, *A Class Act: The Myth of Britain's Classless Society* (Hamish Hamilton, 1997), pp. 3–4.

48. Simon Reynolds, *Rip It Up and Start Again*, p. 288. For an amusing account of a Weller obsessive, and of fandom in general, see David Lines, *The Modfather: My Life with Paul Weller* (Arrow, 2007).

49. Cited in Reed, *Paul Weller*, p. 35.
50. Cited in ibid., p. 75. Matlock in turn invited Weller to join his new band, the Rich Kids, as lead singer and fellow songwriter.
51. Although *Abigail's Party* is Mike Leigh's most famous and popular work, Tom Paulin and Hari Kunzru are among those who have criticised it for being a reactionary, snobbish view of social aspiration. See http://news.bbc.co.uk/1/hi/programmes/newsnight/review/2151325.stm
52. Michael Heatley, *Paul Weller in His Own Words* (Omnibus Press, 1996), pp. 14–5.
53. Cited in Reed, *Paul Weller*, p. 91. In 'Standards', from the album *This Is the Modern World* (1977), Weller warned his young fans of the dangers of too much state power (which he attributed to the Labour Government of the day) with a reference to *1984*.
54. Steve Clarke, 'All Change and Back to 1964', *NME*. 7 May 1977.
55. Cited in Reed, *Paul Weller*, p. 65.
56. Cited in ibid., p. 67.
57. Heatley, *Paul Weller in His Own Words*, p. 57.
58. D. J. Taylor, 'That's Entertainment', in John Aizlewood (ed.), *Love Is the Drug: Living as a Pop Fan* (Penguin, 1994), pp. 264–5.
59. Ibid., p. 266.
60. Ibid., p. 265.
61. Charles Shaar Murray, *NME*, 28 October 1978.
62. Cited in Paolo Hewitt, *The Jam: A Beat Concerto* (2nd ed., Boxtree, 1996), p. 68.
63. Zadie Smith, *White Teeth* (Penguin, 2001), pp. 27–8.
64. Reed, *Paul Weller*, p. 54.
65. Cited in Terry Rawlings, *Mod: A Very British Phenomenon* (Omnibus, 2000), pp. 166–7.
66. Cited in Simon Reynolds, *Retromania: Pop Culture's Addiction to Its Own Past* (Faber, 2011), p. 226.
67. Adrian Thrills, 'Quads? Quods?', *NME*, 14 April 1979.
68. 'The Mod Squad', *Daily Mirror*, 24 August 1979.
69. Cited in Mick Wall, *John Peel* (Orion, 2005), p. 97.
70. 'The Mod Squad'.
71. Cited in Enamel Verguren, *This Is a Modern Life: The 1980s London Mod Scene* (Helter Skelter, 2004), p. 131.
72. Christine Feldman, 'We Are the Mods': A Transnational History of a Youth Subculture* (Peter Lang), p. 43.
73. Ibid., pp. 43–4.
74. Judith Judd, 'Beware the Mods', *Observer*, 13 April 1980.
75. 'The Mod Squad'.

76. Cited in Verguren, *This Is a Modern Life*, p. 117.
77. Cited in ibid., p. 145.
78. Cited in ibid., p. 146.
79. Peter York, 'Mods: The Second Coming', *Harpers & Queen*, September 1979.
80. Reynolds, *Retromania*, p. 201.
81. Feldman, *'We Are the Mods'*, p. 53.
82. Billy Bragg, interview with the author, 20 April 2009.
83. Cited in Dave Thompson, *Wheels out of Gear: 2 Tone, the Specials and a World in Flame* (Helter Skelter, 2004), p. 78.
84. *Quadrophenia* was conceived in 1972 when Townshend recalled happy memories of meeting Mods in Brighton, where the Who played during the disturbances of 1964. 'My idea was to take the band back to our roots. We'd been different then,' he later wrote, 'we'd been subsumed in the Mod gang and we needed to do that again' (Pete Townshend, *Who I Am*, HarperCollins, 2012, p. 236). *Quadrophenia* was a commercial success in Britain and America, reaching No. 2 in the album charts of both countries (despite the fact that the Mod story was lost on many Americans). However, the 1973 *Quadrophenia* tour was hampered by technical problems and the erratic behaviour of Keith Moon, and critical reaction to both the album and tour were patchy. Townshend concluded that as a result it 'had failed to replace *Tommy* as the back-bone of our live show' (ibid., p. 258). Partly as a result of his engage-ment with the musical New Wave, Townshend began to adapt it for cinema in 1978. For an excellent account of the making and reception of the *Quadrophenia* album in 1973, see Dave Marsh, *Before I Get Old: The Story of the Who* (Plexus, pp. 419–33), in which he argues that Jimmy was a metaphor for 'the problems of transition between the sixties and the seventies' (p. 422).
85. *Quadrophenia*, dir. Franc Roddam, 1979; DVD: Universal Pictures UK, 1999.
86. Robert Elms, interview with the author, 30 July 2010.
87. Eddie Piller, interview with the author, 14 May 2012.
88. Humphrey Ocean, interview with the author, 31 August 2011.
89. Stephen Jones, interview with the author, 23 May 2012.
90. For an excellent critique of heavy metal, see Andy Bennett, *Cultures of Popular Music* (Open University Press, 2001), pp. 42–57.
91. K. J. Donnelly, *Pop Music in British Cinema* (BFI, 2001), p. 59.
92. Cited in Ali Catterall and Simon Wells, *Your Face Here: British Cult Movies since the Sixties* (4th Estate, 2002), pp. 170, 184, 182.
93. Cited in ibid., p. 179.

94. Cited in ibid.

95. Julie Burchill and Daniel Raven, *Made in Brighton: From the Grand to the Gutter – Modern Britain as Seen from beside the Sea* (Virgin, 2008), p. 116.

96. NA/MEPO/31/43, Mrs Stuttard to Westminster Council, 4 August 1969; Mrs N. Bliss to Westminster Council, 18 July 1978. The Met's description of the hippies was contained in a standard reply (such was the volume of complaint) dated 19 August 1969. The *Daily Express* publicized the issue (and probably attracted more teenagers to the area) in an article called 'Escape to the Far Out World of Eros Island', 11 August 1969.

97. Sandbrook, *Seasons in the Sun*, p. 558.

98. Mark E. Smith with Austin Collings, *Renegade: The Lives and Tales of Mark E. Smith* (Penguin, 2009), pp. 41–2.

99. Laurie Taylor, 'The Skin-deep Revolution', *The Times*, 31 July 1984.

100. Marcus, *Lipstick Traces*, p. 77.

101. Heatley, *Paul Weller in His Own Words*, p. 18.

102. Jon Savage, *Teenage: The Creation of Youth* (Chatto & Windus, 2007), p. xiv.

103. For a notable contemporary exception to this, see Richard Dyer, 'In Defence of Disco', 1979; reprinted in Jon Savage and Hanif Kureishi (eds), *The Faber Book of Pop* (Faber, 1995), pp. 518–27.

104. Don Letts, interview with the author, 21 March 2012.

105. Jon Savage, 'Letter from London: Britpop', in Artforum, 1995; reprinted in *Time Travel – From the Sex Pistols to Nirvana: Pop, Media and Sexuality, 1977–96* (Vintage, 1997), p. 413.

8 Substance Wrapped in Chequerboard

1. Eric Clapton, cited in John Street, *Rebel Rock: The Politics of Popular Music* (Blackwell, 1986), pp. 74–5.

2. Horace Panter, *Ska'd for Life: A Personal Journey with The Specials* (Pan, 2008), p. xvi.

3. Cited in Special Q Edition, *The Ska Explosion* (Emap, 2004), p. 24.

4. Interview with Margaret Thatcher, *Granada World in Action*, ITV, 30 January 1978.

5. Don Letts, *Culture Clash: Dread Meets Punk Rockers* (SAF Publishing, 2008), p. 78.

6. Brinsley Forde, interviewed for *Reggae Britannia*, BBC4, tx: 11 February 2011.

7. Cited in Dave Thompson, *Wheels out of Gear: 2 Tone, the Specials and a*

World in Flames (Helter Skelter, 2004), p. 19. For a fan's view of the movement, see George Marshall, *The Twin Tone Story* (ST Publishing, 2011).

8. Letts, *Culture Clash*, p. 95. Marley wasn't responsible for the song's creation, admitting in a 1978 interview with Charles Shaar Murray that Lee 'Scratch' Perry, his producer, had written the lyrics.

9. Timothy White, *Catch a Fire: The Life of Bob Marley* (2nd ed., Omnibus, 2006), p. 294.

10. Stuart Copland, interviewed for *Reggae Britannia*.

11. Letts, *Culture Clash*, p. 98.

12. Cited in Thompson, *Wheels out of Gear*, pp. 20–1.

13. Julien Temple (dir.) *The Future Is Unwritten: Joe Strummer* (Parallel Films, 2006).

14. Cited in Sarfraz Mansoor, 'The Year Rock Found the Power to Unite', *Guardian*, 20 April 2008.

15. Melvin Bragg *The South Bank Show: The Final Cut* (Hodder and Stoughton, 2010), p. 133.

16. Cited in Thompson, *Wheels out of Gear*, p. 35.

17. Cited in Mansoor, 'The Year Rock Found the Power to Unite'.

18. Cited in ibid.

19. Cited in Alex Petridis, 'Ska for the Madding Crowd', *Guardian*, 8 March 2002. 'Too Much Too Young', one of The Specials' No. 1 singles, was written by Dammers when he was a teenager.

20. Cited in ibid.

21. Winston James and Clive Harris, *Inside Babylon: The Caribbean Diaspora in Britain* (Verso, 1993), p. 46.

22. National Archives, Cabinet Papers, 'Response to the Report on Police/Immigrant Relations by the Select Committee on Race Relations and Immigration', Draft White Paper. CP (73) 92, 20 September 1973.

23. NA/CK2/181, Baron Hunt, *Seen But Not Served* (Community Relations Council Report, 1976). Hunt's comments were reported in the *Sunday Times*, 3 April 1977.

24. Gurinder Chadha, interviewed for *Two Tone Britain*, Channel Four, tx: 29 November 2004.

25. Special Q Edition, *The Ska Explosion*, p. 142.

26. Panter, *Ska'd for Life*, p. 103.

27. Suggs, interviewed for *Two Tone Britain*.

28. Cited in Petridis, 'Ska for the Madding Crowd'.

29. Panter, *Ska'd for Life*, p. xvi.

30. Cited for Thompson, *Wheels out of Gear*, pp. 91–2.

31. Panter, *Ska'd for Life*, p. xvi.

32. Ibid., p. 106.
33. Pauline Black, interviewed for *Two Tone Britain*.
34. Mark Lamarr, 'The Band', retrieved from The Specials Official Website, http://www.thespecials.com.
35. Antony Taylor, *Down with the Crown: British Anti-monarchism and Debates about Royalty since 1790* (Reaktion, 1999), p. 233.
36. Paul Gilroy, interviewed for *Two Tone Britain*. One measure of the movement's legacy is that race was discussed more openly in youth media than before the Two Tone era; the use of black and Asian models, initiated by Mary Quant, also became more common. See, for example, *i-D*, 'Special Anti-Racist Issue', No. 124, January 1994. The feature included interviews with Norman Jay, Paul Weller, Apache Indian and Veronica Webb, the first black British model to win a major cosmetics contract.
37. Yasmin Alibhai-Brown, *Mixed Feelings: The Complex Lives of Mixed Race Britons* (Women's Press, 2001), pp. 75–7.
38. Angela McRobbie, *In the Culture Society: Art, Fashion and Popular Music* (Routledge, 1999), p. 141.
39. Cited in Petridis, 'Ska for the Madding Crowd'.
40. Panter, *Ska'd for Life*, p. 126.
41. Ibid., p. 130.
42. Neville Staple, *Original Rude Boy: From Borstal to The Specials* (Aurum, 2009), pp. 169–70.
43. Letts, *Culture Clash*, pp. 47–8.
44. *NME*, 9 February 1980.
45. Panter, *Ska'd for Life*, p. 134.
46. Cited in Thompson, *Wheels out of Gear*, p. 117.
47. Pauline Black, *Black by Design: A 2-Tone Memoir* (Serpent's Tail, 2011), p. 206.
48. Ibid., pp. 218–19.
49. Ibid., p. 218. The closest encounter that Two Tone had with an American version of John Peel was Rodney Bingenheimer, a DJ at Los Angeles' KROQ station who vigorously but to no avail championed the movement.
50. Ibid., p. 219.
51. Ibid., p. 220.
52. Terry Rawlings, *Mod: A Very British Phenomenon* (Omnibus, 2000), p. 203.
53. Paul Weller, foreword to Colin MacInnes, *England, Half English* (Hogarth Press, 1986). p 104.
54. Cited in John Reed, *Paul Weller: My Ever Changing Moods* (Omnibus, 2005), p. 151.

55. Owen Hatherley, *Militant Modernism* (Winchester Books, 2008), pp. 36, 124.

56. Owen Hatherley, interview with the author, 14 May 2012.

57. Eric Hopkins, *The Rise and Decline of the English Working Classes, 1918– 1990: A Social History* (Weidenfeld & Nicolson, 1991), p. 142.

58. Paul Weller and John Wilson, *Suburban 100: Selected Lyrics* (Arrow, 2007), commentary on 'The Planner's Dream Goes Wrong', p. 43.

59. Paul Weller, 'The Other Side of Futurism', *The Face*, No. 14, June 1981.

60. Basil Spence, 'Our Debt to Le Corbusier', *Sunday Telegraph*, 29 August 1965; reprinted in Irena Murray and Julian Osley (eds), *Le Corbusier and Britain: An Anthology* (Routledge, 2009), p. 217.

61. Christopher Booker, 'Corbusier: Architect of Disaster for the Millions Who Are Condemned to Live in a Concrete Jungle', *Daily Mail*, 16 March 1987; reprinted in Murray and Osley (eds), *Le Corbusier and Britain*, p. 297.

62. Trellick Tower appears as an emblem of modernity in a number of music videos, including those by Blur, the Verve and Hard-Fi. There are a few measured historical accounts of modernist architecture that address the conservative clichés on this subject: see, for example, Elain Harwood, 'White Light/White Heat: Rebuilding England's Provincial Towns and Cities in the Sixties', in Harwood and Alan Powers (eds), *The Sixties: Life, Style, Architecture – Journal of the Twentieth Century Society*, Number 6, 2002, 40, pp. 55–70; and Bronwen Edwards, 'Brave New London: Architecture for a Swinging City', in Christopher Breward, David Gilbert and Jenny Lister (eds), *Swinging Sixties: Fashion in London and Beyond 1955–1970* (V&A Publishing, 2006), pp. 42–8.

63. Evelyn Waugh, review of Le Corbusier's *The City of Tomorrow*, *Observer*, 11 August 1929; reprinted in Murray and Osley (eds), *Le Corbusier and Britain*, p. 74.

64. Terence Conran and Elizabeth Wilhide, *The Ultimate House Book* (Conran Octopus, 2003), p. 11. Liam Gallagher's comment, 'I never wanted a rock 'n' roll house. I just wanted a normal house', was used to compliment Le Corbusier's view that 'Everybody, quite rightly, dreams of sheltering himself in a sure and permanent home of his own.'

65. Breuer's Whitney Museum of American Art, built in New York in 1964, was the most notable of his American projects.

66. Sir Terence Conran, interview with the author, 19 September 2008.

67. Cressida Lindsay, *No Wonderland* (Ballantine, 1967). The cover showed a Mod male tempting a woman into sexual congress.

68. Derek J. Tidball, 'Perspectives in Community Living', *Vox Evangelica* 11

(1979): 65–80. See also Andrew Rigby, *Communes in Britain* (Routledge, 1974).

69. Brian Harrison, *Finding a Role: The United Kingdom 1970–1990* (Oxford, 2010), p. 221.

70. Eric Klinenberg, *Going Solo: The Extraordinary Rise and Surprising Appeal of Living Alone* (Penguin, 2012).

71. Magda Nico for the Council of Europe, *Lifestyles and Living Conditions in the EU*, 1 November 2009, 17, Table 5.

72. The percentage of people aged between 65 and 74 who live alone has remained constant since 1973, at between 25 and 30 per cent, whilst the percentage of people aged 75 and over living alone rose from 40 per cent in 1973 to 50 per cent by 1993. See *Childhood and Family Life: Socio-demographic Changes*, report of research conducted by the Social Issues Research Centre (Oxford 2008), p. 15.

73. Harrison, *Finding a Role*, p. 226.

74. Conran and Wilhide, *The Ultimate House Book*, p. 12. The quote is from Marjorie Garber, *Sex and Real Estate: Why We Love Houses* (Schocken, 2000).

75. C. L. F. Attfield, *Mean Household Weekly Expenditure on Commodity Categories 1973–2003* (2005), p. 57.

76. Billy Bragg, interview with the author, 20 April 2009.

77. Hugh Aldersey-Williams, *British Design* (MOMA, 2010), p. 35.

78. Dominic Sandbrook, *Seasons in the Sun: The Battle for Britain, 1974–1979* (Allen Lane, 2012), p. 16. For a rare interview with Barney Bubbles, see *The Face*, No. 19, November 1981, pp. 32–6. See also Paul Gorman, *Reasons to Be Cheerful: The Life and Work of Barney Bubbles* (Adelita, 2010).

79. Shaun Ryder et al., interviewed for *100 Greatest Albums*, BBC 2, tx: 17 April 2005. His Mondays' sidekick Bez added: 'It's where I got my Rude Boy dance.'

80. Quoted in Jon Savage 'The Smiths: Deliberately', *Sunday Times*, 8 January 1984.

81. Joe Pernice, *Meat Is Murder* (Continuum, 2007), pp. 22, 44.

82. Suede also worked with Mike Joyce, the Smiths' former drummer on early recordings.

83. Noel Gallagher, interviewed in *Uncut* magazine, March 2007.

84. John Robb, *The Stone Roses and the Resurrection of British Pop* (Ebury, 1997), p. 23.

85. Morrissey interviewed for *Spin* magazine, 1991, cited in Mark Simpson, *Saint Morrissey* (SAF Publishing 2004), p. 179.

86. Ibid., p. 181.

87. Harrison, *Finding a Role*, pp. 221–5.

88. Gordon Heald and Robert J. Wybrow. *The Gallup Survey of Britain* (Croom Helm, 1986), p. 234.

89. *NME*, 15 April 1989.

90. *NME*, 18 November 1989.

91. Cited in Glenn Adamson and Jane Pavitt, 'Foreword' to Adamson and Pavitt, *Postmodernism: Style and Subversion, 1970–1990* (V&A Publishing, 2011), p. 14. Jencks dated the 'death of modernism' to 15 March 1972 when the notorious Pruitt-Igoe housing project in St Louis, Missouri, was dynamited.

92. See Jonathan M. Woodham, 'Margaret Thatcher, Postmodernism and the Politcs of Design in Britain', in Adamson and Pavitt, *Postmodernism*, pp. 238–41.

93. Jon Savage, 'The Age of Plunder', *The Face*, No. 33, January 1983.

94. Harry Cocks, 'Modernity and Modernism', in Francesca Carnevali and Julie Marie-Strange, *Twentieth-Century Britain: Economic, Cultural and Social Change* (2nd ed., Longman, 2007), p. 40.

95. See Robb, *The Stone Roses and the Resurrection of British Pop*.

9 There's a Great Big Crack in the Union Jack

1. Cited in John Harris, *The Last Party: Britpop, Blair and the Demise of English Rock* (4th Estate, 2003), p. 129–30. Gallagher's comment was uttered to explain the image on the band's demo cassette: that of a Union Jack being sucked into a vortex which was later used as a back-drop to their TV performances. An excited McGee said that Gallagher reminded him of the young Paul Weller.

2. Cited in ibid., p. 254.

3. Ibid., p. 298. For first-hand accounts of being involved with the hard-core Mod scene during the 1990s, see Enamel Verguren, *I'm Not Like Everybody Else, Volume 2: The 1990s British Mod Scene* (Shaman, 2010).

4. Anthony Heath et al., 'Who Do We Think We Are? The Decline of Traditional Social Identities', in Alison Park et al. (eds), *British Social Attitudes: The 23rd Report* (National Centre for Social Research/Sage, 2007), pp. 1–34.

5. *Sunday Times*, 21 September 1997. This was twice the level of adults who considered themselves English rather than British at the time.

6. Department of National Heritage, press release, 6 November 1996, cited in Harris, *The Last Party*, p. 328.

7. Michael Bracewell, *The Nineties: When Surface Was Depth* (Flamingo, 2003), p. 15.

8. Neil Spencer, 'Britpop's Morning Glory', *Guardian*, 30 June 1996.

9. 'Touched by the Hand of Mod', *Melody Maker*, 11 November 1994.

10. Styker Maguire, 'London Reigns', *Newsweek*, 3 November 1996.

11. David Kamp, 'London Swings Again!', *Vanity Fair*, March 1997.

12. Ibid.

13. The American edition of *Vanity Fair* instead profiled Julia Dreyfus from *Seinfeld*.

14. Andy Beckett, 'The Myth of the Cool', *Guardian*, 5 May 1998.

15. Stuart Maconie, *Select*, April 1993. The term 'Britpop' had previously been used by John Robb in *Sounds* to describe post-Punk bands like the Stone Roses and the La's, but it was Maconie's essay in *Select* that made it stick.

16. Paul Tunkin, interview with the author, 28 April 2012. Blur took the Blow Up DJs on tour with them.

17. The flag-bearers of British indie in the 1980s sold around 150,000 albums each and even the Stone Roses, regarded as the superstars of British indie music, only sold 800,000 worldwide. Compare that to Michael Jackson's *Bad* (1987), which he considered a flop when it sold 30 million worldwide. I owe this point to Stuart Maconie, *Blur: 3862 Days – The Official History* (Virgin, 1999), p. 107.

18. Ibid., p. 72.

19. Cited in Harris, *The Last Party*, pp. xv, 201.

20. Jon Savage, 'Sounds Dirty: The Truth about Nirvana', *Observer*, 15 August 1993; reprinted in Savage, *Time Travel – From the Sex Pistols to Nirvana: Pop, Media and Sexuality 1977-96* (Vintage, 1997), p. 331.

21. Spencer, 'Britpop's Morning Glory'.

22. Cited in Harris, *The Last Party*, p. 1.

23. Liam Gallagher, interviewed for 'Oasis Millions', BBC3, tx: 19 April 2004.

24. Cited in 'The Battle of Britpop', *NME*, 12 August 1995.

25. Cited in Harris, *The Last Party*, p. 299.

26. See Simon Reynolds, 'Old Turf, New Combatants', *New York Times*, 22 October 1995. Reynolds explained the lack of enthusiasm for Britpop as a combination of hip-hop and grunge's popularity and the parochialism of Britpop, especially the British obsession with class that it exhibited.

27. Toby Young, interviewed for John Dower (dir.), *Live Forever: The Rise and Fall of Britpop* (Passion Pictures, 2003).

28. In a very British way, the dress had been created not by a grand designer but by Halliwell's sister, out of a tea towel, when the Spice Girl rejected the black Gucci dress assigned to her. The dress became one of the most valuable items of pop memorabilia when it was sold at Sotheby's in 1998 to the owners of the Hard Rock Café, Las Vegas.

29. Maconie, *Blur*, p. 118.

30. Damon Albarn, interviewed for Dower, *Live Forever*. Albarn unwittingly echoed the comments of Mick Jagger made to the American press in 1965: see p. 107.

31. Brett Anderson, cited in Harris, *The Last Party*, p. 36.

32. Ibid., p. 139.

33. Rupa Huq, 'Paradigm Lost? Youth and Pop', in Jonathan Rutherford, *Young Britain: Politics, Pleasures and Predicaments* (Lawrence & Wishart, 1998), p. 90.

34. Maconie, *Blur*, p. 152.

35. Balfe was an ex-member of 1980s Indie group, the Teardrop Explodes; see ibid., pp. 13–8.

36. *New York Times*, 2 May 1997.

37. Spencer, 'Britpop's Morning Glory'.

38. Cited by Simon Frith, 'And I Guess It Doesn't Matter Any More: European Thoughts on American Music', in Eric Weisbard (ed.) *This Is Pop: In Search of the Elusive* (Harvard University Press, 2004), pp. 15–6.

39. Maconie, *Blur*, p. 180.

40. Billy Bragg, interview with the author, 20 April 2009.

41. Paul Gorman, *The Look: Adventures in Rock and Pop Fashion* (Adelita, 2006), p. 202.

42. Ashley Heath, 'A Mod, Mod World: The Coolest of British Style Cults Comes Round Again', *Guardian*, 20 January 1995.

43. Ozwald Boateng, interviewed for Dower, *Live Forever*.

44. Ozwald Boateng, interviewed for *Why Style Matters*, BBC4, tx: 8 January 2009.

45. Paul Smith, interview with the author, 24 February 2012.

46. Ibid.

47. Alison Goodrum, *The National Fabric: Fashion, Britishness, Globalization* (Berg, 2005), p. 122.

48. The ongoing global influence of British fashion was apparent not only in the success of figureheads like Smith but also in the recruitment of lesser-known Britons by foreign companies. In 2003, 80 per cent of designers at Louis Vuitton were British-trained, 65 per cent at Levi's and 40 per cent at Givenchy; in global labels' sportswear design the figure was 80 per cent. See Caroline Evans, 'British Fashion', in Michael Higgins, Clarissa Smith and John Storey (eds), *The Cambridge Companion to Modern British Culture* (Cambridge, 2010), p. 221.

49. Gilles Peterson, interview with the author, 14 October 2011.

50. Stephen Jones, interview with the author, 23 May 2012.

51. Christine Feldman, *'We are the Mods': A Transnational History of a Youth*

Subculture (Peter Lang, 2009), p. 181. This preference helps to explain why Quant remained one of the most popular brands for women in Japan, with over 200 stores there in 2000 when Mary Quant Ltd. was bought out by a Japanese company.

52. Ibid., p. 183.

53. Ibid., p. 173.

54. Ibid., p. 167.

55. Ibid., p. 183.

56. Brooks Adams, 'Thinking of You: An American's Growing, Imperfect Awareness', in Norman Rosenthal et al., *Sensation: Young British Artists from the Saatchi Collection* (Thames & Hudson, 1997), p. 37.

57. Richard Shone, 'From Freeze to House: 1988–94', in ibid., p. 13.

58. Richard Shone, 'The Blood Must Continue to Flow', in ibid., p. 9.

59. Alex James, *bit of a blur: the autobiography*, (Little Brown, 2007), p. 150.

60. Shone, 'From Freeze to House', p. 15.

61. Ibid., p. 13.

62. Peter Gay, *Modernism: The Lure of Heresy from Baudelaire to Beckett and Beyond* (Vintage, 2009), pp. 486–7.

63. Quoted in Harris, *The Last Party*, p. 191

64. 'Staying Ahead: The Economic Performance of the UK's Creative Industries', Work Foundation Report, 2004, pp. 30, 32.

65. Cited in Jon Wilde, 'Listening to England', *Livewire*, September 1994.

66. British Market Research Bureau Target Group Index for 2000, quoted in Lydia Kan, *Counting the Notes: The Economic Contribution of the UK Music Business* (National Music Council, 2002), p. 49.

67. M. Brennan, and E. Webster, 'The UK Festival Market Report 2010', from the Festival Awards UK conference, London, 18 November 2010. Sociologists have begun to examine the 'greying' of youth culture and are moving away from the obsession with adolescence that still characterizes historians' approach to the subject; see the pioneering work by Paul Hodkinson and Andy Bennett (eds), *Ageing and Youth Cultures: Music, Style and Identity* (Berg, 2012).

68. See Louise Wener, *Just for One Day: Adventures in Britpop* (Ebury, 2011), p. 133.

69. Ibid., p. 191.

70. The Brighton Institute of Modern Music, which was academically accredited by the University of Sussex, was founded in 2002 and later established colleges in Bristol and Dublin. Among its successful alumni were the Kooks.

71. Roy Wilkinson, 'My Dad, the Revolutionary Disciple of Indie Rock', *Guardian*, 15 October 2011.

72. Roy Wilkinson, *Do It for Your Mum* (Rough Trade Books, 2011), pp. 2–8.

73. Wilkinson, 'My Dad, the Revolutionary Disciple of Indie Rock'.

74. Roger Scruton, 'Youth Culture's Lament', *City Journal*, Autumn 1998. Despite this misreading of the Verve's 'The Drugs Don't Work', Scruton's essay contains some real insights into British youth cultures' origins in a romantic view of urban modernity, and their failure to provide the quasi-religious communality that many seek in them. He concluded that 'rave – in which throngs of drug-fuelled young people dance orgiastically to music pumped up as loud as it can go – is the Holy Communion of youth, and it is a communion without decorum, in which the distance between people is not transcended but denied.'

75. Edward Phelps, 'Young Adults and Electoral Turnout in Britain: Towards a Generational Model of Political Participation', SEI Working Paper, No. 92 (2006). The number of those with no party allegiances rose most among young adults between the ages of 18 and 24 in the period 1992–2005, up to 24 per cent, almost four times higher than it was in 1992.

76. *NME*, 14 March 1998.

77. Harris, *The Last Party*, p. 360.

78. Ray Davies, interviewed by Alan Yentob, *Imagine*, BBC1, tx: 17 July 2011.

79. Douglas Coupland, *Generation X: Tales for an Accelerated Culture* (Abacus, 1992) p. 47; italics in the original.

80. Cited in Harris, *The Last Party*, p. 218.

81. Coupland, *Generation X*, p. 26. He defined Boomer Envy as cultural capital coupled with 'envy of material wealth accrued by older members of the baby-boom generation by virtue of fortunate births'.

82. Chart data compiled for the author by Kelsie Baher of Whitman College, USA, and Goldsmiths College, London, in 2012, using the US Billboard Singles Chart and UK Singles Chart (1964–2004).

83. Frith, 'And I Guess It Doesn't Matter Any More', pp. 15–16.

84. British Council of Shopping Centres Report, 2001, p. 8. The rate of growth was slowed by the recession of 2008. See Zoe Wood, 'Why Developers Have Stopped Building Shopping Malls', *Guardian*, 4 May 2012.

85. Jon Savage, 'Letter from London: Britpop', *Artforum*, October 1995; reprinted in Savage, *Time Travel*, pp. 413.

86. Simon Reynolds, 'Reasons to Be Cheerful: The Case against Britpop', *Frieze*, No. 25, Nov–Dec 1995.

87. Cited in Maconie, *Blur*, pp. 148–9. The controversial photo appeared in April 1993 to coincide with the release of the single 'For Tomorrow'.

88. Cited in *NME*, 12 August 1995.

89. Cited in Stuart Maconie, 'The Blanc Generation', *NME*, 23 December 1989.

90. Cliff Jones, 'Looking for a New England', *The Face*, No. 68, May 1994.
91. Andy Bennett, 'Village Greens and Terraced Streets: Britpop and Representations of Britishness', *Young*, Vol. 5, No. 4, December 1997. For more on this debate, see Andy Bennett and John Stratton, *Britpop and the English Music Tradition* (Ashgate, 2010).
92. Steve White, interview with the author 11 May 2012.
93. Eddie Piller, interview with the author, 14 May 2012.
94. Gilles Peterson, interview with the author, 1 October 2011.
95. Ibid.
96. Nicola Jeal, 'It's a Mod, Mod, Mod World', *Observer*, 27 January 1991.
97. BBC Radio 1 website, Gilles Peterson biography, http://www.bbc.co.uk/radio1/gillespeterson/biography.shtml, retrieved April 2012.

10 As English as Fish and Chips

1. Tony Marcus, 'The War Is Over', *Mixmag*, September 1995. Marcus was interviewing the Scottish/Jamaican artist Clifford Price, aka Goldie, on the launch of his debut studio album, *Timeless*, which established drum 'n' bass as an important genre; it entered the UK charts at No. 7 but didn't register in the United States. The context of Marcus's comment was Goldie's description of rave as 'a British movement'. That, concluded Marcus, 'is something the fascists could never accept. It couldn't have existed without a cross-racial and cross-sexual mix of ideas, technology, sounds and chemicals.'
2. Jenny Jarvie and Adam Lusher, 'Ibiza Tries to Shed Image as Island of Sun, Sea and Sex', *Daily Telegraph*, 10 June 2001.
3. *NME*, 23 November 1996.
4. Mark Simpson, 'Here Come the Mirror Men', *Independent*, 15 November 1994.
5. Terry Rawlings, *Mod: A Very British Phenomenon* (Omnibus, 2000), p. 203.
6. Robert Elms, *The Way We Wore: A Life in Threads* (Picador, 2005), pp. 242–3.
7. Gary Aspden, interviewed for *Casuals* (Cass Pennant & Urban Edge Films Ltd).
8. The original company, J. W. Foster, which sold spiked running shoes, had been founded in Bolton in 1895. Foster's grandsons re-launched it as Reebok in 1960, after which it became linked to modern youth culture. Like the Mini Cooper and other British brands in the 1980s, it fell into foreign hands, the company being bought by Germany's Adidas, and its headquarters are now in the United States. Reebok still provides

the name of Bolton FC's stadium, however. For the pre-American influence of Casuals on trainer fashion in Britain, see Peter Hooton, 'The Good, the Bad & the Ugly', *The Face*, No. 26, November 1990.

9. Bob Morris, interviewed for *Casuals*.

10. Cited in Phil Thornton, *Casuals: Football, Fighting and Fashion – The Story of a Terrace Cult* (Milo Books, 2003), p. 23.

11. Cited in ibid., p. 47.

12. Irvine Welsh claims that the 1950s Hibs player Gordon Smith was 'the first meterosexual' with 'a dandy like elegance evident in both his play and his dress'. See Paolo Hewitt and Mark Baxter, *The Fashion of Football: From Best to Beckham, from Mod to Label Slave* (Mainstream, 2004), p. 27.

13. Cited in Matt Munday, 'When Saturday Comes', *Times Saturday Magazine*, 3 January 2004.

14. Cited in ibid. The quote comes from the Who's manager Pete Meaden and not from Marc Bolan, though the point stands.

15. Cited in Thornton, *Casuals*, pp. 38–40.

16. Ibid., pp. 30–1.

17. Kevin Sampson and Dave Rimmer, 'The Ins and Outs of High Street Fashion', *The Face*, No. 22, 1983.

18. Ibid. The article was actually written a few years earlier but even Britain's most astute style magazine refused to run it, such was the lack of interest in the Casuals.

19. Steve White, interview with the author, 12 May 2012.

20. Thornton, *Casuals*, p. 41.

21. Bev Thompson, interviewed for *Casuals*.

22. Ibid.

23. Reproduced in Thornton, *Casuals*, frontispiece.

24. Eric Dunning, Patrick Murphy and John Williams, *The Roots of Football Hooliganism: An Historical and Sociological Study* (Routledge, 1988), pp. 188–98.

25. In 2006 the number of women attending Premiership matches was 18 per cent of the total and rising, having been no more than single figures even before the era of organised football hooliganism from the 1970s to the 90s; see 'Female Fans: A More Beautiful Game', *Independent*, 29 October 2006. The number of fans attending matches from ethnic minorities rose from 1 per cent in the late 1980s to 5 per cent in 2006, while making up over a third of footballers in the Premiership; see Dave Russell, *Football and the English: A Social History of Association Football in England 1863–1995* (Carnegie Publishing, 1997), p. 181. The Centre for Football Research at the University of Leicester provided the more recent data.

26. Damon Albarn, 'Yob Culture', *Modern Review*, Dec/Jan 1994–95, p. 10.

27. Jonny Owen, interviewed for *Casuals*.

28. For example, the red and black cover of *Man Machine* (1978), with the band dressed in slim shirts and ties, was inspired by the work of the Russian artist and designer El Lissitzky (1890–1941). Lissitzky worked with the Bauhaus leaders while in Weimar Germany and had a huge influence on twentieth-century modernist design, not least on the work of Neville Brody.

29. Steve White, interview with the author, 11 May 2012.

30. Wolfgang Fleur, *Kraftwerk: I Was a Robot* (2nd ed., Sanctuary, 2003), pp. 122–3.

31. Ibid. Backstage that night in Liverpool a young Mancunian group called Orchestral Manoeuvres in the Dark paid Kraftwerk a visit that began a lifelong friendship between the two groups. OMD went on to become an influential electro-pop outfit in the 1980s.

32. Ibid., p. 120.

33. Mark Jenkins, 'The End of the British Invasion', *Slate*, 3 May 2002.

34. See, for example, S. Redhead, 'The End of the Century Party', in Steve Redhead (ed.), *Rave Off: Politics and Deviance in Contemporary Youth Culture* (Aldershot, 1993), pp. 3–4.

35. John Reed, *Paul Weller: My Ever Changing Moods* (Omnibus, 2005), p. 204.

36. Paul Weller, 'Style Counsel: The State of the Nation's Dress', *The Face*, No. 36, April 1983.

37. Cited in Simon Reynolds, *Energy Flash: A Journey through Rave Music and Dance Culture* (Picador, 1998), p. 15 (my italics).

38. Letter to *The Face*, No. 20, May 1990.

39. Nelson George, *Hip-Hop America* (Penguin, 1998), p. x.

40. Ibid., pp. x–xi.

41. Mike Pickering, interview with the author, 25 April 2012.

42. Sheryl Garratt, interview with the author for 'Wasted On The Young', *Analysis*, BBC Radio 4, tx: 27 April 2006.

43. Mike Pickering, interview with the author, 25 April 2012.

44. Cited in Reynolds, *Energy Flash*, p. 56.

45. James Nice, *Shadowplayers: The Rise and Fall of Factory Records* (Aurum, 2010), p. 3.

46. Dave Haslam, *Manchester, England: The Story of the Pop Cult City* (4th Estate, 1999), p. xxviii.

47. David Nolan, *Tony Wilson: You're Entitled to an Opinion* (John Blake, 2010), pp. 144–5.

48. Cited in Rawlings, *Mod*, p. 209.

49. Peter Saville, interview with Mark Fisher, *Fact Magazine*, 1 January 2009.

50. Kelly defined the Hacienda as 'a journey through an industrial landscape boosted by theatre and technology. Visual puns to break your journey. A line of steel columns to warn you; take care, you never know who you might bump into on the disco floor . . . all wrapped in a coat of Pigeon Blue BS409.' Cited in Nice, *Shadowplayers*, p. 3.

51. Ibid., p. 184.

52. Cited in ibid., p. 185.

53. Mike Pickering, interview with the author, 25 April 2012.

54. Ibid.

55. Ibid.

56. Tony Wilson, cited in John Harris, *The Last Party: Britpop, Blair and the Demise of English Rock* (4th Estate, 2003), p. 14.

57. Alan McGee, interviewed for *The Creation Story*, BBC4, tx: October 2011.

58. Sarah Thornton, *Club Cultures: Music, Media and Subcultural Capital* (Polity Press, 1995), p. 15. Thornton describes club-related genres in music and fashion as 'cultures of taste', contradicting those who argue that rave led to the decline of subcultural style.

59. Cited in Sheryl Garratt, *Adventures in Wonderland: A Decade of Club Culture* (Headline, 1998), p. 223.

60. Eddie Piller, interview with the author, 14 May 2012.

61. Robert Elms, interview with author, 28 July 2010.

62. Reynolds, *Energy Flash*, p. 51.

63. Ibid.

64. Tim Willis, 'The Lost Tribes: Rave Culture', *Sunday Times*, 18 July 1993.

65. Rudolf Klein, 'Drugs and Society', *Observer*, 2 July 1967. Klein was referring to the Jagger/Richards drugs bust earlier that year, and argued that the trial had made martyrs of the Rolling Stones.

66. *Daily Telegraph*, 14 August 1967. The combined figures for those young-sters who said smoking was the biggest threat to their well-being was 14 per cent; the figure for alcohol was 15 per cent.

67. NA/HO303/79, Home Office Note, 'Public education about drugs', 8 June 1967. Deciding to place adverts in teen magazines such as *Trend* and *Honey*, the Home Office noted that modern pop culture had glam-ourised narcotics since the Second World War: 'Much publicity has been given recently to pop stars who take drugs and inevitably some of the glamour surrounding these people has been identified with drug-taking. Many adolescents must now consider it smart to take seemingly harmless pep pills. Publicity directed towards them should

therefore carry a large element of de-glamourisation in a similar way to the current anti-smoking publicity.'

68. NA/HO319/86, 'Annual Reports from Probation Officers to Scotland Yard, North East London, 1972–73'. When launching the survey in 1970, the Metropolitan Police had suggested that drug use was 'particularly prevalent among certain groups, e.g. students and immigrants'. The Met's immediate reaction to reports showing that it was becoming widespread among all social classes is not apparent. Despite public interest in the subject there remains no adequate history of drug policy and use in post-war Britain to match Virginia Berridge and Gareth Edwards, *Opium and the People: Opiate Use and Policy in 19th Century and Early 20th Century Britain* (2nd ed., Free Association Books, 1998).

69. Ibid.

70. NA/HO319/86, 'Annual Reports from Probation Officers to Scotland Yard, South East London, 1970–71'.

71. Reynolds, *Energy Flash*, pp. xxiv–xxv.

72. Cited in Andy Miller, *The Kinks Are the Village Green Preservation Society* (Continuum, 2007), p. 88.

73. Cited in Reynolds, *Energy Flash*, pp. 44–5.

74. Cited in ibid. p. 40.

75. Noel Gallagher, interviewed for John Dower (dir.), *Live Forever: The Rise and Fall of Britpop* (Passion Pictures, 2003).

76. Cited in Reynolds, *Energy Flash*, p. 50.

77. Cited in Peter Hook, *The Hacienda: How Not to Run a Club* (Simon & Schuster, 2010), p. 167.

78. Angela McRobbie, *Back to Reality? Social Experience and Cultural Studies* (Manchester University Press, 1997), p. 152.

79. Cited in Reynolds, *Energy Flash*, p. 47. The *New Statesman* article was by former Suedehead and *NME* journalist Stuart Cosgrove.

80. Cited in Matthew Collin, *Altered States: The Story of Ecstasy Culture and Acid House* (2nd ed., Serpent's Tail, 1997), p. 114.

81. Alex Bellos, 'Law or No Law, Youth Keeps Dancing', *Guardian*, 6 May 1995.

82. David Fowler, *Youth Culture in Modern Britain, c.1920–1970* (Palgrave, 2008), p. 3.

83. Office for National Statistics, *Social Trends 29* (1999), p. 219.

84. Cited in Jane Bussmann, 'Sea, Sun and Acid House Rock', *Guardian*, 12 July 1990. Bussmann also noted that 'Britain's newest generation of clubbers are a self-conscious, well-dressed lot; even the boys have travel irons.'

85. *Daily Telegraph*, 10 June 2001.

86. Garratt, *Adventures in Wonderland*, p. 83.

87. *Mixmag*, 'Best of British', April 2007.

88. *Guardian/Mixmag* drug survey, *Guardian*, 15 March 2012.

89. Cited in Adam Sweeting, 'Little Manchester in the USA', *Guardian*, 16 August 1990.

90. Cited in Reynolds, *Energy Flash*, pp. 78–9.

91. Ibid., p. 79.

92. Garratt, *Adventures in Wonderland*, p. 160.

93. Emily King (ed.), *Designed by Peter Saville* (Frieze Publications, 2003), pp. 48–9.

94. Tony Champion, for example, has shown that 'London and the six former metropolitan counties of England changed in their rates of population growth over the past two decades, shifting from an overall loss of 245,000 people between 1981 and 1991 to an overall gain of 270,000 in the 10 years to 2001'; Tony Champion 'The Census and the Cities', *Town & Country Planning*, Vol. 73, No. 1, (2004) 20–2.

95. Michael Pacione, *Urban Geography: A Global Perspective* (Routledge, 2009), p. 81.

96. Interestingly, in the years 1997–2003 the combined population of the three central London boroughs and the City of London grew by around 100,000; see Tony Chapman, 'State of the English Cities – The Changing Urban Scene: Demographics and the Big Picture', Department for Communities and Local Government (Nathan and Urwin, 2006), p. 47.

97. 'City People: City Centre Living in the UK', Centre for Cities, London, p. 28. This despite the facts that the proportion of young homeowners in Britain remained constant, at around 30 per cent of the 18–29 age group, between 1975 and 1990; and that the average age of the first-time buyer rose from 29 to 34, so this migration cannot be dismissed as the yuppie self-interest of a few bankers or bohemians playing the property market. See Jackie Smith, Bob Pannell, Council of Mortgage Lenders et al., *Understanding First-Time Buyers* (University of Cambridge, 2005), p. 20.

98. *Private Eye's* long-running cartoon strip, 'It's Grim Up North London', started in 1993 by 'Knife & Packer', satirised urban gentrifiers, its gay, style-obsessed couple repeating the trope that style and taste were somehow effeminate concerns. For more on this theme, see Frank Mort, 'Soho: Archaeologies of Bohemia', in Mort, *Cultures of Consumption: Commerce, Masculinities and Social Space* (Routledge, 1996), pp. 151–7. The book also contains useful essays on Neville Brody and *The Face*.

99. Robert Elms, interview with author, 28 July 2010.

100. Mike Pickering, interview with the author, 25 April 2012.
101. Nolan, *Tony Wilson*, p. 146.
102. Rawlings, *Mod*, p. 209.

Conclusion: A Heritage of Modernism

1. Nik Cohn, cited in Kevin Davey, 'Pete Townshend: Talking 'bout Regeneration', in Davey, *English Imaginaries: Anglo-British Approaches to Modernity* (Lawrence & Wishart, 1999), p. 85.
2. Cited in Michael Heatley, *Paul Weller in His Own Words* (Omnibus, 1996), pp. 66, 70.
3. See 'Tribal Ungathering', *NME*, 5 December 1998; cited in Rupa Huq, *Beyond Subculture: Pop, Youth and Identity in a Postcolonial World* (Routledge, 2006), p. 9.
4. Robert Elms, interview with the author, 28 July 2010.
5. Andy Bennett, 'Dance Parties, Lifestyle and Strategies for Ageing', in Andy Bennett and Paul Hodkinson (eds), *Ageing and Youth Cultures: Music, Style and Identity* (Berg, 2012), pp. 98, 102–3.
6. Nicola Smith, 'Parenthood and the Transfer of Capital in the Northern Soul Scene', in ibid., pp. 159–60.
7. Jonathan Aitken, *Young Meteors* (Secker & Warburg, 1967), p. 34.
8. 'March of the Middle Class Slows in the Face of Cooler Working Class Credibility', *Daily Telegraph*, 25 January 2007.
9. Ibid.
10. This, as well as a desire for celebrity status, helps to explain why so many pop musicians come from the moneyed classes. One survey in 2010 found that while fewer than one in ten British children attended a fee-paying school, 60 per cent of acts in the British charts were privately educated, up from only one per cent twenty years earlier. Cited by Julie Burchill, *Independent*, 16 December 2010.
11. Owen Jones, *Chavs: The Demonization of the Working Class* (2nd ed., Verso, 2012).
12. *Guardian*, 13 August 2011.
13. Stephen Hale, 'Mods or Modernists?', The Modernist, Issue 1, June 2011, p. 21. Hale was writing about Manchester Mods, and in the context of twentieth-century architecture and design, to which this journal is devoted.
14. Christopher Breward, *Fashion* (Oxford, 2003), p. 224.
15. Glenn Adamson and Jane Pavitt, Introduction to Adamson and Pavitt, *Postmodernism: Style and Subversion, 1970–1990* (V&A Publishing, 2011), p. 95.

16. Cited in *V&A Magazine*, No. 216, Autumn/Winter 2011.

17. Ted Polhemus, *Street Style: From Sidewalk to Catwalk* (Thames & Hudson, 1994), p. 134.

18. Christine Feldman, *'We Are the Mods': A Transnational History of a Youth Subculture* (Peter Lang, 2009), p. 53.

19. Nick Hornby, interview with the author for 'Wasted on the Young', *Analysis*, BBC Radio 4, tx: 27 April 2006.

20. Anne McElvoy, 'Britain Just Got Weller: Meet the Jam Generation', *Spectator*, 13 February 2008.

21. *Guardian*, 21 April 2010.

Further Reading

British youth culture has produced a vast amount of books by journalists, social scientists and those involved in creating it. What follows is a brief selection that I hope readers who want to explore this subject further may find useful. The primary sources used in this book are to be found in the endnotes.

Christine Feldman's *'We Are the Mods': A Transnational History of a Youth Subculture* (Peter Lang, 2009) is one of the more accessible sociological studies and the only one to examine the international appeal of Mod, rather than just looking at the foreign influences that shaped its cosmopolitan outlook. Mixing historical research and interviews with Mods around the world, Feldman's work is also one of the few books on the movement to take women's role in it seriously.

Terry Rawlings' *Mod: A Very British Phenomenon* (Omnibus, 2000), an illustrated overview of the movement from the 1950s to the 1990s, is at its best on the early years. Richard Barnes's *Mods!* (Plexus, 1979) is an account of the 1960s, which has acquired canonical status because the author was involved in the movement's genesis and his book became a guide for the Mod revivalists of the 1970s and 80s, in an age before the internet provided an instant archive for aspirant Mods everywhere.

Paolo Hewitt is the pre-eminent chronicler of the movement. Among his many books, *The Soul Stylists: Six Decades of Modernism – From Mods to Casuals* (Edinburgh, Mainstream, 2000) contains a wealth of original interviews with those involved in it, while *The Sharper Word: A Mod Anthology* (Helter Skelter, 2002) collects excerpts from key sources, ranging from personal testimony to academic studies.

Among the academic studies, one of the best accounts of Mod is still to be found in Dick Hebdige's *Subculture: The Meaning of Style*

(Routledge, 1979). Although rightly criticised by later sociologists for not taking female youth seriously enough, Hebdige's interpretation of Mod as a parody of middle-class lifestyle remains compelling; so too does his analysis of the extent to which British youth cultures have been grounded in a testy but productive dance between black and white youth.

Hebdige also acknowledged the connections between twentieth-century modernism and the youth culture that bears its name. One of the few books to explore that connection in depth is Nigel Whiteley's *Pop Design: Modernism to Mod* (Design Council, 1987). A study of trends in British art, design and architecture from the 1950s to the 1970s, it draws imaginative links between pre-war modernism and the music and fashion of mid-century Britain. Lewis MacAdams' *Birth of the Cool: Beat, Bebop and the American Avant-Garde* (2002) makes similar connections between the jazz, art and literature of mid-century America and Europe and helps to put early Mods into context. For those who want to dig deeper, Martin Daunton and Bernhard Rieger's *Meanings of Modernity: Britain from the Late Victorian Era to World War II* (Berg, 2001) is an interesting historical analysis of how the British perceived what it meant to be modern at the height of their global power, just before youth culture newly defined modernity as that power waned.

Surprisingly few historians have paid attention to youth culture, however, and those that have done so usually downplay its significance. David Fowler's *Youth Culture in Modern Britain, c.1920–1970* (Palgrave, 2008) exaggerates the continuities between pre- and post-war movements, but it does show how youth culture was both a middle- and a working-class phenomenon; it also contains a useful chapter on Mod in the 1960s. Taking a more international perspective, Jon Savage's illuminating *Teenage: The Creation of Youth 1875–1945* (Chatto & Windus, 2007) also shows that youth cultures existed before the 1950s, while reaffirming how different they were to those that emerged in the age of affluence and television.

Critics like Savage have written the best studies of specific movements. John Harris's *The Last Party: Britpop, Blair and the Demise of English Rock* (Fourth Estate, 2003) is an excellent account of Britpop that also looks at the political incorporation of youth culture in the 1990s. All of Simon Reynolds's work repays attention, primarily *Energy*

Flash: A Journey Through Rave Music and Dance Culture (Picador, 1998) and *Retromania: Pop Culture's Addiction to Its Own Past* (Faber, 2011). *Retromania* is a challenging look at the future of youth culture in the twenty-first century, arguing that it has become so historicised by its acceptance into the mainstream and so ubiquitous as a result of the internet that it now struggles to be the creative form of modernism that it was for much of the late twentieth century.

Among all the memoirs of life at the coalface of music and fashion since the 1960s, just a few stand out. Ian McLagan's, *All the Rage: My High Life with the Small Faces, the Faces, the Rolling Stones and Many More* (second edition, Pan, 2000) is an amusing account of being in the legendary Mod group and of the cross-class encounters that 'Swinging London' threw up, while Alex James's *bit of a blur: the autobiography* (Little Brown, 2007) does the same for the 1990s from a middle-class perspective. Robert Elms's *The Way We Wore: A Life in Threads* (Picador, 2005) is part memoir and part history of Mod-related fashions since the 1960s that captures the appeal of dressing-up for British youth. Although memoirs of those involved in music and fashion usually pay tribute to their parents and children, the only one to focus on that subject is Roy Wilkinson's engaging *Do It For Your Mum* (Rough Trade Books, 2011).

Perhaps the best starting point for anyone interested in this book's subject is still the late George Melly's *Revolt into Style: The Pop Arts in Britain* (1970). Written by a Soho jazzman and one of the first journalists employed by the quality press to cover popular music, *Revolt into Style* is a witty, incisive study of modern British youth culture written at the end of its first decade, when few predicted its extraordinary longevity and far-reaching influence.

Credits

Text and lyrics

I would like to thank the following for permission to reproduce the quotations and lyrics that appear within the text:

Thom Gunn, 'Elvis Presley', in *The Sense of Movement*, Faber, 1957 © Thom Gunn, 1957.

Sonia Orwell and Ian Angus (eds), *The Collected Essays, Journalism and Letters of George Orwell, Vol. II: My Country Right or Left, 1940–1943*, Penguin, 1970 © George Orwell, 1937. Reprinted by permission of Random House.

Colin MacInnes, *Absolute Beginners*, Allison & Busby, 1959 © the Colin MacInnes estate, 1959. Reprinted by permission of Allison & Busby.

Andrew Loog Oldham, *Stoned*, Secker & Warburg, 2000 © Clear Entertainment Ltd, 2000. Reprinted by permission of Andrew Loog Oldham.

Andrew Loog Oldham, *2Stoned*, Secker & Warburg, 2002 © Clear Entertainment Ltd, 2002. Reprinted by permission of Andrew Loog Oldham.

Pete Townshend, *Substitute*, Reaction, London, 1966 © Fabulous Music Ltd. Reprinted by permission of Essex Music.

Curtis Mayfield, *Move On Up*, Curtom, USA, 1970; words and music by Curtis Mayfield © 1970. Reprinted by permission of EMI Tunes Ltd, London W1F 9LD.

Tom Wolfe, *The Pump House Gang*, Bantam, 1968 © Tom Wolfe, 1968. Reprinted by permission of Random House Inc.

Paul Weller, *When You're Young*, Polydor, London, 1979; words and music by Paul Weller © Stylist Music Limited/Universal Music Publishing Limited, 1981. Reprinted by permission of Music Sales Ltd.

Zadie Smith, *White Teeth*, Hamish Hamilton, 2000 © Zadie Smith, 2000. Reprinted by permission of Penguin Publishing.

Louise Wener, *Just For One Day: Adventures in Britpop*, Ebury, 2011 © Louise Wener, 2010. Reprinted by permission of Random House.

Roy Wilkinson, *Do It For Your Mum*, Rough Trade Books, 2011 © Roy Wilkinson, 2011. Reprinted by permission of Roy Wilkinson.

Casuals Cass Pennant (dir.) [DVD], UK Cornerstone Media, 2011 © Urban Edge Films. Reproduced by permission of Cornerstone Media.

Every effort has been made to trace copyright holders, and the publisher will be happy to correct any mistakes or omissions in future editions.

Images

Jacket of *Absolute Beginners*, Allison & Busby, 1959 © Roger Mayne. Reproduced courtesy of the Gitterman Gallery
Soho street dancing © Werner Rings/BIPs/Getty Images
Miles Davis © Michael Ochs Archives/Getty Images
Donald Byrd EP cover © EMI Records Ltd
The Flamingo Club © Michael Ochs Archives/Getty Images
Sleeping couple © Leon Morris/Getty Images
Marc Feld © Don McCullin
Jacket of *Horse Under Water* © Penguin
Girl on scooter © Mary Evans
Cathy McGowan © Keystone/1965 Getty Images
The Kinks on *Ready, Steady, Go!* © Val Wilmer/Redferns
The Small Faces & P.P. Arnold © Gilles Petard/Redferns
The Who © Tony Frank/Sygma/Corbis
The Beatles © Harry Hammond/V&A Images/Getty Images
Jacket of *Quant by Quant* © Ballantine Mod Books (1967)
French mods © Terrence Spencer/Time & Life Pictures/Getty Images
Quant football dress © Keystone/Getty Images
John Stephen and Angus Young. Reproduced courtesy of Bill Franks
Terence Conran © Popperfoto/Getty Images
Mods & Rockers fighting on the beach © Keystone/Getty Images
Giles cartoon © Express Syndication. Reproduced courtesy of the British Cartoon Archive
Northern Soul dancers © Mick Gold/Redferns
BIBA sales girls © Caroline Gillies/BIPs/Getty Images
David Bowie © Gijsbert Hanekroot/Redferns
Julie Driscoll © David Redfern/Redferns
Suedehead couple © Keystone Features/Hulton Archive/Getty Images
The Jam © Gered Mankowitz/Redferns
Quadrophenia © WORLD NORTHAL/Album/AKG
Paul Weller © Steve Pyke/Getty Images
Weller, Townshend and Hewitt © Janette Beckman/Redferns
Pauline Black © Kevin Cummins/2009 Getty Images
Specials fans © John Sturrock/ www.reportdigital.co.uk
Casuals. Reproduced courtesy of Neil Primett/80s Casual Classics Ltd
Blur © Kevin Cummins/Getty Images
Blow Up flyer. Reproduced courtesy of Paul Tunkin
John Taylor Quartet EP cover. Reproduced courtesy of Eddie Piller/Acid Jazz Records
Noel Gallagher © Fred Duval/FilmMagic
The Hacienda © Kevin Cummins/Premium Archive/Getty Images
Design Museum © akg/Bildarchiv Monheim
Tube map, *Going Underground*, Mark Wallinger 2008 © London Underground
Jonathan LeRoy. Reproduced courtesy of 'Jump the Gun', www.jumpthegun.co.uk
Ben Sherman © Ben Sherman/Antony Crook
Wiggo © *The Times*/NI Syndication

Index